# A History of the Credit Market in Central Europe

This is the first comprehensive study of loans and debts in Central European countries in the Middle Ages and Early Modern Period. It outlines the issues of debts and loans in the Czech lands, Poland and Hungary, with respect to the influence of Austria and Germany. It focuses on the role of loans and debts in medieval and early modern society, credit markets in these countries, the mechanism of lending and borrowing, forms of credit, availability of loans, frequency of credits dealings, range of lending business, and last, but not least, the financial relationships inside the social classes and between them.

The research presented in the book is based on a wide range of resources including credit contracts and agreements, evidence of loans and debts of courts, accounting of nobility, towns, churches and guilds, merchant diaries and Jewish registers, as well as other financial records. It covers a wide range of historical disciplines including economic and financial history, social history, the history of economic thought as well as the history of everyday life. It also contains a wealth of case studies, which offer, for the first time in English, a comprehensive and representative sample of the most up-to-date Central European research on the history of loans and debts and serves as a basis for a comparison with the other parts of Europe during the same period.

The book is designed primarily for postgraduates, researchers and academics in financial, economic and historical sciences but will also be a valuable resource for students of business schools.

**Pavla Slavíčková** is an assistant professor at the Palacky University in Olomouc, the Czech Republic.

# A History of the Credit Market in Central Europe

The Middle Ages and Early Modern Period

Edited by
Pavla Slavíčková

Routledge
Taylor & Francis Group

LONDON AND NEW YORK

First published 2021
by Routledge
2 Park Square, Milton Park, Abingdon, Oxon OX14 4RN

and by Routledge
52 Vanderbilt Avenue, New York, NY 10017

*Routledge is an imprint of the Taylor & Francis Group, an informa business*

*British Library Cataloguing-in-Publication Data*
A catalogue record for this book is available from the British Library

*Library of Congress Cataloging-in-Publication Data*
Names: Slavíčková, Pavla, 1979– editor.
Title: A history of the credit market in Central Europe : the middle ages and early modern period / edited by Pavla Slavíčková.
Description: 1 Edition. | New York : Routledge, 2020. |
Includes bibliographical references and index.
Identifiers: LCCN 2020017580 (print) | LCCN 2020017581 (ebook)
Subjects: LCSH: Loans – Europe, Central – History. |
Debt – Europe, Central – History.
Classification: LCC HG1642.E86 H57 2020 (print) |
LCC HG1642.E86 (ebook) | DDC 332.1/75309430902–dc23
LC record available at https://lccn.loc.gov/2020017580
LC ebook record available at https://lccn.loc.gov/2020017581

ISBN: 978-0-367-40418-5 (hbk)
ISBN: 978-0-429-35601-8 (ebk)

Typeset in Sabon
by Newgen Publishing UK

# Contents

# Figures

# Tables

# Contributors

Eveline Brugger, Institute for Jewish History in Austria, St. Pölten (Austria)

Marie Buňatová, Czech Academy of Sciences, Prague (the Czech Republic)

Bronislav Chocholáč, Masaryk University, Brno (the Czech Republic)

Piotr Guzowski, University of Białystok (Poland)

János Incze, Masaryk University, Brno (the Czech Republic)

Cezary Kardasz, Scientific Society in Toruń (Poland)

Tomáš Klír, Charles University in Prague (the Czech Republic)

Petr Kozák, Silesian University in Opava (the Czech Republic)

Monika Kozłowska-Szyc, University of Białystok (Poland)

Marzena Liedke, University of Białystok (Poland)

Piotr Łozowski, University of Białystok (Poland)

Anna Paulina Orłowska, Polish Academy of Sciences, Warsaw (Poland)

Hana Pátková, Charles University in Prague (the Czech Republic)

Tereza Siglová, State District Archives, Pardubice (the Czech Republic)

Pavla Slavíčková, Palacky University, Olomouc (the Czech Republic)

Tomáš Sterneck, Czech Academy of Sciences, Prague (the Czech Republic)

Zuzana Vlasáková, University of Pardubice (the Czech Republic)

Petr Vorel, University of Pardubice (the Czech Republic)

Boglárka Weisz, Research Centre for Humanities, Budapest (Hungary)

Birgit Wiedl, Institute for Jewish History in Austria, St. Pölten (Austria)

Zdeněk Žalud, Hussite Museum in Tábor (the Czech Republic)

Roman Zaoral, Charles University in Prague (the Czech Republic)

# Introduction

## Credit in Central European historiography

*Roman Zaoral*

## Theoretical concepts

The study of public finances has received considerable attention during the last decade because of its key role in European state formation by serving as an instrument to extract the capital needed for the realization of political goals from the economic systems that formed the base of all public finances. In this respect, it is worth mentioning the book by David Stasavage (2011) who made a valuable contribution to the debate on the emergence of public credit as a decisive element in the state formation processes that took place in late medieval and early modern Europe. In his work, Stasavage emphasizes the importance of geographic scale of political units and the form of political representation within polities for the access to capital markets and thus the possibility to create funded public debt in order to finance the consolidation or expansion of their relative position within political networks and regions. According to him, the foundation of the public debt was provided by the fiscal revenues originating from direct or indirect taxation.

He argues that intensive forms of representative assemblies facilitated the emergence of such a system. Assemblies did this by both monitoring and modifying expenditures and by helping guard the interests of state creditors. The existence of these credit-friendly assemblies, in turn, was facilitated by two conditions: first, limited geographic size; and, second, the presence of a group of politically influential merchants. Both of these conditions were most common in western European city-states.

Wim Blockmans (1997) pointed out in this debate the importance of scale and timing with respect to local political representative structures. He showed that in the larger Flemish cities such as Ghent or Bruges, the participation of middle classes in town governments and thus control over public finances developed in an earlier stage (the 14th century), whereas these developments in less urbanized regions with smaller urban populations such as Holland and Guelders, which were part of the Holy Roman Empire at that time, did not occur until the 15th century. In this way, it can be stated that the position of urban elites influenced the management of urban finances at large, and urban fiscal systems in particular. The degree to which urban elites were able to monopolize urban government was also determining the room left for other intermediaries to have a say in the financial polities of a town and to function in the management of the fiscal systems that were the basis of most urban finances. The socio-political backgrounds and the inter-play between the political elites, urban officials, and tax farmers are thus an important topic for knowledge of the intricate mechanisms which are at the crossing point of the economic, social, political, and financial developments in the late-medieval urban society.

In the 15th century, the importance of urban middle classes as tax-farmers started to grow; they increasingly gained influence on the financial and fiscal regime, both through political emancipation as well as by serving as finan-cial officials. They also demanded more insight in the financial management, both of indirect taxation and the management of urban debt. They were given a central role in the financial reforms necessary to face the growing tension between economic stagnation and the financial demands. In this way, the impact of these socio-political changes on the management of the urban fiscal systems can be displayed.

The concept of a financial crisis has recently been addressed by what is now known as the 'New fiscal history'. The emergence of public finance, fiscal systems, and the creation of public debt are at the heart of these discussions. In this sense, a financial crisis occurs when expenditure struc-turally outweighs the normal revenues from taxation and the ability to borrow money in order to meet current financial obligations (Bonney 1995, pp. 5–8). The 15th century is generally seen as a period of struc-tural political and economic crisis (Van Uytven 1975; Šmahel 2002). This crisis also had consequences for urban public finance and its management. Each town within the Empire had to pay a fixed percentage of the total tax sum of central direct taxation through a system of repartition and so the increased tax burden had forced several towns to sell annuities on an unprecedented scale because these sums were paid directly through the urban finances (Blockmans 1999, pp. 287, 297–304). Thus, central direct taxation indirectly tapped into the financial resources of the towns which, in turn, led to an ever growing pressure on the urban finances causing an increase of urban indirect taxation to cover the funded debt caused by these annuity sales.

Financial crises and social conflicts directed the aim of restructuring power of the old ruling elites and finally were centred round the wish for a more efficient management of urban financial resources and more intensive control rights for those urban social groups that provided the capital for the realization and protection of 'common' urban interests.

But what was the situation in Central Europe? Why the conditions for credit use were not so favourable here like in the West? A passive trade balance within the triangle between North Italy, Flanders, and Central Europe following from the uneven position in West–East trade relationships and a lack of sea are generally considered a reason why this region was behind. The research shows that besides common features, which became evident with delay in the eastern parts of the Empire, there were also differences: while in the West, the tax basis was rather created by indirect taxes, in the East direct taxes prevailed. While in the West trade activities played an important role, rich burghers in the East instead invested in land estates. In the West, the growing incomes of cities led to the establishment of separate cashes, while in the East, a single-entry accounting prevailed (Zaoral 2014, pp. 281–89).

The aim of this book is to show to what extent is the above mentioned concept of credit reflected by historians dealing with the history of Central European countries, the territory covering the eastern part of the Holy Roman Empire (Austria, Bohemia, Moravia, Silesia), Poland, and Hungary. This region is, among others, characterized by smaller political stability. It is necessary to emphasize at the outset that the medieval lands of these states were not identical with their modern counterparts; the territories of medieval Poland and Hungary, especially, differed drastically from their modern equivalents.

The views of the position of this region within the European economic system oscillate between periphery and semi-periphery. As the region characterized by exporting all or mostly raw materials and importing all or mainly finished goods, Central Europe is usually ranked to periphery (Wallerstein 1976, pp. 229–30). A slightly different view has been formulated by N. J. G. Pounds who divides late medieval Europe into developed, developing, and backward areas using five criteria – reliability of political structure, trade, urban areas density, population growth, and agrarian improvements. In this sense, he puts Bohemia, western Poland, and western Hungary among developing areas, together with eastern Germany, the shores of Scandinavia, the Scottish lowlands, Spain, and southern Italy (Pounds 1978, p. 102, 112). An indicator of the social and economic wealth of the European regions is for him the evaluation of the dioceses for taxation by the Holy See. This shows that France and Italy were taxed much more heavily than for instance Germany and that Germany was taxed heavier than Poland, for instance (Hroch & Klusáková 1996, p. 39).

Central Europe served primarily as a market for the craft products of West European origin and also as a region providing precious metals for the European financial system. It is well documented that precious metal production expanded significantly in the 14th century, especially in Bohemia and Hungary. The growing yields of silver and gold contributed to an increase in purchasing power and thus created better opportunities for the development of long-distance trade and the use of credit. Although a lot has been done, the specific research issues of Central Europe are still not fully integrated into the general European historiographic tradition, and it is no doubt that the particular role of Central Europe in the wider European economy needs to be revisited.

The presented historiographic overview is primarily intended for scholars who come from a different region and cannot use the local languages. That is why main attention is paid to the works of Polish, Czech, Slovak, and Hungarian historians. The works of German-language authors, which often represent a key basis for study of the history of Central Europe, are for these reasons mentioned only marginally. At the same time, it is necessary to call attention to the fact that most works in this field concern the early modern period, which corresponds to the number of extant historical sources in the Central European archives, among which medieval accounts or ledgers are rather rare.

## Areas of research

A true breakthrough in Polish economic historiography was the work of Witold Kula *An Economic Theory of the Feudal System: Towards a Model of the Polish Economy, 1500–1800* (Kula 1962, in English 1976) which drew inspiration from the Annales School. It is an idiosyncratic synthesis of serial history and Marxist theory enriched by Kula with his own perspective on the behaviour of economic participants. Kula examined structural changes and fluctuations within the boom-bust cycle in combination with emphasis on the contradictions of feudal system. He pointed to different starting institutional and social conditions of feudalism as against capitalism (the absence of free market and competition, the existence of non-market phenomena like serfdom and guilds), which forced economic participants to markedly different behaviour from that based on profit maximization and cost minimization. The peasant has used the market in fact only because he received money for amortization of his obligations towards manorial lords. His 'income' therefore did not preferentially depend on market conditions but on crop conditions. That is the reason for the specific logic of behaviour that reacts to price fluctuations in the market in a manner completely contrary to that which modern economics would assume: the peasant sells less during price growth and sells more during price decline. So the key factor in the peasant's decision is not the situation of the market itself but the necessity to provide sufficient cash for repayment of his obligations. Likewise, the economic behaviour of manorial lords did not follow the market but rather the maintenance of their own standard of living and social status (the 'negative market stimulation'). While a period of price growth in capitalism stimulates economic activities and mobilizes reserves, in feudalism it is, on the contrary, the decline of 'national income', mostly caused by non-economic factors (poor harvest, war) which functions as needed stimulation of economic activity.

Within the dynamic of the long-term (*longue durée*), Kula pointed out tendencies in the Polish economy which differ from the countries of early modern Europe. First of all, it is noteworthy that the improving conditions for foreign trade (particularly for corn export) did not affect the total structure of production and consumption in any clear way, no matter how they managed to generate considerable profits for manorial lords. The reason was the general orientation of the Polish aristocratic dominion, which was not focused outwardly on foreign markets but inwardly on the peasant, his unpaid work and the surplus from which it benefited. Moreover, this tendency to form isolated and autarchic dominions was accompanied by a specific economic strategy of owners which was supposed to provide that not only potential expenses but also peasant's potential monetary surpluses got back into the treasury of manorial lords. This way a specific form of closed monetary circle formed which Kula suitably describes as the economic *perpetuum mobile*.

Besides Kula's monograph on the feudal economic model, the theoretical works of Polish historians examined the roots of the economic growth of East-Central Europe during the late Middle Ages (Małowist 1973a) and the origins of capitalism in Europe (Topolski 1965). Likewise, Małowist made an attempt to compare the social-economic structures between East and West in the 13th–16th centuries, placing emphasis on uneven economic development in the different regions of Europe (Małowist 1973b, in English 2010a, 2010b), he dealt with merchant credit (Małowist 1981) and with the circulation of capital in East-Central Europe (Małowist 1985). The role of money in Poland has been studied by Mączak (1976) and Żabiński (1981) who presented a synthesis of the accounting and monetary systems with an economic analysis of the changes they underwent.

The link between economy and reformation was recently studied by Guzowski and Liedke (Guzowski 2010; Liedke& Guzowski 2017) who follow the older works of Bogucka (1972) and Lesiński (1976). The fiscal system in late medieval and early modern Poland was a subject of interest of several Polish historians (Brzeczkowski 1981; Horn 1985, 1986; Sepiał 1998; Filipczak-Kocur 1999; Guzowski 2006; Mikulski 2008). Different strategies of fighting financial crisis in Poland have been recently analysed by Boroda and Guzowski in their common work (2016).

Following the fundamental monograph of Gilomen (1984), Polish historians paid intensive attention to rents, annuity sales, and credit in the towns of the southern Baltic coast: Gdańsk (Samsonowicz 1961, 1964, 1969; Bogucka 1972; Możejko 2004; Grulkowski 2009; Orłowska 2020), Elbląg (Czaja 1987; Girsztowt 2013), Toruń (Czaja 1988; Mycio 1999), comparative study for Greifswald, Gdańsk, Elbląg, Toruń, Rewel (Kardasz 2013), as well as in Prussia (Janosz-Biskupowa 1958; Samsonowicz 1960; Dygo 1988, 2003), in Warsaw (Łozowski 2016) and Sieradz (Łydkowska-Sowina 1989) and in Silesian Wrocław (Goliński 2006) and Świdnica (Goliński 2003). Besides that, Samsonowicz (1991, 1994) is the author of generally designed studies about the role of credit in the economic life of medieval

Poland; Myśliwski (2008) dealt with the changeover to a tax system. From the comparison of these works, it is evident how much the developed Baltic region differed from the Polish inland lagging behind.

Capital importance for consideration of the various forms of credit in Central Europe have, among others, the works of Markus Denzel, focused on payment operations (Denzel 1994) and the system of cashless payment in Europe, including East European peripheries (Denzel 2008), two volumes *Kredit im spätmittelalterlichen und frühneuzeitlichen Europa* and *Von Aktie bis Zoll* edited by Michael North (1991, 1995), as well as the *Banchi pubblici, banchi privati e monti di pietà nell' Europa preindustriale* (Banchi 1991) with several contributions relating to the Holy Roman Empire. Just the study of credit became an exemplary theme of the economic anthropology, the intension of which is to clarify the cultural importance of economic practices (Muldrew 1998).

The management of merchant books and registers have been thoroughly analysed in the collection *Kaufmannsbücher und Handelspraktiken vom Spätmittelalter bis zum beginnenden 20. Jahrhundert* (Denzel, Hocquet & Witthöft 2002) in which Denzel presents trade practices of the Fugger family within the network connecting, among others, Naples with Cracow, Amsterdam with Wrocław and Augsburg with Buda. Central European trade centres and their ties to the West and South are captured in the *Netzwerke im europäischen Handel des Mittelalters* (Fouquet & Gilomen 2010). From the Central European perspective, numerous works of Wolfgang von Stromer on finance still keep special importance (Stromer 1970, 1976, 1982). The role of Italian merchants in Central Europe was thoroughly analysed by Weissen (2001, 2003, 2006).

In Czech historiography, theoretical and legislative fundamentals for the study of credit relations have been elaborated by Urfus (1959, 1975) who focused on the types of credit practices, usury and the changing amounts of interest. Buňatová (2018) and Vorel (2009, 2014) paid attention to the problems of financial and commodity credit, money changing and the trade practice of early modern merchants, presenting them in the broader European context. Besides that, Buňatová (2010, 2011a, 2011b, 2016) wrote extensively about the trade and financial activities of Prague Jews. The Jewish credit in Moravia was studied by Blechová (2015) and Zaoral (2015). Jaroslav Mezník paid special attention to annuity owners in Prague (1972) and in Brno (1960). He is also the author of important studies on the economic character of Prague (1969, 1990) and on money circulation in the Czech lands (1993, 1994). The role of credit in Moravian towns Brno and Olomouc has been presented by Zaoral (2014). The financial economy of the towns České Budějovice and Brno is a subject of the studies by Čechura (1993, 1998), who also examined the financial administration of monasteries (Čechura 1994) and of the royal court (Čechura 2012).

Accounting management and accounting systems used in the Czech lands are a subject of research carried out systematically by Pavla Slavíčková (2014, 2017, see also Slavíčková & Puchinger 2016). Various aspects of financing and credit granting in different social milieus (medieval court funding, town accounts, ledgers and customs registers, cathedral and metropolitan chapter accounts) were dealt in the collective monograph *Money and Finance in Central Europe during the Later Middle Ages* (Zaoral 2016). A special volume was devoted to financial conditions in Moravia between the 1350s and the early 17th century (Borovský, Chocholáč & Pumpr 2007).

Credit in the aristocratic entrepreneurship has been examined by Ledvinka (1985), Bůžek (1989), and Sterneck (2004). Vorel (1998) investigated the role of credit in the financial transactions of Bohemian and Moravian nobility during the journeys abroad. In his later studies, Vorel documented that pressure put on the systemic reduction of the interest rate cannot be fully explained by the influence of German reformation. He argues that it was a more general problem, related to the credit policy of European powers and interwoven with the international banking market (Vorel 2002, 2006). With the creditors of George of Poděbrady, King of Bohemia, dealt Boublík (2007, 2011). Special attention was also paid to the financing of wars against the Hussites (Polívka 1993, 2004). The financial issues of the Prague metropolitan chapter were thoroughly studied by Maříková (2018). Analysing account registers from 1358–1418, Maříková proved that the volume of loans was in comparison with other incomes of the chapter fully negligible.

The first attempts to look into the financial management of subjects appeared in Czech historiography in connection with the study of prices and wages in the 1960s. The widely designed research of the experts from Prague and Brno brought a number of stimulating ideas but the more detailed research of this question was not realized at that time. Besides the classic book published by Procházka (1963), based on the study of land registers and dealing with subject finance in the context of holding tenant farms and the legal status of subjects in property matters, one of the most important contributions represents a study written by Mainušová (1965). Another important work with the analysis of money and corn debts at the Roudnice manor in the 18th century has been published by Křivka (1986). Research of the property and financial aspects of tenant farms in the 16th and 17th centuries continued then in the works of Chocholáč (1989, 1990, 1999, 2001), Holakovský (1993) and Odehnal (2000, 2011, 2013).

In Hungarian historiography a heated response was provoked by a paper of Oszkar Paulinyi published in 1972. Its controversial subtitle Gazdag föld – szegény ország (Rich Land – Poor Country) constantly recurs in debates on this subject and became the title for a collection of Paulinyi's studies on mining history (Paulinyi 2005). Paulinyi drew on the most-cited source of medieval Hungarian foreign trade, the 1457–58 Pressburg thirtieth register, to determine that Hungarian foreign trade ran a deep deficit which could only be settled by the trade in money stemming from precious metal mining and minting the gold florin. His thesis inspired many other Hungarian historians, notably Mályusz in his work about the export of Hungarian livestock to Bavaria (1986) and Kubinyi in the broader designed study (1992).

A milestone in the recent research represents the collective monograph *The Economy of Medieval Hungary* (Laszlovsky et al. 2018), which covers various aspects of economic life, including financial administration, urban and ecclesiastic economy and foreign business interests in late medieval Hungary.

Detailed attention to the system of financial and tax administration in Hungary under Matthias Corvinus and the Jagellonians was paid by Kubinyi (1958, 2001). Recently, two scholars from Hungary (Neumann 2019) and the Czech Republic (Kozák 2019) analysed the register of incomes and expenses of the Buda court of Vladislaus Jagiellon dated back to 1494–95 and made its modern critical edition. Public finances, taxes, king's revenues as well as loans to the king were studied by numerous Hungarian historians: Mályusz (1965), Hermann (1975), Fügedi (1980, 1982), Bak (1987), Engel (1994), Draskóczy (2001, 2014), Kenyeres (2012) and Tóth (2016, 2018).

With the use of the 1427 Catasto, the credit activities of Italian bankers in Hungary were researched by Teke (1984) and Arany (2007, 2014). Numerous studies on this topic come also from Prajda (2013, 2017). The financial administration of Hungarian mining towns was researched by Weisz (2017), as well as by Slovak historians (Štefánik 2013; Dvořáková 2016).

# References

Arany, K. (2007). Siker és kudarc. Két firenzei kereskedőcsalád, a Melanesi-k és a Corsini-k Budán Luxemburgi Zsigmond uralkodása (1387–1427) alatt. *Századok*, 141(4), pp. 943–66.

Arany, K. (2014). *Florentine families in Hungary in the first half of the fifteenth century*. Ph.D. Diss. Budapest: Central European University.

Bak, J. (1987). Monarchie im Wellental: Materielle Grundlagen des ungarischen Königtums im fünfzehnten Jahrhundert. In Schneider, R., ed. *Das spätmittelalterliche Königtum im europäischen Vergleich, Vorträge und Forschungen*. Sigmaringen: Jan Thorbecke Verlag, pp. 347–84.

Banchi (1991). *Banchi pubblici, banchi privati e monti di pietà nell' Europa preindustriale. Amministrazione, tecniche operative e ruoli economici*, 2 vols. Genova: Società ligure di storia patria.

Blechová, L. (2015). The Jewish Credit Trade in the Late Middle Ages: Kroměříž and Olomouc (1353–1417). In Doležalová, E., ed. *In Juden in der mittelalterlichen Stadt – Jews in the medieval town. Colloquia mediaevalia Pragensia*, 7, Praha: Filosofia, pp. 39–56.

Blockmans, W. (1997). The impact of cities on state formation: Three contrasting territories in the Low Countries, 1300–1500. In Blickle, P., ed. *Resistance, Representation and Community*. Oxford: Oxford University Press, pp. 256–71.

Blockmans, W. (1999). The Low Countries in the Middle Ages. In R. Bonney, R., ed. *The Rise of the Fiscal State in Europe, c. 1200–1815*. Oxford: Oxford University Press, pp. 281–308.

Bogucka, M. (1972). Obrót wekslowo-kredytowy w Gdańsku w pierwszej połowie XVII wieku. *Roczniki Dziejów Społecznych i Gospodarczych*, 33, pp. 1–29.

Bonney, R., ed. (1995). *Economic Systems and State Finance. The Origins of the Modern State in Europe 13th to 18th Centuries*. Oxford: Oxford University Press.

Boroda, K. & Guzowski, P. (2016). From king's finance to public finance. Different strategies of fighting financial crisis in the Kingdom of Poland under Jagiellonian rule (1386–1572). In Nigro, G., ed. *The Financial Crises. Their Management, Their Social Implications and Their Consequences in Pre-Industrial Times*. Firenze: Firenze University Press, pp. 451–70.

Borovský, T., Chocholáč, B. & Pumpr, P., eds. (2007). *Peníze nervem společnosti. K finančním poměrům na Moravě od poloviny 14. do počátku 17. století*. Brno: Matice moravská.

Boublík, J. (2007). Půjčky a věřitelé Jiřího z Poděbrad. *Sborník Národního muzea*, A 61, pp. 47–51.

Boublík, J. (2011). Správa královských financí ve středověku. Několik poznámek k době poděbradské. *Numismatické listy*, 66, pp. 17–26.

Brzeczkowski, T. (1981). Ustanawianie podatków nadzwyczajnych w Polsce w XV w. *Roczniki Dziejów Społecznych i Gospodarczych*, 42, pp. 77–104.

Buňatová, M. (2010). Kreditwesen und Handel der Prager Juden im Spiegel des "Liber albus Judeorum" 1577–1601. In Ash, M. G., ed. *Wissenschaft ist Jung II, Wiener Zeitschrift zur Geschichte der Neuzeit*, 10(2), pp. 6–19.

Buňatová, M. (2011a). *Die Prager Juden in der Zeit vor der Schlacht am Weißen Berg. Handel und Wirtschaftsgebaren der Prager Juden im Spiegel des Liber albus Judeorum 1577–1601*. Kiel: Solivagus-Verlag.

Buňatová, M. (2011b). Die Handelsaktivitäten jüdischer Frauen in Prag und ihre soziale und rechtliche Stellung an der Wende des 16. zum 17. Jahrhundert. In Keil, M., ed. *Besitz, Geschäft und Frauenrechte. Jüdische und christliche Frauen in Dalmatien und Prag 1300–1600*. Kiel: Solivagus-Verlag, pp. 144–69.

Buňatová, M. (2016). Die wirtschaftlichen Beziehungen Prager Juden zum Adel in den böhmischen Ländern an der Wende vom 16. zum 17. Jahrhundert. In Hirbodian, S. & Strezt, T., eds. *Juden und ländliche Gesellschaft in Europa zwischen Mittelalter und Früher Neuzeit (15.–17. Jahrhundert). Kontinuität und Krise, Inklusion und Exklusion in einer Zeit des Übergangs*. Wiesbaden: Harrassowitz Verlag, pp. 33–49.

Buňatová, M. (2018). Úvěr a finance v obchodní praxi. Evropa – české země – Praha: směry a perspektivy výzkumu. *Český časopis historický*, 118, pp. 787–821.

Bůžek, V. (1989). *Úvěrové podnikání nižší šlechty v předbělohorských Čechách*. Praha: Ústav československých a světových dějin ČSAV.

Čechura, J. (1993). Finanční hospodaření Českých Budějovic v letech 1396––1416. *Numismatický sborník*, 19, pp. 33–66.

Čechura, J. (1994). *Die Struktur der Grundherrschaften im mittelalterlichen Böhmen unter besonderer Berücksichtigung der Klosterherrschaften*. Stuttgart – Jena – New York: Gustav Fischer Verlag.

Čechura, J. (1998). Srovnání berních knih města Brna z let 1365 a 1422. Poznámky k metodice studia pramenů hromadné povahy. *Časopis Matice moravské*, 117, pp. 341–52.

Čechura, J. (2012). Královská komora a královské finance lucemburské epochy. In Bobková, L. & Šmahel, F., eds. *Lucemburkové. Česká koruna uprostřed Evropy.* Praha: Nakladatelství Lidové noviny, pp. 319–28.

Chocholáč, B. (1989). Zadluženost a poddanské dávky (Příspěvek ke studiu sociálněekonomických problémů poddaných v druhé polovině 16. století na základě rozboru pernštejnských pozemkových knih). *Jižní Morava,* 25, pp. 75–87.

Chocholáč, B. (1990). K hospodaření poddaných na pernštejnském panství v druhé polovině 16. a v první polovině 17. století. *Časopis Matice moravské,* 109, pp. 83–111.

Chocholáč, B. (1999). *Selské peníze. Sonda do finančního hospodaření poddaných na západní Moravě koncem 16. a v 17. století.* Brno: Matice moravská.

Chocholáč, B. (2001). Poddanský úvěr na Moravě v 16. a 17. století. *Český časopis historický,* 99, pp. 59–84.

Czaja, R. (1987). Rynek kupna renty w Elblągu w pierwszej połowie XIV wieku. *Zapiski Historyczne,* 52(3), pp. 7–37.

Czaja, R. (1988). Kredyt pieniężny w Starym Mieście Toruniu do roku 1410. *Roczniki Dziejów Społecznych i Gospodarczych,* 49, pp. 5–19.

Denzel, M. A. (1994).'*La Practica della Cambiatura'. Europäischer Zahlungsverkehr vom 14. bis zum 17. Jahrhundert.* Stuttgart: Steiner Verlag.

Denzel, M. A., Hocquet, J. C. & Witthöft, H., eds. (2002). *Kaufmannsbücher und Handelspraktiken vom Spätmittelalter bis zum beginnenden 20. Jahrhundert.* Stuttgart: Steiner Verlag.

Denzel, M. A. (2008). *Das System des bargeldlosen Zahlungsverkehrs europäischer Prägung vom Mittelalter bis 1914.* Stuttgart: Steiner Verlag.

Draskóczy, I. (2001). Kamarai jövedelem és urbura a 15. század első felében. In *Gazdaságtörténet-könyvtártörténet. Emlékkönyv Berlász Jenő 90. születésnapjára.* Budapest: MTA-BKAE Gazdaság és Társadalomtörténeti Kutatócsoport, pp. 147–66.

Draskóczy, I. (2014). A királyi jövedelmek a 16. század elején Magyarországon: Szempontok bányászatunk és külkereskedelmünk történetéhez. In Orsolya, M., ed. *Historia critica: tanulmányok az Eötvös Loránd Tudományegyetem Bölcsészettudományi Karának Történeti Intézetéből.* Budapest: ELTE Eötvös Kiadó, pp. 75–92.

Dvořáková, D. (2016). Stredoslovenské banské mestá ako venné majetky uhorskej kráľovnej Barbory Celjskej. In *Ars Montana: umělecký a kulturní transfer v otevřeném prostoru česko-saského Krušnohoří na prahu raného novověku.* Praha: ViaGaudium, pp. 367–76.

Dygo, M. (1988). Der Adel und das Geld in den Ostseeländern im 15. und am Anfang des 16. Jahrhunderts. *Studia maritima,* 7, pp. 7–23.

Dygo, M. (2003). Die Wirtschaftstätigkeit des Deutschen Ordens in Preußen im 14.–15. Jahrhundert, in Czaja, R. & Sarnowsky, J., eds. *Die Ritterorden in der europäischen Wirtschaft des Mittelalters.* Toruń: Wydawnictwo Uniwersytetu Mikolaja Kopernika, pp. 147–160.

Engel, P. (1994). Die Einkünfte Kaiser Sigismunds in Ungarn. In Macek, J., ed. *Sigismund von Luxemburg, Kaiser und König in Mitteleuropa 1387–1437. Beiträge zur Herrschaft Kaiser Sigismunds und der europäischen Geschichte um 1400.* Warendorf: Fahlbusch Verlag, pp. 179–83.

Filipczak-Kocur, A. (1999). Poland-Lithuania before partition. In Boney, R., ed. *The Rise of Fiscal State in Europe c. 1200–1815*. Oxford: Oxford University Press, pp. 442–79.

Fouquet, G. & Gilomen,H. J. (2010). *Netzwerke im europäischen Handel des Mittelalters*. Ostfildern: Jan Thorbecke Verlag.

Fügedi, E. (1980). Steuerlisten, Vermögen und soziale Gruppen in mittelalterlichen Städten. In Bátori, I., ed. *Städtische Gesellschaft und Reformation. Kleine Schriften, 2*. Stuttgart: Klett-Cotta Verlag, pp. 58–96.

Fügedi, E. (1982). Mátyás király jövedelme 1475-ben. *Századok*, 116, pp. 484–506.

Gilomen, H. J. (1984). *Der Rentenkauf im Mittelalter*. Habilitationsschrift. Basel: Basel Universität (manuscript available on-line).

Girsztowt, A. (2013). Kobiety na elbląskim rynku renty w okresie średniowiecza. *Komunikaty Mazursko-Warmińskie*, 281, pp. 481–98.

Goliński, M. (2003). W poszukiwaniu motywów sprzedaży rent nowych – przykład XIV-wiecznej Świdnicy. In Michaluk, D. & Mikulski, K., eds. *Miasta i mieszczaństwo w Europie środkowowschodniej do połowy XIX w.* Toruń: Wydawnictwo Adam Marszałek, pp. 321–32.

Goliński, M. (2006). *Wrocławskie spisy zastawów, długów i mienia żydowskiego z 1453 roku. Studium z historii kredytu i kultury materialnej*. Wrocław: Wydawnictwo Uniwersytetu Wrocławskiego.

Grulkowski, M. (2009). Rynek renty w Głównym Mieście Gdańsku w świetle najstarszych ksiąg gruntowych w XIV – XV wieku. In Kizik, E., ed. *Studia i materiały do dziejów domu gdańskiego, 1*. Gdańsk: Wydawnictwo Uniwersytetu Gdańskiego, pp. 21–98.

Guzowski, P. (2006). Klienci czy wierzyciele? Nie tylko o ekonomicznym wymiarze zastawu dóbr królewskich w pierwszej połowie XV wieku. In Dubas-Urwanowicz, E. & Urwanowicz, J., eds. *Patron i dwór. Magnateria Rzeczypospolitej w XVI-XVIII wieku*. Warszawa: Wydawnictwo DiG, pp. 67–86.

Guzowski, P. (2010). W poszukiwaniu gospodarki protestanckiej. In Bagińska, E., Guzowski, P. & Liedke, M., eds. *Studia nad reformacją*. Białystok: Uniwersytet w Białymstoku, pp. 111–35.

Hermann, Z. (1975). Államháztartás és a pénz értéke a Mohács előtti Magyarországon (Megjegyzések Thurzó Elek költségvetési előirányzatához). *Századok*, 109, pp. 301–36.

Holakovský, M. (1993). Finanční hospodaření na selských gruntech v předbělohorských jižních Čechách. *Jihočeský sborník historický*, 62, pp. 70–92.

Horn, M. (1985). Żydzi i mieszczanie na służbie królów polskich i wielkich książąt litewskich w latach 1386–1506. *Biuletyn Żydowskiego Instytutu Historycznego w Polsce*, 135–6, pp. 3–19.

Horn, M. (1986). Chrześcijańscy i żydowscy wierzyciele i bankierzy Zygmunta Starego i Zygmunta Augusta. *Biuletyn Żydowskiego Instytutu Historycznego w Polsce*, 139–40, pp. 3–11.

Hroch, M. & Klusáková, L., eds. (1996). *Criteria and Indicators of Backwardness: Essays on Uneven Development in European History: Seminar of General History of the Institute of World History, Faculty of Arts of Charles University at Prague*. Říčany u Prahy: Variant.

Janosz-Biskupowa, I. (1958). Materiały do dziejów lichwy w Prusach Krzyżackich w poł. XV wieku. *Studia i Materiały do Dziejów Wielkopolski i Pomorza*, 4(1), pp. 355–72.

Kardasz, C. (2013). *Rynek kredytu pieniężnego w miastach południowego pobrzeża Bałtyku w późnym średniowieczu (Greifswald, Gdańsk, Elbląg, Toruń, Rewel) / Monetary Credit Market in the Cities of the Southern Baltic Coast in the Late Middle Ages (Greifswald, Gdańsk, Elbląg, Toruń, Rewel)*. Toruń: Towarzystwo Naukowe.

Kenyeres, I. (2012). A bányakamarák szerepe a Magyar Királyság jövedelmeiben a 15–16. Században. In Mikó, G. et al., ed. *Tiszteletkör. Történeti tanulmányok Draskóczy István egyetemi tanár 60. Születésnapjára*. Budapest: ELTE Eötvös Kiadó, pp. 177–88.

Kozák, P. (2019). *Účty budínského dvora krále Vladislava II. Jagellonského (1494–1495)*. Praha: Scriptorium.

Křivka, J. (1986). *Zadlužení poddanského zemědělství na roudnickém panství v 18. století*. Praha: Academia.

Kubinyi, A. (1958). A királyi kincstartók oklevéladó működése Mátyástól Mohácsig. *Levéltári közlemények*, 28, pp. 35–60.

Kubinyi, A. (1992). Wirtschaftsgeschichtliche Probleme in den Beziehungen Ungarns zum Westen am Ende des Mittelalters. In Eberhard, W., ed. *Westmitteleuropa – Ostmittelaeuropa. Vergleiche und Beziehungen. Festschrift für Fedinand Seibt zum 65. Geburtstag*. München: Oldenburg, pp. 165–74.

Kubinyi, A. (2001). Ernuszt Zsigmond pécsi püspök rejtélyes halála és hagyatékának sorsa (A magyar igazságszolgáltatásnehézségei a középkor végén). *Századok*, 135, pp. 301–61.

Kula, W. (1962). *Teoria ekonomiczna ustroju feudalnego. Próba modelu*. Warszawa: Państwowe Wydawnictwo Naukowe.

Kula, W. (1976). *An economic theory of the feudal system: towards a model of the Polish economy, 1500–1800*. London: New Left Books.

Laszlovsky, J. et al., ed. (2018). *The Economy of Medieval Hungary*. Leiden: Brill.

Ledvinka, V. (1985). *Úvěr a zadlužení feudálního velkostatku v předbělohorských Čechách. Finanční hospodaření pánů z Hradce 1560–1596*. Praha: Ústav československých a světových dějin ČSAV.

Lesiński, B. (1976). Wyderek czyli sprzedaż nieruchomości z prawem odkupu w prawie polskim od XV do XVII wieku. *Czasopismo Prawno-Historyczne*, 28, pp. 19–67.

Liedke, M. & Guzowski, P. (2017). Problemy finansowe ewangelickiej Jednoty Litewskiej w pierwszej połowie XVII w. w świetle akt synodów prowincjonalnych. *Roczniki Dziejów Społecznych I Gospodarczych*, 78, pp. 95–130.

Łozowski, P. (2016). Struktura rynku kredytowego Starej Warszawy w latach 1427–1453. *Roczniki Dziejów Społecznych i Gospodarczych*, 76, pp. 165–208.

Łydkowska-Sowina, U. (1989). Ruch kredytowy w późnośredniowiecznym Sieradzu – pożyczki pieniężne, in Dembińska, M., ed. *Szkice z dziejów materialnego bytowania społeczeństwa polskiego*. Wrocław: Wydawnictwo PAN, pp. 119–35.

Mączak, A. (1976). Pieniądz i społeczeństwo w Rzeczypospolitej XVI–XVII w. *Roczniki Dziejów Społecznych i Gospodarczych*, 37, pp. 63–85.

Mainušová, H. (1965). Obchod gruntovními penězi na strážnickém panství na konci 16. a počátku 17. století. *Ceny, mzdy a měna*, 10, pp. 1–10.

Małowist, M. (1973a). *Wschód a Zachód Europy w XIII–XVI wieku. Konfrontacja struktur społecznogospodarczych*. Warszawa: Państwowe Wydawnictwo Naukowe.

Małowist, M. (1973b). Z problematyki wzrostu gospodarczego Europy Środkowo-Wschodniej w późnym średniowieczu i na początku XVI wieku. *Przegląd Historyczny*, 64(4), pp. 655–80.

Małowist, M. (1981). Merchant credit and the putting-out system: rural production during the Middle Ages. Review. *A Journal of the Fernand Braudel Center*, 4, pp. 667–81.

Małowist, M. (1985). Comments on the circulation of capital in East-Central Europe. In Mączak, A., Samsonowicz, H. & Burke, P., eds. *East-Central Europe in Transition from the 14th to the 17th century*. Cambridge: Cambridge University Press, pp. 109–27.

Małowist, M. (2010a). Merchant Credit and the Putting-Out System: Rural Production during the Middle Ages. In Batou, J. & Szlajfer, H., eds. *Western Europe, Eastern Europe and World Development, 13th–18th Centuries: Collection of Essays of Marian Małowist*. Leiden: Brill, pp. 73–84.

Małowist, M. (2010b). Some remarks on the role of merchant capital in Eastern Europe in the late Middle Ages. In Batou, J. & Szlajfer, H., eds. *Western Europe, Eastern Europe and World Development, 13th–18th Centuries: Collection of Essays of Marian Małowist*. Leiden: Brill, pp. 85–100.

Mályusz, E. (1965). Les débuts du vote de la taxe par les ordres dans la Hongrie féodale. In Csatári, D., Katus, L. & Rozsnyói, A., eds. *Nouvelles études historiques*, 1. Budapest: Akadémiai Kiadó, pp. 55–82.

Mályusz, E. (1986). Bajorországi állatkivitelünk a XIV-XV. században. *Agrártörténeti szemle*, 28, pp. 1–33.

Maříková, M. (2018). *Finance v životě pražské metropolitní kapituly. Hmotné zabezbečení kanovníků optikou účetních rejstříků z let 1358–1418*. Praha: Archiv hlavního města Prahy.

Mezník, J. (1960). Vývoj ceny rent a rentového vlastnictví v Brně ve 14. a 15. století. *Sborník prací Filosofické fakulty brněnské university. Řada C-historická*, 9(7), pp. 203–213.

Mezník, J. (1969). Der ökonomische Charakter Prags im 14. Jahrhundert. *Historica*, 17, pp. 43–91.

Mezník, J. (1972). Vlastnictví rent na Starém Městě počátkem 15. století. *Pražský sborník historický*, 7, pp. 50–61.

Mezník, J. (1990). *Praha před husitskou revolucí*. Praha: Academia.

Mezník, J. (1993). Oběh peněz mezi vrchností, městy a poddanými podle účtů třeboňského kláštera z let 1367–1369. *Sborník prací Filozofické fakulty Ostravské university*, 139, pp. 7–13.

Mezník, J. (1994). Model oběhu peněz v pozdním středověku. In Nesejt, F. & Wolf, V., eds. *Pohledy do minulosti. Sborník příspěvků k šedesátinám Doc. PhDr. Vladimíra Lesáka*. Hradec Králové: Gaudeamus, pp. 149–56.

Mikulski, K. (2008). Poll-tax (pogłówne) in fiscal system of Poland in early modern times 16th–17th century. In Cavaciocchi, S., ed. *Fiscal Systems in the European Economy from the 13th to the 18th Centuries*. Firenze: Firenze University Press, pp. 591–9.

Możejko, B. (2004). *Czynsz gdański w polityce Kazmierza Jagiellonczyka i jego synów, 1468–1516*. Gdańsk: Wydawnictwo Uniwersytetu Gdańskiego.

Muldrew, C. (1998). *The Economy of Obligation. The Culture of Credit and Social Relations in Early Modern England*. Basingstoke–New York: Palgrave.

Mycio, A. (1999). Formy kredytu mieszczańskiego na początku XVII wieku w świetle ksiąg ławniczych Starego Miasta Torunia. *Rocznik Toruński*, 26, pp. 55–70.

Myśliwski, G. (2008). From feudal rents towards a tax system in Central Europe (the thirteenth to the fifteenth century). In Cavaciocchi, S., ed. *La fiscalità nell'economia europea secc. XIII–XVIII*. Firenze: Firenze University Press, pp. 271–8.

Neumann, T. (2019). *Registrum Proventuum Regni Hungariae. A Magyar Királyság kincstartójának számadáskönyve (1494–1495)*. Budapest: MTA Bölcsészettudományi Kutatóközpont Történettudományi Intézet.

North, M., ed. (1991). *Kredit im spätmittelalterlichen und frühneuzeitlichen Europa*. Köln – Wien: Böhlau Verlag.

North, M., ed. (1995). *Von Aktie bis Zoll. Ein historisches Lexikon des Geldes*. München: C. H. Beck.

Odehnal, P. (2000). Měšťané a předměšťané klobučtí. Příspěvek k poznání hospodářských poměrů poddaných na brumovském panství ve druhé polovině 16. století na základě rozboru pozemkových knih. *Časopis Matice moravské*, 119, pp. 45–64.

Odehnal, P. (2011). "Paměť se činí, že se peníze gruntovní pasírují". K hospodaření poddaných na východní Moravě v 17. a počátkem 18. století. *Východní Morava*, 1, pp. 43–64.

Odehnal, P. (2013). Nad zlomkem gruntovní knihy vsi Šanov z druhé poloviny 17. století. *Východní Morava*, 3, pp. 19–35.

Orłowska, A. P. (2020). *Johan Pyre. Ein Kaufmann und sein Handelsbuch im spätmittelalterlichen Danzig*. Köln: Böhlau Verlag.

Paulinyi, O. (2005). *Gazdag föld – szegény ország*. Buza, J. & Draskóczy, I., eds. Budapest: Budapesti Corvinus Egyetem.

Polívka, M. (1993). Dva prameny z norimberských archivů k českým dějinám první třetiny 15. století. I. K držbě hradu v předhusitské a husitské době; II. Zpráva o financování bojů s husity v době obléhání hradu Bechyně v roce 1428. *Táborský archiv*, 5, pp. 20–31.

Polívka, M. (2004). "Liber Tewtonicorum des Ausgebens" – pramen k financování válek proti husitům z let 1428–1431. In Pánek, J., ed. *Vlast a rodný kraj v díle historika. Sborník prací žáků a přátel věnovaný profesoru Josefu Petráňovi*. Praha: Historický ústav Akademie věd České republiky, pp. 231–59.

Pounds, N. J. G. (1978). *An Economic History of Medieval Europe*. London: Longman.

Prajda, K. (2013). Florentine merchant companies established in Buda at the beginning of the 15th century'. *Mélanges de l'Ecole française de Rome. Moyen-Age*, 125-1 (available online only) https://doi.org/10.4000/mefrm.1062

Prajda, K. (2017). Florentines' Trade in the Kingdom of Hungary in the Fourteenth–Fifteenth Centuries. Trade Routes, Networks and Commodities. *Hungarian Historical Review*, 6(1), pp. 36–58.

Procházka, V. (1963). *Česká poddanská nemovitost v pozemkových knihách 16. a 17. století*. Praha: Nakladatelství Československé akademie věd.

Samsonowicz, H. (1960). Studia nad rentą miejską w Prusach w XV wieku. *Zapiski Historyczne*, 25(2), pp. 35–57.

Samsonowicz, H. (1961). Studien über hansischen Kaufmannskapital im 15. Jahrhundert. In Heitz, G. & Unger, M., eds. *Heinrich Sproemberg zum 70. Geburtstag*. Berlin: Forschungen zur mittelalterlichen Geschichte.

Samsonowicz, H. (1964). Formy pracy kupca hanzeatyckiego w XIV– XV w. Z dziejów techniki wymiany towarowo-pieniężnej. *Kwartalnik historii kultury materialnej*, 12(2), pp. 235–77.

Samsonowicz, H. (1969). *Untersuchungen über das Danziger Bürgerkapital in der zweiten Hälfte des 15. Jahrhunderts*. Weimar: Böhlau.

Samsonowicz, H. (1991). Die Rolle des Kredits im Wirtschaftsleben des mittelalterlichen Polen. In North, M., ed. *Kredit im spätmittelalterlichen und frühneuzeitlichen Europa*. Köln: Quellen und Darstellungen zur hansischen Geschichte NF, 37, pp. 159–70.

Samsonowicz, H. (1994). Local credit in mediaeval Poland. *Studia Historiae Oeconomicae, 21*, pp. 51–7.

Sepiał, M. (1998). Zastaw na dobrach ziemskich i dochodach królewskich w okresie panowania Władysława Warneńczyka na Węgrzech (1440–1444). *Zeszyty Naukowe Uniwersytetu Jagiellońskiego, Prace historyczne*, 125, pp. 35–49.

Slavíčková, P. (2014). The double-entry accounting system before 1800 as an example of a cultural transfer failure. In Čapská, V., ed. *Processes of Cultural Exchange in Central Europe, 1200-1800*. Opava: Silesian University, pp. 129–47.

Slavíčková, P. (2017). *Účetnictví mezi tradicí a racionalitou: v českých zemích od středověku do počátku 18. století*. Praha: Scriptorium.

Slavíčková, P. & Puchinger, Z. (2016). Accounting records of the town offices in Bohemia and Moravia: methodology and application. In Zaoral, R., ed. *Money and Finance in Central Europe during the Later Middle Ages*. Basingstoke: Palgrave Macmillan, pp. 155–68.

Šmahel, F. (2002). *Die Hussitische Revolution*. Hannover: Hansche Buchhandlung.

Stasavage, D. (2011). *States of Credit: Size, Power and the Development of European Polities*. Princeton and Oxford: Princeton University Press.

Štefánik, M. (2013). Daňové povinnosti banského a mincového mesta Kremnica v stredoveku. *Historický časopis, 61*, pp. 645–64.

Sterneck, T. (2004). K majetkovému zázemí a domácnosti rytíře Petra Doudlebského z Doudleb. *Husitský Tábor*, 14, pp. 259–362.

Teke, Z. (1984). Az 1427.évi firenzei catasto. Adalékok a firenzei–magyar kereskedelmi kapcsolatok történetéhez. *Történelmi Szemle*, 27(1–2), pp. 42–9.

Topolski, J. (1965). *Narodziny kapitalizmu w Europie XIV–XVII wieku*. Warszawa: Państwowe Wydawnictwo Naukowe.

Tóth, N. C. (2016). A Magyar királyság 1522.évi költségvetése. In Weisz, B., ed. *Pénz, posztó, piac. Gazdaságtörténeti tanulmányok a magyar középkorról*. Budapest: MTA Bölcsészettudományi Kutatóközpont Történettudományi Intézet, pp. 83–148.

Tóth, N. C. (2018). Bakóc Tamás kölcsönei a királynak. In Mária, K., ed. *Hadi és más nevezetes történetek: Tanulmányok Veszprémy László tiszteletére*. Budapest: HM Hadtörténeti Intézet és Múzeum.pp. 81–91.

Urfus, V. (1959). *Zdomácnění směnečného práva v českých zemích a počátky novodobého práva obchodního*. Praha: Československá akademie věd.

Urfus, V. (1960). *Vznik a počátky konkurzního práva v Čechách*. Praha: Československá akademie věd.

Urfus, V. (1975). *Právo, úvěr a lichva v minulosti*. Brno: Univerzita J. E. Purkyně.

Van Uytven, R. (1975). Politiek en economie: de crisis der late XVe eeuw in de Nederlanden. *Revue Belge de philologie et d'histoire*, 53, pp. 1097–1149.

von Stromer, W. (1970). *Oberdeutsche Hochfinanz 1350–1450* Teil III. Wiesbaden: Franz Steiner Verlag.

von Stromer, W. (1976). Die oberdeutschen Geld- und Wechselmärkte. Ihre Entwicklung vom Spätmittelalter bis zum Dreißigjährigen Krieg. *Scripta Mercaturae*, 10, pp. 23–51.

von Stromer, W. (1982). Hartgeld, Kredit und Giralgeld. Zu einer monetären Konjunkturtheorie des Spätmittelalters und der Wende zur Neuzeit. In Barbagli Bagnoli, V., ed. *La moneta nell'economia europea secoli XIII–XVIII: atti della "settima Settimana di studio" (11–17 aprile 1975)*. Firenze: Le Monnier, pp. 105–25.

Vorel, P. (1998). Úvěr, peníze a finanční transakce české a moravské aristokracie při cestách do zahraničí v polovině 16. století. *Český časopis historický*, 96, pp. 754–78.

Vorel, P. (2002). Frühkapitalismus und Steuerwesen in Böhmen (1526–1648). *Anzeiger der philosophisch – historischen Klasse. Österreichische Akademie der Wissenschaften*, 137, pp. 167–82.

Vorel, P. (2006). *Monetary Circulation in Central Europe at the Beginning of the Early Modern Age – Attempts to Establish a Shared Currency as an Aspect of the Political Culture of the 16th Century (1524–1573)*. Pardubice: Univerzita Pardubice, Filozofická fakulta.

Vorel, P. (2009). *Stříbro v evropském peněžním oběhu 16.–17. století (1472–1717)*. Praha: Rybka Publishers.

Vorel, P. (2014). Směnné kursy jako nástroj mocenské politiky v Římsko-německé říši počátkem čtyřicátých let 16. století. *Český časopis historický*, 112, pp. 379–401.

Wallerstein, I. (1976). *The Modern World-System: Capitalist Agriculture and the Origins of the European World-Economy in the Sixteenth Century*. New York: Academic Press.

Weissen, K. (2001). *Florentiner Bankiers und Deutschland (1275–1475). Kontinuität und Diskontinuität wirtschaftlicher Strukturen*. An unpublished habilitation thesis. Basel.

Weissen, K. (2003). I mercanti italiani e le fiere in Europa centrale alla fine del Medioevo e agli inizi dell'età moderna. In Lanaro, P., ed. *La pratica dello scambio. Sistemi di fiere, mercanti e città in Europa (1400–1700)*. Venezia: Marsilio, pp. 161–76.

Weissen, K. (2006). Florentiner Kaufleute in Deutschland bis zum Ende des 14. Jahrhunderts. In Irsigler, F., ed. *Zwischen Maas und Rhein. Beziehungen, Begegnungen und Konflikte in einem europäischen Kernraum von der Spätantike bis zum 19. Jahrhundert. Versuch einer Bilanz*. Trier: Kliomedia Verlag, pp. 363–401.

Weisz, B. (2017). Az alsó-magyarországi bányavárosok kiváltságai a Zsigmond-korban. In *URBS: magyar várostörténeti évkönyv XII*. Budapest: Főváros Levéltára, pp. 21–48.

Żabiński, Z. (1981). *Systemy pieniężne na ziemiach polskich*. Wrocław-Warszawa-Kraków-Łódź-Gdańsk: Zakład Narodowy im. Ossolińskich.

Zaoral, R. (2014). Taxes, loans, credit and debts in the 15th–century towns of Moravia: a case study of Olomouc and Brno. *Economics World*, 2(4), pp. 281–9.

Zaoral, R. (2015). Financial conditions in early 15th–century Olomouc in the light of the Jewish Register. In Doležalová, E., ed. *Juden in der mittelalterlichen Stadt – Jews in the medieval town. Colloquia mediaevalia Pragensia*, 7, Praha: Filosofia, pp. 131–7.

Zaoral, R., ed. (2016). *Money and Finance in Central Europe during the Later Middle Ages*. Basingstoke – New York: Palgrave Macmillan.

# Loans and debts as a part of royal finances

Part I

Loans and debts as a
part of royal finances

# Chapter 1

# Loan transactions in the Kingdom of Hungary up to the end of the 14th century

*Boglárka Weisz*

## Introduction

The earliest known credit transaction in Hungary was a loan from the church to the king in the 12th century. Borrowing money became common in the 13th century, initially from the church and from landowners. Townsmen only appeared in significant numbers among lenders at the end of the 13th century, although Jews were prominently involved throughout the century. This was the period when coins started to be minted in substantial quantities and there was an upsurge in trade and the circulation of money. Initially, loans were not secured against estates (except loans from Jews, which always required collateral), but the mortgages first appear in the middle of the 13th century. Townsmen established a firmer presence in the credit market during the 14th century, leading to the emergence of a new form, the annuity. All forms of credit used in the Kingdom of Hungary were established by the end of the 14th century, and did not change substantially even in the rapid proliferation and increasing amounts of credit in the 15th century (Lederer 1932). Here, I first concentrate on the loans taken out by Hungarian kings, whom they borrowed from, and how they repaid them, and then I present the types of loans and the social position of the lenders.

## Hungarian kings' borrowings

The first known royal loan in Hungary came from the church. Pannonhalma Abbey, out of money received from the sale of an estate, granted Géza II (1141–1162) a loan of 40 marks of silver, and was later rewarded by a royal grant of land (ÁÚO I, p. 61). Andrew II (1205–1235) took out somewhat larger loans. He needed the money primarily to finance participation in the Fifth Crusade, on which he departed in the summer of 1217, returning only the following year (Veszprémy 2006, p. 101). The lenders were Hungarian churches, clergymen, Hungarian noblemen and Italian merchants. Hungarian monasteries provided the king with valuable jewels which he took to sell on his journey. From the Diocese of Veszprém, he took the crown of Queen

Gisella (HO V, p. 8), wife of Stephen I (996/1000–1038), and from the Benedictines of Tihany, a precious-stone-encrusted chalice, mentioned as a *scyphus* (PRT X, p. 519). Priests provided large sums to Andrew II for his outward and return journeys (ÁÚO XI, p. 155). Italian merchants lent him silver, which he also used to finance the expedition, and the rent on the ships he hired from Venice, Ancona and Zara may also be interpreted as a loan (Robbert 1985, p. 431, Robbert 1995, p. 21). On his return from the Holy Land, the king borrowed 200 silver marks from Bán Atyus of Slavonia (ÁÚO XI, p. 161), probably to cover the costs of the campaign and to repay previous loans. Andrew repaid the loans in silver, by grants of land, and sometimes by the granting the annual salt tax. Andrew's son Béla IV (1235–1270) was obliged to take out loans on several occasions, mainly to finance military operations and defensive works during the Mongol Invasion. Like his father, Béla mostly sought financial assistance from churches, settling the loans with grants of estates (PRT II, p. 321), but private individuals were also featured among his lenders (HO VII, p. 83). Another Árpádian king, Ladislaus IV (1272–1290), took valuables from the diocese of Veszprém with the intention of selling them to finance military campaign expenses, granting an estate in return (CD V/2, pp. 265–6). After the extinction of the house of Árpád in 1301, the Angevin kings frequently borrowed from Italian merchants. Charles I (1301–1342) took a loan of 300 ounces of gold from Florentine merchants to settle his affairs in Hungary. In exchange, his grandmother, Queen Mary of Naples, pledged a gem-encrusted crown as collateral (MDE I, p. 174; Huszti 1941, pp. 57–9). Although we have no record of loans from the later stages of his rule, we may be sure that they continued to form part of his finances. Two new types of loan were added to the royal borrowing mechanism during the reign of his son, Louis I (1342–1382). Firstly, burghers of Hungarian towns, and even the towns themselves, appeared among royal creditors (DF 238 959). Secondly, the king started to mortgage royal castles and domains (the earliest was Óvár in the 1350s [today Mosonmagyaróvár], Sopron vm I, 354.). These two forms of finance were to provide the backbone of royal loans in the 15th century. For example, in 1363, Louis I mortgaged the castle of Köpcsény (today Kittsee, Austria) to the Wolfurtis for 6000 golden florins, Bishop Stephen of Zagreb standing as guarantor (HO VII, p. 410). The mortgage deed has not survived but later contracts make it clear that the king acted with the agreement of his wife Elizabeth (maybe previously his mother Elizabeth) and the barons (1380: Frangepán I, pp. 89–91), although they did not involve a guarantor (1382: DL 6134). The date of redemption was not specified in the mortgage deeds. Louis I mostly borrowed to finance foreign military expeditions, often experiencing the need in the midst of the campaign when he was not in a position to mortgage anything and the lender had to trust the king's word. In this case, the lender was not disappointed. On his Neapolitan campaign, for example, Marmonya, a knight of the royal court, gave the king 500 golden florins to pay his soldiers' bounty. This loan (together with Marmonya's other services) was repaid by a grant of land (1364: CDCr XIII, pp. 331–5). Louis I also had recourse to foreign loans to finance the campaign and found willing lenders among Italian towns (1380: MDE III, pp. 339–40, 374–86, 402–11, 420–3).

A form of 'loan' that emerged in the 13th century and found particular favour among Hungarian kings and queens was the leasing of royal revenues (Weisz 2010, p. 86; Weisz 2013, pp. 207–19) such as minting, tolls, customs duties [thirtieth, Hungarian: *harmincad*, Weisz 2018, pp. 259–60], for which the tenant paid rent in instalments. The tenant bore the costs of the operation and kept the revenue. Tenants bore liability for the source of revenue, and were obliged to sell land and other property if they did not pay their dues. The buyer subsequently enjoyed royal protection (1268: MES I, p. 551; 1369: DL 100 189). The lease system may be conceived as a kind of loan provided by the tenant, who was 'repaid' within a short time, although from the king's point of view, the rent payment could be interpreted as a credit to the tenant, necessitating the tenant's liability to the extent of his own property.

In addition to borrowing money, kings often had purchases made for themselves on domestic or foreign credit and paid for goods after receiving them. This form of purchase was already present in the royal court during the Árpádian age, and one of the most detailed sources on the practice is an account book written by Syr Wulam in the 1260s (Zolnay 1964). This is the documentation of a transaction worth 1500 silver marks, telling us about goods purchased for Stephen, 'junior king of Hungary' (1262–1270), and loans taken out by persons close to the king secured against pledges of chattels.

## Lenders

Kings initially borrowed from churches who, in the Árpádian age, also lent to other churches and to individuals. The increasing demand for money necessitated some compromises in the church's prohibition of interest. In Hungary, King Coloman (1095–1116) passed a law prohibiting men of the church from being 'usurers' *(feneratores)* (Decreta online, pp. 140, 151) but this only applied, in accordance with canon law, to collecting interest and not to lending money. There are several 13th-century records of church loans granted to private individuals who, in most cases, paid their debts by transferring title to an estate (1229: DF 200 627; 1256: ÁÚO VII, p. 433) but there is no record whether it was the mortgaged estate itself or was used to redeem the mortgaged estate. The churches certainly started to take mortgages against loans of money in the 13th century, and this practice became universal in the 14th century (1256: PRT II, p. 305; 1301: ZO I, p. 120; 1346: DF 210 167; 1351: AO V, pp. 509–10). In addition to landowners, townsmen (1378: CD IX/5, p. 285) also appeared among the borrowers, and loans were also provided to clergymen who provided collateral in the form of valuables, religious objects or land (1307: DF 200 084).

Starting in the Árpádian age, landowners lent money to other landowners, taking mortgages on their estates. Mortgaging usually took place before a place of authentication *(loca credibilia)* (1261: ÁÚO VIII, pp. 13–4), a county authority (1298: HO VII, pp. 267–8, 1338: CD VIII/4, pp. 367–8), or even the king (1301: CD VII/4, p. 262; 1346: HO II, pp. 84–6), and these institutions made out the associated documents. The documents concerning the mortgaged estate were also taken by the mortgagee as security. The estate remained in the lender's possession until it was redeemed by repayment of the principal *(debitum principale)*, an act performed before the same office that had overseen the mortgage. Upon repayment of the loan, the lender was required to return the estate and its documents together with the mortgage deed, which thus lapsed (1358: DL 94 081). In most cases, the mortgage was given for a fixed term (anything from a few months to 20 years), and at the end date, the amount borrowed had to be repaid. If the borrower was unable to pay, the amount was increased, indeed doubled (1334: DL 2804), or the parties could agree that the unredeemed estate (or a part equivalent in value to the loan) became the property of the mortgagee (1334: DL 2804; 1351: DL 68 898). There were also cases where the mortgage was made for an indefinite period (1351: AO V, pp. 425–6; 1365: DL 5380). The amount repayable did not increase with the passage of time but the mortgagee took the estate's income, providing the borrower with a motive to repay the loan whenever he could. The assignment of the mortgaged estate's revenue was therefore equivalent to payment of interest on an interest-free loan. The lender sometimes retained the revenue from the mortgaged estate until the end of the term even if the loan was repaid early (1269: UB I, p. 352; 1352: UGDS II, pp. 88–9). The revenue did not count as repayment of the loan (1338: MES III, p. 327), and many mortgage deeds expressly prohibited redemption before time. If the loan agreement provided for the original owner to retain the estate revenues, the borrower was obliged to pay the mortgagee a fixed annual sum (1351: DL 101 904), and thus paid interest. We know of mortgage deeds that provided for the reverse: revenue from the mortgaged estate had to be offset against the amount repayable (1352: DF 253 444; 1358: Teleki I, pp. 106–7) but this had to be explicitly stated for it to be enforced. In that case, the lender received no interest on his money. The terms of the mortgage could also state which of the estate revenues were not due to the lender. These were, for example, taxes, tolls, and revenue in kind (1346: DF 263 089). There was even a case where the borrower, upon redemption, had to pay half the costs of the new buildings put up by the lender on the mortgaged estate, failing which the lender could remove half of the buildings he had built (1365: CDCr XIII, pp. 487–8) or half of them would remain in his ownership (1351: DF 252 706).

The borrower/mortgagor guaranteed that the estate would remain in mortgage, meaning that the lender could take and retain possession of the land without hindrance for the term of the mortgage, failing which the lender would have to provide another estate of equal value. This stipulation arose from the need to obtain the consent of the neighbours and relatives, who had a right of pre-emption that extended to taking a mortgage on the estate. If the original owner died, a mortgaged estate could pass to his heirs and be divided among them, but only together with the loan which meant that they had to pay it back and the mortgagee had the right of pre-emption over the estate. The mortgagee could also pass on mortgage on the estate but only in such a way that the new owner of the mortgage provided the right of redemption. In many cases, debtors repaid the loan by assignment of the estate (1346: DL 90 653) or payment with another estate (1365: Zichy III, p. 276). If the value of the assigned estate was higher than the amount of the loan, the lender had to pay the difference (1346: CDCr XI, p. 297). Several mortgage deeds, however, expressly prohibited redemption in land, meaning that the lender demanded to be repaid in cash. One mortgage deed concerning a loan given in golden florins even stipulated repayment in golden florins (1363: DL 5253). Stipulations of redemption in cash (1304: AO I, p. 88) and payment in the debtor's his own money (1364: Héderváry I, pp. 59–60), meaning that he could not mortgage the estate to another lender, appear in the 14th century. Moreover, there were cases where the mortgagor could not re-mortgage the estate even after redemption to someone other than the previous mortgagee. Nonetheless, as we have already seen, even some 14th-century borrowers repaid their loans by assigning the mortgaged estate, re-mortgaging the property, or mortgaging another property. Mortgages were not confined to estates and could be given on property such as a mill (1364: DL 89 371) or a vineyard (1358: CD IX/2, pp. 705–7). Movable property could also be pledged as collateral, such as expensive clothes (1364: Krassó III, pp. 67–8), as could a source of income, such as a toll (1362: CD IX/3, pp. 315–16; 1376: DL 26 868) or 'vineyard duty' (*tributum montis, Bergrecht,* 1370: DL 58 587). The mortgagor/pledger and the mortgagee/pledgee could be either a man or a woman.

Some of the loans did not involve the direct provision of collateral. In some cases, the borrowers undertook to provide a mortgage of an estate if they could not repay the loan within the time limit (1341: DL 87 119), and in others, there was no such stipulation concerning the debt (1364: Sopron vm I, pp. 354–5) and the borrower merely undertook to pay it back by the due date (1329: DL 50 879). In such cases, however, especially where large amounts or tenant peasants were concerned, a guarantor was provided (1330: CD VIII/ 3, p. 509) or the peasant's lord gave a guarantee (1374: DL 103 337). There was also a case where someone became in sudden need of a loan when abroad which he repaid upon his return by assigning an estate

(1304: AO I, pp. 90–2) or the lender had to pursue his debt (1360: DL 38 831).

Private landowners also lent money to the churches against mortgages. In most of these cases, the date of redemption was not given (1346: Zichy II, pp. 186–7). Loans to churches did not always involve a mortgage, and the mode of repayment also varied. In interesting example, the archbishop of Esztergom borrowed money from Tamás Bedey to renovate the cathedral. Bedey subsequently purchased a piece of land that the archdiocese wanted but could not afford it and waived repayment of the loan on the sole condition that the archdiocese did not later challenge the purchase (CD VIII/1, pp. 175–7). Landowners also sold commodities – most commonly wine – on credit (1341: AO IV, pp. 118–9) but commercial credit was much more common among townsmen.

The first record of lending by a townsman dates from the late 13th century. A citizen of Esztergom lent money to a non-townsman, taking a mortgage on a meadow (1275: ÁÚO IX, pp. 132–3). Such loans become more common in the 14th century but always much less common than loans between landowners. Townsmen also lent to churches, but somewhat rarely. In the 14th century, towns as municipal bodies, as well as individual townsmen, provided mortgage credit to persons from outside the town (1352: UGDS II, pp. 88–9). These cases were similar to mortgage transactions between landowners, involving places of authentication which made out the documents for the transactions. Townsmen provided loans to foreigners as well as Hungarians. In these cases, the mortgaged estate was also in a foreign land (1364: DF 241 339).

Townsmen most often lent to citizens of, or persons owning property in, the same town, in exchange for which they took a mortgage on a property in the town. If the mortgagee made any improvements during the term of the mortgage (erecting new buildings, for example), the borrower was obliged to reimburse him for it upon redemption (1352: DL 87 265). The mortgagee could also extend the loan against an annuity *(purgrecht/Burgrecht)* connected with the property, usually three times a year. The borrower made his repayments by paying the annuity until he had paid as much as the loan, whereupon the property was returned to him (1346: DF 238 714). In this case, he repaid the loan without interest. The annuity could be sold – for ten times the amount – and the seller undertook to pay the rent to the buyer in future (usually in three instalments a year, in all towns) and his obligation persisted even after the amount of the loan had been repaid (1363: DF 238 808). Although this concerned a purchase, it may have involved a hidden loan, one that was disadvantageous to the seller, because the amount invested could be recovered several times over. If the property was of sufficiently high value, it could be encumbered with several mortgages, and there were even cases where it was re-mortgaged together with the annuity obligation, so that the lender was paying the annuity to the beneficiary of the annuity (who did not own the building), while the borrower undertook to repay the loan by the due date (1358: Zichy III, pp. 119–20). In this case, the annuity was smaller than the loan, so that interest was due on the loan but the borrower was relieved from paying the annuity at least for a while. The transaction was attested before the town judge in accordance with the particular customs of the town *(secundum usum et consuetudinem nostre civitatis ab antiquo approbatam)*.

The mortgage deed was made out by the town notary who charged a fee for the service (Ost, p. 79). The loan was entered into the municipal register and, if such was in use, the land register. Under municipal law, if the loan was not repaid after a year and a day, ownership of the collateral property passed to the lender, who could sell it freely. Besides land and buildings, chattels could be also pledged as collateral (1356: DL 51 725). The municipal body could also lend to citizens of the town, sometimes without collateral (1375: DL 105 414). The requirement for a mortgage on town property to be transacted before the municipal authority was aimed at safeguarding the authority's rights of supervision over properties within and around the town. This ensured that rights attaching to properties in the town would be acquired only by persons the municipal authority approved of. In 1355, for example, the municipal authority of Pozsony (today Bratislava, Slovakia) extended this rule to certain wine-growing estates it held to be important for the town, when Louis I granted to the citizens and *hospites* of the town exclusive rights of purchase or mortgage on the Prácson estate of Heiligenkreuz Abbey and any other of its estates and vineyards in the town or within the boundaries of Pozsony (DF 238 745).

Commercial credit also appeared in the Kingdom of Hungary in the Árpádian age, although the records of these transactions are fragmentary. The number of sources increases sharply in the 15th century, probably indicating a substantial rise in the volume of commercial credit. One of the scattered records from the Árpádian age concerns the debt that a citizen of Esztergom owed to a merchant of Gent, almost certainly for the price of the Gent broadcloth he had taken receipt for. The debtor was obliged to hand over his vineyard to the merchant (MES I, p. 606). The increase in trade conducted on credit in the 14th century was due to expansion of the merchant class which consisted mostly of traders who had come to the Kingdom of Hungary from abroad and gained citizenship of a Hungarian town. It involved credit that merchants extended to their customers (DL 6728, Teke 1995, p. 134) and purchase of goods on credit by the merchants themselves. The borrower in a commercial credit transaction was liable to the extent of his entire wealth. One driver of commercial credit was the acquisition of the staple right by an increasing number of towns and the accompanying growth of wholesale trade. When a merchant who sold goods in a town that held the staple right wanted to recover a debt from beyond the municipal boundaries, he was obliged to seek the town's permission (DF 269 235).

We find good illustrations of the spread of commercial credit in letters of exemption prohibiting *repressalia* and in a contract made in 1394 by which Kassa (today Košice, Slovakia) and Cracow permitted their merchants to sell goods freely in each other's towns. If either of these towns wished to terminate the agreement, it was obliged to give notice to the other town four months in advance, so that goods could be sent home and debts collected (DF 269 218).

Most of the information we have on Árpádian-age creditors in the Kingdom of Hungary concerns Jewish lenders, particularly the regulation of their activities (Berend 2001, pp. 116–20). The first to regulate credit transactions between Christians and Jews was King Coloman who fitted the legal constraints to the amount of the loan. If the loan was less than three *pensae*, collateral security had to be provided whether the loan was given by Christian to Jew or Jew to Christian, and Jewish and Christian witnesses were required for the transaction. For loans above three *pensae*, there were additional requirements: the amount of the loan and the names of the witnesses had to be put in writing and both parties had to apply their seals (Decreta online, pp. 132–3). This *cartula sigillata* guaranteed fair dealing to both parties (Kumorovitz 1960, pp. 11–2). A charter of privilege by which Béla IV regulated the rights of Jews (1251) also covers secured loans provided by Jews, and its provisions centre around the items acceptable as collateral and their redemption. There is no mention of the document and seals prescribed by Coloman. There are several possible reasons for this. Béla IV's charter was a Hungarian adaptation of an Austrian charter of privilege issued by Prince Frederick II of Austria (1230–1246) of 1238, and a slightly revised version of 1244. It is primarily concerned with the items of collateral provided to secure loans and only in one case mentions the credit document without prescribing its form. Jews could take almost anything – including real estate – as collateral but not church vestments (although this was permitted in the case that a senior clergyman wished to pledge it as collateral) or clothes that were bloody or damp. If no action had been taken in the matter after a year and a day, the collateral came into the Jew's ownership. Otherwise, if the item of collateral was worth less than the loan and the interest, it could be sold after one year. The Christian could redeem the pledge without paying the interest but was required to pay the interest within one month, failing which the interest was subsequently compounded (MZSO I, pp. 288–91). The Buda Synod of 1279 also prohibited the pledging of votive objects and church property (real or movable), except with the permission of a bishop, a chapter or a convent (RHMA pp. 565–602). Examples of such prohibitions also appear later, suggesting that these items were frequently pledged as collateral.

There is good evidence from 1371 that in Pozsony (and possibly other towns with large Jewish communities), a 'Jewish register' *(Judenpuech)* was in use in the late 14th century. This recorded every loan, whatever the amount, and even the interest, which amounted to two pfennigs (or less) weekly on each font, and for amounts of less than one font, one pfennig a week on sixty pfennigs or three schillings (MZSO I, pp. 82–3). The use of the Jewish register also required Christian and Jewish witnesses and the seals of the witnesses. The Buda Statute Book also regulated Jews' credit transactions, prohibiting the charging of interest but without specifying a penalty, leaving that to 'Judgement Day' (Ost, p. 126). The ban on interest therefore cannot be regarded as real. It also covered items of collateral (banning the pledge of church items) and the deed of pledge *(phanntt prieff)*. The latter had to be presented at the city hall once a year and the judge notified those affected (Ost, pp. 127–8). Thus, Buda also applied the rule that after the passage of a year and a day, the item of collateral passed into the ownership of the pledgee if the pledger did not make a statement concerning the collateral within this time. In Buda, such a statement could be made via the city judge. If a pledge nonetheless passed into the Jew's ownership, it could be offered for sale in the street of the Jews (in der juden gassen) on one day of the week (Ost, pp. 126–7). The deed of pledge was, in Buda, drafted by the city notary, who could charge Jews twice as much for the service as he did Christians (Ost, p. 79).

Louis I ordered the expulsion of the Jews from Hungary in 1360 and they were able to return only after 1367. The Christians who owed money to Jews saw their chance to get rid of their debts simply by not repaying them. In 1365, the municipal authority of Sopron approached Prince Rudolph IV of Austria (1358–1365) in the matter. The prince declared the credit documents concerning debts owed by citizens of Sopron to Jews who had fled into his country null and void unless the Jews could obtain a charter to the contrary from the Hungarian king (Házi I/1, p. 132). The Jews naturally made some effort to recover their money and those who had fled from Pozsony to Haimburg requested the aid of the Haimburg municipal authority in settling their affairs. An agreement was eventually reached with the Pozsony judge that those who presented their credit documents within one year could press their claim to recover the debt (1368: MZSO I, pp. 76–7). After the return of Jews, Louis I intervened several in the matter of Jewish loans. In 1378, for example, he informed the municipal authority of Pozsony that the Jews could demand repayment only in the currency in which they had made the loan, with an exception being made for interest. In the same year, however, he ordered that interest on loans be waived (MZSO I, p. 96). The Jews' clients included Hungarian and foreign subjects, clergy and laity, and towns.

The lease system, greatly favoured by monarchs, was also used by the churches. A lease could be granted on an estate or a house and involved all of its revenues. The lease period was usually between two and ten years. The rent had to be paid at specified times, usually once or twice a year for a long-term lease, and if payment was not made in time, twice the amount became payable (1352: DL 87 266; 1358: MES IV, pp. 205–6). Leases were also granted on sources of permanent revenue, most frequently tolls or tithes (1367: CD IX/7, p. 260; 1366: DF 238 833), or even on the total revenue of a church. In 1384, for example, Palatine Miklós Garai took a lease on the revenue of the archdiocese of Kalocsa for five years and had to pay the rent in three instalments to a Florentine merchant based in Buda, Maruccio di Paolo (Lederer 1932, pp. 258–9, DL 7350). The lease system also became common on townsmen's urban property in the second half of the 14th century.

## Conclusion

By the end of the 14th century, loans secured by guarantee, pledge of movable property, various types of mortgage, loans given against an annuity, commercial credit, and the lease system had all become established as forms of credit in the Kingdom of Hungary. The procedures for credit transactions became fully standardised in the 14th century. They involved written contracts and a specified institution depending on the parties or on the type of collateral. In most cases, loans were given for interest of varying amounts. Lenders included the king, the church, landowners, citizens and towns, and borrowers could also belong to any of these categories. The largest loans were taken out by the monarch (although to a much lesser extent that occurred in and after the 15th century) and by the churches, the latter being required to obtain the pope's consent for borrowing. Some debtors attempted to repay loans by taking out new ones but, in fortunate circumstances, they repaid them. The loan became an accepted and permanent form of the circulation of money.

## References

### Archival sources – unpublished

DF = Magyar Nemzeti Levéltár Országos Levéltára, Diplomatikai Fényképgyűjtemény.
DL = Magyar Nemzeti Levéltár Országos Levéltára, Diplomatikai Levéltár.

### Archival sources – published

AO = Nagy, Gy. Nagy, I. (1878–1920). *Anjoukori okmánytár, Codex diplomaticus Hungaricus Andegavensis I–VII*. Budapest: Magyar Tudományos Akadémia.
ÁÚO = Wenzel, G. (1860–1874). *Árpádkori új okmánytár, Codex diplomaticus Arpadianus continuatus, I–XII*. Pest–Budapest: Eggenberger Ferdinánd Akadémiai Könyvtársulás.
CD = Fejér, Gy. (1829–1844). *Codex diplomaticus Hungariae ecclesiasticus ac civilis I–XI*. Budae: n.p.
CDCr = Smičiklas, T. et al. (1904–1990). *Codex diplomaticus regni Croatiae, Dalmatiae et Slavoniae I–XVIII*. Zagreb: n.p.

Decreta online = Bak, J. (2019). *Online Decreta Regni Mediaevalis Hungariae. The Laws of the Medieval Kingdom of Hungary.* [Online] Available at: https:// digitalcommons.usu.edu/lib_mono/4/.

Frangepán = Thallóczy, L. & Barabás, S. (1910–1913). A Frangepán család oklevéltára. Budapest: Magyar Tudományos Akadémia.

Házi = Házi, J. (1921–1943). *Sopron szabad királyi város története I/1–II/6.* Sopron: Székely, Szabó és Társa.

Héderváry = Radvánszky, B. & Závodszky, L. (1909–1922). *A Héderváry-család oklevéltára I–II.* Budapest: Magyar Tudományos Akadémia.

HO = Nagy et al. (1865–1891). *Hazai okmánytár, Codex diplomaticus patrius I– VIII.* Győr–Budapest: Sauervein Géza.

Krassó = Pesty, F. (1882). *Krassó vármegye története III.* Budapest: Athenaeum.

MDE = Wenzel, G. (1874–1876). *Acta extra Andegavensia. Magyar diplomácziai emlékek az Anjou-korból I–III.* Budapest: Magyar Tudományos Akadémia.

MES = Knauz, F. et al. (1874–1999). *Monumenta ecclesiae Strigoniensis I–IV.* Esztergom–Budapest: Horák–Argumentum.

MZSO = Friss, Á. et al. (1903–1980). *Magyar-zsidó oklevéltár, Monumenta Hungariae Judaica I–XVIII.* Budapest: n.p.

Ost = Mollay, K. (1959). *Das Ofner Stadtrecht. Eine deutschsprachige Rechtssammlung des 15. Jahrhunderts aus Ungarn.* Budapest: Akadémiai Kiadó.

PRT = Erdélyi, L. & Pongrác, S. (1902–1916). *A pannonhalmi Szent-Bendek-rend története I–XII/B.* Budapest: Stephaneum.

RHMA = Endlicher S. L. (1849). *Rerum Hungaricarum monumenta Arpadiana.* Sangalli: Scheitlin–Zollikofer.

Sopron vm. = Nagy, I. (1889–1891). *Sopron vármegye története. Oklevéltár I–II.* Sopron: Litfass Károly.

Teleki = Barabás, S. (1895). *Codex diplomaticus sacri romani imperii comitum familiae Teleki de Szék, A római szent birodalmi gróf Széki Teleki család oklevéltára I–II.* Budapest: Athenaeum.

UB = Wagner, H. & Lindeck-Pozza, I. (1955–1985). *Urkundenbuch des Burgenlandes und der angrenzenden Gebiete der Komitate Wieselburg, Ödenburg und Eisenburg I–IV.* Wien–Graz–Köln: Böhlau.

UGDS = Zimmermann, F., Werner, C. & Gündisch, G. (1892–1991). *Urkundenbuch zur Geschichte der Deutschen in Siebenbürgen I–VII.* Hermannstadt – Köln – Wien – Bucureşt: n.p.

Zichy = Nagy, I. et al. (1871–1915). *A zichi és vásonkeői gróf Zichy-család idősb ágának okmánytára, Codex diplomaticus domus senioris Comitum Zichy de Zich et Vasonkeő I–XI.* Pest–Budapest: n.p.

ZO = Nagy, I. et al. (1886–1890). *Zala vármegye története, Oklevéltár I–II.* Budapest: Zala vármegye közönsége.

## Literature

Berend, N. (2001). *At the Gate of Christendom: Jews, Muslims and 'Pagans' in Medieval Hungary c. 1000–c. 1300.* Cambridge: Cambridge University Press.

Huszti, D. (1941). *Olasz-magyar kereskedelmi kapcsolatok a középkorban. (A Római Magyar Történeti Intézet kiadványai 3).* Budapest: Magyar Tudományos Akadémia.

Kumorovitz, L. B. (1960). *Die erste Epoche der ungarischen privatrechtlichen Schriftlichkeit im Mittelalter (XI–XII. Jahrhundert).* Budapest.

Lederer, E. (1932). *A középkori pénzüzletek története Magyarországon (1000–1458).* Budapest: Magyar Tudományos Akadémia.

Robbert, L. B. (1985). Venice and the Crusades. In Zacour, N. P. & Hazard, H. W., eds. *The Impact of the Crusades on the Near East, (A History of the Crusade 5).* Madison and Wisconsin: University of Visconsin Press, pp. 438–51.

Robbert, L. B. (1995). Venetian participation in the Crusade of Damietta. *Studi Veneziani,* 30, pp. 15–33.

Teke, Zs. (1995). Firenzei üzletemberek Magyarországon 1373–1403. *Történelmi Szemle,* 37, pp. 129–50.

Veszprémy, L. (2006). II. András magyar király keresztes hadjárata, 1217–1218. In Laszlovszky, J., Majorossy, J. & Zsengellér, J., eds. *Magyarország és a keresztes háborúk. Lovagrendek és emlékeik.* Máriabesnyő-Gödöllő: Attraktor, pp. 99–112.

Weisz, B. (2010). Kamaraispánok az Árpád-korban. *Turul,* 83, pp. 79–87.

Weisz, B. (2013). Entrate reali e politica economica nell'età di Carlo I. In Csukovits, E., ed. *L'Ungheria angioina.* Roma: Viella, pp. 205–36.

Weisz, B. (2018). Royal Revenues in the Árpádian Age. In Laszlovszky, J., Nagy, B., Szabó, P. & Vadas, A., eds. *The Economy of Medieval Hungary.* Leiden–Boston: Brill, pp. 255–64.

Zolnay, L. (1964). István ifjabb király számadása 1264-ből. *Budapest Régiségei,* 21, pp. 79–114.

Chapter 2

# Loans and debts of the Bohemian kings in the Middle Ages

## From the last Přemyslids until the end of the pre-Hussite period (1262–1419)

*Zdeněk Žalud*

## Introduction

The loans of medieval rulers are extraordinary incomes which, at some points of reign, supplemented insufficient regular incomes. From the historical sources, we are often worse informed about the credit terms than about consequence of a loan, that is about debt and conditions of its payment, often in the form of a pledge. Medieval rulers of Bohemia and Moravia from the Přemyslid dynasty, who became the last bearers of the kingship in Central Europe at the beginning of the 13th century, used their revenues not only for the purpose of government, but also for prestige promotion and propaganda. In Italy, Ottokar II Přemysl, called the 'king of iron and gold', was rumoured to have 200,000 golden marks and 800,000 silver marks in his four castles in four towers, not to mention golden and silver dishes, jewels, and countless decorations (Kuthan 1993, p. 39). According to the Description of Germany (*Descriptio Theutoniae*) from about 1290, the Bohemian king had a revenue of 100,000 silver marks annually and an unknown author, describing Eastern Europe in 1308, argues that Bohemian kings are mighty not thanks to number of inhabitants, but because of monetary resources flowing from silver mines used for the hiring of mercenaries (Žemlička 2011, 246; Jan 2015, p. 13).

The key concept for the better understanding of medieval royal economy in Bohemia is the royal chamber (*camera regis*), which denotes not only the place, where the royal revenues were directed, but also the summary of king's property and incomes flowing from it (Žemlička 2011, pp. 246–7). The Bohemian exile Pavel Stránský, only in 17th century, tried to aptly express what the revenues of Bohemian kings are based on. His words are, however, applicable for the High and Late Middle Ages as well: 'Regular royal incomes in Bohemia flow partly from annual pay of monasteries and free towns, partly from golden and silver mines, partly from duties and partly from real estates, called chamber or alimental or land registry estates' (Žemlička 2011, pp. 232–3). One part of the regular royal revenues originated not only from taxation of various economic activities of subordinated institutions, but also from real estates, which were managed by kings via their loyal administrators. During the high-medieval colonisation in Central Europe, the structure of pays, levies, and burdens transformed from natural taxes into pecuniary taxes. Kings monopolised some rights connected with revenues – since then the so-called royal rights (*iura regalia*) – they could also lease or pledge them. Royal incomes and expenses fluctuated depending on wars, paying of wealthy dowries, recompenses, occupation of new territories, etc. Extant records of these fluctuations are so unsatisfactory that it is usually difficult to associate these tendencies with particular amounts of money.

> Accounts of the Bohemian king and his court do not survive before the second half of the 14th century and the later situation for Czech lands is, unfortunately, not satisfactory either. Therefore, it is not surprising that studies on the finances of earlier periods are based on documents, forms, letters and narrative sources rather than accounting books.
>
> (Žalud 2016, p. 59)

In spite of dismal state of historical records, we often ascertain loans and debts of Bohemian kings of high and late middle ages. We should remember that 'ordinary revenues of the majority of the medieval rulers often barely sufficed for their everyday needs and did not allow them to accumulate substantial reserves. Therefore, it would be mistaken to attribute to medieval rulers some budgetary irresponsibility' (Postan 1979, p. 431). It is rather appropriate to speak about the chaotic complexity of royal financial transactions. A large part of regular incomes did not come to the royal chamber in order to be distributed but was sent by the kings directly from its source to recipients or creditors. The contemporary researcher is neither able to find out how the repayments of debts were supervised nor to discover the financial value of property of pledge in relation to amounts which were paid from it as payment of debts. That is why the following study presents the first and only rough outline (or chronological survey) of the finance-flow between Bohemian kings as debtors, on the one hand, and their creditors, on the other.

## Loans and debts of the last Přemyslids

The expansion of silver production in the Bohemian-Moravian highlands from the late 1230s and the expanding power of Ottokar II Přemysl, king of Bohemia (1253–1278) to the Alpine lands and the Venetian region in the 1260s and 1270s started trade connections between Italy, especially Venice and Bohemia. The Bohemian king set three currency reforms in 1253, 1260–1261, and 1268–1270 in order to make trade contacts with Venice easier (Zaoral 2019, pp. 213–14). The first loans of the king Ottokar

II Přemysl from abroad are documented in 1262 in Italy. The king's creditors were financiers of Florence (the papal banker Dulcis de Burgo and his business partners) and it cannot be ruled out that king's debts were covered by the Bohemian export of precious metals to Venice (Žemlička 2011, p. 349). Before introducing Prague groschen in 1300, the kings of Bohemia were able to multiply their incomes by regular re-coinage or coin renewal (renovatio monetae), pursued twice a year. In the Czech lands, there were about 12 mints that produced royal coins, mostly leased to burghers (Jan 2015, pp. 496, 501). The leading royal officers of these mints – the so-called urburéři – were certainly the main regular creditors of Bohemian kings.

The sources of Bohemian royal economy – the royal chamber – were considerably exhausted by Ottokar's war with the King of the Romans Rudolph I of Habsburg and with rebellious nobility between 1276 and 1278 (Žemlička 2011, pp. 246, 450). In the early 1280s, the Czech lands seemed to have to pay 15,000 silver marks from the taxation to Otto V the Long, Margrave of Brandenburg, for the returning of the Přemyslid prince and the heir of the Bohemian throne, Wenceslaus II (Jan 2015, pp. 46, 61). His successful politics and territorial expansion of the kingdom from the 1290s was conditioned by increasing of silver production in Bohemia after the discovery of silver ore in Kutná Hora (Zaoral 2019, p. 216). Florentine merchants Rinieri, Apardo, and Cyno called the Lombardian anticipated fabulous gains from conducting business in the lands of the 'silver' king. That is why they 'acted as a bank and rented the office of mint master and a mine from the king, including royal income from smelted precious metals (so-called urbura) with the aim of carrying out a complete monetary reform' (Zaoral 2019, p. 216). The introduction of the Prague groschen in 1300, that should maintain permanent value, finished the period of inflationary regular recoinage.

The Florentines carried on business in real estate and lent the king as well as his nobility huge amounts of money. Apardo became an administrator of the royal economy in the office of chamberlain (subcamerarius). It seems that loans from the Florentine consortium were never repaid during the reign of the last Přemyslids – one of the merchants' claims the amount of 28,000 silver marks from their successor King John the Blind (of Luxembourg) in 1311. The burdensome financial situation of the royal economy after 1305 was result of expensive foreign policy and the war with the Roman King Albert I of Habsburg. The terminally sick Wenceslaus II ordered his heir as well as his most important courtiers to settle royal debts. After the premature death of Wenceslaus III in 1306, his royal treasure carried to the expedition to Poland was stolen and his successor, the Bohemian king Rudolph I of Habsburg, started to pay the old debts by instalments of 1000 silver marks per week from the royal income from smelted precious metals and from the royal chamber (de urbura et fisco regio) (Jan 2015, p. 499).

During the anarchy in Bohemia after Rudolph's death in 1307, the amounts from precious metals in Kutná Hora as well as other royal incomes and real estates became the means of haggle over the political benefits of aristocracy, namely Raimund of Lichtenburg, Henry of Lipa, and John of Wartenberg. The Bohemian nobility began to look for a more capable successor than Henry of Carinthia and the young king John the Blind (of Luxembourg) had to take over the indebted kingdom (Žalud 2016, p. 61).

## Kings of Bohemia from the House of Luxembourg and their extraordinary incomes

John the Blind exploited his regular financial resources – especially taxes, king´s mining revenue (*urbura*), and coinage – but made use of incomes from mercenary service, alliance agreements, from booty, and ransom. He also extended the Bohemian kingdom to Lusatia and Silesia, imposing taxes on his new subjects. During his reign, King John amassed a disorganized and vast tangle of debts and their repayment by John's successors – Emperor and King Charles IV and Wenceslaus, Duke of Luxembourg – was in some cases prolonged until 1370s. John's last will from 1340 shows that the blind king was aware of the problem and appealed to his successors to continue repaying his debts. Among the executors of his last will, we can find royal financiers from the upper social classes – his uncle Baldwin, Archbishop of Trier, Rudolph, Duke of Saxony, noble Peter of Rosenberg and Vaněk of Wartenberg – as well as Abbots of Cistercian monasteries in Bohemia, etc. Some important financiers, however, are not named in that document: Frenzlin (Franz) Jacobi from the patrician family of Prague, Gisco (Gisilbert) of Reste from Silesia, and Arnold of Arlon from the County of Luxembourg (Žalud 2016, pp. 66–72). Many of the royal real estates and revenues were pledged, the burden of older royal debts was growing and so John's heir of throne, Prince Charles, observed the almost complete pledging of real estates and castles in 1330s. Prince Charles tried to improve unfavourable situation of royal economy and established the annual taxation of monasteries in Moravia and later in Bohemia (Borovský 2005, p. 123), yet he could not avoid taking out loans from the nobility as well as from wealthy patricians (Šusta 1946, pp. 216–19). Charles' complicated cooperation with his father by ruling in Bohemia and Moravia was finished by an agreement at the beginning of 1342. King John should stay beyond the kingdom two years in exchange of revenue of 5000 silver marks (Šusta 1946, pp. 370–2). It seems that indebtedness of the kingdom did not decreased considerably during this period and so Charles forced his father to promise not to alienate other royal real estates, especially towns and castles, in the presence of pope Clement VI in Avignon in 1344 (Šusta 1946, p. 415). The commitment was not fulfilled: increased expenses on the Charles' election the King of the Romans in 1346 caused cancellation of such a restriction. Charles had to buy votes of the electors – except for his father – and that is why several capable financiers, especially Arnold of Arlon and Rainhard of Schönau, were employed. Their loans were assured mostly by deeds of pledge. The vote of Charles great-uncle, Baldwin, Archbishop of Trier, was secured by pledging almost the whole County of Luxemburg (Knake 2010, p. 396).

Charles ascension to the throne of the King of the Romans coincides with the crushing defeat of his cavalry and the death of his father at the battle of Crécy. Over three years, Charles had to assert his rank in Germany against the Wittelsbach party and abundant deeds of pledge helped him to recruit political followers (Bender 1967). He 'contracted nearly a third of all the pledges in the Middle Ages' (in total about 1100 pledge contracts) but 'strictly avoided pledging his own hereditary territory' (Isenmann 1999, p. 254). However, we must confess that pledging policy of Charles IV in his Central European domains remain unresearched. If we should mention only one important Charles' financier from the first period of his rule (1346–1378), it would be Dietrich of Portitz, who rose from humble beginnings to the title of archbishop of Magdeburg (1361–1367) and was an important personality at the court of Charles IV. Never named to the office of chamberlain (*subcamerarius*), Dietrich as the king's main creditor got an extraordinary privilege from him in 1357. Charles pledged him all royal revenues from the Bohemian kingdom till the repayment of his financial claims. Dietrich's nephew was elevated to the Bohemian nobility and became the burgrave of Vyšehrad in 1360 (Fajt 2015, pp. 144–96). After Dietrich's departure for Magdeburg, his position in the administration of the royal finances was taken by Bohemian noblemen, honoured with title 'Master of the royal chamber' (*magister camerae regalis*): Zbyněk Zajíc of Hasenburg, Bušek the Younger of Velhartice, Boreš V. of Riesenburg, Hašek of Zvířetice, and Těma of Colditz (Kavka 1991, pp. 23–36). An accommodating creditor of the often-indebted king and (from 1355) emperor was his younger brother John Henry, margrave of Moravia (1322–1375). Thanks to Adolf Nuglisch, we have Charles' revenues from the Holy Roman Empire relatively well documented. The emperor's two campaigns to Italy in 1355 and 1368 were especially lucrative: the first 'Romzug' brought him – according to Nuglisch – more than 565,000 golden florins, the second provided him with more than 311,000 golden florins (Nuglisch 1899, pp. 112, 115).

The most complicated military and diplomatic operation of Charles' territorial politics was conquest of the Margraviate of Brandenburg in 1373. Although the land was conquered by armed forces, the circumspect emperor prepared for the defeated Wittelsbach Margrave Otto financial compensation of 500,000 guilders. The main creditors of this munificent amount were Bohemian towns, the margrave of Moravia along with his adult sons (64,000 florins), whereas Charles' domain in the Upper Palatinate (in Bavaria) were given to the Wittelsbachs as a pledge (Kavka 1993, pp. 150–5). Charles IV paid for the election of his first son Wenceslaus IV as King of the Romans in 1376 with another huge amount of 120,000 florins, which was later collected from the free imperial cities in form of an extraordinary tax (Rapp 2007, p. 224; Kavka 1993, pp. 176–92). Such ambitious foreign politics was not conceivable without considerable credits. According to F. Kavka and F. Šmahel, Charles IV drew from his pledged family domains (Bohemia, Moravia, etc.) ca 50,000 threescore groschen, whereas his deeds of pledge in the Roman Empire brought him credits of 445,000 silver marks, 270,000 halers, and 698,000 golden florins. These enormous deeds of pledge weakened economic potential of the royal chamber until the reign of his successor, King Wenceslaus IV. The slow repayment of the pledges, which dragged on for years, brought financial losses to the royal chamber (Šmahel 1995, p. 208).

Between 1330 and 1350, the production of silver ore in Kutná Hora declined from 20–30,000 kg annually to ca 10,000. Moreover, the constant outflow of precious metals from the Bohemian kingdom abroad weakened the economic potential of the land. Both rulers, Charles as well as Wenceslaus, tried to compensate these losses by the debasement of the quality of the Prague groschen and of its small change, they both strived for restriction of metal export, but in vain. The value of Prague groschen in relation to Hungarian ducat was depreciated by 42 per cent during Charles' reign and by 50 per cent during Wenceslaus' reign, to 1419 (Šmahel 1995, pp. 210–11). However, the evaluation of this development is not unequivocal nowadays (Čechura 2012, p. 325).

Just as his father, Wenceslaus IV was inventive in relation to the means of the enrichment of the royal chamber. It is documented by the loan of 20,000 guilders from his expectant brother-in-law King Richard II of England in 1381 (Bartlová & Bobková 2003, p. 304), yields of three papal tithes in 1380–1400 (in sum ca 4200 threescore Prague groschen) or by his one-time amortization of Christian debts towards Jews in the free imperial cities in Germany, which made him a profit of 40,000 golden florins (Šmahel 1995, p. 219; Hruza 2005, p. 125). On the one hand, Wenceslaus collected valuables (or treasure) and protected them at his royal castles, on the other hand, he callously exploited repeated taxation of royal towns and monasteries, often during a single year. The king was afflicted by several political disasters – prisoner of the Bohemian nobility in 1395, deposition from the kingship of the Romans and war with Ruprecht of Palatinate in 1400, prisoner of his brother Sigismund in 1402 – accompanied by economic disasters – the pillaging of Kutná Hora, the most important mining town in Bohemia, along with the loss of valuables in 1403, substantial debasement of the quality of the Prague groschen and of its small change in 1407 (Castelin 1953, pp. 142–3). According to F. Šmahel, repeated debasement together with lack of precious metals in Bohemia caused a profound decline of the royal finances as well as of the Bohemian coin system in 1417–18 (Šmahel 1995, pp. 214, 220).

Delineation of the economic situation of the royal chamber is more explicit at the end of the 14th century. Not only charters, forms, and narrative sources are preserved, but also extensive remains of royal registers of real estates, the arrangement of the collection of taxes from royal towns and monasteries, and a roll of expenditures of the royal chamber in 1418. This roll shows that about 55 per cent of royal incomes from towns and monasteries was sent by kings directly from their sources to creditors. We are able to gain precise data; however, such lists of revenues are not all-inclusive (Šmahel 1995, pp. 217–19). From the royal registers of real estates, we can gain a realistic idea about the amount and social status of the royal creditors under Wenceslaus IV. The dukes and margraves of Moravia held the highest position among them, then the Bohemian Lords – Jan Krušina of Lichenburg, Těma of Colditz, Boček of Poděbrad, Petr Zmrzlík of Svojšín or Jan Ťavák of Schwamberg – but the most numerous was lesser nobility and rich townspeople – Jan of Lestkov, Zikmund Huler, Mikuláš called the Poor of Lobkovic, Jan of Chotěmic, Jan Sádlo of Smilkov, Vlášek of Kladno, Filip Lout of Dědice, Petr of Netvořice or Konrád of Vechta. Many of them became holders of important royal castles and strongholds or court offices. The most important financial offices of the king remained the chamberlain (*subcamerarius*) and the Masters of the royal chamber (*magistri camerae regalis*) but we are not able to distinguish their official authority more clearly nowadays.

After the debasement of 1407, it seems the king took into account the descending value of coins when he issued some deeds. Real estates, that were pledged by Wenceslaus at that time, got two monetary values: the first, lower, in case of redeeming it by Wenceslaus himself, the second, higher, in case of redeeming it by his successors. These options are documented for the pledged estates Potštejn and Kostelec nad Orlicí (1409), Dvůr Králové nad Labem (1410), and for some properties in Moravia in 1413. In this troubled era associated with plundering companies, many people of noble birth, but impoverished, became robbers or mercenaries. That is why Wenceslaus often used his revenues as soldier's pay or as recompense.

## Conclusion

From the beginning of the 15th century, a social and religious ferment with trade unrest and armed robberies, ongoing debasement of the currency, inconsiderate royal taxation, debts paid over long terms, and increasing royal deeds of pledge – it all together caused and intensified the crises of the royal finances. After Wenceslaus death in 1419, the royal chamber of his legitimate successor Sigismund, king of Hungary, later also Emperor and King of Bohemia, was exhausted by the 14-year-long Hussite wars. Sigismund was forced not only to alienate royal real estates, but also to pledge church property at that time. The Hussite wars dramatically changed the ownership in the Bohemian kingdom: a considerable reduction of royal property and dissipation of the property of the Catholic Church.

This process, however, started already under the reign of Wenceslaus IV or even sooner, during the 14th century. According to Miloš Prokop, Wenceslaus had at his disposal ca 30 castles in 1418, but almost $2/_3$ of them were pledged; he had also about 35–40 fiefdom castles, but many of them were pledged too (Prokop 2004, pp. 147–9). The total sum of Sigismund's pledges reached almost 490,000 threescore Prague groschen but its real value was much higher. During the Hussite wars, Bohemian church institutions lost more than 350,000 threescore groschen (Šmahel 1996, p. 64). It is perhaps obvious from the foregoing presentation that despite the long-lasting and destructive power of the Hussite wars, the revolutionary outcome of the Hussite period was conditioned also by the excessively ambitious or sometimes even reckless financial politics of Sigismund's predecessors.

## References

Bartlová, M. & Bobková, L. (2003). *Velké dějiny zemí Koruny české IV.b: 1310–1402*. Praha: Paseka.

Bender, K. (1967). *Die Verpfändung von Reichseigentum in den ersten drei Regierungsjahren Karls IV. von 1346 bis 1349*, Dissertation, Hamburg.

Borovský, T. (2005). *Kláštery, panovník a zakladatelé na středověké Moravě*. Brno: Matice moravská.

Castelin, K. (1953). *Česká drobná mince doby předhusitské a husitské*. Praha: Nakladatelství Československé akademie věd.

Čechura, J. (2012). Královská komora a královské finance lucemburské epochy. In Bobková, L. & Šmahel, F., eds. *Lucemburkové: česká koruna uprostřed Evropy*. Praha: Nakladatelství Lidové noviny, pp. 319–28.

Fajt, J. (2015). *Der lange Schatten Kaiser Karls IV. Zur Rezeption der luxemburgischen Herrschaftsrepräsentation in den nordöstlichen Territorien des Heiligen Römischen Reichs*. Prag: Národní galerie.

Hruza, K. (2005). Anno domini 1385 do burden die iuden… gevangen. Die vorweggenommene Wirkung skandalöser Urkunden König Wenzels (IV.). In Herold, P. & Hruza, K., eds. *Wege zur Urkunde. Wege der Urkunde. Wege der Forschung. Beiträge zur europäischen Diplomatik des Mittelalters* (Forschungen zur Kaiser- und Papstgeschichte / Beihefte zu J.F. Böhmer, Regesta Imperii 24). Wien: Böhlau, pp. 117–67.

Isenmann, E. (1999). The Holy Roman Empire in the Middle Ages, in: Bonney, R., ed. *The Rise of the Fiscal State in Europe c.1200–1815*. New York: Oxford University Press, pp. 243–80.

Jan, L. (2015). *Václav II. Král na stříbrném trůnu 1283–1305*. Praha: Argo.

Kavka, F. (1991). Správci financí Karla IV. Příspěvek k dějinám české královské komory. *Numismatické listy* 46/5–6, pp. 138–50.

Kavka, F. (1993). *Vláda Karla IV. za jeho císařství (1355–1378). Země České koruny, rodová, říšská a evropská politika. II. díl (1364–1378)*. Praha: Univerzita Karlova – Karolinum.

Knake, S. (2010). »Mietekiese« der Kurfürsten Korruption bei römisch-deutschen Königswahlen 1346–1486. In Grüne, N. & Slanička, S., eds. *Korruption: historische Annäherungen an eine Grundfigur politischer Kommunikation*, Göttingen: Vandenhoeck & Ruprecht, pp. 387–408.

Kuthan J. (1993). *Přemysl Otakar II. Král železný a zlatý, král zakladatel a mecenáš.* Vimperk: Tina.

Nuglisch, A. (1899). *Das Finanzwesen des deutschen* Reiches *unter Kaiser Karl IV.* Dissertation, Strassburg.

Postan, M. M., Rich, E. E., & Miller E. (eds.) (1979). *The Cambridge Economic History of Europe. Volume III, Economic History and Policies in the Middle Ages.* Cambridge: Cambridge University Press.

Prokop, M. (2004). Držba hradů v Čechách v letech 1418–1478 jako zdroj poznání majetkových poměrů české šlechty, panovníka a církve. *Husitský Tábor: sborník Husitského muzea, 14.* Tábor: Husitské muzeum, pp. 147–226.

Rapp, F. (2007). *Svatá říše římská národa německého. Od Oty Velikého po Karla V.* Praha – Litomyšl: Paseka.

Šmahel, F. (1995). *Husitská revoluce 1*, Praha: Univerzita Karlova – Karolinum.

Šmahel, F. (1996). *Husitská revoluce 4*, Praha: Univerzita Karlova – Karolinum.

Šusta, J. (1946). *Karel IV. Otec a syn. 1333–1346* (České dějiny, dílu II. část 3.), Praha: Jan Laichter.

Zaoral, R. (2019). Mining, Coinage, and Metal Export in the Thirteenth Century: The Czech Lands and Italy in Comparative Perspective. In Nagy, B., Vadas, A., & Schmieder F., eds. *The Medieval Networks in East Central Europe: Commerce, Contacts, Communication.* Oxon – New York: Routledge, pp. 211–226.

Žalud, Z. (2016). Financiers to the Blind King. Funding the Court of John the Blind (1310–1346). In Zaoral, R., ed. *Money and finance in Central Europe during the later Middle Ages.* Basingstoke, Hampshire, New York: Palgrave Macmillan, pp. 59–75.

Žemlička, J. (2011). *Přemysl Otakar II. Král na rozhraní věků.* Praha: Nakladatelství Lidové Noviny.

# Chapter 3

# Income and expenditures of the Hungarian Royal Chamber during the first ruling years of King Vladislaus Jagiellon

## Analysis of an accounting register from the years 1494–1495

*Petr Kozák*

At the very end of the Middle Ages, the accounts kept at the court of the Hungarian sovereigns, along with most of the Hungarian royal archives, were destroyed. Unfortunately, only fragments of the originally rich material are available today. By far the most important source from this group is traditionally considered to be the rare preserved income and expenditure account of the Hungarian king, namely the kingdom, from 1494–1495, the original of which is now stored in the National Széchényi Library in Budapest, Hungary. The manuscript contains an overview of the income of Hungarian throne for the two accounting periods and a concurrent inventory of the ruler court's expenditure, with a final balance sheet written by an official of the Hungarian royal treasurer, Bishop Sigismund Ernuszt of Pécs. The aim of the study will be to present, at least in general, the source – well known especially to Hungarian historians – and the interpretative pitfalls associated with it. The importance of the accounting register from 1494–1495 is also illustrated by the fact that it has recently been published twice in the form of a source critical edition (Kozák 2019; Neumann 2019).

Until recently, the income and expenditure account of the Hungarian royal treasury from 1494–1495 generally served as a source documenting the decline in royal income after the death of Matthias Corvinus and the takeover of the government by the new Jagiellonian dynasty (see, e.g. Soltész 1905; Fógel 1913, pp. 13–28; Hermann 1975). However, as Tibor Neumann (2019, pp. 8–25, 50–67) has newly shown with a detailed analysis of preserved accounting and other related sources, reality was much more complicated. In order to understand the interpretative potential and limits of the surviving accounting register, the following questions need to be asked: 1. What is the manuscript, what were the circumstances of its origin (including the general historical context)? 2. What did the structure of the income of Hungarian kings in the second half of the 15th century look like? 3. Which of these royal incomes were registered (and which were not) in the surviving register? The idea that the account book from 1494–1495 sums up all the income (and expenditure) of the Kingdom of Hungary and the Hungarian royal court, which can be easily summed up to provide an uncomplicated picture of the financial condition of the late medieval Hungarian state, seems hardly sustainable in light of the newest findings.

The system of financial management of the Kingdom of Hungary, as it operated in the mid-1490s, was the result of reforms enforced during the reign of King Matthias Corvinus. Their aim was to maximize the income part of the sovereign's budget (Kalous 2009, pp. 90–4). The chief architect of the renovation of the financial and tax system was John Ernuszt, a Viennese Jew, and from the mid-15th century, a Buda burgher who worked his way up to head of the office of Hungarian royal treasurer (*thesaurarius*). The above-mentioned Sigismund Ernuszt, bishop of Pécs and royal treasurer of Hungary from 1494–1496, was one of his sons. The treasurer's office was directly subordinated to the ruling monarch; during the reign of Matthias Corvinus, the influence of the estates on its operation was greatly reduced. It was an extensive, centralized institution at the end of the Middle Ages. The royal treasurer had a vice-treasurer (*vicethesaurarius*) at his disposal, a number of scribes, secretaries, and accountants. He also used the services of a system of tax collectors (in numbers approaching one to two hundred persons). Collectors (*dicatores proventuum*) were sent, usually in twos, to individual counties that formed the backbone of the kingdom's administrative system. In addition to the office of the central treasury, ispáns of salt, mining and coin chambers, as well as crown tax administrators, that is thirtieth (*tricesima, tricesimatores*), which was a fixed customs duty on foreign trade, were under the authority of the treasurer. Research has so far identified a total of 450 officials who were in the service of the Hungarian royal treasurer between 1458 and 1500 (Kubinyi 1957, p. 29).

We can reasonably assume that the accounting system introduced during the office of the Hungarian royal treasurer was quite sophisticated, and that besides the main accounting records there were numerous, variously extensive specialized registers (e.g. Neumann 2019, pp. 20, 62), as it was around 1500 in Jagiellonian Poland, for example (Kozák 2014, pp. XV–XIX; Bołdyrew & Bołdyrew 2014). Unfortunately, we can only get an idea of what it was like thanks to a few preserved pieces of accounting records. The extent of the preservation of the accounting sources associated with the operation of the Hungarian royal court was fundamentally affected by a catastrophe in 1526, during which almost the entire (medieval) archive of Hungarian rulers was destroyed. After the Battle of Mohács, when the young Jagiellonian King Louis fell on the run, the country plunged into chaos. Queen Maria of Habsburg had the most valuable archive, including the Hungarian crown archive, loaded onto ships to protect everything essential in the northwest of the country in Bratislava, which was, as it was judged, outside the reach of the Ottoman sultan's troops. Unfortunately, somewhere in the bend of the Danube near Esztergom, the ship with the archive sunk to the bottom of the river. Written documents of royal authorities from before 1526 have thus mostly been preserved in the archives of recipients – church institutions, towns, aristocratic family archives – and authorities with notarial powers (Kalous 2009, pp. 94–6). From the presumed extensive, internally structured accounting agenda of the Hungarian royal treasurer (or for the older period of its institutional predecessors), only one comprehensive volume of accounting records was preserved from the time when the Hungarian royal treasury was headed by Bishop Sigismund Ernuszt. This is the aforementioned volume documenting royal income and expenditures for the years 1494–1495. Only a fraction of accounting records from 1525 and 1526 is available today, which treasurer Alexius Thurzó was in charge of managing (Engel 1809; Fraknói 1877). In addition, a balance sheet from the years 1522–1523 is available to researchers; this is from when the personally absent Jagiellonian King Louis, who was in the Bohemian lands at the time, was represented by Palatine Stephen Bátori (C. Tóth 2010, pp. 231–58).

The oldest completely preserved (covering two complete accounting periods) account, recording the income and expenditure of the Hungarian crown, and thus the Hungarian monarch and his court, is represented by the register from 1494 to 1495, when Pécs Bishop Sigismund Ernuszt, son of John Ernuszt, architect of financial administration reform from the time of King Matthias Corvinus, was in charge of the operation of the Hungarian royal treasury. This account book was preserved thanks to a combination of lucky coincidences. An important coincidence is that the account register is not likely to have been deposited in the royal archives as other volumes arising from the activities of the royal treasury. It is not a 'standard' product of a continually maintained accounting agenda, but rather a retroactively (artificially) created cartulary of a certain portion of royal income and expenses of the given accounting period, which was intended to serve primarily in the investigation of Sigismund Ernuszt and his deputy, vice-treasurer Emeric Dombai, accused in the summer of 1496 of extensive embezzlement of the monarchs' finances. While the original register from the time of Ernuszt's office as royal treasurer probably ended at the bottom of the Danube, a copy of it remained, which was most likely compiled, as convincingly demonstrated by Tibor Neumann (2019, p. 57), in just two to three weeks between mid-July and mid-August 1496.

The case of the fall of royal treasurer Sigismund Ernuszt has repeatedly attracted the attention of historians (recently, e.g. Kubinyi 2001, pp. 316–18; Fedeles 2011, pp. 34–7). Most recently, Tibor Neumann (2019, pp. 8–18, 50–60) attempted to analyse the events of the time. The basic outline of the story is roughly as follows. Sigismund Ernuszt, holder of an extraordinarily profitable bishopric, was one of the leading barons of the kingdom and a person close to the ruling monarch. At a certain point, he, Chancellor

Thomas Bakóc, and the first among Hungarian dignitaries, Palatine Stephen Szapolyai, became persons to whom the Hungarian estate society projected all the disagreements it had with the ruler. At the end of spring and the beginning of summer of 1496, the controversial moments focused primarily on the issue of the collection of certain taxes. The departure of Sigismund Ernuszt from the office of royal treasurer was in fact an attempt by the royal court to unblock negotiations and induce the estates gathered at the assembly to approve the collection of a special tax, namely the one-florin tax (*contributio unius floreni*). However, the monarch's compromise did not lead to the desired goal. On the contrary, tensions increased, Bishop Ernuszt was accused by the nobility of misusing taxes already levied by the Hungarian assembly, and the accumulated frustration even resulted in a violent uproar in early July. In mid-July 1496, the King seemed to comply with the pressure of the nobility and instructed Bishop Ernuszt to present the accounts to prove that the tax collection and the use of the funds thus obtained was correct. The composition of the committee of inquiry, which was not exactly impartial to the accused, led to the accusation of Sigismund Ernuszt and his deputy (vice-treasurer) Emeric Dombai for the embezzlement of royal finances. King Vladislaus, who had little room for maneuver, had to sacrifice his servant in the end. Ernuszt and Dombai were arrested. Dombai, who was subsequently indicated as the chief architect of the embezzlement, was unable to pay his way out and remained imprisoned in the fortress of Timișoara. Ernuszt was interned at the Siklós Castle in Baranya County under the supervision of the ispán of Temes, Joseph Somi, and his rights (including property rights) concerning his clerical functions were suspended. However, he managed to negotiate a ransom for his release. Ludovicus Tubero mentioned the sum of 280,000 florins. Antonio Bonfini, a contemporary of the day, even mentioned a fabulous 400,000 florins. Both amounts are likely to be exaggerated but the cost of freedom was probably not negligible. Additionally, at the end of October 1496, the townspeople of Levoča informed the city council of Bardejov that Bishop Ernuszt was to set out on a journey to Buda with a caravan of nine wagons loaded with gold and valuables. After paying the fine, Sigismund Ernuszt was released, and he was also allowed to take charge of the administration of the diocese. However, until his death in 1505, he no longer held any royal office; his career at court was finished. At the time King Vladislaus strengthened his position, gaining finances as well as (in terms of an exemplary hard procedure) respect within the Hungarian estate society.

The foregoing indicates that there is one circumstance that must be considered essential, that is the fact that the preserved accounting register from 1494 to 1495 is not a list of all the income and expenditures of King Vladislaus. In fact, it is 'only' a record of income and expenditure of the monarch that: 1. Fell under the authority of the Hungarian royal treasurer; 2. Were also subject to the supervision of the Hungarian estates (Kozák

2019, pp. 22–3; Neumann 2019, pp. 18–19, 61). Therefore, the sum of the registered amounts with the subsequent income and expenditure balance sheet of the budget is by no means a reflection of the whole of the Kingdom's fiscal potency, it merely captures one part, albeit a very significant part. This was already pointed out in the late 1950s by András Kubinyi, who also offered an analysis of the structure of the content of the account register. He also noted that, relatively (compared to the traditional estimates for the period of the reign of Matthias Corvinus), the lower amounts entering the royal treasury in 1494–1495 reflect the fact that, despite the assumptions supported by the suggestive title 'Registrum omnium proventuum regalium', it does not record all the financial sources of the monarch and their management (Kubinyi 1958, pp. 46–8).

Ernuszt's codex is therefore no more than an account of taxes approved by the Hungarian estates, which fell within the jurisdiction of the royal treasurer. Moreover, it is a secondary compilation from other accounts kept during the office of the treasurer for the purposes of the commission, whose task was to investigate the economy of the use of tax funds, the collection of which was subject to the consent of the Hungarian assembly. It was not by chance that the one-florin tax was at the centre of interest, because King Vladislaus's (repeated) demand for its approval by the estates triggered a wave of displeasure in the spring and summer of 1496, and became, as we already know, a formal cause to charge tax officers with embezzlement. It was also the record of the one-florin tax that largely determined the structure of the analysed account book, as the register is divided into two main, unequally extensive blocks corresponding to two 'accounting years'. The first year began on 30 January 1494, on the day of the appointment of Bishop Ernuszt to the office of royal treasurer, and ended on 15 July 1495. The second year started after this date and ended with the end of 1495. While the first 'year' lasted about a year and a half, the second 'year' was only about six months. The reason was, as Tibor Neumann pointed out, the mechanism of collection and processing of the one-florin tax. The second one-florin tax during Ernuszt's term of office was approved by the Hungarian assembly in June 1495, with the first income from it expected after 15 July 1495. This was the reason for the start of a new 'accounting year'. Similarly, the third approved one-florin tax from the time of Ernuszt's office (which could not yet be concluded at the time of the bishop's investigation) was approved by the estates in October 1495, with the fact that it was to be collected after 1 January 1496. This is why the second 'accounting year' ended with the end of the calendar year of 1495. 'Accounting years' are therefore an artificial element created for the purpose of compiling a register for the needs of the investigating estates commission (Kozák 2019, pp. 22–3; Neumann 2019, pp. 19–21, 61–3). The issue that makes it difficult to interpret the data in the register is that according to the logic of the administration of the one-florin tax, royal treasury clerks also included other categories of income and expenditure in the codex within one or another 'accounting year', guided by the effort to balance the income and expenditure side for each of the two separate accounting periods. This often disrupted the chronological sequence of recorded data and the natural link between certain income and expenditure items. Moreover, the day-to-day running of the treasury did not make any distinction between money that came from income approved by the estates and funds that the monarch obtained from other sources. Since it was not always technically possible to separate the two groups, from time to time the surviving register also contains royal income whose collection was not under the influence of the estates. However, the record of this income is fundamentally random and unsystematic in the preserved source (Neumann 2019, pp. 22–4, 64–6).

As in other European monarchies of the period under review, the incomes of Hungarian monarchs can be divided into two basic groups: 1. Taxes, the collection of which was subject to the consent of the estates; 2. Regular royal income, the collection and utilization of which was not influenced by the estates. The mentioned one-florin tax, which was levied by the nobility from Hungary and Transylvania, fell under the first group at the end of the 15th century. The core of the one-florin tax was the older direct tax (*lucrum camerae*) levied from a precisely specified number of tax units – serf gates (*porta*). In the case of Slavonia, however, ravaged in the first half of the 1490s with domestic wars, mainly by repeated Ottoman raids, the tax burden was lower; only half a florin, that is the half-florin-tax (*contributio medii floreni*) was paid from a predefined number of serf gates. The first group included a special tax of Transylvania Saxons and the urban extraordinary tax. The second group consisted of a mix of income, which included ordinary royal taxes from cities, a regular tax from Saxon cities in Transylvania (*census*), profits of the royal treasury from salt and coin chambers and ore mining, twentieth (*vigesima*), thirtieth (*tricesima*) and the Transylvania fiftieth (*quinquagesima*), taxes levied by specific ethno-political units of the Cumans and Jazygians, and finally, income that the monarch had from his own royal domains (Kalous 2009, pp. 92–4; Neumann 2019, pp. 21–2, 63–4).

The register therefore records the one-florin tax and the half-florin-tax, collected and accounted for in the years 1494–1495. The first 'accounting year' also registered income from royal cities (particularly the extraordinary tax), amounts levied for the king from Transylvania by Saxons and Székelys, money paid to the treasury from the Jews (*taxa Iudeorum*), or additional payments from the previous accounting period. The provisor of Buda sent a one-off amount collected from the Cumans and the Jazygians, which basically substituted the one-florin tax, by which the Cumans and the Jazygians were set free. In the second 'accounting year', income other than from the one-florin tax is almost absent (a total of eight records are the sum of all possible income that cannot be broken down into coherent chapters). While in the first 'accounting year' the one-florin tax accounted for more than half of the income recorded in the register, in the second 'accounting year' it represented almost the entire income component of the monarch's budget. However, we must reiterate that the surviving register only records part of the income, namely that which the Hungarian estates had the right to control and which fell under the authority of the Hungarian royal treasurer. This means that all the king's income from Croatia and the rest of Dalmatia, sums managed by the captains of Senj and the provisors of Belgrade, or the ispán of Temes as the captain general of the Lower Parts, are missing, as the treasurer had no direct influence on their collection. Similarly, income that the monarch received from his own royal domains, administered for him by the provisor of Buda Castle, the castellan of Komárom and the castellan of Tata, was not under the immediate supervision of the royal treasurer. Tibor Neumann also pointed out that in addition to income received by the king in the form of payment in kind, some of the income managed by the royal treasurer was absent from the register – specifically income that the king had from the salt monopoly, mining and coinage (Neumann 2019, pp. 22, 64). These were not negligible amounts, as shown by research of the time of the reign of King Matthias Corvinus, when the average yields of salt, mining and coinage chambers amounted to up to 140,000 florins (Kalous 2009, p. 93).

Income that was subject to control by the estates and fell under the jurisdiction of the Hungarian royal treasurer was estimated in the preserved register by authorized officials from the royal treasury at 197,484 and a half florins in the first, and 136,634 florins in the second 'accounting year'. In total, the amount slightly exceeded the sum of 313,939 florins in the period 1494–1495. Just the one-florin tax accounted for 106,158 and a half florins in the first 'accounting year', and 125,629 florins in the second. The system of accounting records was not particularly complicated, the income and expenditure components were free of complicated rubrication and originally appeared to form a simple series of chronologically ordered entries. A higher degree of formalization of records de facto only occurs in the case of the record of the one-florin tax, or the half-florin-tax (for Slavonia). In this case, the scribe rubricated the sections according to individual counties (Slavonia and Transylvania were treated collectively). Each 'county account' had a fixed structure: 1. Planned amount of the tax; 2. Sums actually levied to the royal treasury (after deducting the costs of the salaries of the county staff); 3. Settlement of the said remuneration for collectors and county court and administrative officials; 4. Record of unpaid tax with a brief explanation of why it was not paid. In addition to actually levied sums (see above), we therefore also have ideal expectations of the collection of the one-florin tax and half-florin-tax. For the first 'accounting year', the treasury office planned a tax revenue of 206,585 florins, and up to 219,586 florins for the second year. The actual revenue of this tax authorized by the estates was thus de facto only half of the planned amount (namely 51% and 57%

respectively). There are multiple reasons for this situation. The owners of some estates held royal documents that exempted them from paying the tax. The collection of part of the tax was delegated directly to other persons as a form of payment of their claims against the royal treasury. Some of the taxpayers at the time were rebels against the royal authority. Others were unable to honour their obligations simply because their estates suffered from hold-outs of various armies in recent years. Antonín Kalous (2009, p. 94) offered the hypothesis that Vladislaus's predecessor, King Matthias Corvinus, simply overstepped the kingdom's fiscal policy and sucked the country dry, which naturally resulted in a decline in tax revenues after his death. It is true that the sums are not always perfect in the source, which can be attributed to the rush in which the register was compiled. However, we can undoubtedly get a basic idea of the amount of registered income.

Expenditure recorded in the 1494–1495 accounting register reveals the tendency of the compilers to show the dissatisfied estates that a substantial part of taxes approved by them were actually used by the monarch (and the royal treasurer) to defend the kingdom against an internal and external enemy, and as compensation for important representatives of the estates society, including the Hungarian palatine, the voivode of Transylvania, or aristocrats at the head of the south Hungarian banates. A large part of the records is thus related to expenses for the operation and reconstruction of forts on the Hungarian–Ottoman border. However, they particularly document the course of military actions both against the Ottoman neighbour, and opposition lead by Bosnian Duke Lawrence Újlaki. In November 1494, the army of King Vladislaus attacked the footholds of Újlaki and his allies, in the middle of December, good-walled Újlak (Ilok in present-day Croatia) was captured, where the monarch and his entourage publicly celebrated thereafter this military victory. In early 1495, Lawrence Újlaki was besieged at the castle of Németújvár (Güssing in present-day Austria), where he surrendered in the hopeless situation. At the end of February 1495, he and other geneats had to humble themselves before the triumphant king (Fedeles 2012). Accounting records provide valuable information on ammunition and weapon supply (on land and water), and more generally logistics and tactical leadership of military campaigns. There is also evidence of accolades, in which young noblemen were awarded the title of knight. Details of the circumstances of the ceasefire with the Ottoman Empire, which occurred in the King's presence in 1495 in Pécs, the residential city of Bishop Ernuszt (Baczkowski 1997, pp. 335–7), are also interesting. The variety of types of expenditure items is much more diverse, however. Among other things, the pages of the account book depict the daily government 'functioning' of the Hungarian-Bohemian Jagiellonian personnel union, because Vladislaus Jagiellon was not only a Hungarian (and Croatian) monarch, but also King of Bohemia. The income and expenditure balance sheet is passive. Expenditure exceeded income by 20–30 thousand florins (depending on the corrections of subtotals). However, this in itself does not say much about the real status of 'state' finances at the given time. The real (total) amount of Hungarian income of King Vladislaus was, as we know, different (higher). On the other hand, the expenditure was certainly also higher than that shown in the preserved accounting register. Caution is therefore appropriate.

The income and expenditure register of the King (Kingdom) of Hungary for the years 1494–1495, from January 1494 to the end of December 1495, is undoubtedly an extraordinary source in terms of its significance. At the same time, it is a tricky material whose interpretation is not always easy. It is not the product of a continuously maintained accounting agenda. In fact, it is a compilation of various (other) accounting registers, compiled by officials of the Hungarian royal treasury in the summer of 1496 in association with the investigation of the (then already former) royal treasurer Sigismund Ernuszt, accused by the Hungarian estates of financial embezzlement. Despite the suggestive title 'Registrum omnium proventuum regalium', only some of the income and expenditure of the Hungarian monarch was recorded on the pages of the analysed account book. The records were adjusted multiple times to meet the need to present before the investigating estate commission the correct settlement of a key income item, namely the one-florin tax approved by them. The numerical data offered by the accounting source can therefore not be accepted separately and uncritically. The historical context and the knowledge that the 1494–1495 account book is a mere (albeit significant) piece of the mosaic is also a key factor here.

## References

Baczkowski, K. (1997). Europa wobec problemu tureckiego w latach 1493–1495. *Studia Historyczne*, 40, pp. 313–40.

Bołdyrew, A. & Bołdyrew, A. (2014). Royal bills as the source of the history of taste and food in Poland of the last Jagiellons. Basic sources and research possibilities. *Piotrkowskie Zeszyty Historyczne*, 15, pp. 11–27.

C. Tóth, N., ed. (2010). *Politikatörténeti források Bátori István első helytartóságához (1522–1523)*. Budapest: Magyar Országos Levéltár.

Engel, J. Ch., ed. (1809). Fragmentum libri rationarii super erogationibus aulae Regis Hungariae Ludovici II. de anno 1526. In Engel, J. Ch., ed. *Monumenta Ungrica*. Viennae: Antonius Doll, pp. 185–236.

Fedeles, T. (2011). *"Eztán Pécs tűnik szemünkbe". A város középkori históriája (1009–1526)*. Pécs: Pro Pannónia.

Fedeles, T. (2012). *A király és a lázadó herceg. Az Újlaki Lőrinc és szövetségesei elleni királyi hadjárat (1494–1495)*. Szeged: Szegedi Középkorász Műhely.

Fógel, J. (1913). *II. Ulászló udvartartása (1490–1516)*. Budapest: Magyar Tudományos Akadémia.

Fraknói, V., ed. (1877). II. Lajos király számadási könyve (1525. január 12–július 16). *Magyar Történelmi Tár, 22*. Budapest: Magyar Tudományos Akadémia, pp. 45–236.

Hermann, Zs. (1975). Államháztartás és a pénz értéke a Mohács előtti Magyarországon (Megjegyzések Thurzó Elek költségvetési előirányzatához). *Századok*, 109, pp. 301–36.

Kalous, A. (2009). *Matyáš Korvín (1443–1490). Uherský a český král*. České Budějovice: Veduta.

Kozák, P., ed. (2014). *Účty dvora prince Zikmunda Jagellonského, vévody hlohovského a opavského, nejvyššího hejtmana Slezska a Lužic, z let (1493) 1500–1507: Kritická edice pramene*. *Rationes curiae Sigismundi Iagellonici, ducis Glogoviensis et Opaviensis, Silesiae et Lusatiarum summi capitanei, de annis (1493) 1500–1507: Editio critica*. Praha: Scriptorium.

Kozák, P., ed. (2019). *Účty budínského dvora krále Vladislava II. Jagellonského (1494–1495)*. Praha: Scriptorium.

Kubinyi, A. (1957). A kincstári személyzet a XV. század második felében. *Tanulmányok Budapest múltjából*, 12, pp. 25–49.

Kubinyi, A. (1958). A királyi kincstartók oklevéladó működése Mátyástól Mohácsig. *Levéltári Közlemények*, 28, pp. 35–60.

Kubinyi, A. (2001). Ernuszt Zsigmond pécsi püspök rejtélyes halála és hagyatékának sorsa (A magyar igazságszolgáltatás nehézségei a középkor végén). *Századok*, 135, pp. 301–61.

Neumann, T., ed. (2019). *Registrum proventuum regni Hungariae. A Magyar Királyság kincstartójának számadáskönyve (1494–1495)*. Budapest: Magyar Tudományos Akadémia.

Soltész, G. (1905). *Az 1494. és 1495. évi királyi számadások művelődéstörténeti vonatkozásai*. Budapest: Barcza József.

Chapter 4

# The beginnings of royal pledging in the Kingdom of Hungary

*János Incze*

## Introduction

> Then, it is known to all what great and frequent dangers attended
> and arose in the affairs of the royal majesty and the whole country by
> the pledging and temporary alienation of the real and just revenues
> of the Holy Crown of the kingdom to diverse persons, as was done
> hitherto.
>
> (Decreta regni, pp. 177–9)

With these words, the first article of the royal decree promulgated at the diet
of 1514 begins. Its prominent place assigned in the decree shows clearly how
pressing the issue of pledged and alienated royal revenues and possession
became for the crown of Hungary in the early 16th century. In accordance
with this as well, the measures prescribed by the decree reflect the severity
of the problem. It was decided at the diet that half of pledged and alienated
royal possessions and revenues had to be returned to the king after his
remaining debts had been cleared away. Four years later, even more drastic
measures were taken at another diet, as a new decree ordered that not only
half of pledged and leased royal rights and revenues had to be returned to
the king, as had been formerly decided, but all of it (CIH, p. 756).

While similar regulations concerning the recovery of pledged royal
possessions emerged in other parts of Central Europe in this period, the
problem gained special importance in Hungary because of the looming
Ottoman threat and because of how great a financial challenge this posed to
the kingdom (Ludwig 1984, pp. 113–17, 121; Matuszewski 1997, pp. 52–
3; Isenmann 1999, pp. 253, 265). On the one hand, the royal revenues
had dwindled during the Jagiellonians' rule in comparison to the earlier
period. This was partly because the number of taxable tenants dropped in
the southern regions of the kingdom, but also because not all royal revenues
were collected for the treasury owing to various military and fiscal reforms
of the late 15th century. Finally, the continuous putting in pledge and alienation of the royal domains and revenues had also greatly contributed to the

emergence of this situation (Neumann et al. 2019, pp. 57–9; Fógel 1913, pp. 14–15. Pálosfalvi 2018, p. 455). On the other hand, not only were the revenues lower, but expenses became so high that it was not always possible to meet them, sometimes not even the treasury's basic expenditures. For fending off the Ottoman danger, a chain of castles and forts were erected alongside the southern border already in the first part of the 15th century and later extended with new ones. This defence system could fulfil its purpose entirely only if armed troops were stationed in the castles. To this end, a permanent army was established in the kingdom which was, at that time, one of the earliest on the continent, but its costs represented an enormous financial burden for the kingdom. The most severe financial troubles came forward when, besides paying the castles' garrisons, troops were raised for planned military campaigns and their wages had to be covered as well. The case of the year 1522 is known from closer research and it shows a gloomy picture. That year, the royal revenues most likely remained short of the expenditures by a small margin despite the extraordinary tax levied for recruiting mercenaries (C. Tóth 2016, pp. 124, 126–7, Pálosfalvi 2018, pp. 4, 455). Considering all this, it is understandable that the recovery of pledges became such a cardinal issue for a treasury that was striving to complement its revenues by almost all possible means. Despite the ordinances of the diets their stipulations were not completely fulfilled, partly because some of the royal possessions were pledged exactly for military service (Kubinyi 2006, p. 306; Pálosfalvi 2018, p. 460).

This is how crucial the issue of the pledged royal lands became in late medieval Hungary before the Ottoman conquest. The aim of the present study is to trace back the roots of this process and to present the emergence of pledging in the royal finances, and to highlight under what circumstances it could become an important element of these finances.

## King Louis I's finances

The name that initially pops up concerning royal pledging in the Kingdom of Hungary is Sigismund of Luxembourg (1387–1437) and this is not by coincidence. During his half-century-long reign in the country, he had managed to conclude several hundreds of transactions of pledge, in which a high number of royal castles were involved. Even one of medieval Hungary's most infamous transactions of pledge is related to him. In 1412, he put in pledge a region to the king of Poland in such way that it could be recovered only 360 years later (Incze 2016, p. 266). Nonetheless, despite pledging becoming somewhat inseparable from his name, it was certainly not Sigismund who established this form of raising extraordinary revenues in the country. This is proven by one of his many transactions by which he contracted a loan based on his predecessor King Louis I' (1342–1382) pledging of Steničnjak

(Sztenicsnyák) castle (DL 34052, Frangepán I, pp. 131–2). Characteristic of Sigismund, he demanded a loan greater than the original sum for which the castle was given in pledge by Louis. His demand for credit was backed up by threatening the widow of the original pledge holder that he would grant the castle to someone else if his request was not met (Frangepán I, p. 140; Engel 1977, p. 158). The most interesting aspect emerging from this case perhaps was not how Sigismund dealt with the whole situation, but the fact that it reveals that his predecessor had to tackle financial problems and that he similarly tried to overcome them by pledging. The initial transaction concluded in 1380 leaves no doubt that Louis pledged the castle for a loan – a sum as high as 10,000 Hungarian golden florins. This might be somewhat unexpected in light of the literature's frequent statements according to which Louis treasury seemed inexhaustible, or the prevailing notion that due to his prosperous financial situation he never had to resort to melting down or pawning his treasures (Engel 2003b, p. 315; Engel 2001, p. 157; Csukovits 2019, p. 108). The renowned Hungarian medievalist, Pál Engel, also noted this discrepancy and suggested that it was characteristic only of Louis' last years of his reign when probably the outputs of gold production had dropped off, causing such financial difficulties for the treasury that they could never be overcome (Engel 2001, p. 187). Though admittedly, the transaction from 1380 belonged to Louis' later ones, he had been pledging from much earlier in his reign – at least from the first part of the 1360s. Furthermore, specialists date the beginning of the gold production decline to somewhat later that his reign, the beginning of the 15th century (Batizi 2018, p. 176; Paulinyi 2005, p. 185). This entire discussion reflects precisely how much uncertainty surrounds the topic of royal finances during King Louis' rule. It is telling in regard to the whole situation that the source material is so scarce that it only allows estimates for the revenues Sigismund had, whereas in the case of Louis not even such estimations are possible (Engel 2003a, p. 426; Kubinyi 2006, p. 23).

What seems unequivocally accepted is that the salt and the precious metal monopoly, the tax of the royal towns and of the hospes settlements, the extraordinary levy, and the revenues related to the royal estates were among Louis' most important sources of income. Out of these, he could expect the highest yields from the precious metal mining, particularly from gold production (Engel 2003b, p. 315; Bertényi 1987, p. 219). The Kingdom of Hungary possessed vast mineral and metal wealth and, already in the second part of the 13th century, a boom was registered in the silver mining industry, while gold appeared only as a by-product of it. This first 'golden age' of the country's precious metal mining was stopped by the fights for the throne that broke out after the extinction of the Árpád dynasty's male line in 1301. After Louis's father, Charles I (1301–1342), had risen to power and managed to stabilize his rule around 1320, new mines with large resources have been discovered and a new prosperous era began in the precious metal mining activity. At this time, especially the gold mining started to flourish, and despite the fluctuation in the output caused by the discovery of new mines and the closing of older, inundated ones, a highly significant amount of gold in the continent was produced by Hungary in the 14th century. On the top of that, silver mining was also thriving to such extent that only Bohemia produced more of it during this period. Calculations in scholarship estimate the yearly output of gold to 2–2.5 tons, and around 10 tons of silver (Batizi 2018, pp. 172–6; Štefánik 2012, pp. 224–5; Paulinyi 2005, pp. 184–5).

The journey of the queen mother, Elisabeth, to Italy in 1343 is commonly seen by the historiography as proof of this substantial wealth. That year, Robert of Anjou (1309–1343), the king of Naples died, and his testament named Joana, his granddaughter, to be his successor. King Louis' brother and Joana's husband, Andrew, lived in Naples since 1333 and was also a candidate to the throne. After Robert's death, Queen Elisabeth set out on a journey to Italy to facilitate her son Andrew's rise to power in Naples. If we can accept the information of a contemporary chronicler, Elisabeth carried with her more than six tons of silver and more than five tons of gold on the diplomatic journey. Nonetheless, even this great fortune proved not to be enough for her expenses so Louis sent another large amount of gold to her (Csukovits 2019, pp. 30–2; Engel 2001, pp. 156, 159–60). In line with this as well, one of Louis' letters from 1366 is often mentioned, in which he wrote to one of his barons that if the money sent for paying soldiers is not enough, then he should send word of how much was needed, and it would be sent. Finally, Louis and his mother visited a number of pilgrimage sites abroad and lavished them with sumptuous gifts which shows precisely what financial possibilities the dynasty possessed at the time (Csukovits 2019, pp. 107–13; Engel 2001, p. 186).

## A new element of the royal extraordinary revenues

It is not entirely clear when Louis resorted to the fundraising method of pledging for the first time. What can be stated with greater certainty is that putting royal possessions in pledge was more characteristic of the last two decades of his rule than the early phases. Presumably, Altenburg (Óvár) Castle of Moson County was one of the earlier examples of his pledging. The only piece of evidence attesting that Altenburg was given in pledge is in fact about its redemption. In 1364, Eglolf Wolfurt informed the king about the redemption of the castle from his brother Conrad. The text does not provide any further details on when and under what conditions the deal between Conrad and Louis was struck. Moreover, the situation is further complicated by the fact that Altenburg was in the Wolfurt family's possession as part of their office already from 1350. Even Conrad himself is mentioned in 1357 as comes of Altenburg, supposedly around that time he became the pledge holder for it (DL 5313; Sopron vm., p. 354).

This was not the only transaction that Louis concluded with the Wolfurts. Kittsee (Köpcsény), another castle in Moson County, was similarly pledged to the family. We know about the transaction because, in 1363, Stephen, the bishop of Zagreb and vicar of Slavonia, promised in his and in some of his relatives' names that by February 1364, they would manage to issue a charter with the royal grand seal. The document would contain that Eglolf Wolfurt and his brother Rudolph took in pledge the castle Kittsee from the king at a value of 6,000 florins. Also, in the case that the charter could not be issued by the deadline, Bishop Stephen and his relatives themselves would have to pay back the 6,000 florins to the Wolfurts. Finally, if the bishop and his relatives would not prove able to get the charter issued nor pay the money back then they would have to provide a recompense from their own domains (DL 5256; HO, 410). It was uncommon that certain persons stood as guarantors behind the pledgings of kings, but it was not completely unparalleled either. From the many transactions of King Sigismund, there is one with a resemblance to this. In that case, a royal *familiaris* guaranteed similarly with his own possessions that before a given deadline the creditors of the king would receive royal domains for the money they lent (CD X/6, p. 842; ZsO XIII, 1429). Furthermore, it was he to whom the credit was handed over. It remains unclear whether Bishop Stephen was similarly more deeply involved in the deal concluded between the Wolfurts and the king, or if his role was restricted simply to the issuing of the charter. The reason behind Louis not being able to use the great seal when the charter of the pledging was issued is that he simply did not have it. That year (1363), he personally led a military expedition to Bosnia and during the siege of a castle, the great seal was allegedly stolen (or lost) from the archbishop of Esztergom's tent. In order to prevent the stolen seal being used for falsification and forgeries, a new grand seal was produced, and all documents on which the stolen seal was hanging had to be resealed with the new (Csukovits 2019, p. 78. AOklt XLVII. 659).

The Wolfurts, the pledge holders of the two royal castles, were a knightly kindred from the Vorarlberg region that King Louis came to know from his Italian military expeditions. Ulrich Wolfurt, the brother of Eglolf, Rudolph and Conrad, had a prominent role in Louis' campaigns to Naples, as he was the Hungarian king's most highly favored mercenary captain. It shows how much trust Louis placed in him that after the first campaign to Naples, the king left the city with Ulrich in charge acting as a governor (Veszprémy 2008, p. 166). After the Neapolitan Wars were over, the brothers moved to Hungary where they received offices from the king (Engel 1996, pp. 155–6, 179, 226). It was suggested that even Altenburg Castle was pledged to them as a recompense for Ulrich's military accomplishments (Csukovits 2019, p. 43). Most probably, the pledging was concluded several years after the Neapolitan campaigns finished; there is information preserved only on

Conrad being the castle's pledge holder, no such information existing for Ulrich. Still, since Louis donated royal domains years after his troops left the Italian Peninsula – for the grantees' 'Apulian merits' – the possibility cannot be completely ruled out (Csukovits 2019, p. 50).

It was more than mere coincidence that the Wolfurts – who provided military service to Louis – became pledge holders of royal property. Waging war was a central element of Louis' four-decade reign in the Kingdom of Hungary. The bellicose ruler organized military campaigns almost in every direction (to Naples, Venice, Lithuania, Serbia, etc.), and he himself took part in a minimum of sixteen of these. Only from the second part of the 1370s, his appetite for war began to diminish and in 1377, he led a military campaign abroad for last time (Csukovits 2019, p. 106; Kubinyi 1982, p. 31). The almost regular wars must have caused difficult periods for the treasury; especially the Italian Wars could be proven very costly as mercenaries like the Wolfurts were hired in large numbers for these campaigns (Veszprémy 2008, p. 171). Due to the mounting expenditures, Louis had no choice but to raise loans, sometimes in the middle of a military expedition (for example, see the study of Boglárka Weisz in the present volume). By that time, it was already a common practice for members of the royal court, and members of the high clergy, to secure the loans they contracted by pledges of lands (DL 3924, AOklt XXXI, 929; DL 94077; DL 37556; DL 87228; Lederer 1932, 44). It was only a matter of time until the king himself would also resort to this fundraising method. War-related expenses burdening the treasury's resources most heavily, it is presumable that Louis' pledges aimed to cover these directly or indirectly. However, it must be emphasized that the field of military expenditures was not the only one with which the money of the pledges was associated.

Only fragmentary evidence is left regarding Louis' two financial deals struck with the Wolfurts. His first known pledging for which a charter has come down to us with full details of the transaction is from 1372 and concerns the castle of Sirok. The wording of the charter is not ordinary as it completely lacks the terms commonly used to denote pledging (*obligare*, *impignorare*). Based on its wording, it is no wonder that for a long time this transaction was regarded as the very first royal castle pledging in the Kingdom of Hungary (Fügedi 1986, p. 114). In this case the castellan of the very same castle (Sirok) became the pledge holder of it for 2000 florins lent to the king and which the ruler needed for the refurbishment of that castle (DL 6047, 6049). Another instance reveals a different field of outlays with which Louis' pledging was associated. Just two months before he died, he gave in pledge a number of settlements in Pozsony County to Temlin Szentgyörgyi, for an earlier loan and for the expenses of diplomatic assignments. According to the document, Szentgyörgyi and another envoy travelled twice to Bavaria on Louis' order and the journeys' expenses were covered by Szentgyörgyi himself. With the pledging, Louis intended to clear away his debt from the loan and the diplomatic journeys (DL 6939).

The sample-pool of Louis' pledges is not large enough to perform a painstaking comparison with his successor's pledging practice but, nonetheless, certain patterns are vaguely traceable. It was King Louis who laid down the foundations of royal pledging in Hungary and it was he who chose the more advantageous form of pledging for the royal possession – a practice that later became widely used by the future kings of Hungary. This form lacked a deadline for redeeming the pledge; in this case the ruler did not risk losing the property due to not being able to meet the deadline. The elaboration or precise description of the need for pledging was often bypassed by some of the Hungarian king's charters of pledging, in a way that the justification was phrased too vaguely in many cases (DL 7519, 33412, 13189). This practice also had its beginnings in King Louis' reign. The already mentioned 10,000 florins loan raised from the pledging of Steničnjak was allegedly needed by Louis for his own advantage, without anything more specific being revealed about why it was necessary (Frangepán I, pp. 89–91).

Certain decisions of Louis regarding how and for what he used pledging (refurbishing royal castles, covering services of his adherents) proved to be a desirable model for the successors to his throne. Moreover, even his choice of pledge holder turned out to be influential since he began to undertake transactions of pledge (Steničnjak) with the prominent Croatian family, the Frankopan, which later became the most important pledge holder of his heir to the throne (Incze 2018, p. 168).

Finally, it is not known precisely how many transactions of pledge King Louis made. Nonetheless, it seems almost certain that he was among the Hungarian kings with the fewest pledgings. The number of pledged royal castles can serve as a good indicator of this. The four castles known at this point as being put in pledge by Louis seems like a negligible number compared to the more than 80 pledged castles of King Sigismund. Also, King Matthias I (1458–1490) and Wladislas II (1490–1516) had considerably more castle pledges than Louis (Incze 2018, p. 82; DL, 15508, 30860, 16156, 88716, 103835, 88828; Fógel 1913, 14–15). This can be explained by Louis father's cautious alienation policy, one that which Louis would also follow. As a result, only 18 castles were transferred into private hands during his whole reign (Fügedi 1986, pp. 113–14).

## Conclusion

Despite the golden age of precious metal mining in Hungary, the royal treasury of King Louis seems to have experienced shortages more often than merely in the last years of his rule. Most likely, the expenses of the countless wars in which the kingdom was involved could not always be met with the ordinary revenues. To fill this financial void, besides other methods of raising extraordinary funds, Louis chose one that was already well known by some members of the royal court: loans secured by pledges of land. Louis, as the ruler who introduced pledging into the royal finances of the Hungarian kings, shaped its form and had an influence on its later evolution. That is why certain elements of his pledging practice reappear in that of his successors. Moreover, even his choice of pledge holders proved to be influential since it was he who initiated this set of interactions with the family that later became his successor's largest pledge holder.

Pledging as a tool of raising funds was mostly characteristic of the second part of his reign and the small amount of known transaction is not only the consequence of the loss of sources, but it is also an indication of the limited usage of pledging by King Louis. After his death, on the foundation laid down by him, a new era began in royal pledging when its importance and extensive usage reached heights unimagined before.

## Funding

This chapter was supported by the Expro-Project: "Od performativity k institucionalizaci. Řešení konfliktů v pozdním středověku (strategie, aktéři, komunikace) (Konflikt)" (identification number: GX19-28415X), funded by the GAČR (Grantová agentura České Republiky).

## References

### Archival sources

AOklt – Piti, F. & Sebők, F., eds. (2007, 2017). *Anjou-kori oklevéltár XXXI 1347, XLVII 1363*. Budapest-Szeged: Szegedi Középkorász Műhely.
CD – Fejér, G., ed. (1844). *Codex Diplomaticus Hungariae ecclesiasticus ac civilis*, X/6. Buda: Typis typogr. Regiae Universitatis Ungaricae.
CIH – Nagy, G. et al., eds. (1899). *Corpus Iuris Hungarici. Magyar törvénytár, 1000–1526 évi törvényczikkek*. Budapest: Franklin társulat.
DF – *Magyar Országos Levéltár – Diplomatikai Fényképgyűjtemény* (Collectio Diplomatica Hungarica).
DL – *Magyar Országos Levéltár – Diplomatikai Levéltár* (Collectio Diplomatica Hungarica).
Frangepán I – Thallóczy, L. & Barabás, S., eds. (1901). *Codex diplomaticus Comitum de Frangepanibus I. A Frangepán család oklevéltára. 1333–1527*. Budapest: Magyar Tudományos Akadémia.
HO – Ipolyi, A. & Nagy, I., eds. (1880). Dezső Véghely. *Hazai okmánytár. Codex diplomaticus patrius VII*. Budapest: MTA.
Sopron vm. – Nagy, I., ed. (1889). *Sopron vármegye története. Oklevéltár első kötet 1156–1411*. Sopron.
ZsO – *Zsigmondkori oklevéltár 1387–1424, I–XIII*. Budapest: Magyar Országos Levéltár.

## Literature

Bak, J. M., Banyó P. & Rady M., eds. (2012). *Decreta regni medievalis Hungarie. The Laws of the Medieval Kingdom of Hungary 1490–1526.* Salt Lake City: CEU Dept. of Medieval Studies.

Batizi, Z. (2018). Mining in medieval Hungary. In Laszlovszky J. et al., eds. *The Economy of Medieval Hungary.* Leiden: Brill, pp. 166–81.

Bertényi, I. (1987). *Magyarország az Anjouk korában.* Budapest: Gondolat Könyvkiadó.

Csukovits, E. (2019). *Az Anjouk Magyarországon II. I. (Nagy) Lajos és Mária uralma (1342–1395).* Budapest: MTA Bölcsészettudományi Kutatóközpont, Történettudományi Intézet.

Engel, P. (1977). *Királyi hatalom és arisztokrácia viszonya a Zsigmond korban (1387–1437).* Budapest: Akadémiai Kiadó.

Engel, P. (1996). *Magyarország világi archontológiája 1301–1457.* Budapest: Magyar Tudományos Akadémia.

Engel, P. (2001). *The Realm of St Stephen. A History of Medieval Hungary, 895–1526.* London: I. B. Tauris.

Engel, P. (2003a). A magyar királyság jövedelmei Zsigmond. In Csukovics E., ed. *Honor, vár, ispánság.* Budapest: Osiris, pp. 426–33.

Engel, P. (2003b). Társadalom és politikai struktúra az Anjou-kori Magyarországon. In Csukovics E., ed. *Honor, vár, ispánság.* Budapest: Osiris, pp. 302–19.

Fógel, J. (1917). *II. Lajos udvartartása 1516–1526.* Budapest: Magyar Tudományos Akadémia.

Fógel, J. (1913). *II. Ulászló udvartartása (1490–1516).* Budapest: Magyar Tudományos Akadémia.

Fügedi, E. (1986). *Castle and Society in Medieval Hungary (1000–1437).* Budapest: Akadémiai Kiadó.

Incze, J. (2016). 360 Years in Pledge. The pledging of the Spiš Region. In Bagi D. & Barabás G., eds. *Hungaro-Polonica. Young Scholars on Medieval Polish-Hungarian Relations.* Pécs: Történészcéh Egyesület, pp. 265–90.

Incze, J. (2018). *"Our Lord the King Looks for Money in Every Corner". Sigismund of Luxembourg's Pledgings in Hungary.* Ph.D. Diss., Central European University, Budapest.

Isenmann, E. (1999). The Holy Roman Empire in the middle ages. In Bonney R., ed. *The Rise of the Fiscal State in Europe, c. 1200–1815.* Oxford: Oxford University Press, pp. 243–80.

Kubinyi, A. (1982). I. Lajos király és kora. In Marosi E., et al., eds. *Művészet I. Lajos király korában (1342–1382).* Budapest: MTA Művészettörténeti Kutatócsoport, pp. 15–36.

Kubinyi, A. (2006). A Jagelló-kori magyar állam. *Történelmi Szemle,* 48(3–4), pp. 287–308.

Lederer, E. (1932). *A középkori pénzüzletek története Magyarországon (1000–1458).* Budapest: Kovács J.

Ludwig, M. (1984). *Besteuerung und Verpfändung königlicher Städte im spätmittelalterlichen Polen.* Berlin: Duncker & Humblot.

Matuszewski, J. (1997). Die Verpfändung der Krongüter und das Nutzungssystem der Herrschaftsgüter der Regierenden im Polen des 15. und 16. Jahrhunderts. In

Leitsch W. et al., eds. *Polen und Österreich im 16. Jahrhundert*. Vienna: Böhlau Verlag, pp. 47–63.

Neumann, T., Tóth C. N. & Pálosfalvi T. (2019). Két évszázad a sztereotípiák fogságában. In Fodor P. & Varga Sz., eds. *Több mint egy csata: Mohács. Az 1526. évi ütközet a magyar tudományos és kulturális emlékezetben.* Budapest: MTA Bölcsészettudományi Kutatóközpont, pp. 11–74.

Pálosfalvi, T. (2018). *From Nicopolis to Mohács: A History of Ottoman-Hungarian Warfare, 1389–1526. Ottoman Empire and Its Heritage.* Leiden: Brill.

Paulinyi, O. (2005). Mohács előtti nemesfémtermelésünk és. In Buza J. & Draskóczy I., eds. *Gazdag föld - szegény ország. Tanulmányok a magyarországi bányaművelés.* Budapest: Budapesti Corvinus Egyetem, pp. 183–229.

Štefánik, M. (2011). Italian involvement in metal mining in the central Slovakian Region, from the thirteenth century to the Reign of King Sigismund of Hungary. *I Tatti Studies*, 14/15, pp. 11–46.

Tóth, C. N. (2016). A Magyar királyság 1522.évi költségvetése. In Weisz B., ed. *Pénz, posztó, piac. Gazdaságtörténeti tanulmányok a magyar középkorról.* Budapest: MTA Bölcsészettudományi Kutatóközpont Történettudományi Intézet, pp. 83–148.

Veszprémy, L. (2008). *Az Árpád- és Anjou-kor csatái, hadjáratai.* Budapest: Zrínyi Kiadó.

Chapter 5

# King's debts and king's creditors in Poland in the first half of the 15th century

*Piotr Guzowski*

Clientelism, which is associated primarily with the early modern era, not only in Polish historiography, seems to be a concept that can as well be successfully applied to the late Middle Ages. Wojciech Fałkowski, when writing about the policy of Vladislaus III and the knights accompanying the king abroad, characterized the mechanism of making a career in the following way:

> [...] a trip to Hungary with a detachment of knights and a certain amount of cash to lend to the ruler became a real investment. [...] *Consiliarus et servitor noster fidelis, sincere nobis dilectus*, according to the royal records, received measurable benefits for his fidelity, usefulness and helpfulness; the greater the benefits, the more his services and assistance were recognized. This in turn depended on the knight's position with the king, which was determined by a combination of several components: the offices held, personal authority and position within the elite of power as well as individual and direct contacts with the ruler. Maintaining a high position over a longer period of time required not only great dexterity, but also high fixed expenses and the ability to skilfully find support with other participants of this game. And the game was all about access to the king, his grace and favour, and about creating political support in a narrow circle of advisors and in broad milieus of the noble *communitas*.
>
> (Fałkowski 2004, pp. 11–12)

Therefore, if we take into account the obvious differences resulting from the specificity of the period, it seems justified to make an attempt at explaining some social and political phenomena as being part of the patron–client relationship. This is facilitated, on the one hand, by advanced prosopographical work, especially concerning the 15th century, and on the other hand, by the degree of recognition of the phenomenon in subsequent centuries as well as, consequently, by the methodology already developed. Nevertheless, the nature of the preserved sources including their number and scope largely determine the scope of research possibilities by limiting them to the monarch's court and possibly the clergy.

The pledge of royal estate fits into a wide range of different types of patron–client relationships. It is one of the many elements that permanently binds people who are in an asymmetric relationship. The element may not be the most important or decisive one, but definitely of considerable economic importance. The aim of this chapter is to present the scale of the phenomenon entailing the pledge of royal estate in the first half of the 15th century, to draw attention to the financial aspect of this area of monarchical activity, as well as to indicate new, non-economic, interpretative possibilities. The source basis consists of 203 preserved pledge documents issued by Vladislaus Jagiellon between 1386 and 1434, and published in the most important diplomatic collections (Akta grodzkie i ziemskie, 1870–1883, vols 2, 4, 5, 7; Kodeks dyplomatyczny Małopolski, 1905, vol. 4; Kodeks dyplomatyczny Polski, 1852, vols 1–2; Zbiór dokumentów małopolskich, 1962–1975, parts 6–7; Kodeks dyplomatyczny Wielkopolski, 1908–1990, vols 5–9). There are approximately 2,500 documents issued by Vladislaus Jagiellon that we are aware of so the pledge documents subject to analysis constitute less than 8% of the available resources (Gąsiorowski 1974). Undoubtedly, the source material that we have used cannot be regarded as complete.

The pledge documents subject to analysis are a kind of random sample, yet they can be considered a sufficient basis for drawing conclusions about the phenomenon. The activity of Vladislaus Jagiellon will also be compared to a similar activity of his son, Vladislaus III, during his reign both in Poland and in Hungary, that is between 1440 and 1444, as known from Marcin Sepiał's research (Sepiał 1998). In late medieval Poland, the most common type of pledge was the so-called 'pledge involving control where the pledger gives the pledged asset to the pledgee for possession (and use)' (Rymaszewski 1962, p. 119).

In the practice of 15th-century courts, the pledged assets 'were almost everything of value' (Rymaszewski 1962, p. 117), hence all kinds of movable property: jewels, ornaments, books, robes, etc., and real property: landed estates, agricultural lands, forests, ponds, mills (Matuszewski 1979) as well as gains, such as from customs duties or pensions. Two types of pledge involving control prevailed:

- a strict usufruct pledge (to be redeemed), in which 'the value of the profits collected by the pledgee does not reduce the pledger's debt' (Rymaszewski p. 120), hence the pledgee collected gains from the pledged goods until the pledger returned the sum borrowed from the pledgee;
- a pledge subject to control, in which 'the pledgee held the goods in pledge until the value of the profits derived from the goods reached the sum of the claims' (Rymaszewski 1962, p. 121), that is the gains from the pledged goods represented the depreciation of the debt (Sepiał 1998, p. 36).

In the royal practice, it is extremely rare to find a pledge subject to control which concerned the pledge of gains from, for example the salt mines (*żupy*). The pledge for redemption was dominant, which made it possible to circumvent the canonical ban on usury. The pledger returned the amount borrowed, while the profits collected from the pledged goods by the pledgee were an obvious type of interest, although interest was never mentioned in such circumstances.

The monarch made the assignment in his own name and that of his successors to the pledgee and his legal heirs, who had the goods at their disposal until the sum lent was repaid in full. Then the pledge would be returned to the king but until then, the pledgee could hold, possess, and use the pledge, although almost always the king indicated that he kept the right to stop by at the estate (Sepiał 1998, pp. 36–7).

The general picture of the analysed pledges made by Vladislaus Jagiellon is as follows: there were 202 pledge documents for the total amount of: 32,619 marcs, mentioning 151 individual pledgees (plus the Lviv Archcathedral Chapter). In some cases, royal estates were not pledged to individuals, but to brothers, or father and son together. The documents contain information about at least 270 villages, 11 castles, and 16 towns which were pledged.

The number of preserved records issued in particular years manifests great diversity. The king did not often resort to this type of transactions, just four times a year on average. However, there were years, mainly in the first part of the reign: co-rule with Jadwiga and the beginnings of independent reign, where there is no trace of such transactions (1388–1389, 1393–1395, 1398, 1400, 1403, 1407). On the other hand, the end of this monarch's reign resulted in a significant increase in the intensity of this phenomenon. In 1431, Jagiełło issued 25 pledge records and in 1433, as many as 36. There is also an increase in the volume of pledges issued in the years 1410–1411, 13 and 12 records, respectively (see Figure 5.1).

The frequency of the records overlaps with the amounts of pledges. On average, there were four pledges per calendar year during the reign, with a total value of approximately 665 marcs, except that there were years when the king did not resort to this type of transactions (or the sources have not been preserved) and years when the pledges amounted to substantial sums, such as 2,600 marcs in 1410 or 4,775 marcs in 1433.

As regards the unit value of the pledge, it amounted to approximately 160 marcs on average, although it could generally range from 20 to 1,000 marcs (see Figure 5.2). The majority of the records covered relatively small amounts, up to 100 marcs (127 records or 63%), while larger amounts were less frequent (between 101 and 200 marcs – 16.5%, between 201 and 300–6%, between 301 and 400–5.5%, between 401 and 500–4.5%, above 500 marcs – 4.5%).

The most numerous records with the lowest values in total involved the amount of 7,815 marcs, which was only less than 1,000 marcs more than 9

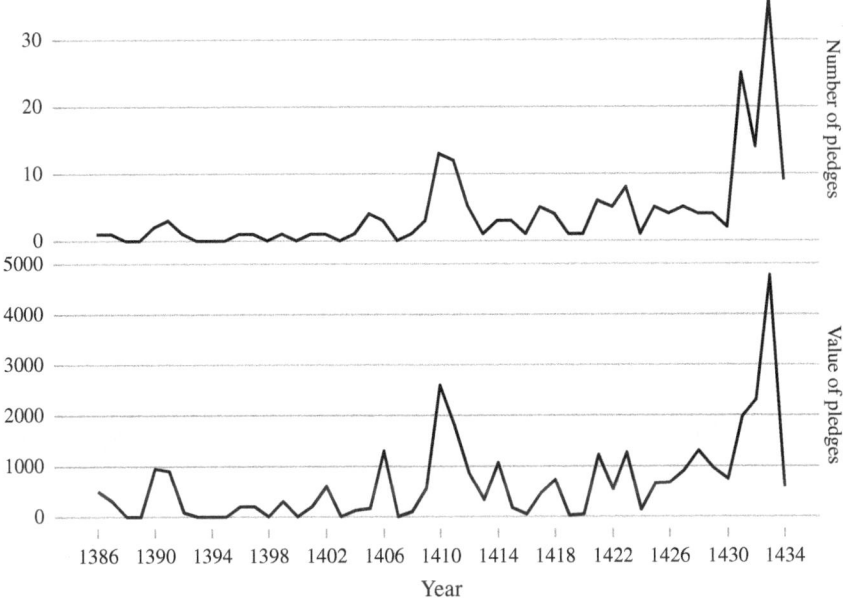

*Figure 5.1* Number and value of pledge records issued by Vladislaus Jagiellon in specific years of his reign.

Source: *Akta grodzkie i ziemskie* (1870–1883), vols. 2, 4, 5, 7; *Kodeks dyplomatyczny Małopolski* (1905), vol. 4; *Kodeks dyplomatyczny Polski* (1852), vols. 1–2; *Zbiór dokumentów małopolskich* (1962–1975), parts 6–7; *Kodeks dyplomatyczny Wielkopolski* (1908–1990), vols. 5–9.

records for amounts exceeding 500 marcs (6,950). Pledges of medium value were much lower: 101–200 marcs – 5,972, 201–300 marcs – 3,280, 301–400 marcs – 4,212 and 401–500 marcs – 4,390 (see Figure 5,2). Interestingly, such a structure of the size of the pledges does not differ from the practices of the gentry (Morawski 1993, p. 93).

Once the frequency of issuing pledge documents during the year is traced (see Figure 5.3), it turns out that the royal activity in this field was permanent, although both in terms of the number of pledges issued and their value, the 'peak season' was March (31 records for the amount of 5,715 marcs) and November (23 records for the amount of 4,080 marcs), whereas both January and December were 'low season' months (January: 9 records for the amount of 1,080 marcs, December: 7 records for the amount of 820 marcs).

Vladislaus Jagiellon issued pledge documents to at least 151 people (142 individuals, 3 siblings, and 1 family) and the Lviv Archcathedral Chapter. The vast majority of creditors (75.5%) received a pledge from this king once in their lifetime (see Figure 5.4). The others acted as creditors twice (17%), three times (4.1%), four times (2%), five times (0.7%) or six times (0.7%).

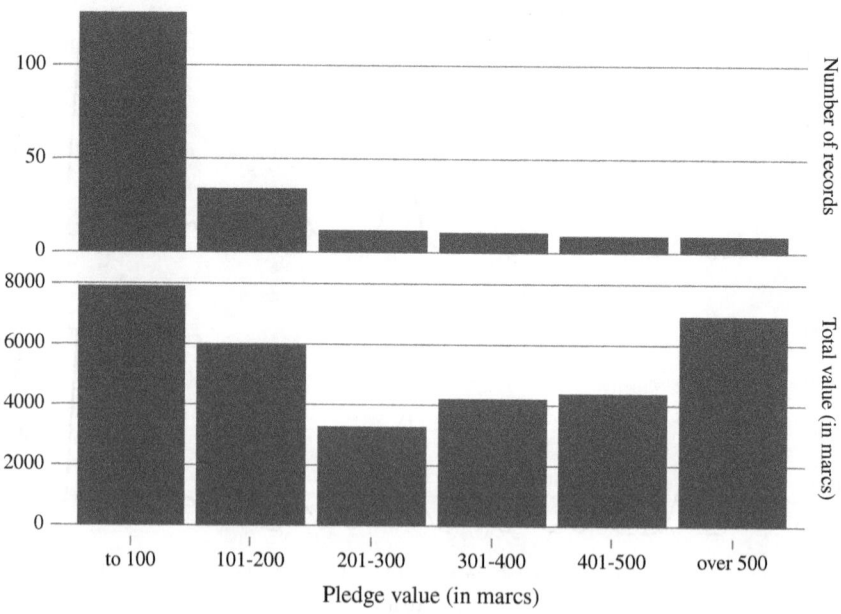

*Figure 5.2* Number of Vladislaus Jagiellon's records by pledge value.

Source: *Akta grodzkie i ziemskie* (1870–1883), vols. 2, 4, 5, 7; *Kodeks dyplomatyczny Małopolski* (1905), vol. 4; *Kodeks dyplomatyczny Polski* (1852), vols. 1–2; *Zbiór dokumentów małopolskich* (1962–1975), parts 6–7; *Kodeks dyplomatyczny Wielkopolski* (1908–1990), vols. 5–9.

Slightly more than half (52.5%) of the royal claims relate to individuals who acted as pledgees only once (17,122 marcs in total). More than 32.2% of the total debt was covered by documents issued to individuals twice (10,492 marcs), 7.7% three times (2,510 marcs), 5.8% four times (1,902 marcs), 0.9% five times (300 marcs) and 0.9% six times (290 marcs).

If the average value of the pledge record in individual groups of pledgees is considered (isolated by the frequency of acting as a pledgee), the differences are insignificant: in the most numerous groups the value ranges from 139.4 to almost 210 marcs. The average value of pledges of individuals acting as pledgees five and six times differs from this, but these are single cases.

It can be inferred from the analysis of the reasons why the king issued the documents that they were usually remuneration for various types of service (the provided reasons are rather terse: for merit, for service, for faithful service, for participation in the war, and also to strengthen the pledgee in his previous and current attitude) rather than real money loans. Hence, the pledges were non-cash transactions. An intermediate option can be encountered at times, when the king simultaneously remunerates for service and confirms the fact of taking out a loan. For example, on 30 June 1433, the king recorded a pledge of 200 marcs of the villages of Rączyna

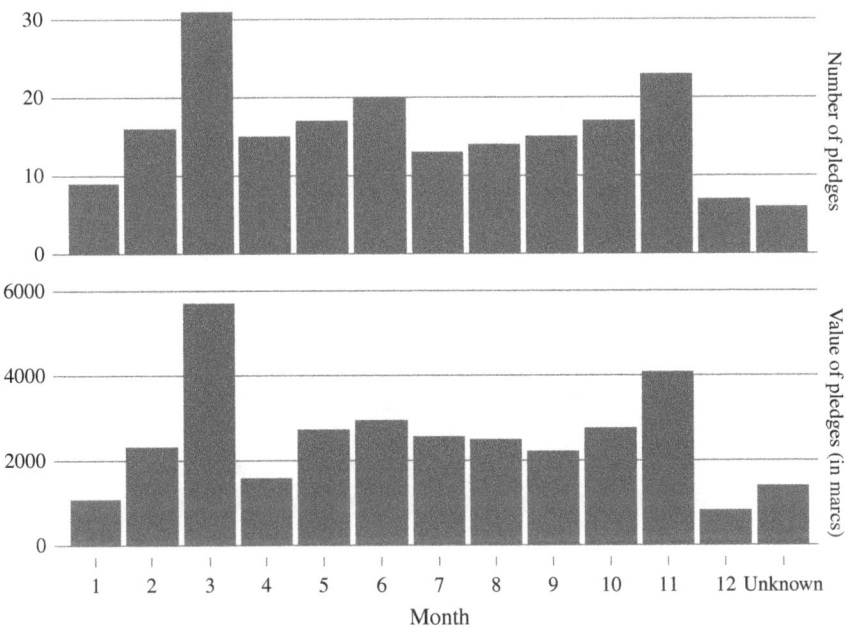

*Figure 5.3* Pledge documents issued by Vladislaus Jagiellon in specific months of the year.

Source: *Akta grodzkie i ziemskie* (1870–1883), vols. 2, 4, 5, 7; *Kodeks dyplomatyczny Małopolski* (1905), vol. 4; *Kodeks dyplomatyczny Polski* (1852), vols. 1–2; *Zbiór dokumentów małopolskich* (1962–1975), parts 6–7; *Kodeks dyplomatyczny Wielkopolski* (1908–1990), vols. 5–9.

and Zagórze to the benefit of Jan Koniecpolski for his wartime merits and loan (Zbiór dokumentów małopolskich, 1962–1975, 7, no. 2147). There are also incidents when the ruler, having purchased some valuable items, instead of paying cash to the owner, recorded their value against the royal estate: for example, on 17 April 1434, to the benefit of Jan of Oleśnica, 100 marcs as a pledge for a velvet, sable-lined overcoat of the castle of Solec and the villages being part of the castle (Zbiór dokumentów małopolskich, 1962–1975, 7, no. 2168); on 3 November 1431 to the benefit of Michał Wapowski 50 marcs as a pledge of the village of Tarnowce for three horses (Zbiór dokumentów małopolskich, 1962–1975, 7, no. 2090).

Both the low frequency of pledging of the royal estate (four times a year on average) and the value of liabilities are proof not so much of the perfection and efficiency of the fiscal administration of the time, but rather of the well-thought-out royal policy and a relatively low financial deficit level. Maybe this also manifests minor needs of the court. Makeshift calculations made by Hubert Wajs demonstrate that the consumption of Jadwiga's court cost the royal treasury about 30 marcs per week (Wajs 1993, p. III). It seems highly unlikely that pledges for small sums of money could result from the

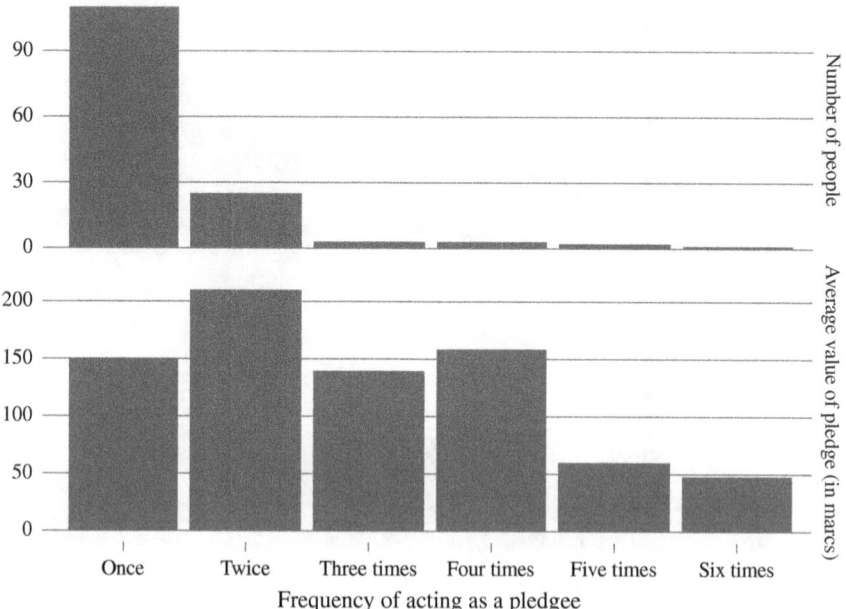

*Figure 5.4* Frequency of acting as a pledgee in the analysed documents concerning Vladislaus Jagiellon.

Source: *Akta grodzkie i ziemskie* (1870–1883), vols 2, 4, 5, 7; *Kodeks dyplomatyczny Małopolski* (1905), vol. 4; *Kodeks dyplomatyczny Polski* (1852), vol 1–2; *Zbiór dokumentów małopolskich* (1962–1975), parts 6–7; *Kodeks dyplomatyczny Wielkopolski* (1908–1990), vols 5–9.

king's urgent need for a quick cash injection. This could be a more realistic option with larger amounts of money. Both parties were probably more prone to pay and receive remuneration in the form of a pledge rather than in cash; the ruler did not dispose of the money (which he might not have had), and the pledgee was given a chance to draw a sum from the royal estate, significantly exceeding the contractual value of the pledge.

While assuming that there is more than just economics to the phenomenon of pledging royal goods by Vladislaus Jagiellon, we will refer here to the definition and characteristics of clientelism (Mączak 2003, pp. 40–51). Firstly, according to the general wording of the definition of clientelism, there is a situation of disposition of resources. The king has two kinds of resources; firstly, the material resources in the form of royal goods, which he can give away or pledge. Moreover, it is the king who largely enables access to the public sphere.

Secondly, direct relations and personal ties tended to develop between the king and the pledgees. The pledgees mainly included central officials (e.g. the marshal/*marszałek* of the kingdom, Jan of Oleśnica, the subchancellor/

*podkanclerzy*, Klemens of Łaskażew), officials of the lands (voivodes/ *wojewodowie*, castellans/*kasztelanowie*, chamberlains/*podkomorzy*, etc.) as well as court officials and court servants (*familiares* of various kinds). All of them had close ties to the monarch. Some of these people's biographies can be found in the Polish Biographical Dictionary (PSB), whose authors, writing the dictionary at a time when the term *clientelism* was still absent in Polish scientific literature, summarized their characteristics in the following way: 'he stood faithfully by his lord ruler' (Piotrowicz 1939, pp. 306–7) or 'he was a supporter of the dynasty and enjoyed the special trust of the court' (Górski 1963, p. 483). Yet, it should also be noted that only a few people such as: Klemens of Moskorzewo, Piotr Szafraniec, Domarat of Kobylany, Jan of Szczekociny, Andrzej of Donabórz or Paszko Złodziej appeared with great frequency as witnesses on Jagiellon's perpetual documents, which may provide proof that they belonged to the circle of royal advisors or at least to the wider elite ruling the country (Sułkowska-Kurasiowa 1982; Klimecka 1990).

Undoubtedly, in the case of relations between the king and the pledgees, the existence of 'reciprocity' is a fact. The pledgees served the king as soldiers, deputies, administrators or in any other capacity. They also performed political functions. It is not without reason that the greatest intensity of the phenomenon of the pledge is connected with the last years of Vladislaus Jagiellon's reign and his succession efforts. Among the 35 lay witnesses mentioned on the Jedlnia privilege, 10 are royal pledgees: Piotr Szafraniec, Piotr Bniński, Domarat of Kobylany, Jan of Oleśnica, Piotr of Pieskowa Skała, Piotr Korczbok, Stanisław of Szczkowo, Paweł of Bogumiłowice, Abraham of Zbąszyno, Zawisza of Oleśnica (*Volumina legum*, 1859, vol. 1, p. 42).

The importance of the time factor is also easily discernible. Although the vast majority of pledgees appeared in this role only once, a pledge usually tied for life. This is most evident in people who received pledge documents several times as exemplified by the most frequent pledgees in the documents, such as Jakub of Malice, Pełka of Służowo, Piotr Szafraniec, and Piotr Korczbok. Jakub of Malice, referred to as *familiaris*, received subsequent pledge records from the king in the years 1411 – the village of Buczyków for the amount of 60 marcs (Zbiór dokumentów małopolskich, 1974, vol. 6, no. 1757), 1421 – the hamlet (*pustkowie)* of Okno for the amount of 40 marcs (Zbiór dokumentów małopolskich, 1962–1975, vol. 7, no. 1905), 1422 – the village of Buczyków again for the amount of 20 marcs (Zbiór dokumentów małopolskich, 1962–1975, vol. 7, no. 1929), 1423 – this time Okno already being a village for the amount of 20 marcs (Zbiór dokumentów małopolskich, 1962–1975, vol. 7, no. 1936), 1431 – the village of Rynkaszów for the amount of 20 marcs (Zbiór dokumentów małopolskich, 1962–1975, vol. 7, no. 2093) and 1433–5 villages: Buczyków, Okno, Semenów, Cerkwica, and Nastaszyn for the amount of 110 marcs (Zbiór dokumentów małopolskich, 1962–1975, vol. 7, no. 2151). Hence, there are 6 pledges issued over 22 years with a total value of 290 marcs recorded for 5 villages. It is also worth noting that at the end of Jagiellon's reign, *familiaris* Jakub was already the *wojski* of Przemyśl, that is an official reporting to the castellan (Przyboś 1987, p. 163).

In May 1415, the king renewed the burnt (and thus earlier) pledge document worth 100 marcs for the village of Makuniów in the Przemyśl poviat to his knight Pełka of Służowo (Zbiór dokumentów małopolskich, 1974, vol. 6, no. 1795). A few months later (in November) *strenuus miles* Pełka received another pledge of the same village for the amount of 20 marcs (Zbiór dokumentów małopolskich, 1974, vol. 6, no. 1801). The next two come from 1433, from the beginning and end of the year, amounted to 50 marcs twice and concerned the same village of Makuniów (Zbiór dokumentów małopolskich, 1962–1975, vol. 7, nos 2120, 2154).

The two cases of pledging royal estate were by no means connected with covering the royal debt. Rather, they were a form of remuneration for service, probably military. The situation was slightly different in the case of more affluent pledgees. A different scale, as regards both the value of the pledge and the type of service, referred to a similar practice of burdening the same places. Multiple pledges of the same estate that the pledgees had held before were very beneficial from their point of view. According to M. Sepiał, 'Increasing the amount that the king had to repay in order to recover the estate reduced the likelihood of redemption in the absence of money in the treasury' (Sepiał 1998, p. 47).

In the years 1410 and 1411, Piotr Szafraniec, the chamberlain of Cracow, lent the king money twice, in the amounts of 200 and 100 marcs. The pledge comprised the town and castle of Chęciny and 11 villages (Zbiór dokumentów małopolskich, 1962–1975, vol. 7, no. 1747; Kodeks dyplomatycznym Małopolski, 1905, vol. 4, no. 1128). In 1421, he saved the royal budget again at the request of Vladislaus Jagiellon with another 200 marcs (Zbiór dokumentów małopolskich, 1975, vol. 7, no. 1915) (another pledge of Chęciny and the neighbouring villages), and in 1425, for his merits not only as chamberlain of Cracow, but also as governor (*starosta*) of Sieradz, he received a pledge record for 300 marcs of the village of Fajsławice (Zbiór dokumentów małopolskich, 1975, vol. 7, no. 1989).

Piotr Korczbok (Korzbok), the chamberlain of Poznań, was rewarded at least three times between 1426 and 1433 by the king with pledges for the following amounts: twice 100 marcs and once 140, of the town, the castle of Babimost and the villages belonging to them (Kodeks dyplomatyczny Wielkopolski, 1990, vol. 9, no. 1306; Kodeks dyplomatyczny Polski, 1852, vol. 1, no. 172; Kodeks dyplomatyczny Wielkopolski, 1908, vol. 5, no. 468). Since the beginning of the 15th century, Korczbok had been a royal courtier, fulfilling diplomatic missions several times (Gąsiorowski 1969, pp. 159–60). Numerous examples of this kind can be found in the records. For instance, three out of four pledges issued between 1429 and 1434 to Piotr Bniński, the castellan of Gniezno, referred to the town of Mosina (Kodeks dyplomatyczny Wielkopolski, 1982, vol. 5, nos 506, 530, 543), while Paweł of Bogumiłowice, the castellan of Połaniec and later on a Cracow judge, received in 1410 and in 1421 two pledges of the town of Stopnica (Zbiór dokumentów małopolskich, 1974, vol. 6, no. 1746; 1975, vol. 7, no. 1710), and Piotr of Smolice was awarded two pledges in 1421 and 1423 of the village of Targowiska (Zbiór dokumentów małopolskich, 1975, vol. 7, nos 1912, 1934), etc.

As usual, the most questionable is the issue of the 'informality' of a relationship involving clientelism. It cannot be said in this case that the issue of pledges remained in the private sphere, but it cannot be closed within the formal rigours of governance, either. Until 1440, there were no formal restrictions on the distribution of royal estate, hence the law did not regulate this phenomenon, and it remained somewhat in the sphere of custom (Matuszewski 1985, pp. 101–20). Vladislaus Jagiellon's rule was, in a way, groundbreaking. Assignments, perpetual and lifelong, as well as pledges, had been unheard of on such a significant scale before (Luciński 1970, pp. 21–43). On the other hand, at the time of assuming the throne, Vladislaus Jagiellon was the first monarch who was forced to resort to this type of transactions in order to ensure the sustainability of the dynasty's rule in the country.

Pledges during Vladislaus Jagiellon's reign were both a form of remuneration for faithful service to the king and a way to quickly obtain cash. Whether they referred to less influential knights or mighty lords, they meant strong ties with the ruler and his policy. Sometimes they tied the gentry and the monarch throughout several generations.

The custom, initiated by Jagiellon, of offering royal estate as a pledge, not yet dangerous during his rule, and not really significantly affecting the finances of the state, was brought to a pathological form by his son, Vladislaus III who, during only four years of joint reign in Poland and Hungary, issued pledge documents for a total of almost 122,000 marcs (Sepiał 1998, p. 38) even though the Statutes of 1440 forbade a pledge of the great government of Cracow. This practice continued later on as well (Boroda & Guzowski 2016). Kazimierz Tymieniecki made a calculation that during the entire reign of Kazimierz Jagiellończyk, 406 records of new pledges were registered in the Crown Metric (Metryka Koronna), while for Jan Olbracht there were 131 of them (Tymieniecki 1934, p. 106).

Although both historians of the time and later historians assessed the phenomenon as extremely negative (Kiryk 1967, p. 10; Sucheni-Grabowska 1967, pp. 27–32, as well as the works cited above; from a slightly different point of view: Matuszewski 1979, no. 6)., from the point of view of both the king and his pledgees, the matter did not look so unambiguously. When writing about clientelism at the 17th-century French court, A. Mączak stressed the role of the monarch's tactics in shaping it: '[...] grant graces as short-term as possible so that the applicants would have to come back for them all the time. Using the vocabulary of the business: not sale, not emphyteusis, but short term lease' (Maczak 2003, pp. 105–6). In the circumstances of the Crown, in the 15th century, this was not always possible, for example because of the life-long nature of many offices. However, the pledge was perfectly fit for purpose. It combined the elements of a medieval feudal system – domain state (Ormrod 1995; Bonney 1999) with modern financial and political operations. The king did not permanently dispose of domain elements. Although the pledges may have served as an apparent, hidden assignment, the king himself valued the services rendered to him, chose the estate as well as, in fact, the period for which it was pledged. The king was able to redeem the estate at any time or, more likely, allow another pledgee to redeem it. In the period between 1447 and 1501, as many as 360 previous pledges were recorded in the Crown Metric (Tymieniecki 1934, p. 106). Moreover, the creditors of Jagiellon came into possession of the royal estate as a result of redemption of previously pledged villages or towns. In this way, the king was able to use the phenomenon, seemingly of a purely economic nature, for political purposes. His creditors were also aware of this and many of them, after the death of the old monarch, were bound to his sons in exactly the same manner. They became the creditors of the dynasty. Or, perhaps, its clients.

## Funding

This chapter was prepared as part of the project: Financial capacity of Jagiellonian states in the 16th century in the comparative perspective (no. 2017/27/L/HS3/03242) financed by the National Science Centre, Poland.

## References

Akta grodzkie i ziemskie z czasów Rzeczypospolitej Polskiej z Archiwum tak zwanego bernardyńskiego we Lwowie. (1870–1883). vols 2, 4, 5, 7. Lwów: Galicyjski Wydział Krajowy.

Bartoszewicz, J., ed. (1852). Kodeks dyplomatyczny Polski, 1, 2. Warszawa: Typis Stanislai Strąbski.

Bonney, R. (1999). The rise of the fiscal state in Europe c. 1200–1815. In Bonney, R., ed. The Rise of the Fiscal State in Europe c. 1200–1815. Oxford: OUP, pp. 1–23.

Boroda, K. & Guzowski, P. (2016). From king's finance to publicfinance. Different strategies of fighting financial crisis in the Kingdom of Poland under Jagiellonian rule (1386–1572). In The Financial Crises. Their Management, Their Social Implications and Their Consequences in Pre-Industrial Times. Firenze: Firenze University Press, pp. 451–70.

Fałkowski, W. (2004). Możnowładztwo polskie wobec króla. Zabiegi i działania polityczne wokół monarchy w XV stuleciu. In Fałkowski, W., ed. Kolory i struktury średniowiecza. Warszawa: Wydawnictwo DiG, pp. 9–26.

Gąsiorowski, A. (1969). Piotr Korzbok. In Polski Słownik Biograficzny, 14. Wrocław – Warszawa – Kraków: Zakład Narodowy im. Ossolińskich, pp. 159–60.

Gąsiorowski, A. (1974). *Itinerarium Króla Władysława Jagiełły 1386–1434*. Warszawa: Państwowe Wydawnictwo Naukowe.

Gąsiorowski, A. & Jasiński, T., eds. (1990). *Kodeks dyplomatyczny Wielkopolski*, 9. Warszawa – Poznań: Państwowe Wydawnictwo Naukowe.

Górski, K. (1963). Jan ze Szczekocin. In *Polski Słownik Biograficzny*, 10. Wrocław–Warszawa–Kraków: Zakład Narodowy im. Ossolińskich, p. 483.

Kiryk, F. (1967). *Jakub z Dębna na tle wewnętrznej i zagranicznej polityki Kazimierza Jagiellończyka*. Wrocław–Warszawa–Kraków: Zakład Narodowy im. Ossolińskich.

Klimecka, G. (1990). *Czy rzeczywiście doradcy Władysława Jagiełły?* In Kuczyński, S. K., ed. *Społeczeństwo Polski Średniowiecznej*, 4, Warszawa, pp. 214–35.

Kuraś, S. & Sułkowska-Kuraś, I., eds. (1974). *Zbiór dokumentów małopolskich*, 6. Wrocław: Zakład Narodowy im. Ossolińskich.

Kuraś, S. & Sułkowska-Kuraś, I., eds. (1975). *Zbiór dokumentów małopolskich*, 7. Wrocław: Zakład Narodowy im. Ossolińskich.

Luciński, J. (1970). *Rozwój królewszczyzn w Koronie od schyłku XIV wieku do XVII wieku*. Poznań: Polskie Towarzystwo Przyjaciół Nauk.

Matuszewski, J. S. (1976). Czy pierwsi Jagiellonowie roztrwonili dobra królewskie? In *Sprawozdania z Czynności i Posiedzeń Naukowych Łódzkiego Towarzystwa Naukowego*, 33, pp. 1–7.

Matuszewski, J. S. (1979), *Zastaw nieruchomości w polskim prawie ziemskim do końca XV stulecia*, Łódź: Uniwersytet Łódzki.

Matuszewski, J. S. (1982). Obowiązek służby wojskowej zastawników królewszczyzn w piętnastowiecznej Polsce. *Czasopismo Prawno-Historyczne*, 34(1), pp. 101–13.

Matuszewski, J. S. (1985). Statut Władysława Warneńczyka z 1440 r. w procesie ograniczania królewskiego dyspozycji domeną ziemską w Polsce. *Czasopismo Prawno-Historyczne*, 37(2), pp. 101–21.

Mączak, A. (2003). *Nierówna przyjaźń. Układy klientalne w perspektywie historycznej*. Wrocław: Fundacja na Rzecz Nauki Polskiej.

Morawski, Z. (1993). *Ziemia, urzędy, pieniądze. Finanse szlachty łęczyckiej w końcu XIV i w pierwszej połowie XV wieku*. Warszawa: Neriton.

Ohryzko, J., ed. (1859). *Volumina legum 1*. Petersburg: nakładem i drukiem J. Ohryzki.

Ormrod, M. (1995). The West European monarchies in the Later Middle Ages. In Bonney, R., ed. *Economic Systems and State Finance*. Oxford: Clarendon Press, pp. 123–62.

Piekosiński, F., ed. (1905). *Kodeks dyplomatycznym Małopolski*, 4. Kraków: Wydawnictwa Komisyi Historycznej Akademii Umiejętności w Krakowie.

Piekosiński, F., ed. (1908). *Kodeks dyplomatyczny Wielkopolski*, 5. Poznań: Poznańskie Towarzystwo Przyjaciół Nauk.

Piotrowicz, K. (1939). Domarat z Kobylan. In *Polski Słownik Biograficzny*, 5, Kraków: Polska Akademia Umiejętności, pp. 306–7.

Przyboś, K. (1987). *Urzędnicy województwa ruskiego*, Wrocław: Zakład Narodowy im. Ossolińskich.

Rymaszewski, Z. (1962). Zastaw w świetle praktyki sądów małopolskich w XV wieku. *Zeszyty Naukowe Uniwersytetu Łódzkiego. Nauki Humanistyczno-Społeczne*, 1(26), pp. 113–33.

Sepiał, M. (1998). Zastaw na dobrach ziemskich i dochodach królewskich w okresie panowania Władysława Warneńczyka na Węgrzech (1440–1444). *Zeszyty Naukowe UJ MCCXIX, Prace historyczne*, 125, pp. 36–49.

Sucheni-Grabowska, A. (1967). *Odbudowa domeny królewskiej w Polsce 1504–1548*. Wrocław: Zakład Narodowy im. Ossolińskich.

Sułkowska-Kurasiowa, I. (1982). Doradcy Władysława Jagiełły. In Kuczyński, S. K., ed. *Społeczeństwo Polski Średniowiecznej*, 2, Warszawa: pp. 188–220.

Tymieniecki, K. (1934). Wpływy ustroju feudalnego w Polsce średniowiecznej. *Roczniki Dziejów Społecznych i Gospodarczych*, 3, pp. 77–112.

Wajs, H. (1993). *Wstęp*. In Wajs, H., ed. *Rachunki królewskie z lat 1393–1395 i 1412 r. Rachunki podrzęctwa krakowskiego. Rachunki stacji nowosądeckiej*. Warszawa: Wydawnictwo DiG, pp. I–XI.

# Chapter 6

# The political and economic relevance of Jewish loans for the dukes of Austria during the late Middle Ages

*Eveline Brugger*

## Introduction

The *Judenregal* (right to the Jews), originally defined as an exclusive regal right, was a much-coveted prerogative among the territorial princes of the Empire for both political and financial reasons during the late Middle Ages (Toch 2013, pp. 48–9). The dukes of Austria, officially enfeoffed with the *Judenregal* in 1331 (Brugger & Wiedl 2005, p. 278, no. 338), actually managed to establish almost exclusive sovereignty over the Jewish population of their lands in the first half of the 13th century. The close attachment of the Jewish subjects to their duke was cemented with Duke Frederick II's privilege for the Austrian Jews in 1244 (Brugger & Wiedl 2005, pp. 35–7, no. 25). This ducal privilege accommodated the immigration of Jews into the duchy and created a valid legal basis for this group that was to last until medieval Jewish settlement in Austria came to a violent end in the early 15th century.

The privilege was issued with the clear intention of promoting and legally safeguarding Jewish settlement in Austria, with economic utility – unsurprisingly – being the duke's first priority. The numerous provisions concerning Jewish pawnbroking and moneylending leave no doubt that as far as the duke was concerned, the only desirable occupation for Jews in Austria was the money business – other occupations were not mentioned at all, indicating that while they were not forbidden, they were of no interest to the duke (Chazan 2010, p. 124). The privilege simultaneously established a direct attachment of the Austrian Jews to their duke by subordinating them to his chamber, that is the ducal treasure, going so far as to establish that financial penalties levied for attacks against the Austrian Jews were to go largely to the duke. Based on this charter, the Austrian dukes granted their Jews protection and favours; in exchange, the Jews had to pay them substantial taxes and accept ducal control of their business (Brugger 2016, pp. 268–9).

## Jewish moneylenders between duke and nobility

The dukes of Austria were not the only territorial princes who encouraged Jews to go into the credit business. At a time of intense debate on the general morality of interest-taking, the disapprobative stance of most ecclesiastical authorities (Gilomen 2018) could not diminish the demand for credit which was part and parcel of the general development towards a more money-based economy. Jewish moneylenders were often seen as one (albeit not the only) way to resolve that problem, even though the majority of loans were at all times granted between Christian parties (Lohrmann 1990, pp. 249–50). The well-established stereotype of a Jewish 'monopoly' on moneylending on interest has been thoroughly debunked (Brugger et al. 2013, pp. 156–8); a study of the Austrian source material that focuses on the credit business in general (as opposed to studying Jewish loans exclusively) shows that Christian creditors found various ways to circumvent ecclesiastical prohibitions on interest-taking or ignored them altogether (Brugger 2004, pp. 23, 107–9).

At first, these sources mostly resulted from contacts between the Christian and Jewish social elites; written sources concerning lower-class business transactions only became more numerous in the course of the 14th century. This should not be seen as an indication that Jewish-Christian business relations were restricted to the upper social classes of both groups in this period. On the contrary, the aforementioned first ducal privilege for the Austrian Jews indicates that the 'smaller' pawnbroking business was the norm, not the exception: ten of the 31 paragraphs dealt with pawnbroking, while only one touched upon bigger credit transactions between Jews and Christian noblemen. However, the smaller business transactions (pawnbroking and short-term loans for small sums of money) were not yet considered important enough to warrant a written record, which is illustrated by the fact that debt inventories and similar sources which shed light on smaller Jewish business transactions in other parts of Europe did not exist in Austria at the time (Brugger 2016, p. 269).

For that reason, the bulk of the surviving source material on Jewish business from the 13th and first half of the 14th centuries consists of charters documenting financial dealings between the elite of Jewish financiers and noble debtors. The economic changes of the period caused financial struggles for many noble families, although some also proved remarkably apt at working the new, more money-based system in their favour. However, Jewish moneylenders were hardly ever the first choice of Austrian noblemen who needed to raise money. The nobility was well aware that failure to settle their debts could lead to the loss of pawned goods, which usually meant land: fields, vineyards, and houses were the most common pledges. Noble families tried to avoid losing landed estates that way and often preferred to borrow from their family members so that unredeemed pledges would remain part of the family property. With a few exceptions, members of the nobility regarded the services of Jewish moneylenders as a last resort if no other solution was available (Brugger 2004, pp. 107–8). Another factor in this reluctance was the close connection between the Austrian Jews and the duke – since the Jews were direct subordinates of the ducal chamber, indebtedness to them could render a debtor more dependent on the duke's benevolence than many nobles were comfortable with.

Those misgivings were hardly baseless since the Austrian dukes repeatedly interfered in loan transactions on behalf of their Jewish subjects. By putting pressure on noble debtors to repay their Jewish loans, the dukes tried to prevent economic damage to their Jews which, in turn, would have affected their own profits from the Jewish tax (Brugger 2004, pp. 39–41). During the early period of Habsburg rule in Austria, which was a time of power struggles between the new ruling family and the nobility of the land, Duke Albrecht I even went a step further: Leutold of Kuenring, instigator of a rebellion of the Austrian nobility against the duke, had to submit to Albrecht I in 1295 and to promise (among other things) to compensate the duke's Jews for everything 'he had taken from them or owed them'. If the Jews should put too much financial pressure on Leutold, the duke promised to appoint an arbiter (Brugger & Wiedl 2005, pp. 94–5, no. 89) – a clear threat to the influential nobleman that it was entirely up to the duke to decide how much access to Leutold's property his Jewish creditors were getting, thus making sure that Leutold would not risk opposing Albrecht I any more (Lohrmann 1990, p. 117).

It is therefore not surprising that it was mostly families from the lower ranks of the Austrian nobility, risen to a position of power in the duke's service, who were willing to use the financial services of the duke's Jewish subjects. The most spectacular example in this regard was the Lower Austrian *ministerialis* Kalhoch of Ebersdorf: in 1298, Kalhoch purchased the ducal office of chief chamberlain – an office whose holder exercised vicarious jurisdiction over the Austrian Jews since 1244. Kalhoch had raised the required sum in part through a loan from his Jewish lender of many years, Lebman from Vienna. However, he subsequently found himself having trouble paying the money back; in late 1305, he resorted to the drastic measure of pawning the office of chief chamberlain including all income arising therefrom (explicitly including all revenue coming from the Jews) for seven years to his creditor Lebman to cover a debt of 800 pounds of Viennese pence. However, Lebman could only claim the income from the office, while the corresponding authority of the chamberlain was transferred to another ducal official, the *Hofmarschall* Dietrich of Pillichsdorf, until such a time that the office was redeemed – presumably a condition imposed by the duke, whose approval was required for this arrangement (Brugger 2004, pp. 69–81). Kalhoch, who managed to establish his family among the elite of the Austrian nobility, could only take such financial risks because his loyalty to the dukes ensured that the dukes would not use his debts to a Jewish creditor against him.

Considering how keen the dukes of Austria were on Jewish moneylenders doing business in their territory, there is surprisingly little evidence of the dukes themselves taking out loans with their Jewish subjects. In 1225, the Jew Teka stood surety for Duke Leopold VI of Austria for 2000 marks which the duke had to pay the king of Hungary as part of a peace treaty, but even though Teka owned a house in Vienna, he was mostly active in the service of the Hungarian king and can hardly be considered an Austrian Jew (Wiedl 2010, p. 242). In the course of the 14th century, some Austrian dukes seem to have used nobles as middlemen, who would take out loans with Jewish creditors for which the duke ostensibly stood surety, while the wording of the debt instruments suggests that the real debtor was in fact the duke himself (e.g. Brugger & Wiedl 2005, p. 253, no. 298). It is not entirely clear why the Habsburg dukes were so coy about being indebted to Jewish moneylenders, given that such debts were hardly an unusual occurrence for territorial princes during that timeframe. Reversely, there is frequent evidence of the dukes repaying their own debts to Austrian nobles by amortizing the Jewish loans of the nobleman in question, although not always by redeeming them outright. Since Jewish creditors had no way to enforce repayment from the duke himself, debt instruments from the middle of the 14th century onwards often contained the debtor's formulaic promise not to transfer the debt to the duke – a provision that was very likely demanded by the Jewish creditors, although there was little they could do if the duke still decided to take over the debt (Brugger 2012, pp. 339–40).

While the Habsburg dukes hesitated to take out direct loans with their Jewish subjects, they readily pledged their revenues from the Austrian Jewry to their Christian creditors. The Jewish tax in particular could be pawned to ducal retainers and allies alike, especially during times of war. In 1320, the Austrian duke Frederick the Fair, who was fighting against Ludwig the Bavarian for the German crown, affirmed a debt of 1200 marks in silver owed to his ally, the archbishop of Salzburg. Duke Frederick promised to ensure that the chamberlain would settle two-thirds of the sum from the Viennese Jewish tax (Wiedl 2012a, pp. 375–7). From then on, the dukes frequently used mortgages on the Jewish tax as a comparatively safe way to raise money, especially since the holder of the *Judenregal* not only had the right to collect the regular annual Jewish tax, but also to levy special taxes as an extraordinary measure. When Dukes Albrecht III and Leopold III found themselves in massive financial difficulties during the 1370s, they signed the entire financial administration of their lands, including the Jewish tax, over to a consortium of three ducal officials and two citizens of Vienna for the duration of four years (Lackner 2002, pp. 45–9). In such a context, the Austrian Jews became a source of ducal income among many that could be pledged at will – a concept that could be reconciled with the ducal promise of protection for the Jews because of their special status as subordinates of the duke's chamber (Toch 2013, pp. 104–6).

## Ducal protection of Jewish credit business

The privilege of 1244 had granted the ducal chief chamberlain vicarious jurisdiction over the Austrian Jews. However, the chamberlain rarely appears as a judge in documentary sources relating to Jewish affairs; much more commonly, he corroborated credit transactions between members of the nobility and of the Jewish economic elite with his seal (Brugger 2004, pp. 85–6). The consultation of the chief chamberlain was supposed to ensure that the documented agreement was binding for both sides, which was fundamentally in the interest of all involved parties.

The chamberlain also occasionally supported Jewish creditors in their efforts to collect their receivables from noble debtors, sometimes in collaboration with the *iudex Iudeorum*[1] (justice of the Jews): for example, Duke Frederick the Fair tasked the acting chamberlain Reinprecht of Ebersdorf and the Viennese *iudex Iudeorum* During Piber to assist all Jews resident in Austria in collecting their receivables in 1317 (Brugger & Wiedl 2005, p. 198, no. 209). From the perspective of the territorial prince, it was important to ensure that the income of his Jewish subjects – especially of the economic elite of Jewish financiers – was not diminished as a result of their financial dealings with Christians since that would have reduced the revenues the duke could expect from the Jewish tax.

Their close connection to the Austrian duke, and his financial interest in furthering their profits from credit transactions, was an important factor in the prospering of Jewish communities in Austria during the 13th century. However, their dependency on ducal protection left the Austrian Jewry in a precarious situation during the first half of the 14th century, which brought about the first major persecutions of Jews in the Duchy of Austria (Brugger et al. 2013, pp. 208–19). Unlike most German cities, Austrian towns had little power over the Jewish community in their midst, which also meant no financial profit and therefore no reason to value or protect them, while Jewish credit business was often seen as unwelcome competition and Jewish privileges were considered an unfair economic advantage over Christians (Wiedl 2013, pp. 201–8). It is therefore no coincidence that the first persecutions were carried out by the citizenry of the towns where the Jews lived, not by any secular or ecclesiastical authority.

An assault on a group who was under the protection of the duke and so closely linked to him that it technically belonged to his treasure constituted a direct challenge to the duke's authority which he could not tolerate. While ducal protection usually proved too slow or ineffective to prevent outbreaks of anti-Jewish violence, the dukes often attempted to punish the attackers afterwards, although the severity of their reaction depended on a number of political and economic factors that had little to do with the Jews themselves (Brugger 2016, pp. 270–8). Still, by learning from the experiences of previous persecutions, Duke Albrecht II was able to keep the Jews of Austria mostly safe during the period of the Black Death (Brugger & Wiedl 2010, pp. 94–8, no. 645–7), which was accompanied by massive outbreaks of anti-Jewish violence (usually instigated by municipal authorities or even territorial rulers) in many other territories of the Holy Roman Empire in the middle of the 14th century (Müller 2004, pp. 256–7).

The general willingness of the Austrian dukes to protect their Jews and to punish their attackers earned them harsh criticism from the clergy. Duke Albrecht II was reproachfully dubbed 'patron of the Jews' (*fautor Iudeorum*) (Brugger & Wiedl 2010, p. 98, no. 647), an epithet which had already been used for his older brother and predecessor Duke Rudolph III (Brugger & Wiedl 2005, pp. 156–7, no. 147). In the latter text, the Cistercian author Ambrose of Heiligenkreuz also turned the commonplace stigmatization of Jewish moneylenders as usurers into a vehicle for polemical criticism of the ruler's policies by explicitly accusing the duke of protecting 'his most beloved Jews' in order to profit from their usury (Wiedl 2012b, pp. 319–20).

Not only the clergy was aware of the fact that the Jews played a mostly financial role for the duke – municipal authorities repeatedly tried to use the Jewish population of their city as a bargaining chip when they were quarrelling with the duke over legal or financial matters. During the widespread persecutions that followed an alleged Jewish host desecration in the Lower Austrian town of Pulkau in 1338, the city of Vienna forced the Viennese Jewish community to agree to a severe reduction of interest rates on Jewish loans in return for protection. The privilege of 1244 had allowed the Austrian Jews a weekly interest rate of eight pence per pound but, in 1338, the Jewish community had to 'voluntarily' lower the maximum weekly interest rate on loans taken out by Viennese citizens to three pence per pound. In spite of the financial losses they were bound to suffer from the lower profit margins of Jewish moneylenders, Dukes Albrecht II and Otto had to agree to the reduction in order to keep the Viennese Jewry safe (Brugger 2013, pp. 194–5). Although both the Hebrew and the ducal charters (Brugger & Wiedl 2005, pp. 336–8, nos 439–40) were addressed to the citizens of Vienna only, the interest rate of eight pence subsequently disappeared almost completely – albeit as part of a larger-scale development that was limited neither to Jewish loans nor to Austria, since interest rates were generally declining during the 14th century (Wenninger 1991, p. 290).

## Ducal encroachment on Jewish credit business and its limits

While there is no evidence that Jews in the Duchy of Austria fell victim to violent persecution during the second half of the 14th century, ducal protection of Jewish business was weakening. The persecutions had demonstrated to the Christian population that the Jews were vulnerable and that the protection they received from the dukes had its limitations – but more importantly, the dukes themselves were beginning to lose interest in protecting Jewish business as the economic relevance of Jewish moneylenders waned (Wiedl 2009, p. 301). The Jews became one source of ducal income among many, while their status as a group under the direct protection of the duke lost significance. An early indicator of the gradual loosening of ducal protection was a ducal charter, issued in 1330 for the chamberlain Reinprecht of Ebersdorf. The charter gave the chamberlain permission to take the money which Dukes Albrecht II and Otto owed him from the Jewish tax and, in case he shouldn't get his money, to hold the wealthiest Jews captive until they had paid Reinprecht the sum he was owed (Brugger & Wiedl 2005, pp. 316–17, no. 407).

Social markers of the Jewish loan clientele were shifting as well: the surviving sources indicate that a growing number of Christian clients now came from lower classes, no longer from the nobility and the urban elites (Toch 2008, pp. 197–9). This might partly be due to the fact that financial transactions between Jews and lower-class Christians were now more likely to be recorded because of the emergence of *Judenbücher* (*libri Iudeorum*), which documented Jewish loans, during the second half of the 14th century (Wiedl 2013, pp. 218–19). However, it may also indicate a gradual decline in the social status of the majority of the Jewish population, especially since Christian credit business was growing steadily at the same time, which diminished the importance of Jewish moneylenders (Brugger 2016, pp. 278–9).

At the time, more and more rulers throughout the Empire were considering the option of alleviating their financial problems by seizing Jewish property (Toch 2013, p. 64). In Austria, Dukes Albrecht III and Leopold III started to extort money from rich Jewish subjects by holding them captive until they paid huge sums as ransom (Brugger et al. 2013, p. 220). Another indication that Jewish business interests were no longer the dukes' main concern after the middle of the 14th century was the growing number of *Tötbriefe* ('killing letters'), ducal decrees which cancelled the debts of persons or institutions without any compensation for the Jewish moneylender in question (Brugger 2012, pp. 331–3). They were most often issued to the benefit of Austrian nobles – usually because the duke owed the nobleman in question money for his services. Sometimes, they were also used as a means of punishing Jews who left the duke's territory without explicit permission (Lohrmann 1990, pp. 217–20). Duke Rudolph IV (1358–1365), who placed great importance on stressing his sole right to rule over 'his' Jews (up to the point of including it in his famous falsification of imperial privileges for Austria known as the *Privilegium maius*), was especially quick to issue 'killing letters' for the purpose of punishing the 'flight' of a Jew from his lands – an accusation that was facilitated by the general mobility of the Jewish economic elite. Rudolph often chose to take over outstanding Jewish loans instead of simply annulling them; in some cases, he acted so aggressively that his brothers and successors Albrecht III and Leopold III considered it necessary to rescind their late brother's decrees in order to encourage a wealthy Jewish financier to return to their territory (Brugger 2012, pp. 335–7).

The severe ducal extortion policies generally seem to have been abrogated in the mid-1380s because they had brought the Jewish population to the limits of their economic capabilities (Lohrmann 1990, pp. 291–2). New ducal privileges for the Jews, granted by Dukes Wilhelm and Albrecht IV in 1397 and 1401, can thus be regarded as attempts at damage limitation, as the dukes realised that they had to enact countermeasures if they did not wish to lose the Jewish population as a source of income altogether. The aforementioned privileges confirmed the old rights of the Jews in Austria, offering the Jewish population protection from violence and plunder and promising Jewish creditors the eschewal of ducal debt cancellations as well as the assistance of the Austrian *Landmarschall* in the collection of their receivables (Brugger & Wiedl 2018, pp. 191–2, no. 2147, pp. 233–5, no. 2220).

Ducal mandates tasking the *Landmarschall* with the support of Jewish creditors were indeed issued both in 1397 and in 1401 (Brugger & Wiedl 2018, p. 186, no. 2141, pp. 239–40, no. 2227). The *Landmarschall* had already been deployed on occasion as a ducal representative in Jewish tax issues in the last third of the 14th century. The collection of debts owed to Jews by the nobility may have been a particular responsibility in his remit; it would explain why *Landmarschall* Rudolph of Wallsee-Enns was already instructed to assist Jewish moneylenders in the early 1380s (Brugger & Wiedl 2015, p. 373, no. 1771). In a privilege issued in 1402, Dukes Wilhelm and Albrecht IV not only aimed to regulate the stagnating collection of the Jewish tax, but also tasked the Austrian *Landmarschall* above all other officials with the protection of the rights of the Jews – a task which remained his responsibility until the end of Jewish settlement in medieval Austria (Brugger & Wiedl 2018, pp. 256–7, no. 2255).

Matters of authority relating to Jews also became a factor in the conflicts concerning the guardianship of the underage Duke Albrecht V that arose between representatives of the other Habsburg lines after Duke Albrecht IV's death in 1404 (Niederstätter 1996, p. 239). Of particular interest in this context is a statement by the Austrian territorial estates dated September 1406 which prescribed that the guardian should uphold the old rights of the Jews in Austria, including assisting them in the collection of debts (Lampel 1927, p. 163, no. 18295). At a time when a growing number of territorial rulers or municipal authorities throughout the Empire decided to expel their Jewish population altogether (Wenninger 1981), there was still (some) interest in preserving the economic capability of the Austrian Jewry in general, and of Jewish moneylenders in particular, during the early years of the 15th century.

## Conclusion

Even though the Austrian dukes set great store by their role as protectors of all Jews living in the Duchy of Austria, their efforts to coax their Jewish subjects into the credit business left no doubt that other Jewish occupations were of little interest to them, and that the Jews could only expect concrete ducal support in their function as moneylenders. Regular Jewish taxes and the growing number of extraordinary levies were another factor that made it necessary for the Jewish communities to make profits from moneylending in order to remain able to satisfy the dukes' financial demands and therefore keep the territorial princes interested in their continued protection.

Ducal interest in Jewish moneylending proved to be a mixed blessing for many Jewish businessmen and –women in Austria: on the one hand, the economic elite of wealthy Jewish financiers were often granted generous privileges, in some cases even a special legal status, in return for even higher taxation (Lohrmann 1990, pp. 294–6); on the other hand, the dukes regarded their Jewish subjects mostly as a financial commodity and often did not hesitate to exploit them accordingly with little regard to the impact that measures like the pawning of Jewish levies or the annulment of Jewish loans had on individual Jewish businesspeople or communities as a whole. Only when the growing financial burdens began to endanger the 'usefulness' of the Austrian Jews as a source of ducal income on the whole did the dukes start to reconsider their previous policies to a certain degree, albeit without deviating from their basic view of the Jews as a financial resource until Duke Albrecht V brought Jewish life in Austria to a violent end through the persecution campaign known as the 'Vienna Gesera' which he initiated in 1420 (Brugger et al. 2013, pp. 221–4).

## Funding

Research for this chapter was funded by the Austrian Science Fund (FWF): P32395 and preceding projects P28609, P24404, P21236, P18453, P15638.

## Note

1 On the office of the *iudex Iudeorum* see the chapter by Birgit Wiedl in this volume.

## References

Brugger, E. (2004). *Adel und Juden im mittelalterlichen Niederösterreich*. St. Pölten: NÖ-Inst. für Landeskunde.

Brugger, E. (2012). »So sollen die brief ab und tod sein«. Landesfürstliche Judenschuldentilgungen im Österreich des 14. Jahrhunderts. *Aschkenas*, 20(2), pp. 329–41.

Brugger, E. (2013). Between a rock and a hard place: rulers, cities, and 'their' Jews in Austria during the persecutions of the fourteenth century. In Price, M. & Utterback, K. eds. *Jews in Medieval Christendom – »Slay Them Not«*. Leiden: Brill, pp. 189–200.

Brugger, E. (2016). Neighbours, business partners, victims: Jewish-Christian interaction in Austrian towns during the persecutions of the fourteenth century. In Shoham-Steiner, E., ed. *Intricate Interfaith Networks: Quotidian Jewish-Christian Contacts in the Middle Ages*. Turnhout: Brepols, pp. 267–86.

Brugger, E., Keil, M., Lichtblau, A., Lind, C., & Staudinger, B. (2013). *Geschichte der Juden in Österreich*. Vienna: Ueberreuter.

Brugger, E. & Wiedl, B. (2005). *Regesten zur Geschichte der Juden in Österreich im Mittelalter, Band 1*. Innsbruck: Studien Verlag.

Brugger, E. & Wiedl, B. (2010). *Regesten zur Geschichte der Juden in Österreich im Mittelalter, Band 2*. Innsbruck: Studien Verlag.

Brugger, E. & Wiedl, B. (2015). *Regesten zur Geschichte der Juden in Österreich im Mittelalter, Band 3*. Innsbruck: Studien Verlag.

Brugger, E. & Wiedl, B. (2018). *Regesten zur Geschichte der Juden in Österreich im Mittelalter, Band 4*. Innsbruck: Studien Verlag.

Chazan, R. (2010). *Reassessing Jewish Life in Medieval Europe*. Cambridge: Cambridge University Press.

Gilomen, H. (2018). Das kanonische Zinsverbot und seine theoretische und praktische Überwindung? Mitte 12. bis frühes 14. Jahrhundert. In Maleczek, W., ed. *Die römische Kurie und das Geld*. Ostfildern: Jan Thorbecke, pp. 405–49.

Lackner, C. (2002). *Hof und Herrschaft. Rat, Kanzlei und Regierung der österreichischen Herzoge (1365–1406)*. Vienna: Oldenbourg.

Lampel, J. (1927). *Quellen zur Geschichte der Stadt Wien, Abteilung I, Band 10*. Vienna: Gerold&Co.

Lohrmann, K. (1990). *Judenrecht und Judenpolitik im mittelalterlichen Österreich*. Vienna: Böhlau.

Müller, J. (2004). 'Erez gezerah' – 'Land of Persecution': Pogroms against the Jews in the »regnum Teutonicum« from c. 1280 to 1350. In Cluse, C., ed. *The Jews of Europe in the Middle Ages (Tenth to Fifteenth Centuries)*. Turnhout: Brepols, pp. 245–60.

Niederstätter, A. (1996). *Das Jahrhundert der Mitte. An der Wende vom Mittelalter zur Neuzeit*. Vienna: Ueberreuter.

Toch, M. (2008). Economic activities of German Jews in the Middle Ages. In Toch, M., ed. *Wirtschaftsgeschichte der mittelalterlichen Juden. Fragen und Einschätzungen*. Munich: Oldenbourg, pp. 181–210.

Toch, M. (2013). *Die Juden im mittelalterlichen Reich*. 3rd ed., Munich: Oldenbourg.

Wenninger, M. (1981). *Man bedarf keiner Juden mehr. Ursachen und Hintergründe ihrer Vertreibung aus den deutschen Reichsstädten im 15. Jahrhundert*. Vienna: Böhlau.

Wenninger, M. (1991). Juden und Christen als Geldgeber im hohen und späten Mittelalter. In Ebenbauer, A. & Zatloukal, K., eds. *Die Juden in ihrer mittelalterlichen Umwelt*. Vienna: Böhlau, pp. 280–99.

Wiedl, B. (2009). Jews and the city: parameters of Jewish urban life in late medieval Austria. In Classen, A., ed. *Urban Space in the Middle Ages and the Early Modern Age*. Berlin: De Gruyter, pp. 273–308.

Wiedl, B. (2010). Die Kriegskassen voll jüdischen Geldes? Der Beitrag der österreichischen Juden zur Kriegsfinanzierung im 14. Jahrhundert. In Dornik, W., Gießauf, J. & Iber, W., eds. *Krieg und Wirtschaft von der Antike bis ins 21. Jahrhundert*. Innsbruck: Studien Verlag, pp. 241–60.

Wiedl, B. (2012a). Jüdisches Geld in der Kriegsfinanzierung Friedrichs des Schönen. *Aschkenas*, 20(2), pp. 371–95.

Wiedl, B. (2012b). The host on the doorstep: perpetrators, victims, and bystanders in an alleged host desecration in fourteenth-century Austria. In Classen, A. & Scarborough, C., eds. *Crime and Punishment in the Middle Ages and Early Modern Age: Mental-Historical Investigations of Basic Human Problems and Social Responses*. Berlin: De Gruyter, pp. 299–346.

Wiedl, B. (2013). Codifying Jews: Jews in Austrian town charters of the thirteenth and fourteenth centuries. In Price, M. & Utterback, K., eds. *Jews in Medieval Christendom – 'Slay Them Not'*. Leiden: Brill, pp. 201–22.

# Part 2

# Credit market in medieval and early modern towns

# Chapter 7

# Written sources concerning debts and loans in late medieval Czech towns

*Hana Pátková*

## Introduction

Towns in medieval Bohemia developed relatively later than towns in west and south Europe and the surrounding regions. They were unable to build on the legacy of ancient town settlements; however, they were often linked to an older settlement, which was usually a settlement with production and market functions, which was converted into the form of a legal town, governed by town law. The 13th century was an important period in relation to the origin of towns, even though they also continued to originate subsequently (well-arranged by Hoffmann 1992, pp. 31–42; Hoffmann 2009, pp. 21–60). With regard to town law, both North German, so-called Magdeburg law, and South German law was enforced in the territory of Bohemia. The law of mining towns had certain particularities, Bohemian mining towns were governed by the law of the town of Jihlava, and subsequently by the law of the town of Kutná Hora (Haas 1952; Hoffmann 1975).

## The beginnings of town official documents

The oldest evidence of official papers originating in towns comes from the 13th century. The oldest town seals, demonstrating that the town was able to issue documents, have been preserved from the 1240s (Vojtíšek 1928; Čarek 1985). Sporadic documents have survived from the second half of the 13th century. The oldest mention of a town ledger dates from the turn of the 1270s and 1280s; this ledger was allegedly kept in Prague, or more precisely Prague Old Town. However, it has not survived and it is not certain whether it actually existed (Vojtíšek 1953a). There is also information from as early as the end of the 13th century about town scribes, a list of duties of the scribe of Prague Old Town has survived from 1296. He was to write Charters and letters for the town and its residents and be involved in collection of town taxes. Major changes in regard to written sources occurred in the 14th century. The oldest actually preserved town ledger – the ledger of Prague Old Town – was kept from 1310 (Archiv hlavního města Prahy, ms. 986;

Pátková 2011). Town ledgers from other towns have also survived. Five of them from the period before 1350 have been preserved in Prague Old Town, Nový Bydžov, Louny, Litoměřice, and Kolín (Pátková 2011; Kapras 1907; Herold 1971; Kocánová & Tomas 2006; Bláhová 1978; Vojtíšek 1953b), however, it is certain that these ledgers were kept quite commonly. The number of preserved ledgers rises steeply from the middle of the 14th century and they were also commonly kept in smaller towns. It is evident from the content of the oldest five ledgers that the content of the ledgers soon began to be specialised. As well as ledgers with a mixed content, a number of more or less specialised volumes, kept depending on the needs of the specific town in the specific period, originated depending on the type of administration. With regard to the relationship to the topic of the chapter, that is debts and loans, their utilisation is quite diverse. Ledgers of privileges and statutes (*liber privilegiorum, statutorum*) have quite a limited evidential value. Loan administration only appears in these if it is affected by a town statute. Market ledgers (*libri contractuum, libri emptionum et venditionum, libri traditionum*), which record purchase and sale, particularly purchase and sale of real estate, are a much more abundant source. And, finally, specialised types of ledger, recording debt administration – ledgers of entries or obligations (*libri obligationum, libri cautionum*) – were also created in some towns. Ledgers of pledges (*libri additionum*), which contain records of claims raised by creditors, are similar to these. Testaments, usually preserved in volumes of testaments, record debts and receivables of specific town residents. Ledgers originating during administration of the financial and economic affairs of the town are a completely separate group. This mainly concerned collection of various types of taxes, of which there were several in medieval Bohemian towns – either intended for the territorial lord, or the lord of the town, or intended for the needs of the town itself. Written sources originating on the basis of activities by other institutions residing in the town must also be taken into consideration. This particularly concerned guilds and brotherhoods. These corporations collected regular contributions from their members and could also provide them with a loan or contribution if necessary. However, sources arising from the activities of individuals also very rarely survived, these being several fragments of merchant's ledgers. However, these existed in much greater numbers, as evidenced by mentions of lost papers in other sources, particularly in testaments.

This very general outline must be followed by a more detailed description of various types of sources.

## Charters

A very broad range of various legal actions was recorded in writing in the form of charters, from the 13th century to the end of the Middle Ages. While charters are the only type of written document surviving from the

13th and the beginning of the 14th centuries, they exist in parallel to other sources in the 14th and 15th centuries, particularly official ledgers. However, their present is very inconsistent in the town environment, only a fragment of the original number has evidently survived. With regard to the fact that in most cases this concerned acquisitions between individuals, private persons – residents of the town, the probability of survival of such documents is less than of documents intended for the town as a whole. With regard to preserved IOUs and quittances, most of these are simple. Paper was quickly established as a writing material and printed seals appear alongside appended seals. The form of deed does not contain any decorative formulations as for example the IOU from Jan of Bezdědice for the town of Domažlice dated 1420 (Monasterium).

These deeds could be issued by individuals – debtors, possibly along with their guarantors, and also very frequently by the town council, even if this concerned a loan to the town or if this was affair of an individual burgher (compare the debt of Klatovy burgher Jan owed to the monk of local Dominican monastery dated 1411) (Monasterium).

A fairly common way to obtain a loan in late medieval towns in Bohemia was sale of so-called permanent payments. These payments, usually linked to real property and most often a house, were sold most commonly for ten times their annual value. They were irrevocable. Sometimes they were restricted to a lifetime, but very often they were truly permanent, unlimited. Documents in the form of deeds have also been preserved regarding these business transactions and were often issued by the town council under the town seal, even though this concerned a transaction between two individuals (e.g. Kutná Hora burgheress Merl Schikactmertlin and burgher Ondřej Polner from 1398 (Monasterium). Survival of such documents is quite random, more of them are known from České Budějovice (Šimeček 1959), Vodňany (Šimeček 1960), and Kutná Hora.

The list of documents must also include testaments. Most – if they survived – have been preserved in testament ledgers in Bohemian towns; however, they also existed in the form of papers. Most of the surviving paper testaments were from České Budějovice and Soběslav (Hradilová 1992), which did not have testament ledgers. They have a very simple form in both towns – they are written on paper, the seal is additionally printed as usual, the script is more common, and the text does not contain decorative formulations. However, testaments issued under appended seals are also known from late medieval Bohemia. The testament informs, in more or less detail, of the debts and receivables of a deceased person. Written records of wills were not binding in late Bohemian medieval towns, this probably occurred more in cases of complicated inheritance or more complicated division of property by the testator (Testaments 2006). Comprehensiveness cannot therefore be assumed in relation to this matter. On the other hand, testaments often record information about places for which there are no other sources (e.g. surrounding towns where similar written documents did not survive but where the testator had business contacts), and also about rural inhabitants, whose appearance in sources is otherwise sporadic. Deeds from towns and burghers are recorded, with more or less comprehensiveness, in summarising editions of documents (Codex diplomaticus et epistolaris regni Bohemiae 1904; Regesta diplomatica necnon epistolaria Bohemiae et Moraviae 1855; Regesta Bohemiae et Moraviae aetatis Venceslai IV, 1967), municipal chartularies were issued for some more important towns such as in Žatec, České Budějovice, Ústí nad Labem, Krupka, Český Krumlov, Plzeň, and Most (Schlesinger 1892; Köpl 1901; Hieke-Horčička 1896; Müller 1929; Schmid-Picha 1908, 1910; Strnad 1891, 1905; Schlesinger 1876). Specialised editions also made the town privileges of Bohemian towns available (Codex iuris municipalis, 1886–1961).

## Town ledgers

Official ledgers kept for the needs of the town and its residents – that is town ledgers are more substantial sources from the aspect of preserved data. These have been preserved in Bohemia from a fairly late date – from 1310, whereas only five of them from the period up to 1350 (Pátková 2016b) have survived. The number of surviving ledgers increased to 51 from the period between 1350 and 1400, and 232 volumes dating up to 1500 have survived (according to Nový 1963, passim). The analogical type of written document was commonly widespread in surrounding German lands, where traces of their existence appear at the end of the 12th century (Koln am Rhine), they appear in other towns by the end of the 13th century, and also survive from towns belonging to the lands of the Bohemian crown earlier than in Bohemia itself (Görlitz, Wroclaw) (for information regarding the situation in Germany see the project of records of town ledgers *Index librorum civitatum*). Nevertheless, town ledgers became widespread in Bohemia and became a very important source for the modern historian. However, their survival is random as a result of fires in Middle Ages such as the fire of the town hall in Prague Old Town in 1399 resulted in only four ledgers from the 14th century surviving in Prague Old Town or fires of the royal towns of Domažlice and Čáslav caused that nearly the entire medieval archives were lost. Also subsequent and modern losses as well as disasters such as destruction of part of the archive of the town of Prague in May 1945, and the tendency to throw away 'old and unneeded' papers, particularly at the end of the 18th and sometimes even in the 19th century, had a destructive impact and was something that affected the archives of the royal towns such as Hradec Králové (Vojtíšková & Šebesta 2013) or Žatec, the best-preserved type of sources of town provenience.

During the 14th and 15th centuries, these ledgers developed into fairly diverse materials. Modern Czech diplomatic therefore created several classification systems according to which these ledgers are classified into several groups depending on their content or the town body that kept them (Nový 1963, pp. 21–7; Pátková 2016a, pp. 135–6, comment 225; Čarek & Lůžek 1968). From the aspect of keeping ledgers, this concerns the fact that judicial ledgers, kept by the municipal court, and council ledgers, kept by the town council, can be distinguished in Czech towns. Both these groups can overlap from the aspect of content, it depended on the competence of the court of law and the council in the specific town and the specific period.

Classification by content is fundamental for research of financial obligations, debts, and loans. The most commonly classified groups are: I. Town administration ledgers in the narrower sense of the word – this includes ledgers of privileges and statutes (*libri privilegiorum et statutorum*); various office ledgers – forms, copy ledgers (*formularium, liber copiarum*), etc., and also a large group of financial ledgers, kept for administration of the town's economic management. II. Town judicial ledgers – these contain disputable and indisputable civil matters, criminal justice matters. III. Ledgers for the transmitted public competence of the town – orphan ledgers (*libri orphanorum*), hospital ledgers, and church expense ledgers.

If we proceed in order along the individual groups, we must state that the ledgers of statutes and privileges did not contain much data. These are essentially cases when a provision concerned matters of debts. Several provisions from the 14th century concerning debts and lien were published on the basis of the town ledgers of the Old Town (Archiv hlavního města Prahy, ms. 986; ms. 993) and other sources by Emil Franz Rössler in the 1840s (Rössler 1845, passim, and pp. LXIII–LXIV). This group of ledgers is similar to legal ledgers, of the towns we can mention the legal ledger of Kamenice nad Lipou, a smaller subject town in South Bohemia established in the 1460s (Krčilová, Martínek & Martínková 2004). With regard to the specific homogeneity of town law, these provisions are usually of a similar content. With regard to the separate chapter devoted to the legal framework of the debt administration, there is no need to pursue this matter further.

### Financial ledgers

In the broadest sense of the word these are ledgers used to administer the town's finances. Several types of these ledgers can be distinguished. (Nový 1960; Beer 1915) Ledgers used during collection of various taxes and allowances, whether these were intended for the territorial lord or nobility, or whether these were for the needs of the town – tax ledgers and registers, etc. Debt matters only essentially appear here in limited numbers – this mainly concerned arrears of various allowances. A specific register of arrears dating from 1486–1487 survived in Kutná Hora and there were undoubtedly more similar written documents (Archiv města Kutná Hora, ms. I D 4). Another large group of data is town quantities, usually recording income and expenditure chronologically according to the official terms of office of individual burgomasters. A ledger recording the debts of resigning town councillors owed to new town councillors has also exceptionally survived (České Budějovice, 1390s; Archiv města České Budějovice, ms. D 8). A list of townspeople owing the town for municipal real estate dating from 1511 to 1514 from Kutná Hora is also unique (Archiv města Kutná Hora, ms. I D 8). The financial ledgers of auxiliary municipal authorities recording specialised administration (trade in wine in České Budějovice; the office of the Prague Bridge in Prague Old Town, etc.) have survived in some towns. Ledgers originating directly in relation to a loan that the town provided to the monarch and in which its residents participated are of greater significance. Such a ledger survived in České Budějovice and dates from 1394 (Archiv města České Budějovice). From the aspect of form, these ledgers or registers are very simple, they have the form of a notebook or file, are written on paper, and record the names of specific persons and the relevant amounts.

As for the group of municipal justice ledgers, four types in particular are of interest in relation to debt administration: ledgers for debts or books of obligations, which, as the name implies, are especially kept for this type of administration, ledgers of pledges and also market ledgers, and, finally, testament ledgers.

In regard to the first type, it must be mentioned that very few of these specialised ledgers have survived, we can chiefly mention several ledgers from Prague. Specialised ledgers were created at Prague Old Town in the 1370s at the latest. A justice ledger for minor debts from 1370 to 1371 has been preserved from this period (Archiv hlavního města Prahy, ms. 988). This is followed in order by a ledger of minor debts dating from 1400 to 1499 (Archiv hlavního města Prahy, ms. 998) and a ledger of major debts from 1400 to 1483 (Archiv hlavního města Prahy, ms. 997). The boundary between a major and minor debt was the amount of 10 stacks of 60 Prague grosses (about ledgers Kremličková 1952).

Prague Old Town also has so-called registration ledgers where debt obligations form part of the administration. These have survived from 1471 to 1518 (Archiv hlavního města Prahy, ms. 94), 1518 to 1535 (Archiv hlavního města Prahy, 2098), and 1518 to 1538 (Archiv hlavního města Prahy, ms. 99). The ledger of town rights, marriage contracts, and quittances from 1518 to 1552 comes from the very end of the monitored period (Archiv hlavního města Prahy, ms. 534), and quittances are recorded in a separate section of the ledger. Debt administration also appears in ledgers with mixed contents, the so-called white ledgers of registration, contracts, and other entries from 1452 to 1535 (Archiv hlavního města Prahy, ms. 2141). The second Prague town, Prague New Town, has a similar series of ledgers for debts of less than ten stacks of 60 grosses from 1377 to 1417 (Archiv hlavního města Prahy, ms. 2070, 2073, 2077, 2078). These ledgers are essentially kept chronologically on the basis of the dates when the municipal court went into session. Such notably specialised ledgers do not appear in other Bohemian towns. They were probably not kept in smaller towns and they may have existed in larger towns but probably disappeared over time. This is evidenced by the fact that larger towns in Moravia (Brno, Olomouc, Znojmo) and in Eger have similar ledgers (Nový 1963, pp. 39–49, 128–34, 190–200, 69–81). Ledgers of pledges recorded notification of claims before the town court or council. A specialised ledger of pledges regarding debts from Kutná Hora from 1514 has survived (Archiv města Kutná Hora, ms. E b/10), and this category can also include some ledgers from the Prague towns – the ledger of contracts, pledges, and levies of Prague Old Town from 1518 to 1558 can also be classified with these fairly late ledgers (Archiv hlavního města Prahy, ms. 2155), along with two ledgers from Prague New Town, these being – from the 16th century – the ledger of pledges, quittances, and town rights from 1518 to 1538 (Archiv hlavního města Prahy, ms. 554), and, finally, the ledger of pledges from 1490 to 1518 (Archiv hlavního města Prahy, ms. 2097).

The majority of the surviving books are therefore not specialised in this manner, records concerning debts are mixed among other administrative items. This is also the case of Prague Old Town, where a judicial ledger from 1351 has survived (Archiv hlavního města Prahy, ms. 987); records concerning debts are mixed in among other entries of various content. The ledger is basically kept chronologically according to the sessions of the town court (Třikač 1996).

The aforementioned market ledgers are a very frequent type where one can often find entries about sale of the so-called permanent payments among entries about sale of real estate. Permanent payments were very common in Bohemian late medieval towns. This system was abolished during the Hussite Revolution period but, with regard to the fact that there was no substitute for it in economic life, it very quickly reappeared. Records in Prague market ledgers provided most of the information on this phenomenon for a basic study by B. Mendl (Mendl 1932) which is also important because some of the used ledgers were destroyed during the fighting in Prague in May 1945. A specific debt usually originated during sale of real estate; payment of the entire price at once was not a common occurrence in late medieval Bohemian towns. It was much more common to pay part of the price and gradually pay off the remainder at specified intervals. Records of payments can sometimes be found as additional entries next to the original entry. Payment of the entire amount and therefore settlement of the obligation is usually graphically expressed by crossing out the entry so that the original text remains visible. Commemorative ledgers which contain mixed entries of various content, which is related simply by the need to record this information in writing for future memory or books that can be called civil justice ledgers in modern terminology, are much less specialised. The abovementioned types of ledgers are generally widespread and have survived from even very small locations, for instance Hošťka in North Bohemia (Nový 1963, p. 68) or Kaplice in the southern part of the country (Nový 1963, p. 93).

With regard to testament ledgers as stated above, testaments have survived in some towns in the form of papers. However, most of them are preserved in the form of ledgers. The testament ledgers themselves have survived quite inconsistently, testaments are sometimes also mixed in among other entries of a different nature. When working with a testament one must remember that most deceased people did not create a testament; this usually originated in relation to more complicated inheritance or property relations which meant that written records of acquisition were necessary. Testaments are a very generous source from the aspect of research of debt administration. They record the receivables and debts of the deceased, and also record the method these were handled in. Receivables were specifically the subject of bequests and donation, whether to specific people or church institutions, however, these did not receive cash and the question is to what degree they were able to utilise these receivables. A very common type, though a fairly complicated from the research aspect, is ledgers identified as commemorative ledgers (*liber memorabilium, memorialis*). These are very common particularly in smaller towns where the administration of town authorities was not very extensive and so specialised ledgers were not created like they were in bigger towns. These ledgers have a mixed content and they can contain various entries which needed to be recorded in writing for more permanent preservation. In these, debt administration is mixed among other types of records and there are often long intervals between entries, especially in the ledgers of small towns, which complicates evaluation of the evidential value of these ledgers and the comprehensiveness of the entries. An example of such a book is the commemorative ledger of the town of Čelákovice in Central Bohemia, with records from 1366–1557 kept chronologically according to the session of the town court (Archiv města Čelákovice, 12).

## Guilds and brotherhoods

Town corporations – guilds and religious brotherhoods – were also involved in loan administration. They were able to loan their members money from their resources. The existence of guilds and brotherhoods is documented in Bohemian towns from the first half of the 14th century. Written documentation kept by these corporations – mostly ledgers demonstrating guild management – would certainly be a suitable source but they have only been preserved very sporadically. Only several of these ledgers and their fragments from medieval Bohemia have survived, yet thousands of them must have existed (Pátková 2006). The archive documents of the guild of artists of Prague Old Town, including ledgers, are exceptionally well-preserved (Pátková 1996; Benátská 2011; Chytil 1906). The oldest artistic guild ledger contains records from 1348 to 1527, including accounts, but does not allow systematic monitoring of loans within the terms of the guild environment (Pátková 1996).

Accounting records were also kept by individuals in late medieval towns. The so-called merchant's ledgers must be mentioned at this point. Only several fragments, the records of two merchants selling cloth and one selling spices dating from the 14th century, are known from Bohemia (Graus 1956), the recently identified specialised records of a Prague merchant (Musílek 2016) which means we cannot assume their extensive use. However, future findings of unknown material cannot be precluded. A ledger kept from 1455 (Třeštík 1956) has survived in a neighbouring land – from the town of Eger. Of course not only merchants kept such records. References to a 'register' which individual burghers kept and in which they kept detailed records of their debts, receivables, and possibly other similar administration appear in various sources. Similar mentions can also be found in testaments, where these 'registers' are commonly referred to for detailed records of the testator's property. Thousands of similar documents must have existed but practically nothing has survived. The merchant's ledger of the Runtingers from the relatively close Bavarian town of Regensburg (Graus 1956, p. 644; Bastian 1935–1944) mentions the Bohemian territory only very marginally.

## Other institutions active in the town

After this summary of sources concerning the town, its residents, and originating as a result of the activities of the lord of the town, the town itself, and its residents, we must also briefly mention the activities of other – essentially out-of-town – institutions, active in the town.

Town residents were naturally able to enter into financial relations with these institutions. Church institutions – monasteries, chapters and churches – are particularly important in this aspect. Sources regarding financial transactions between them and burghers may be stored in their archives. They may be in the form of the abovementioned papers or may be bound in a ledger. So-called expenditure ledgers are important in this field. These contained records of the management of churches (Zilynská 1998; Kůrka 2010). Their survival is fairly random; the accounts of the Parish Church of Saint Nicholas in Prague Old Town from the 15th century have survived in Prague, with its great number of churches (Opatrný 1957); these ledgers have not been preserved in most towns. Surviving materials include ledgers from Kutná Hora, Ústí nad Labem, Kaplice, and the ledger from Jičín (Francek 1981), and also the ledger from Tábor from the beginning of the 16th century (Vandrovcová 2010).

## Acknowledgment

This study was supported by the programme Progres Q07 implemented at the Faculty of Arts, Charles University.

## References

### Archival sources

Archiv hlavního města Prahy.
*Archiv města Čelákovice.* Státní okresní archiv Praha-východ.
*Archiv města České Budějovice.* Státní okresní archiv České Budějovice.
*Archiv města Kutná Hora.* Státní Okresní archiv Kutná Hora.
*Archivní katalog.* Archiv Hlavního města Prahy. http://katalog.ahmp.cz/pragapublica
Čelakovský, J., Friedrich, G. & Haas, A., eds. (1886–1961). *Codex iuris municipalis regni Bohemiae.* Part 1–4. Prague.
*eBadatelna.* Státní oblastní archiv v Praze. http://ebadatelna.soapraha.cz/
Erben, K. J., ed. (1855). *Regesta diplomatica nec non epistolaria Bohemiae et Moraviae.* Prague.
Friedrich, G., ed. (1904–1907). *Codex diplomaticus et epistolaris regni Bohemiae.* Prague: Sumptibus comitiorum Regni Bohemiae.
*Index Librorum Civitatum.* www.stadtbuecher.de
Jenšovská, V., ed. (1967). *Regesta Bohemiae et Moraviae aetatis Venceslai IV.* Part I/ 1. Prague: Sumptibus Academiae scientiarum Bohemoslovacae.
*Monasterium.* www.monasterium.net

### Literature

Bastian, F. (1935–1944). *Das Runtingerbuch 1383–1407 und verwandtes Material zum Regensburger-Südostdeutschen Handel und Münzwesen.* Regensburg: G. Bosse.
Beer, K. (1915). Über Losungsbücher und Losungswesen böhmischer Städte im Mittelalter. *Mitteilungen des Instituts für österreichisches Geschichtsforschung,* 36, pp. 31–95.
Benátská, K. (2011). *Cechovní kniha pražských malířů od 1490.* Thesis, Faculty of Arts, Charles University in Prague.
Bláhová, M. (1978). Nejstarší městská kniha města Kolína. In: *Z pomocných věd historických. In memoriam Zdeňka Fialy.* Praha: Karolinum, pp. 117–49.
Čarek, J. (ed.1985). *Městské znaky v českých zemích.* Praha: Academia.
Čarek, J. & Lůžek, B. (1968). Názvosloví městských knih v severozápadních Čechách. *Sborník archivních prací,* 18, pp. 452–77.
Chytil, K. (1906). *Malířstvo pražské 15. a 16. věku a jeho cechovní kniha staroměstská z let 1490–1582.* Praha: ČAVU.
Francek, J. (1981). Úřad kostelníků v Jičíně a jejich kniha záduší z let 1431–1508. *Sborník archivních prací,* 31, pp. 75–104.
Graus, F. (1956). Tři zlomky českých kupeckých knih z doby předhusitské. *Československý časopis historický,* 4, pp. 644–54.

Haas, A. (1952). Právní oblasti českých měst. *Časopis Společnosti přátel starožitností*, 60, pp. 15–24.

Herold, V. (1971). O nejstarší městské knize lounské. *Sborník archivních prací*, 21, pp. 32–92.

Hieke, W. & Horčička, A., eds. (1896). *Urkundenbuch der Stadt Aussig bis zum Jahre 1526*. Prag: VGDB.

Hoffmann, F. (1975). K oblastem českých práv městských. *Studie o rukopisech*, 14, pp. 27–67.

Hoffmann, F. (1992). *České město ve středověku*. Praha: Panorama.

Hoffmann, F. (2009). *Středověké město v Čechách a na Moravě*. Praha: NLN.

Hradilová, M. (1992). Soběslavské kšafty z let 1455–1523. *Táborský archiv*, 4, pp. 47–107.

Kapras, J. (1907). *Kniha svědomí města Nového Bydžova z let 1311–1470*. Nový Bydžov: Obec Nový Bydžov.

Kocánová, B. & Tomas, J. (2006). *Městská kniha Litoměřic (1341)–1562 v kontextu písemností městské kanceláře*. Ústí nad Labem: Univerzita J. E. Purkyně.

Köpl, K. (1901). *Urkundenbuch der Stadt Budweis in Böhmen I. 1251–1391*. Prag: Calve.

Krčilová I., Martínek, Z. & Martínková, L., eds. (2004). *Práva a privilegia města Kamenice nad Lipou 1462–1798*. Pelhřimov-Brno: MZA.

Kremličková, M. (1952). *Staroměstské soudní knihy pro dluhy pod 10 kop z let 1370–1391 a 1400–1440*. Thesis, Faculty of Arts, Charles University in Prague.

Kubů, F. (2006). *Chebský městský stát; počátky a vrcholné období do počátku 16. století*. České Budějovice: Veduta.

Kůrka, P. B. (2010). *Kostelníci, úředníci, měšťané*. Praha: Historický ústav.

Mendl, B. (1932). Z hospodářských dějin středověké Prahy. *Sborník příspěvků k dějinám hlavního města Prahy*, 5, pp. 161–390.

Müller, A. (1929). *Quellen- uns Urkundenbuch des Bezirkes Töplitz-Schönau bis zum Jahre 1500*. Prag: VGDB.

Musílek, M. (2016). Zlomek knihy vydání. v níž jsou jména Židů. "Nově objevený" rukopisný zlomek kupeckého rejstříku a jeho výpověď pro pražský obchod ve středověku. *Pražský sborník historický*, 44, pp. 141–66.

Nový, R. (1960). Městské finanční knihy doby předhusitské a husitské. *Zápisky katedry čsl. dějin a archivního studia*, 4, pp. 29–41.

Nový, R., ed. (1963). *Městské knihy v Čechách a na Moravě 1310–1526*. Praha: Karolinum.

Opatrný, J. (1957). *Záduší kostela sv.Mikuláše na Starém Městě pražském*. Thesis, Faculty of Arts, Charles University in Prague.

Pátková, H. (1996). *Cechovní kniha pražských malířů 1348–1527*. Praha: Koniasch Latin Press.

Pátková, H. (2006). "Volumus eciam. quod liber in pergameno fiat." Úřední knihy středověkých bratrstev a cechů v Čechách. *Archivní časopis*, 56, pp. 184–92.

Pátková, H. (2011). *Under collaboration of Aleš Pořízka and Věra Smolová. Liber vetustissimus Antiquae Civitatis Pragensis*. Praha: Scriptorium.

Pátková, H. (2016a). Městské knihy a jejich význam. In *Historické a historiografické problémy středověku*. Praha: Historický ústav, pp. 135–41.

Pátková, H. (2016b). Die Stadtbücher in Böhmen bis 1350. *Krakowskie Studia z Historii Państwa i Prawa*, 9(3), pp. 271–8.

Rössler, E. F. (1845). *Das altprager Stadtrecht aus dem XIV. Jahrhunderte. Prag:* Tempsky.

Schlesinger, L. (1876). *Das Stadtbuch von Brüx bis zum Jahre 1526.* Prag: VGDB.

Schlesinger, L. (1892). *Urkundenbuch der Stadt Saaz bis zum Jahre 1526.* Prag-Wien-Leipzig: VGDB; Brockhaus.

Schmid, V. & Picha, A. (1908. 1910). *Urkundenbuch der Stadt Krummau in Böhmen I-II.* Prag: Calve.

Šímeček, Z. (1959). Renty a rentovní listiny v Českých Budějovicích. *Právněhistorické studie, 5, pp. 49–75.*

Šimeček, Z. (1960). Rentovní listiny ve středověkých Vodňanech. *Jihočeský sborník historický,* 29, pp. 1–7.

Strnad, J. (1891. 1905). *Listář královského města Plzně a druhdy poddaných osad.* Plzeň: Městské historické muzeum.

Sturm, H. (1951). *Eger. Geschichte einer Reichsstadt.* Augsburg: Kraft.

Testamenty (2006). *Pozdně středověké testamenty v českých městech.* Praha: Archiv hlavního města Prahy.

Třeštík, D. (1956). Nejstarší obchodní kniha z Čech. *Zápisky katedry čsl. dějin a archivního studia,* 1, pp. 25–6.

Třikač, J. (1996). Staroměstská kniha soudní z let 1351–1367. *Pražský sborník historický,* 29, pp. 5–58.

Vandrovcová, J. (2010). *Táborské kostelní účty z let 1509–1510.* Thesis, Faculty of Arts, Charles University in Prague.

Vojtíšek, V. (1928). *O pečetech a erbech měst pražských a jiných českých.* Praha: Památkový sbor hl. m. Prahy.

Vojtíšek, V. (1953a). O nejstarších městských knihách českých, pražské a novobydžovské. In *Výbor rozprav a studií Václava Vojtíška.* Praha: Academia, pp. 341–66.

Vojtíšek, V. (1953b). *O nejstarších knihách města Kolína nad Labem. In Výbor rozprav a studií Václava Vojtíška.* Praha: Academia, pp. 109–15.

Vojtíšková, J. & Šebesta, V. (2013). *(Králové)hradecké městské kanceláře do roku 1620.* Ústí nad Orlicí: Optis.

Zilynská, B. (1998). Záduší. In *Facta probant homines.* Praha: Scriptorium. pp. 535–48.

# Chapter 8

# Monetary credit market in the cities of the southern Baltic coast in the late Middle Ages (Greifswald, Gdańsk, Elbląg, Toruń, Rewel)

*Cezary Kardasz*

## Introduction

The colonization and urbanization of the south-eastern coast of the Baltic Sea integrated these areas into the Latin culture and the European economic system. Settlers from Germany brought along to Baltic cities credit forms and institutions known in Western Europe (Sprandel 1975, p. 55). The 14th century saw a significant development of credit markets. At that time, the purchase of rents became the most popular form of raising and investing capital in cities located on the southern coast of the Baltic Sea. The flexibility of this legal form enabled its rapid evolution and expansion. From the 12th century, lifetime contracts concluded with monasteries to the credit transaction, a fully developed form used in the 14th and 15th centuries. Late medieval source materials, in addition to the basic form of rent transactions, contain information on number of other rent types used according to the needs of counterparties – from perpetual rents, which disappeared in the 14th century, arising when the original creditor sought to recover the invested cash from older rents, through *ratione muri* rents used in the acquisition or reconstruction of a property, to lifetime rents which played an important role in municipal economy (Kardasz 2013, pp. 31–42).

## Social aspects of credit markets in Baltic cities – social structure of the participants

The degree of development of the capital market is one of the basic indicators of economic advancement. The social scope of the market – the percentage of the entire public, as well as individual social and professional groups participating in it – allows us to determine the degree and dynamics of its development, and, in turn, the city and country in which it operates. It is assumed that the wider the group of market participants, the higher the degree of socio-economic development. It is not only the social scope that is important here, but also the degree and nature of market share of particular social and professional groups and institutions (merchants, craftsmen, women and minors, clergy and the Church, as well as municipal authorities).

The condition of the source base and the dynamics of this phenomenon make us dependent on estimates when trying to determine the social scope of the credit market in Baltic cities in the Middle Ages (Cf. Wenner 1972, p. 51). The analysis of credit records shows that a monetary credit enjoyed moderate interest among the society. In Greifswald, over the period 1300–1442, 3,129 people were recognised as being creditors or debtors at least once. At that time, five generations of the town's inhabitants could be active on the market; in Elbląg, over the period 1330–1417, it was 3,008 people. With some caution, we can estimate the percentage of inhabitants of the studied cities who were active on the credit market at 10 to 20% of the total population. In Greifswald and Rewel, it was about 10%, a higher percentage was recorded in the Old Town of Elbląg (20%).

Debtors prevailed on all studied markets. The percentage of people in both groups was low (5–7%). This clearly demonstrates a specialisation of credit market activity resulting from the economic situation of particular groups. The clear division between those granting credit and those incurring debts was not associated with high prevalence on the market. The majority of both creditors and debtors (50–60%) have granted or taken out a loan only once. However, creditors outnumbered debtors on the market.

The identified merchants constituted from 10 to 20% of market participants but they contributed almost half of the capital to the market. The average value of loans granted by the representatives of this group was a result of its financial capacity and demand for loans. Merchants dominated both among those granting high loans and in the group of those making high financial commitments. This indicates high income and investment activity on the market. However, a significant part of the loans granted by the representatives of this group were small and medium transactions, which proves the influence of demand on the value structure.

The share of craftsmen in the markets was between 10 and 20%. Like merchants, they often appeared on the market only once, yet in contrast to them, they took out debts much more often than they granted loans. The average value of debts and investments, compared to the representatives of the merchant stratum, is much lower in this group. There were some significant differences with regard to wealth within the group, which were reflected also in the nature of activity on the credit market. There were numerous representations of craftsman's related to trade (coopers), food industry (bakers, butchers), and metal's craft (goldsmiths, blacksmiths). The representatives of these crafts stood out from the group in terms of the amount of loans taken out.

Women and minors were present on the credit markets of all the studied towns. They accounted for 10 to 15% of all participants. Their market share is characterized by low prevalence on the market and a visible advantage of the granted credit value over debt. Representatives of these groups granted high loans, which, combined with their low prevalence on the market, indicates searching for financial security. The activity of women, chiefly widows and minors, on the market was associated with local factors (e.g. epidemics). With the exception of Greifswald, we do not observe an increase in investments made by these groups in the examined cities in late 1340s and early 1350s, which indicates that they were not directly affected by the plague outbreak of that period.

When talking about the market share of minors, it is impossible to ignore the capital introduced to the credit market on their behalf by municipal authorities. Based on the analysis of the sources from Toruń and Gdańsk, it can be concluded that there are clear differences in this field. The authorities of Toruń, having at their disposal the capital of minors, granted low-interest loans to merchants suffering from the negative effects of the downturn in Hanseatic trade in late 14th century.

Clergy and church institutions were a permanent element of the late medieval capital market. The market share of these groups in the studied urban centres ranged from 0.4 to 15.4%. Representatives of the clergy and church institutions were relatively rare on the credit market – they usually appeared once or twice, mainly as creditors. However, the only exception to this rule were municipal hospitals, which made repeated appearances on the market. The representatives of this group invested large sums of money on the market – this particularly applies to institutions.

Apart from church institutions, municipal authorities were some of the most important institutional participants of the credit market in late medieval cities (cf. Huang 2019). In the studied cities, the share of municipal authorities in the turnover of the credit market ranged from 0.1 to 8.8% in the case of granted loans and 1.4 to 4.7% of the debt value. Municipal councils were mainly active on the credit market as debtors, seeking capital to cover growing expenses. A characteristic feature of their market share is the high value of transactions concluded which could be associated with their high credibility as debtors. However, the market share of municipal authorities was not limited to borrowing only to meet current needs. The example of Rewel's authorities shows that they sometimes also conducted extensive lending operations related to the investment of capital belonging to church institutions that remained under their patronage.

When reflecting on the social side of credit market in late medieval cities, it is impossible to ignore the question of the allocation of the funds obtained in this way. It can be stated that part of the credit was earmarked for investments – the borrowed money was used, for example for the purchase of real estate, commercial activity, modernisation of the workshop – however, we cannot unfalteringly determine the scale of this phenomenon. In Höxter, a city in Westphalia, at the turn of the 14th century, only in less than 10% of cases the moment of selling a rent can be linked to the purchase or reconstruction of a house or workshop, and in 50% of cases the debt was the result of a bad economic situation (Rüthing 1986, p. 244). Studies on the rent market in other regions show that non-economic factors such as family situation, marital status or age may have played a significant role in making a decision whether to be active in this field and thus allocate the capital.

## Economic aspects of credit markets in Baltic cities – credit market as an indicator of the city's economic position

The credit market, as a place to invest and raise capital, was an important part of the city-wide economic system. It is still disputed which of its elements determined the turnover and thus reflect the economic situation of the time. A large number of researchers assume that the development of the market for rent purchase was determined by the supply of merchant capital, which was dependent on economic conditions (Richter 1971, p. 8; Wenner 1972, pp. 20, 94). Senior researchers assumed that the more prosperous the economic situation, the higher the profits from commercial activity and, consequently, the higher the turnover on the rent market. As Helen Haberland has shown, at certain times the value of turnover was determined by the demand for loans (Haberland 1974, p. 262).

When considering the relationship between the demand and supply of capital in the rent purchase market, we must also take account of the fact that the sources containing the entries of rent transactions do not inform us of the total supply of capital and demand for credit, the number and value of transactions concluded were the resultant of these factors (Czaja 1987, p. 22). The amount of capital obtained from trade was higher than the value of rents bought at that time, as not all capital was invested in their purchase. Similarly, the demand for credit could at certain times exceed the amount for which the rents were sold – due to the lack of free cash, only part of it could be satisfied. The increase in the turnover of the rent market was not always synonymous with good economic situation. Studies on the rent market in Elbląg prove that in the periods of stagnation in commercial activity, the withdrawn capital was invested in the purchase of rents (Kardasz 2008, p. 311). However, turnover fluctuations on the rent market can be used to capture certain tendencies in the economic life of the city, as in the period of a long-term crisis the inflow of capital to the market would be impossible, which would result in a clear decline in the turnover.

The analysis of the types of purchased rents can provide information on the economic location and the course of the economic situation. The emergence and functioning of the secondary rent market is another stage of capital market development in the city (Gilomen 2010, p. 65). The older and more stable the market, the greater the share of old rents in it, and the newer and more dynamically developing the market, the newer rents (Goliński 2003, p. 40).

In all the studied cities, the so-called new rents, which constituted about 80% of the market, were most frequently used. The share of old rents in the total number of contracts ranged from 0.7% in Rewel to 2.3% in Greifswald. The weakness of the secondary market indicates that the capital market of the examined cities in the 14th and the first half of the 15th century was still in the initial phase of development. This makes it very difficult to use the relations between the types of rents as an indicator of economic location. In Greifswald and Rewel, we often encounter rents related to the purchase of real estate, which indicates a close relationship between the rent market and the real estate market.

Another indicator used in research on the credit market and economic location is the amount of interest rate. Ahasver von Brandt treated the rent market as a place to invest merchant capital, granting them a decisive influence over its development. Using a simple correlation between demand and supply, he found that in periods of economic prosperity, increasing profits of merchants resulted in increased investments that lead to a supply-over-demand advantage and a drop in credit prices, whereas during the crisis, demand for credit exceeded supply, resulting in an increase in interest rates, that is a drop in the price of rents (Brandt 1935, pp. 19–20). However, this view has several shortcomings. The amount of interest is a function of the degree of social and economic development, and the low cost of credit indicates that the development of the money-goods economy is advanced and the credit market is developed but, in the late Middle Ages, the interest rate was not a simple result of the capital demand and supply ratio. The Church, territorial rulers, and municipal authorities often established the applicable or maximum interest rate by way of administration. In such cases, the amount did not fully reflect the real economic situation of the city. More importantly, the increased supply of merchant capital and the ensuing increase in the turnover on the rent market did not always result from the economic boom. During the crisis, attempts were made to invest the capital withdrawn from commercial operations in the purchase of rents, and the downturn did not encourage the incurring of liabilities, so the supply could exceed demand. Under certain circumstances, therefore, falling interest rates could indicate an economic depression.

All throughout the period under review, the markets of the studied cities – in line with the pan-European trend – have seen a fall in the interest rates on rent loans. At the beginning of the 14th century, it was usually 10%, a value which continued until the 1360s. Apparently, interest rates fell in Livonian cities to 6.6–5% at the turn of the 14th century. In Prussia, in 1386, the maximum interest rate was lowered by administration from 10 to 8.33%. This amount, with the exception of Elbląg, was valid until the end of the 15th century. In Elbląg, as early as in the 1380s, probably due to the large supply of merchant capital, the interest rate on rents fell below 8%,

*Table 8.1* Structure of credit market value in selected cities (in percentages)*

| City value of the transaction | Greifswald | | Gdańsk | | Elbląg | | Toruń | | Rewel | |
|---|---|---|---|---|---|---|---|---|---|---|
| | *1* | *2* | *1* | *2* | *1* | *2* | *1* | *2* | *1* | *2* |
| ≤ 30 marks | 2.2 | 11.6 | 14.25 | 60.25 | 19.5 | 52 | 4 | 28.5 | 9 | 45 |
| 30–99 marks | 22.8 | 39.4 | 26.5 | 26 | 47.5 | 38 | 17.25 | 33.5 | 23.5 | 31 |
| ≥ 100 marks | 75 | 49 | 59.25 | 13.75 | 33 | 10 | 78.75 | 38 | 67.5 | 24 |

* 1 – Value of transactions; 2 – Number of transactions.

at the beginning of the 15th century a rate of 1:15 (6.66%) was commonly used there.

Having analysed the structure of the credit market value one may draw conclusions about its social scope and the role of credit in the economic activity of particular groups, and, indirectly, also about the origin of capital on the market and economic situation. It should be assumed that craftsmen were looking for a small credit (≤30 marks) and a large credit (≥100 marks) was sought by merchants. This assumption is confirmed by share analyses of identified representatives of individual social groups on the credit market and source information indicating the ownership and income of individual social groups. The annual cost of living, including food, accommodation, fuel, and clothing for a family of five in Rostock at the end of the 14th century amounted to about 35–40 Lübeck marks, while the average income of a craftsman amounted to 30–50 marks. (Hauschield 1973, p. 158; Hammel 1981, pp. 44–6). The bricklayer's daily rate was 3 solidi, which gave the amount of about 13 marks annually. The basic annual salary of a city scribe in the 15th century Elbląg was 12 Prussian marks. The flautist employed by the city council earned 0.25 marks per week (Pelech 1987–1989, Nos 82, 211, 772, 1100). We can see that a loan of 30 marks, with an interest rate of 2–3 marks per year, was the maximum financial capacity of a craftsman from that time. The merchants' income depended on the direction and object of trade and the economic situation but on average amounted to 15% to 25% of the invested sum (Stark 1985, pp. 131–40). Thus, the market share of transactions of a certain amount will not only allow to make conclusions about the social scope of medium- and long-term credit, it may also indicate the location of particular social groups.

The structure of transaction values concluded in Gdańsk and Elbląg was dominated by small transactions (≤ 30 marks). In Rewel, they accounted for less than half of all concluded transactions; in Greifswald and Toruń, they remained on the margin of the credit market. In all the cities, the value of turnover was determined by large transactions (≥ 100 marks) or, as in the case of Elbląg, large and medium transactions.

The structure of credit market value was not static. In the examined period, the average value of one transaction increased in all studied cities. This process was associated with a drop in interest rates and rising inflation in the 15th century. The social structure of market participants also influenced the structure of the value of concluded transactions – in the periods of increased merchant activity there was an increase in the market share of high value transactions.

## Economic prosperity on the southern coast of the Baltic Sea in the late Middle Ages and its conditions

The period until mid-14th century was a time of relatively stable growth and a successful economic situation, interrupted only by short periods of downturn. There are clear analogies in the economic situation of the cities of the Wendish Quarter, Pomerania, Prussia, and Livonia. These concern both long-term trends, such as the economic recovery in the 1330s and the prosperity after the Treaty of Stralsund, as well as its short-term collapses, such as the crisis in the 1340s. These phenomena were associated with political events concerning the entire Baltic area – the end of the 1320s crisis, the end of the war with Denmark and the opening of trade opportunities after signing the peace treaty, the conflict with the counts of Holstein. The exception was the plague outbreak of the late 1340s, the effects of which were almost unnoticeable in Prussia and Livonia. As the crises of 1380s intensified, the role of local and regional factors became increasingly important, which, combined with the general crisis tendencies, determined the situation of individual cities.

The first symptoms of the approaching economic collapse appeared in Elbląg in the early 1380s. At that time, the percentage of merchant capital invested in the credit market clearly increased, which was a consequence of the withdrawal or/and exclusion of Elbląg merchants from long-distance trade and the search for safe investments. This was mainly due to an increasing competition of Gdańsk merchants and difficulties accessing the sea. At that time in other cities of the Baltic area, we can still observe a relatively stable situation related to the effects of the Treaty of Stralsund (1370) (Hammel 1988, p. 92).

The economic situation of Greifswald was similar to that of Elbląg at the turn of the 14th century. Both cities experienced a period of economic growth and prosperity in the first half of the 14th century but in the second half of the century they found themselves in a crisis which resulted in the exclusion of these towns from long-distance trade. The reasons for these phenomena lay at the local (ports) and regional level (stronger neighbours). The unfavourable trend in the economic situation in this period undoubtedly accelerated these phenomena. This argument is confirmed by the fact that the economic collapse began in Greifswald almost two decades after it took place in Elbląg.

The situation of Toruń was utterly different. Until the beginning of the 15th century, the city had remained strongly linked to Silesia economically and acted as an intermediary between the Sudeten-Carpathian area and the Baltic Sea basin. The first symptom of the crisis was that merchants in the late 1380s became increasingly interested in loans. Due to difficulties in trade with Slovakia and Russia and the downturn in Hanseatic trade, trade income was declining, and some of the merchants sought capital to survive the impending crisis. However, the symptoms of the downturn were visible in Toruń only at the beginning of the 15th century and its effects were aggravated by the aftermath of the war of 1409–1411 (Sarnowsky 1993, p. 454). Although in the 1440s Toruń experienced a short-term economic recovery, the city waited until the end of the 15th century to reverse the long-term unfavourable trend.

Among the analysed Prussian cities, Gdańsk clearly stood out from other cities in terms of economic location at the turn of the 14th century. It quickly rebuilt the damage it incurred at the beginning of the century and in the second half of the 14th century the merchants of Gdańsk, at the expense of the inhabitants of Elbląg and Toruń, were gaining an increasingly strong position in Prussian trade. This related to contacts with Polish lands and relations with the cities of Western Europe. Research indicates a clear intensification of economic contacts of Cologne with Gdańsk at the beginning of the 15th century, whereas at the same time the relations with Elbląg (late 14th century) and Toruń (after 1411) (Hirschfelder 1994, p. 222) were dying out. The analysed source material does not indicate an economic slowdown in Gdańsk at the end of the 14th century. A slight increase in the number of unpaid rents, which may indicate that the economic situation deteriorated, occurred in the Main City of Gdańsk only in the 1430s.

The influence of regional factors on the economic location of the city is clearly visible on the example of the Livonian city of Rewel. In Rewel, a period of economic downturn associated with pirate activity at the end of the 14th century took place along with other surveyed cities, yet unlike in Prussian or Pomeranian cities we do not observe a downturn at the turn of the 14th century. The signs of crisis are not to be seen in Rewel until the mid-1420s – at the same time, due to economic differences, there was a clear increase in tension between Wendish, notably Lübeck, and Livonian cities (Misāns 2003, p. 36).

## Credit markets in Baltic cities against the backdrop of the region and Western Europe (selected aspects)

About 15% of inhabitants of the 14th-century Stade are mentioned on the credit market (Ellermeyer 1975, p. 47). In Lübeck, as early as at the turn of the 13th century, one-third of the city's residents were active on the rent and real estate market (Haberland 1974, p. 23). In the mid-14th century in Hamburg, the share of the city's inhabitants mentioned as creditors or debtors is estimated at about 50–60% (Wenner 1972, p. 52). The social scope of credit markets in Baltic cities of 10 to 20% ranks them among the small and medium-sized Hanseatic cities.

In all analysed cities, the secondary market was very underdeveloped. In Hamburg, the share of old rents on the market in the second half of the 14th century was 22–32% so it was ten times higher than in Greifswald (Baum 1976, p. 87). In Poland in the 14th to 15th centuries, the old rent was barely known (Lesiński 1966, p. 189).

Compared to the cities of similar size and economic potential and smaller Hanseatic cities, the level of loan interest rates in the analysed cities in the second half of the 14th and early 15th centuries shows no clear differences. A similar situation can be observed in Silesia where the prevailing rate of 10% in the 14th century went slowly down in the second half of the century only to reach 7% in Wrocław at the beginning of the 15th century (Beyer 1901, p. 83; Goliński 2003, p. 36). At that time, lower interest rates were applied in the largest trade and craft centres of the Baltic area. In Hamburg at the turn of the 13th century, they ranged from 12.5 to 6.66%, the most commonly applied was 8.33%, and from 1303 6.66% (Richter 1971, p. 61). In Lübeck at the same time, the interest rate was 6.25%, falling to 5% in the decades that followed (Haberland 1974, pp. 202–3). In the cities of the Kingdom of Poland at the beginning of the 14th century, the most common interest rate amounted to 12.5% (Cracow). In the second half of this century, it amounted to 10% (Lviv, Poznań), and dropped to 8.33% in the middle of the 15th century (Lesiński 1966, p. 185).

In the value structure of rent transactions in the examined cities, small transactions prevailed, however, the turnover was determined by contracts for higher amounts. In Hamburg, which is best documented in this respect in 1471–1490, small rents (with a value of up to 10 marks) accounted for 70% of concluded transactions, with a share in turnover amounting to 32%, medium-sized transactions (from 10.1 to 50 marks) accounted for 28% of all concluded transactions concluded and their value amounted to 57% of total turnover, large rents (above 50 marks) accounted for only 2% of concluded transactions and the turnover of 11% (Gabrielsson 1971, p. 42). This comparison confirms the conclusions from the analysis of the social scope – in the 14th and 15th centuries credit markets in the examined cities were at an initial stage of development.

## Conclusion

In the 14th–15th centuries Baltic cities in Prussia and Livonia, rents constituted a commonly used credit form. Merchants clearly dominated credit markets. However, the scale and nature of their participation was locally determined and depended on the economic situation of the city. The market share and its nature of other social groups showed clear analogies.

The period of up to the 1380s in all the examined cities was characterised by a successful economic situation. As crisis intensified on a European scale, local conditions played an increasingly important role. As early as in the 1380s the first symptoms of the crisis were traceable in Elbląg, and a decade later in Greifswald. At the beginning of the 15th century, Toruń became also affected by the crisis which, until that time, had been competing with Gdańsk as it had strong ties with Polish lands and Silesia. In Rewel, clear symptoms of the crisis are visible in the mid-1420s. Gdańsk clearly stands out in comparison with other Prussian cities as the signs of crisis appeared there only in the 1430s.

The degree of development of credit markets in individual cities over the period of the 14th–15th centuries varied: from the relatively underdeveloped and having an insignificant social scope market in Rewel, through a more developed market in Elbląg, which was in serious crisis at the turn of the 14th century, to the large and developed market in 15th-century Gdańsk. Comparing the situation on credit markets in the selected cities on the southern shore of the Baltic Sea, the Reich, the Kingdom of Poland and Silesia proves the existence of a number of locally conditioned differences in the degree of their development. In the late Middle Ages, credit markets in the analysed urban centres were underdeveloped compared with the situation in Hamburg or Lübeck but showed clear analogies with the situation in Silesian cities. In the 14th–15th centuries, the capital market in Polish cities was much less developed. The degree of development and social range of the credit market in the late medieval Baltic cities represented a function of their social structure and economic location.

## Funding

Text prepared as a part of the project, no. UMO-2016/21/B/HS3/03099, financed by the National Science Centre, Poland.

## References

Baum, H. P. (1976). Hochkonjunktur und Wirtschaftkrise im spätmittelalterlischen Hamburg. *Hamburger Rentengeschäfte 1371–1410*, Hamburg.

Beyer, O. (1901). Schuldwesen der Stadt Breslau im 14. und 15. Jahrhundert mit besonderer Berücksichtigung der Verschuldung durch Rentenverkauf. *Zeitschrift des Vereins für Geschichte und Alterthum Schlesies, 35*, pp. 68–143.

Brandt, A. (1935). *Der Lübekcker Rentenmarkt von 1320–1350*. Kiel.

Czaja, R. (1987). Rynek kupna renty w Elblągu w pierwszej połowie XIV wieku. *Zapiski Historyczne, 52*, 3, pp. 7–37.

Czaja, R. (2006). Strefa bałtycka w gospodarce europejskiej w XIII–XV wieku ze szczególnym uwzględnieniem Prus Krzyżackich. In Gawlas, S., ed. *Ziemie polskie wobec Zachodu. Studia nad rozwojem średniowiecznej Europy.* Warszawa: Wydawnictwo DiG, pp. 195–245.

Ellermeyer, J. (1975). *Stade 1300–1399. Liegenschaften und Renten in Stadt und Land. Untersuchungen zur Wirtschaft – und Sozialstruktur einer hansischen Landtstadt im Spätmittelalter.* Stade: Selbsverlag des Stader Geschichtes- und Heimatsvereins.

Gabrielsson, P. (1971). *Struktur und Funktion der Hamburger Rentengeschäfte in der Zeit von 1471 bis 1490.* Hamburg: Christiana.

Gilomen. H. J. (2010). Kredit und Innovation im Spätmittelalter. In Hesse Ch. & Oschema K., ed. *Aufbruch im Mittelalter. Innovationen in Gesellschaften der Vormoderne. Studien zu Ehren von Rainer C. Schwinges.* Ostfildern, pp. 35–68.

Goliński, M. (2003). *Wokół socjotopografii późnośredniowiecznej Świdnicy 2.* Wrocław: Vydawnictwo Uniwersytetu Wroclawskiego.

Haberland, H. (1974). *Der Lübecker Renten – und Immobilienmarkt in der Zeit von 1285–1315. Ein Beitrag zur Sozial – und Wirtschaftspolitik der Hansestadt.* Lübeck.

Hammel, R. (1981). Vermögensverhaltnisse und Absätzmöglichkeiten der Bäcker in hansischen Seestädten am Beispiel Lübeck. Ein Beitrag zur hansischen Gewerbegeschichte des späten 14. Jahrhunderts. *Hansische Geschichtsblätter,* 99, pp. 33–60.

Hammel, R. (1988). Häusermarkt und wirtschaftliche Wechsellagen in Lübeck von 1284 bis 1700. *Hansische Geschichtsblätter,* 106, pp. 41–107.

Hauschield, U. (1973). *Studien zu Löhnen und Preisen in Rostock im Spätmittelalter.* Köln: Böhlau.

Hirschfelder, G. (1994). *Die Kölner Handelsbeziehungen im Spätmittelalter.* Köln: Kölnisches Stadt Museum.

Huang, A. (2019). A Source Collection on Urban Annuities, 14th–18th Centuries: An Introduction to the Data. *Vierteljahrschrift für Sozial- und Wirtschaftsgeschichte,* 106(1), pp.67–80.

Kardasz, C. (2008). C. Kardasz, Rynek kupna renty w Elblągu w latach 1361–1417. *Komunikaty Mazursko-Warmińskie,* 261(3), pp. 299–318.

Kardasz, C. (2013). *Rynek kredytu pieniężnego w miastach południowego pobrzeża Bałtyku w późnym średniowieczu (Greifswald, Gdańsk, Elbląg, Toruń, Rewel).* Toruń: Towarzystwo Naukowe.

Lesiński, B. (1966). *Kupno renty w średniowiecznej Polsce na tle ówczesnej doktryny i praktyki zachodnioeuropejskiej.* Poznań: Uniwesytet im. Adama Mickiewicza.

Misāns, I. (2003). Riga, Dorpat und Reval im Spannungsfeld zwischen den wendischen und preußischen Städten vom Ende des 14. bis zur Mitte des 15. Jahrhunderts. In Dybaś, B., ed. *Prusy i Inflanty między średniowieczem a nowożytnością. Państwo – społeczeństwo – kultura.* Toruń: Wydaw. Uniwersytetu Mikolaja Kopernika, pp. 29–43.

Pelech, M., ed. (1987–1989). *Nowa księga rachunkowa Starego Miasta Elbląga 1404–1414,* 1–2. Warszawa: Państ. Wydaw. Naukowe.

Richter, K. (1971). *Untersuchungen zur Hamburger Wirtschafts- und Sozialgeschichte um 1300.* Hamburg: Christians.

Rüthing, H. (1986). *Höxter um 1500. Analyse einer Stadtgesellschaft.* Padeborn: Verlag Bonifatius-Druckerei.

Sarnowsky, J. (1993). *Die Wirtschaftsführung des Deutschen Ordens in Preußen (1382–1454).* Köln: Böhlau.

Sprandel, R. (1971). Der städtische Rentenmarkt in Nordwestdeutschland im Spätmittelalter. In Kellenbenz H., ed. *Öffentliche Finanzen und privates Kapital im späten Mittelalter und in der ersten Hälfte des 19. Jahrhunderts.* Stuttgart: Gustav Fisher Vlg., pp. 14–23.

Sprandel, R. (1975). *Das mittelalterliche Zahlungssystem nach hansisch-nordischen Quellen des 13.–15. Jahrhunderts.* Stuttgart: Hiersemann.

Stark, W. (1985). *Untersuchungen zum Profit beim Handelskapital in den ersten Hälfte des 15. Jahrhunderts.* Weimar: Böhlau.

Wenner, H. J. (1972). *Handelskonjunkturen und Rentenmarkt am Beispiel der Stadt Hamburg um die Mitte des 14 Jahrhunderts.* Hamburg: Christians.

Chapter 9

# Rural credit and monetarisation of the peasantry in the late Middle Ages

The Eger city state c. 1450

*Tomáš Klír*

## Introduction

On the threshold of the early modern period, we record deep changes in the social, economic, and demographic regimes of European peasant society. The early modern peasantry seems to us in comparison with the late medieval as strongly monetarised, commercialised, oligarchised, and also saturated with sophisticated credit regimes. This was accompanied by changes in economic management, improvement living standards, and the beginnings of consumer society. The causes of the peasantry transformation are sought through the combined effects of external and internal factors that have generated an increasing financial burden on peasant households and the need to regularly obtain high amounts of cash. Attention is drawn to demographic growth, the price revolution, state fiscalism, changes in the practice of property disposition, and inheritance law and the difficult position of the primary heirs of farmsteads within the primogeniture. However, our knowledge is very erratic. While the social and economic structures and processes within the early modern peasantry are well known in detail, the situation in the late Middle Ages is rather modelled and remains hypothetical (for the Czech Lands in particular Kostlán 1987; Cerman & Zeitelhofer 2002; Chocholáč 1999, 2005; Procházka 1963; Čechura 1990; Míka 1960, pp. 208–21). The lack of late medieval data is characteristic of the whole of Central Europe (Cerman 2008). The Eger (Cheb) city state is the exception where we can see inside the peasant economy thanks to the unique interplay of fiscal and court records (Klír et al. 2016). Our question is what was the degree of monetarization of the Eger peasantry and what was the nature and extent of the peasant credit market in the late Middle Ages?

We narrow our view to a relatively short but sufficiently representative period of 1435/1442–1456 because the highest quality source base is available for this period. In doing so, we build on previous studies (Klír et al. 2016; Klír 2018, 2019). We will focus only on the 'subject' farmsteads that prevailed in the Eger city state (95%); we leave aside 'free' farmsteads.

## Region and sources

In the late Middle Ages, the Eger region had the status of an imperial pledge to the Bohemian king (1322), later the Crown of Bohemia, and its territory was already more or less stabilised geographically (after 1413). Territorial power was in fact executed by the city council in Eger (Cheb), which was materialised by the annual collection of the land tax and organisation of the land militia. Eger's city state in the 15th century had a size of around 400 km², included 11 parishes with approximately 130 rural settlements, 1,000 farmsteads and roughly 10,000 denizens (Klír et al. 2016, pp. 31–58, 124–7; Klír 2019, pp. 344–6). In terms of geographical and market conditions, its entire territory can be divided into several zones, from the agro-climatically optimal part of the Eger Basin along the River Eger (400–500 m a.s.l.) to foot-hill, climatically harsh and agriculturally unfavourable areas (500–650/700 m a.s.l.). Agricultural production in the Eger city state was characterized by a three-field fallow system and, especially in the Eger Basin, market-oriented cattle breeding (Klír 2018, pp. 177–9, 201–2, 224; Klír 2019, pp. 345–6).

The period of 1435/1442–1456 was relatively calm, defined, on the one hand, by the so-called Hussite and on the other the Hungarian wars. At the same time, it was a period of a power vacuum when the power of the Eger city council peaked (Klír et al. 2016, pp. 19–21). We judge according to the geographically relatively close Nuremburg data that the period after 1440 until 1465 was also abnormally stable as whole also in the Eger city state, in terms of crop yields, demography, and prices (Bauernfeind 1993, pp. 178–201).

The main source for knowledge of the Eger peasantry in the late Middle Ages are the fiscal sources. They are the registers of the land tax (1392–1757) and registers of the city tax (1390–1758). Thanks to this high-quality source base, we are informed on the monetary value of all of the real estate and moveable property in the countryside and in the city. For the 'subject' tenants, we know not only the amount of the land tax, but also the land rent (Klír et al. 2016; Klír, in print). The so-called debt protocols, kept at the Eger city court, are crucial for understanding the credit market (*Schuldprotokolle*, 1387–1496).

All of the peasant households which held a farmstead paid the land tax. The land tax was property, progressive, and the tax rate fluctuated most often in the range of 1.5–3.0%. The amount of the tax was determined according to the monetary value of the (1) tenure right to the farmstead; (2) horses, cattle, and sheep; (3) the so-called non-farmstead plots; (4) other rights, properties, and moveable property (Klír et al. 2016, pp. 144–57, 175–7; Klír 2018, pp. 181–2).

All of the members of the city community (burghers) paid the city tax. In the 15th century, the city tax was assessed both as a fee for a fireplace (chimney) and further as a progressive tax for all the real and moveable property (tax rate of 1.5–2.0%). The rural properties of the burghers were also subject to the city tax.

The tenants had a relatively wide disposition, family property and inheritance rights to the 'subject', that is 'purchased' farmstead. The farmstead was usually passed as whole to only one of the heirs (the so-called primary heir), and the remaining members of the family received an ideal share from its monetary value. A distinction was made between full-fledged peasant farmsteads ('Hof') and smallholder/ cottager farmsteads ('Herberge') which usually did not own a team of horses. Full-fledged peasant farmsteads predominated in the Eger city state (77–80%; Klír et al. 2016, pp. 146–50; Klír 2018, pp. 184–91; Klír 2019, p. 346; cf. Procházka 1963; Cerman 2008, pp. 58–64).

In addition to inalienable land, firmly bound to 'subject' farmsteads, there were other, independent and separately taxed plots in the Eger city state, subject to 'fief' law, which the holder could relatively freely dispose of (so-called non-farmstead plots). Their absolute share in the land fund was relatively low (estimated at 2–5% of fields, ca 25% of meadows) but the economic importance was high (Klír et al. 2016, pp. 152–4; 2018, p. 185).

The landlords' rights in the late medieval Eger city state were extraordinarily fragmented and dispersed. Estates in the sense of economically consolidated dominions were lacking. Land rent most often had in-kind nature (grain); the labour rent was minimal. This all indicates a relatively weak landlord control of the property transfers of peasant land (Klír et al. 2016, pp. 159–61, 237–41; Klír 2018, pp. 187–8).

Feudal rent was comprised of the land rent, land tax, and church tithe. The land rent had a fixed nature; it reflected the size of the peasant holding and favoured some 'subject' farmsteads. The land tax was progressive and in principle respected the level of commercialisation and monetarisation of the farmsteads. Both forms of feudal rent drew on the seasonal agricultural surplus and were complementary in time and physically. The land rent drew directly from the grain surplus (collection on St Michael); the land tax indirectly on the animal surplus (collection after St Martin). The church tithe was of an extremely variable nature, compared to the rent of the land, it was 10–25% (Klír, in print). The analysis of land rent, land tax, and church tithe showed that the feudal rent as a whole was set to a minimum production level of farmsteads, below which they did not reach even in the agriculturally unfavourable years in the monitored time segment. Most peasants thus surely had an available surplus in hand, the specific amount of which fluctuated year-on-year (Klír, in print).

## Monetarisation

The question is how much cash the peasants needed to pay feudal rent (external factor) and how much to potentially pay siblings or buy a farmstead, livestock, and non-farmstead plots (internal factor). The first part of the question is answered by the analysis of the above-mentioned land tax

*Table 9.1* Indicative price of grain and livestock in the Eger city state in 1438 and 1456

| Commodity | Draught horse | Cow | Calf | Sheep | I 'Kar' of grain (ca 3 hectolitres) |
|---|---|---|---|---|---|
| Price | 120–140 gr. | 50–55 gr. | 8 gr. | 7 gr. | 15 gr. |

*Note:* gr. – Prague groschen.

*Source:* Klír 2018, pp. 191–3; cf.Vaniš 1981; Míka 1959.

and land rents in the register of the land tax from 1469 (*Klosteuerbuch*, 1469). The second part of the question is answered by an analysis of monetary value of the properties in the tax register from 1438 and taxation book from 1456 (Klír et al. 2016; Klír 2018, pp. 188–98). An essential prerequisite for the interpretation is naturally knowledge of the prices of grain and cattle (Table 9.1).

As far as the cash necessary to pay the feudal rents, the situation of individual families varied enormously. Considering that our aim is a comparison with the early modern situation, we can simplify reality to the average values (Table 9.2). The land tax had an exclusively monetary form, representing for the 'Hof' farmstead on average an annual burden of 28.5 Prague groschen and for 'Herberge' farmstead 11.5 Prague groschen. Land rent was mostly in kind and, therefore, did not force most peasants to raise cash. Only one-fifth of the peasant farmsteads had to pay the land rent in cash, on average each was required to pay 29.5 Prague groschen annually. If the land tax met with a cash land rent, the average financial burden was 68 groschen. We can summarise that in the monitored period the average peasant household in the late medieval Eger city state needed to acquire at least 30–60 Prague groschen of cash each year. That corresponded to the price of one and a half cows, or 8–16 hectolitres of rye. At the same time, low prices mean that the annual reproduction of the peasant farmstead was not extremely expensive.

The average monetary value of the tenure right to a 'subject' farmstead, the livestock and non-farmstead plots is shown in Table 9.2. The relatively low price of the tenure right for the farmsteads is striking. It was true for the 'subject' farmsteads that the value of the tenure right was about half the value of all property, the other half was the value of livestock. If the peasant households also owned non-farmstead plots, then the value of the tenure right was on average one-third of the overall value, the second third was the livestock, and the third was the non-farmstead plots (1:1:1). Or, the average 'subject' farmstead in and of itself could be acquired for the price of 10–12 cows, or 3 draught horses.

The contrast to the early modern price relations is clear. Although the early modern situation has not yet been analysed for the Eger city state,

Table 9.2 Overview of average monetary values of peasant property (1438, 1456) and cash and in-kind burdens on Eger 'subject' farmsteads of the year (1469)

| | | | 'Subject' farmstead | | Number of cases |
|---|---|---|---|---|---|
| | | | 'Hof' farmstead | 'Herberge' farmstead | |
| Average price | Purchase right | 1438 | 11 ss 45 gr. | 5 ss 18 gr. | 609 / 86 |
| | | 1456 | 13 ss 42 gr. | | 632 |
| | Horses and cattle | 1438 | 11 ss 38 gr. | 3 ss 28 gr. | 820 |
| | | 1456 | 12 ss. 11 gr. | | 655 |
| | 1 ploughed 'Morgen' (ca 0.57 ha)* | | 2 ss 12 gr. | | 81 (1438) / 75 (1456) |
| | 1 meadow 'Morgen' (ca 0.57 ha)* | | 4 ss 30 gr. | | 86 (1438) / 111 (1456) |
| Average annual land tax (1438) | | | 28 gr. | 11.5 gr. | 763 |
| Average annual land rent only in cash (22.5% of farmsteads) | | | 29.5 gr. | | 132 |
| Average annual land rent only in grain (71% of farmsteads) | | | 6.8 grain 'Kar' (ca 20 hectolitres) | | 416 |
| Church tithe | | | 10% – 30% of the amount of the land rent | | 31 |

Notes: gr. – Prague groschen; ss – threescore Prague groschen

* – only a minority of peasant families owned this

Source: Klír et al. 2016; Klír 2018, pp. 190–6; Klír, in print.

we can help by comparison with other well-known regions. For example, for the area of the Saxon town of Grimma near Leipzig, it was established on the basis of data from the Turkish tax registers of 1542 that the livestock value was only about 10% of the total value of the peasant property (Schirmer 1996, p. 62). Similar relations are also supported by data from the oldest land registers for Bohemia or Moravia (Míka 1960, pp. 213–18, 352–405; Chocholáč 1999, pp. 72–97). Horses and cattle were less than one-tenth of the estimated price of rich farmsteads in the grain areas. The ratio of the monetary value of horses and cattle to the estimated value of the courtyard with land fluctuated around 1:8 (Hanzal 1963, pp. 42–4).

Thus, although the norms of property disposition and inheritance law in the late medieval Eger city state did not in principle differ from those we know in early modern Bohemia, their economic and social consequences for the functioning of peasant communities were fundamentally different – due to different price relations and demographic regime. Thanks to the relatively low value of the tenure right to the 'subject' farmstead, the position of the primary heir apparent in the Eger city state was not in any way economically burdensome because the obligations to the other heirs could be relatively easily and immediately settled in natural commodities, non-farmstead plots, or relatively attainable cash. Model considerations as well as specific examples show that neither a loan nor repayment of shares was necessary in most cases.

We can formulate the hypothesis that the late medieval peasantry of Eger was not forced to be in intensive interaction with the market. We speak of course on the level of the average because the Eger city state was not homogeneous and it is necessary to count with differences between the agriculturally advantageous and foothill zones, or the small and large farmsteads. The hypothesis of generally low level of the monetarization and commercialization of the peasantry will be tested in the next chapter using a credit market analysis.

## Credit market

The relationship between the peasant society and the credit market has attracted the long-standing systematic attention of historians, as shown by the number of monographs, volumes, and a special issue of the journal 'Continuity and Change' from 2014 (e.g. Briggs & Zuijderduijn 2018; Schoefield & Lambrecht 2009). At this point, we will use the established methodological framework to examine the nature, structure, availability, function and importance of the credit market in the late medieval Eger countryside.

Knowledge of the Eger credit market is made possible by the protocols of the city court. The Eger city court sat relatively regularly, namely on Mondays and Fridays, extraordinarily on Wednesdays. A wide spectrum of people who had receivables from Eger burghers – not only the Eger burghers themselves, burghers from other towns or Jews, but also the peasantry – 'subject' and 'free' tenants from the countryside could turn to the court. The city court and its protocols were a key institutional element providing guarantees for debt recovery and the efficient functioning of the urban-rural credit regime. What is important is that the peasantry was given the same guarantees as the inhabitants of the city, which was an incentive to enter the credit market.

The court protocols recorded (1) the petitions of the creditors on the debtors; and (2) to a lesser extent also the declarations of the debtors on the specific obligation, repayments and guarantees. In the first case, we see formal and informal credits, which failed. In the second case, they are formal credit, specifically loans, regardless of whether they were repaid. Those recorded were mainly those loans, with which the creditor wanted to secure his rights and the enforceability of the debt. It is thus not surprising that records of Jewish creditors predominate. The creditor usually was satisfied with the admission of the debtor himself before the city court, only in one case is also the presence of his landlord documented.

The subject of our analysis are the petitions from 1442–1456 and the declarations of the debtors from 1435–1456 (*Schuldprotokolle*, 1429–1439; 1439–1452; 1452–1470).

### The testimony of the petitions

When the creditor turned to court, he first brought the first petition, and if the claim was not paid, it was followed by the second and finally the third petition, forfeiture of the pledge, or other remedial action was accepted. Both the amount due (principal) and interest ('damage' of the creditor) were regularly recorded. It is fundamental that even small debts, less than 10 Prague groschen, were discussed before the court in the period in question, so the earlier city council's resolution was not applied, namely that only the enforcement of debts from a certain amount of money was to be recorded in the books (*Schuldprotokolle*, 1387–1416, pp. 1–3).

We have identified, among the 12,276 petitions from 1442 to 1456, a total of 257 (2.1%) cases when the plaintiff came from a rural settlement or market village, whether from Eger city state or outside of it (Table 9.3). Of these petitions, 165 were primary; the rest were repeated petitions. Among the plaintiffs, it was possible to identify 133 unique individuals. The majority of them were peasants. In the registers of the Eger land tax, it was possible to find 61 plaintiffs – peasants directly in the year of the petition. Among the other plaintiffs, a significant share were rural millers (9% of the plaintiffs; 17% of the petitions) and even parish priests were represented.

The first question is what type of credit the claims concerned. Was it a failed loan, or a sale on credit? The specific cause of the debt can only be traced exceptionally in the protocols – unpaid wages occurred three times, an unspecified trade transaction twice, loaned money twice, likely an unpaid inheritance share once, debt created by the sale of grain twice, and of dill once. Nevertheless, a total of 47 primary petitions (28.5%) were brought against burghers – butchers, six petitions concerned Eger millers and five weavers (c.f. *Losungsbuch*, 1446). On the level of the general tendency, we therefore assume that the petitions relate predominantly to sale credit that

*Table 9.3* Amount of the debt for claims sued by plaintiffs from outside Eger before the city court in 1442–1456

| Amount of the debt (Prague groschen) | Primary petitions | | | |
|---|---|---|---|---|
| | number | % | Eger 'butchers' | %* |
| 7–30 | 50 | 31.6 | 12 | 24.0 |
| 31–60 | 47 | 29.7 | 17 | 36.2 |
| 61–120 | 31 | 19.6 | 12 | 38.7 |
| 121–300 | 23 | 14.6 | 6 | 26.1 |
| 300–3,600 | 7 | 4.4 | 0 | 0.0 |
| Total | 158 | 100.0 | 47 | 29.7 |

\* – share within the shown monetary category.

Source: *Schuldprotokolle*, 1439–1452; 1452–1470.

failed, or that they were unpaid wages. In other words, among the plaintiffs, there are mainly the suppliers of the city market for meat, grain, and wool (both direct producers and intermediaries). In this case, the credit market and its institutional security by the city court indirectly helped to supply the city efficiently, as they compensated for seasonal fluctuations and secured agricultural commodities even in a situation of cash shortage.

The second question is how much the individual petitioned debts amounted to. This also tells us how much money the peasants were getting at one time by selling their products. The amount of monetary debt varied in a wide range from seven groschen to 60 threescore Prague groschen. Nevertheless, a total of 61% of the debt can be considered to be small, not exceeding one threescore Prague groschen. Another 20% of the debts were between one and two threescore of Prague groschen. The boundary of 10 threescore Prague groschen was crossed only exceptionally (three cases). Receivables from Eger butchers had the highest representation in the category of a half to two threescore Prague groschen. This range corresponds to the assumption that normal trade with agricultural, especially livestock, products was behind the large part of the petitioned claims.

The third question is how much interest was associated with the credit. We unfortunately do not know the time between the creation of the debt and the deadline for its payment. The records of the petitions listed the interest rate for loaning the money in 119 of the cases (72%); in 46 cases, it was interest-free debt. In total volume, the amount of the petitioned debts was 295 threescore Prague groschen, of which 177 threescore was connected with an interest in the amount of 43 threescore (24%). The interest rate fluctuated in a wide range of 7–79%. Most often, the interest was in the interval of 7–20% and 21–40%, only exceptionally it exceeded 60% (Figure 9.1). The analysis did not show a convincing dependence of the amount of interest on the size of the principal, the occupation of the debtor, the social status of the plaintiff or creditor, the number of petitions, or the year of the petition.

The fourth question is what the property positions of the plaintiffs (peasants) and defendants (burghers) were. We have determined the status of the peasants based on the land tax attributed in the year of the petition, the status of the burghers according to the city tax register from 1446. Of the statistical methods, we have used quintile analysis, that is we ranked all taxpayers according to the prescribed tax and divided them into five categories from the poorest to the richest (Klír 2018, pp. 202–4; 2019, p. 347). In total, we have evaluated the status of 54 plaintiffs in 69 petitions and 31 defendants in 62 petitions (Figure 9.2). The richest peasants predominated among the plaintiffs. The status of the defendant burghers was more balanced, with moderately wealthy and very wealthy burghers represented equally. It follows that the city's foodstuffs market was mainly supplied by the richest peasants who were willing to sell to the burghers on credit.

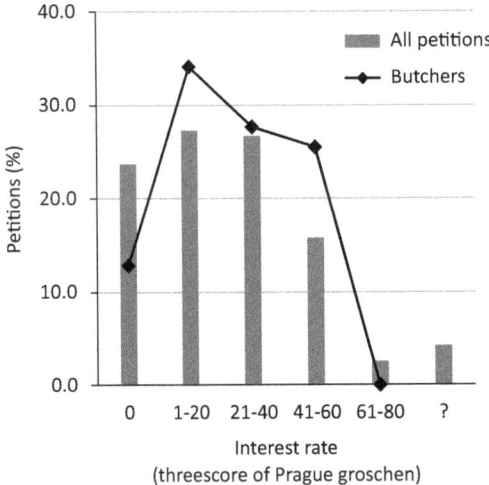

*Figure 9.1* Amount of the interest for loaning money.

*Source: Schuldprotokolle,* 1439–1452; 1452–1470.

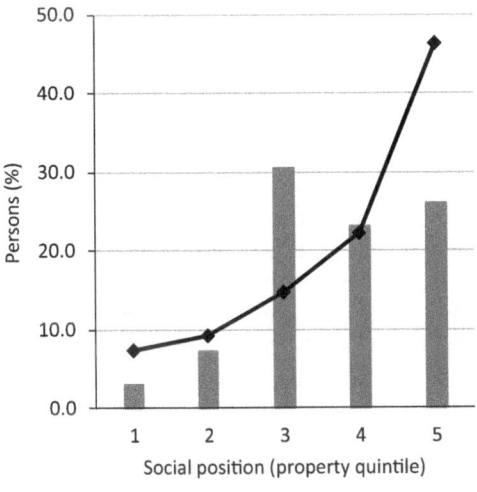

*Figure 9.2* Social status of the creditors and debtors in the Eger city state, 1442–1456 (sale on debt).

*Source: Klosteuerbücher,* 1442–1456; *Losungsbuch* 1446; 1439–1452; 1452–1470.

## The testimony of the records of the loans

The protocols also contain records of the loans. In them, among others, the term of the anticipated repayment was listed, or the repayment calendar, often also a pledge. The interest rate for loaning the money was never given; many records were later crossed out, that is the loan was repaid.

We have analysed the protocols from 1435–1456 which contained a total of 779 declarations of debtors on the acceptance of the financial obligation. Of this number, only 36 (4.6%) concerned peasants, demonstrating their low level of involvement in the market with formal loans. We identified the peasants according to the predicate and then searched in the registers of the Eger land tax (*Klosteuerbuch*, 1435; 1438; 1441–1456).

The records of the loans show the reverse direction of the flow of economic resources than the records of the petitions. In 86% of the records, the peasant was the debtor and the burgher the creditor. Behind a total of 31 records of loans, there were 23 individual peasants because some peasants bound themselves to debts repeatedly. We most often encounter individual peasants (61%), the representation of a 'society' of the two peasants and a 'society' of a peasant with a burgher was approximately equal (17 and 22%). The Eger Jews predominate among the creditors (61%); the rest fall to burghers. A declaration where a peasant was the creditor of another peasant was not recorded even once.

Some studies point to the important role of millers in the rural credit market (Guzowski 2014, p. 134). In the analysed court protocols, millers only occurred twice among individual debtors. Rural millers did not appear among the creditors.

Regarding the social status of the peasants and the burghers in the year of the record of the declaration, we again relied on the testimony of the land tax registers, the city tax register of 1446 and the quintile analysis. The result of the analysis was not surprising (Figure 9.3). Only the richest peasants borrowed money through a formal credit market. The creditors also came from the ranks of the wealthiest burghers. Among the peasants we find tenants of 'subject' farmsteads, in one case the holder of a 'free' farmstead.

The amount of the loan was not usually enormously high or extremely low (Figure 9.4). The minimal loan was 40 Prague groschen, the maximal 26 threescore Prague groschen. Most often, peasants borrowed amounts from one to three threescore Prague groschen and then from six to ten threescore Prague groschen. The loans to 6 threescore were repaid at once with exceptions; higher amounts were in half of the cases divided into two to four instalments. It follows that the rich peasants did not have a problem to suddenly get the amount of up to 6 threescore but higher amounts were already difficult to put together.

Loans were of a short-term nature. If the debt was repaid at once, the loan never exceeded one year, usually repaid within six months (Figure 9.5). Most of the debts paid in instalments were also paid within one year. The first instalment followed within six months of granting the loan. The longest loan was repaid in four instalments over two years.

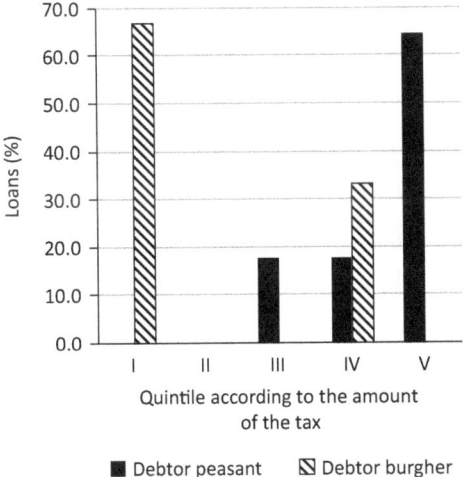

*Figure 9.3* Social status of the debtors in the Eger city state, 1435–1456 (loans).

*Source: Klosteuerbuch,* 1435; 1438; 1441–1456; *Losungsbuch,* 1446; *Schuldprotokolle,* 1429–1439; 1439–1452; 1452–1470.

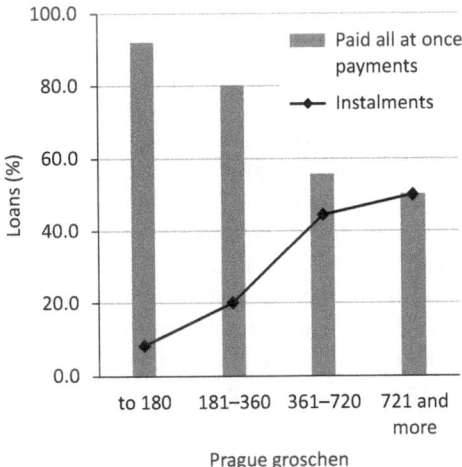

*Figure 9.4* Nominal amount of the loans of the peasants in the Eger city state, 1435–1456.
*Source: Schuldprotokolle,* 1429–1439; 1439–1452; 1452–1470.

One third of the records also stated the pledge that the debtor guaranteed to the creditor (eleven times). The mention of the pledge was more common with nominally higher debts. The peasants secured the loans with non-farmstead plots (five times) or all the property (four times), less already the farmstead (once) or a house in the city (once).

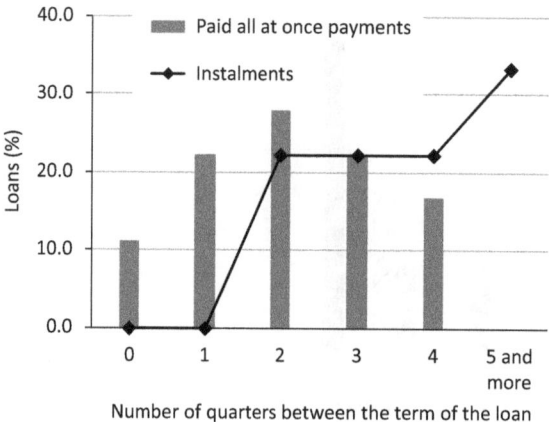

*Figure 9.5* Length of the repayment of peasant loans.

Source: *Schuldprotokolle*, 1429–1439; 1439–1452; 1452–1470.

We do not know the precise purpose of any of the loans but we can esti-mate thanks to the price relation. The most frequent amount of 1–3 three-score Prague groschen corresponds in price of one horse, several cows or one 'Morgen' of a non-farmstead field (ca 0.57 ha). Loans falling into the second most frequent interval of 6–12 threescore corresponded to the prices of all of the livestock animals on an average farmstead, two 'Morgen' of non-farm meadows or four 'Morgen' of fields, or half the amount for which it was possible to acquire the tenure right to a good 'subject' farmstead.

An important testimony is borne by the ratio of the borrowed amount to the total value of the debtor's assets, respectively its ratio to the land tax (Figures 9.6 and 9.7). In 72% of the cases, the loan was less than a tenth of the total value of the property; more than a quarter of the value of the property in 17% of the cases. In 61% of the cases, the amount of the loan was up to four times the amount of tax paid each year. The loan surpassed ten times the annual land tax amount in 22% of the cases.

To sum up, the short repayment period, the relatively low amount of the loaned amounts, its ratio to the annual land tax, and the total value of the property suggest that mainly seasonal bridging loans or investment loans in non-farm plots were entered in the court protocols.

The flow of capital from the countryside to the city is also documented. The court protocols from 1435–1456 contain five records in which peasants lent cash to the Eger burghers. The analysis of their social status showed a fact that was not surprising – the creditors were rich peasants and, on the contrary, the debtors were poor burghers (Figure 9.3). The amount of the loans was in the range of the cash that the peasants could obtain on a one-off basis (two to seven threescore Prague groschen). Peasants in the role

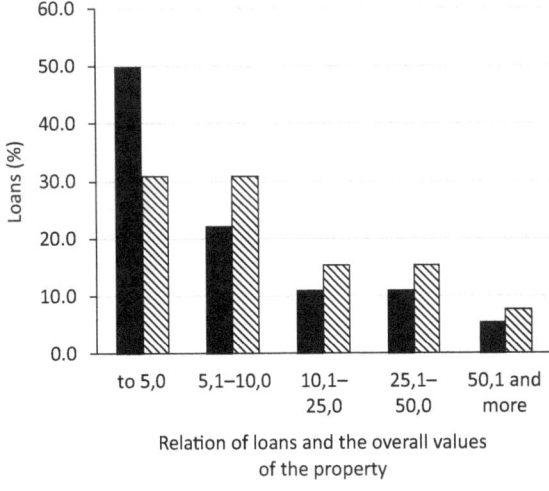

*Figure 9.6* Ratio of the nominal amount of the loan and the total amount of the peasant's property in the Eger city state, 1435–1456.

Source: *Schuldprotokolle*, 1429–1439; 1439–1452; 1452–1470.

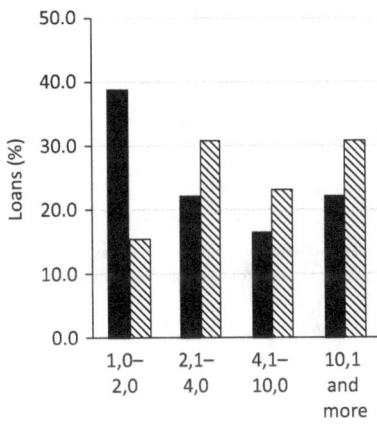

*Figure 9.7* Ratio of the nominal amount of the loan and the land tax in the Eger city state, 1435–1456.

Source: *Schuldprotokolle*, 1429–1439; 1439–1452; 1452–1470.

of creditors illustrate the close interaction of the rural and urban economy as well as financial entrepreneurship. We assume that the peasant-creditors were among the rural elite, as its basic characteristics were precisely plural economic activities and income diversity (e.g. Čechura 1994, p. 115; Aparisi 2015, pp. 337–9, 352).

### Geographical aspects

Sales on credit and loans had different spatial reach. In the first case, the credit area was equal to the local market area of the city of Eger, with the perimeter ranging between 12 and 18 km (Figure 9.8). The spatial reach of loans was

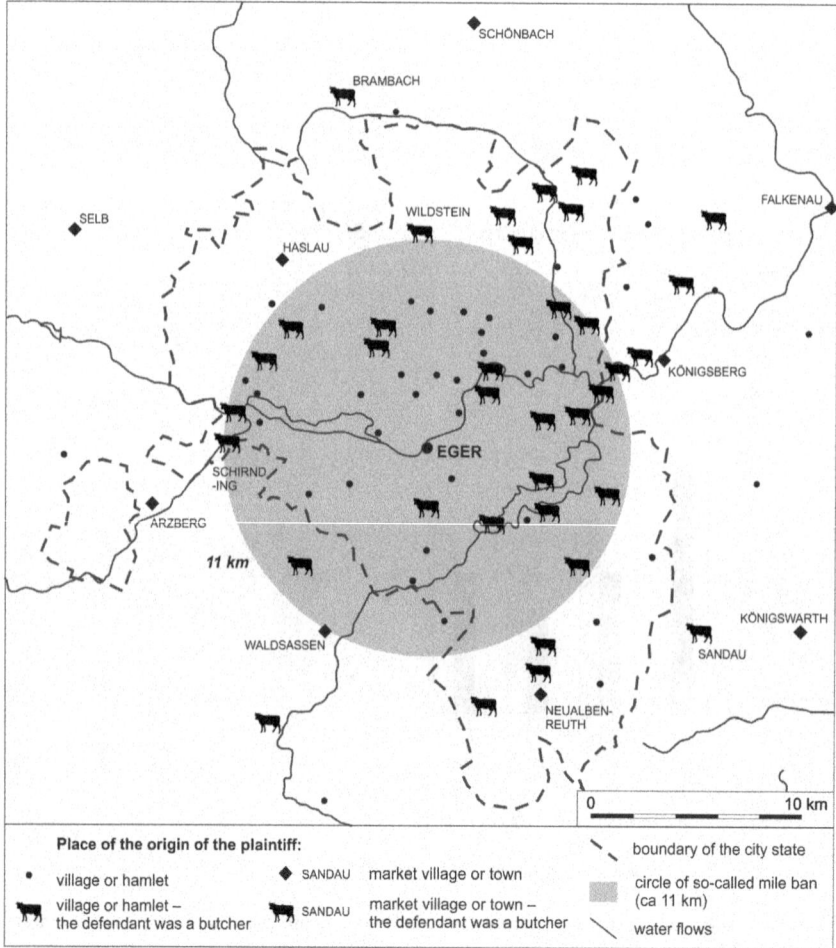

*Figure 9.8* The origin of the creditors from outside of the city of Eger who sued Eger burghers (1442–1456). Predominantly sale on credit.

Source: *Schuldprotokolle, 1439–1452; 1452–1470.*

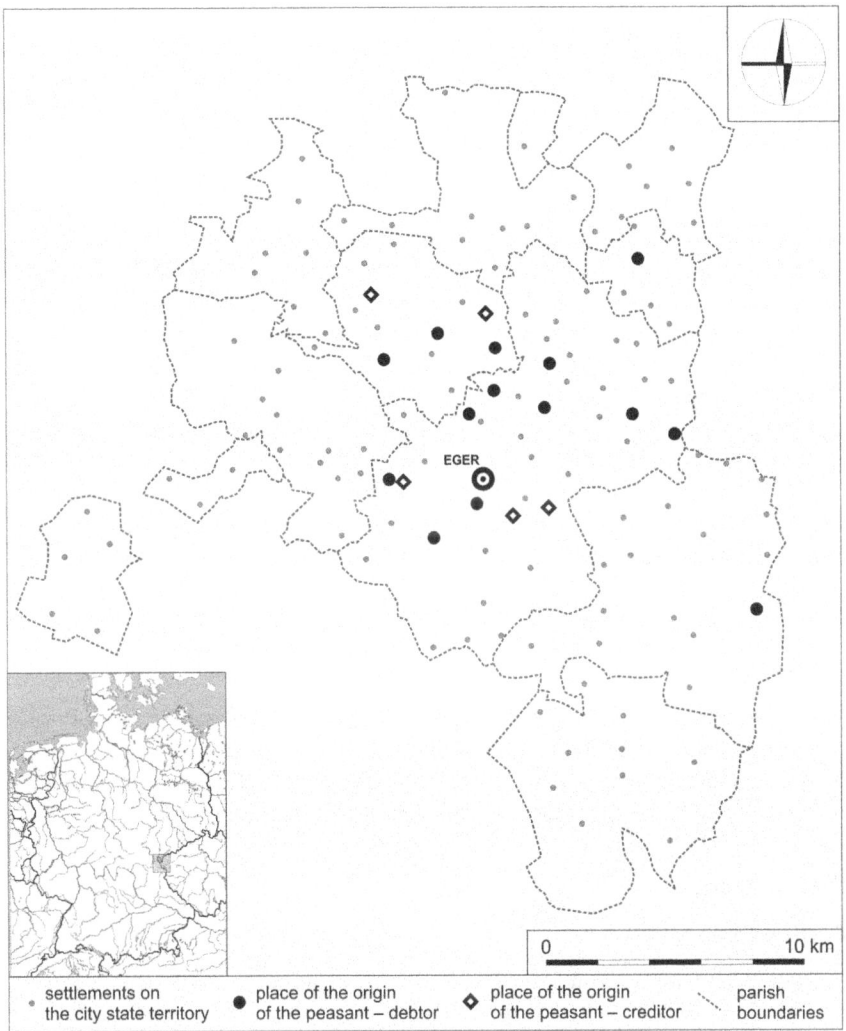

*Figure 9.9* The origin of the rural debtors and creditors (1435–1456).

*Source: Schuldprotokolle, 1429–1439; 1439–1452; 1452–1470.*

smaller, reaching 6–8 km from the city of Eger and overlapping with the most fertile and commercialized zone, interwoven with dense information, social and economic networks linking the richest peasants to the city (Figure 9.9).

## Conclusion

The rate of commercialization and monetarization of the late medieval peasantry of Eger (c. 1450) was low compared to the early modern period. As for the external factors that forced the peasants to acquire cash, it was mainly the land tax, namely to a bearable degree. As for the internal factors, the peasant needed cash for the annual reproduction of his farmstead or for the payment of inherited shares. But even this was not burdensome given the price range. We tested the hypothesis that the average peasant household needed cash only to a small extent by analysing the credit market.

The credit market in the Eger city state was institutionally secured by the city court, which provided guarantees not only to the burghers, but also to the peasants in the countryside. The relevant protocols make it possible to identify both formal loans (repaid and failed) and informal sales on credit (failed). The involvement of the peasantry in the loan market appears to be small and limited to the richest peasants. We find peasants mostly in the role of debtors (85% of the cases); their creditors were wealthy burghers. If, on the other hand, the peasant appeared as a creditor (15%), his debtor was a poor burgher. Loans were of a short-term nature, mostly not enormously high. The peasants were far more active in selling agricultural commodities to burghers, especially meat, on credit. This sale credit artificially increased the inflow of economic resources from the countryside to the city because market transactions could have been realized even in the absence of cash.

## Funding

This work was supported by the European Regional Development Fund-Project 'Creativity and Adaptability as Conditions of the Success of Europe in an Interrelated World' (No. CZ.02.1.01/0.0/0.0/16_019/0000734). Text translated by Sean Mark Miller (Prague). Special thanks to Martin Janovský (Prague).

## References

### Archival sources

*Klosteuerbuch* (1435). Fonds 1 (the city of Cheb), book Nr. 1066, State District Archive Cheb.

*Klosteuerbuch* (1438). Fonds 1, the city of Cheb, book Nr. 1067, State District Archive Cheb (copy from 1769; edition by Klír et al., 2016).

*Klosteuerbücher* (1442–1456). Fonds 1, the city of Cheb, books Nr. 1069–1083, State District Archive Cheb.

*Klosteuerbuch* (1469). Fonds 1 (the city of Cheb), book Nr. 1096, State District Archive Cheb.

*Klosteuerbuch (Schätzungsbuch)* (1456). Fonds 1, the city of Cheb, book Nr. 1084, State District Archive Cheb (edition by Klír et al., 2016).

*Losungsbuch* (1446). Fonds 1, the city of Cheb, book Nr. 1424, State District Archive Cheb.

*Schuldprotokolle* (1387–1416). Fonds 1, the city of Cheb, book Nr. 894, State District Archive Cheb.

*Schuldprotokolle* (1429–1439). Fonds 1, the city of Cheb, book Nr. 896, State District Archive Cheb.

*Schuldprotokolle* (1439–1452). Fonds 1, the city of Cheb, book Nr. 897, State District Archive Cheb.

*Schuldprotokolle* (1452–1470). Fonds 1, the city of Cheb, book Nr. 898, State District Archive Cheb.


## Literature

Aparisi, F. (2015). Village entrepreneurs: The economic foundations of Valencian rural elites in the fifteenth century. *Agricultural History* 89, pp. 336–57.

Bauerfeind, W. (1993). *Materielle Grundstrukturen im Spätmittelalter und der Frühen Neuzeit. Preisentwicklung und Agrarkonjunktur am Nürnberger Getreidemarkt von 1399 bis 1670*. Neustadt a. d. Aisch: Stadtarchiv Nürnberg.

Briggs, Ch. D. & Zuijderduijn, C. J., eds. (2018). *Land and Credit: Mortgages in the Medieval and Early Modern European Countryside*. Cham, Switzerland: Palgrave Macmillan.

Cerman, M. (2008). Social structure and land markets in Late Mediaeval Central and East-central Europe. *Continuity and Change*, 23, pp. 55–100.

Cerman, M. & Zeitelhofer, H., eds. (2002). *Soziale Strukturen in Böhmen. Ein regionaler Vergleich von Wirtschaft und Gesellschaft in Gutsherrschaften, 16.–19. Jahrhundert*. Wien: Verlag für Geschichte und Politik; München: Oldenbourg Wissenschaftsverlag.

Čechura, J. (1990). Die Bauernschaft in Böhmen während des Spätmittelalters: Perspektiven neuer Orientierungen. *Bohemia*, 31, pp. 283–311.

Čechura, J. (1994). *Die Struktur der Grundherrschaften im mittelalterlichen Böhmen unter besonderer Berücksichtigung der Klosterherrschaften*. Stuttgart – Jena – New York: Walter de Gruyter GmbH & Co KG.

Chocholáč, B. (1999). *Selské peníze: Sonda do finančního hospodaření poddaných na západní Moravě koncem 16. a v 17. století*. Brno: Matice moravská.

Chocholáč, B. (2005). Güterpreise, Verschuldung und Ratensystem: Eine Fallstudie zu den finanziellen Transaktionen der Untertanen bei Besitzübertragungen in Westmähren im späten 16. und im 17. Jahrhundert. In Cerman, M. & Luft, R., eds. *Untertanen, Herrschaft und Staat in Böhmen und im "Alten Reich". Sozialgeschichtliche Strukturen*. München: Oldenbourg, pp. 89–125.

Guzowski, P. (2014). Village court records and peasant credit in fifteenth- and sixteenth-century Poland. *Continuity and Change* 29, pp. 115–42.

Hanzal, J. (1963). Poznámky ke studiu ceny poddanské nemovitosti v 16.–17. století. In *Příspěvky k dějinám cen nemovitostí v 16.–18. století*. Praha: Univerzita Karlova, pp. 39–48.

Klír, T. (2018). Sociálně-ekonomická mobilita rolnictva v pozdním středověku. Chebsko v letech 1438–1456. In Nocuń, P., Fokt, K. & Przybyła-Dumin, A., eds. *Wieś miniona, lecz obecna. Ślady dawnych wsi i ich badania*. Chorzów: MGPE, pp. 159–231.

Klír, T. (2019). Socioeconomic mobility and property transmission among peasants: The Cheb region (Czech Republic) in the Late Middle Ages. In Brady, N. & Theune, C., eds. *Settlement Change across Medieval Europe: Old Paradigms and New Vistas*. Leiden: Sidestone, pp. 341–55.

Klír, T. (in print). *Rolnictvo na pozdně středověkém Chebsku. Sociální mobilita, migrace a procesy pustnutí.* Praha: Karolinum.

Klír, T., et al. (2016). *Knihy chebské zemské berně z let 1438 a 1456.* Praha: Filozofická fakulta Univerzity Karlovy, Ústí nad Labem: Filozofická fakulta Univerzity Jana Evangelisty Purkyně v Ústí nad Labem, Dolní Břežany: Scriptorium.

Kostlán, A. (1987). "Cenová revoluce" a její odraz v hospodářském vývoji Čech. *Folia Historica Bohemica,* 11, pp. 161–212.

Míka, A. (1959). Nástin vývoje cen zemědělského zboží v Čechách v letech 1424–1547. *Československý časopis historický,* 7, pp. 545–71.

Míka, A. (1960). *Poddaný lid v Čechách v první polovině 16. století.* Praha: Nakladatelství Československé akademie věd.

Procházka, V. (1963). *Česká poddanská nemovitost v pozemkových knihách 16. a 17. století.* Praha: Nakladatelství Československé akademie věd.

Schirmer, U. (1996). *Das Amt Grimma 1485–1548. Demographische, wirtschaftliche und soziale Verhältnisse in einem kursächsischen Amt am Ende des Mittelalters und zu Beginn der Neuzeit.* Beucha: Sax-Verlag.

Schofield, P.R. & Lambrecht, T., eds. (2009). *Credit and the rural economy in North-western Europe, c. 1200–c. 1850.* Turnhout, Belgium: Brepols.

Vaniš, J. (1981). Ceny v Lounech v druhé polovině 15. století. *Hospodářské dějiny,* 8, pp. 5–93.

# Chapter 10

# The credit market in Old Warsaw in the late Middle Ages

*Piotr Łozowski*

## Introduction

This chapter presents the results of research on the credit market of late medieval Old Warsaw. Since its establishment at the end of the 13th century, the city has experienced a systematic social and economic development: from a centre of about 4,000 inhabitants in the 15th century to one of the largest and most important cities in Central and Eastern Europe with a population of 100,000 (Bogucka & Samsonowicz 1986, p. 119; Kuklo 2009, p. 233). This modern blossoming would have been much slower (or impossible) without the solid medieval root, which was based mainly on trade in wood, grain, fur, and other forest products floated down the Vistula River to Toruń and Gdańsk from where it was transported to London, Bruges, and Amsterdam (Samsonowicz 1972). Therefore, the period of the late Middle Ages seems to be an extremely valuable research topic as it offers the possibility to observe economic indicators during the development of the town. The credit market is one of the most important indicators, best represented in sources. The chapter is divided into two parts: one presents the functioning of Warsaw market on a general scale (value of loans, duration of contracts, interest rates, security methods, moment of conclusion and repayment); the other covers the social background in the form of market activities of craftsmen, merchants, and other social estates. Obtaining such a precise and diverse picture allows for referring not only to the discussion about the economic crisis of the late Middle Ages in Poland (Guzowski 2008), but also about the social and territorial scope of the credit instrument, the horizontality of the market (Schofield 2002), the level of trust between creditor and debtor observed, for instance, through changes in interest rates and the duration of contracts (Nightingale 2007; van Zanden, Zuijderduijn & de Moor 2012), or the well-known 'de Soto problem' (de Soto 2000).

The source of the deliberations is formed by six preserved court records from 1427–1527. It should be noted that there is no jury record from 1473–1496 and the fact that the completeness of the council records increased significantly only at the end of the 15th century. Studying Old Warsaw market, we come across a basic problem for almost all credit analyses, that is the possibility of capturing only a fragment of the entire loan movement, due to voluntary agreement registration in city books. Importantly, despite the obvious imperfections of the material, it was possible to separate a group of 1,558 contracts involving 1,647 people with a total value of 1,337,447 groszes,[1] which, given the size of the city, constitutes a convenient basis for drawing a conclusion on the economic condition of Old Warsaw. In order to better describe the long-term changes, a period of 100 years was assumed from the beginning of the oldest surviving city book in 1427.

## Economic and legal background

The Warsaw credit market registered in court records was based on simple debt obligations concluded between the burghers as a declaration of payment of a specified amount of money to a person on a specified date, with the simultaneous reservation of consequences resulting from non-performance of the agreement. Rent contracts (*census*) appeared sporadic-ally: in total we registered 182 entries constituting 12% of all transactions and 15% of their total value. The creditor was usually the town jury or council and the agreement itself took the form of a new repurchase rent. There was no turnover in old rents or life annuities. If the obtained picture of low popularity of annuities is true and does not result from disappear-ance of a separate annuity book (there is no strong evidence of its existence), then the Warsaw credit market should be regarded as less developed than in Prussian towns such as Toruń, Elbląg, Gdańsk (Kardasz 2013), or Western and Southern Europe (Zuijderduij 2009) where annuity was an extremely popular instrument.

The value of loans taken out in Old Warsaw in the late Middle Ages amounted to 920 groszes according to the average and 270 groszes according to much more reliable median indications. In the course of the analysed century, the median contract value increased from 240 groszes in the first half of the 15th century to 300 groszes in the years 1457–1527, thus illus-trating the trade in increasingly larger capital. 73% of the contracts did not exceed the amount of 600 groszes, which was a credit for consumption or for supporting small investments in craft workshops, home development, or small trade. The second group of 27% included contracts concluded mainly by the merchants, exceeding 600 groszes and fulfilling a typical investment and trade role. The proportion between groups is reversed if we look at the share in the total market value where consumer contracts (up to 600 groszes) covered only 16% of the turnover, while investment contracts (above 600 groszes) covered as much as 84%. On the one hand, this shows the market based on the number of small credit agreements and, on the other hand, it shows the scale of wealth differences between the lower and middle strata and the elites, as well as the economic importance of the wealthiest groups.

The median of the contract in both groups was 210 and 2,580 groszes (3.5 and 43 *sexagenae*) so the elites participating in the distant trade used the amounts more than twelve times higher.

In order to better capture the real value of the agreements, we will use their relationship to the prices of farming-food products, commercial products, and exemplary bare-bones baskets. The amount of 3.5 *sexagenae* made it possible to buy, according to the prices in the Warsaw district, registered in the court books from 1427–1453: stack (*acervus*) of rye and wheat or about 40 bushels of each of these cereals, 4 stones of pepper, 2 barrels of herring, 4 barrels of salt, about 400 pieces of hewn wood, and a horse. Correspondingly, for the sum of 43 *sexagenae*, one could buy 10 stacks, 10 lasts or more than 500 bushels of rye and wheat, 57 stones of pepper, 32 barrels of herring, 54 barrels of salt, almost 5,200 pieces of hewn wood, and 14 horses. Assuming the prices registered in Cracow in the second half of the 15th century and at the beginning of the 16th century (Pelc 1935), for 3.5 and 43 *sexagenae* there could be bought, respectively: 11.5 and 143 bushels of oat, 9 and 107 barrels of beer, and 0.5 or 6 barrels of wine, 2.4 and 30 pounds of saffron or 105 or 1,290 elbows of canvas. It is also worthwhile to convert it into the so-called bare-bone baskets. An average family of four needed about three such baskets; the price of a single basket in Cracow and Lvov in the first quarter of the 16th century oscillated between 32–33 grams of silver (Malinowski 2016, pp. 3, 5). The amount of 210 groszes converted into the amount of bullion (1 grosz = 0.78 Au) allowed the purchase of five baskets which not only provided food for the whole family, but also allowed the purchase of more than the minimum quantity of selected goods. This short list shows the enormous scale of trade opportunities offered by the elite but also confirms that, apart from satisfying consumption needs, the representatives of the community (e.g. craftsmen) could occasionally take part in small trade. In the case of investments in the real estate market, the amount of 210 groszes covered only half of the price of an average wooden house in Old Warsaw (480 groszes) so it could be used only to carry out minor renovation and construction works. Similarly, a trade credit was used primarily for trade or investments in wooden houses, as the purchase of a tenement house at the market square should have involved (Łozowski 2020).

Some researchers are convinced that the dynamics of interest rate changes are closely related to the stability and health of the urban economy which ultimately influences the level of credit risk by raising or lowering interest rates. In Old Warsaw, the rent received on borrowed capital ranged from 2.4 to 10% per annum but the most common (61% of records) was one mark per annum on 10 *sexagenae* groszes, that is 8%. It is worth noting that this interest rate functioned mainly in the second half of the 15th century, while after 1500, it was reduced to 6.66%. Relating this fact to the afore-mentioned assumption, we can conclude that the Old Town credit market is still developing and the credit risk reduction resulting from the stability of economic life is resulting in a simultaneous increase in trust between the creditor and the debtor.

Data analysis showed that the credit market of *civitatis Antiquae Varsoviae* was mainly based on short-term contracts. In total, 30% of all records did not exceed three months, over 55% were within the six-month period, and as much as 86% lasted less than a year. Only 14% of contracts were concluded for a period longer than 12 months, of which 7% were within one to two years. The average duration of the transaction was 9.7 months, with slight changes in this value during the analysed century. The loan term systematically increased from an average of seven months in the years 1427–1453, through 10 months between 1454 and 1485, to 11 months at the beginning of the 16th century which can be seen as another proof of market stability and lenders' lack of fears about the borrower's insolvency as well as a positive assessment of their future financial standing by debtors. As regards the status of burghers' budgets and long-term revenue and expenditure forecasting, the correlation between the duration of a contract and its value provides a great deal of valuable information. It turns out that the smallest transactions (2 *sexagenae*) were concluded for a six-month period with the amount doubling in relation to the six- / twelve-month period (4.3 *sexagenae*). The liabilities lasting one to two years amounted to 5.3 *sexagenae*, while the repayment of loans of the highest value was spread over more than 24 (9 *sexagenae*) and 36 months (as many as 12 *sexagenae*). Based on the results obtained, we can see that townspeople were able to accumulate a cash surplus of 4 *sexagenae* per year. The issue of predicting future income and repayment of liabilities is related to the use of the instalment system. In the Warsaw credit turnover, it was present only in 20% of contracts. If repayment was scheduled in instalments, two (61%) or three (25%) parts were most often chosen. The main factor influencing the application of instalment payments was the duration of the agreement. Among liabilities lasting up to two years, the division into two and three parts prevailed, while loans exceeding the limits of 24 or 36 months were divided into four or more instalments.

The material stored in the books enables the identification of the day of the beginning of the loan agreement in the case of 95% of entries and the declaration of the repayment date appeared in 60% of the transactions. Using this data, we are able to identify the moments of the highest demand for cash on a yearly basis and the periods of payment of liabilities. Observing the indications presented in Figure 10.1, we can see three distinct moments of credit registration intensification: January (14%), April and May (13 and 11%) and October (12%). It seems that the increased financial needs of townspeople at the beginning of the year should be associated primarily with the need to buy additional food in a difficult winter period. The spring summit could, to a large extent, be associated with the beginning of the trading and sowing season, while the end of the year with the obligation to pay rents and prepare provisions for the coming winter. At the same time,

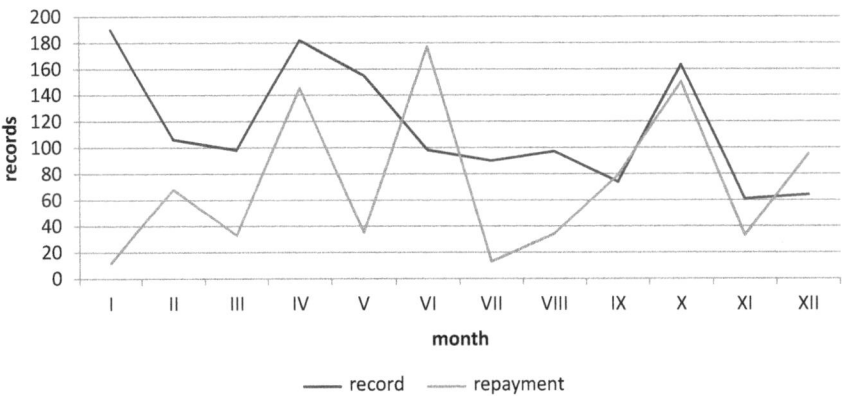

*Figure 10.1* Number of credit records depending on the month in Old Warsaw in 1427–1527.

it is also worth noting the reduced interest in loan trading in the summer when, apparently, the townspeople had enough money in the context of their activities. An almost identical rhythm of court records can be observed in other late medieval Polish medium-sized and small towns (Bartoszewicz 2003), which shows that the system of three peaks (hungry gap, spring, and autumn) was characteristic for them. The repayment of the liability was most often made in April (17%), June (20%), and October (17%). The analysis of exact daily dates showed close connection with both the Warsaw fair system and the days of patrons of local churches – extremely popular terms were: St George and St Wojciech (Adalbert, April 23), St John the Baptist (June 24, patron of the Warsaw Collegiate Church), St Hedwig (October 15), and on a slightly smaller scale St Michael (September 29), St Martin (November 21) and Christmas (December 25). Interestingly, the presented regularity did not occur at the moments of notation, which were made throughout the month. The sketched picture of the scheme of taking out and settling credit agreements was maintained without major changes in the 15th and first quarter of the 16th century.

Capital investment in the credit market is burdened with the risk of debtor's insolvency, therefore various ways of securing the borrowed cash were used. One of the most probable was the entry of the contract in the town books; however, this form was repeatedly supplemented with additional clauses. First of all, the level of a debtor's creditworthiness conditioned the state of his possession and, to some extent, his position in the municipal hierarchy, therefore there was a simple relationship where greater affluence increased the chance of obtaining a higher credit. The majority of the group of proprietors had one property in the form of a house, on which it was possible to secure up to a few loans. If the property status expanded to include other houses, gardens, lands, etc., then the possibilities of using these goods to obtain funds for other investment purposes automatically grew. Therefore, the accumulation of real estate is so characteristic, for example, of a group of merchants. However, we should not forget the 'de Soto problem', the role played on the part of borrowers by the institutional framework organizing the system of securing contracts. The lower the risk of a rapid loss of ownership, the greater the interest of potential debtors in a specific form of credit.

In Old Warsaw, the additional security clause concerned 60% of all loans registered in the court records. The catalogue of assurance formulas focused on several categories: real estate (e.g. house, garden, parcel, land, malt house), financial penalties, additional rent collected in case of delayed repayment, third party guarantees, or pledge on movables. The most popular was the security on real estate goods: the house (34%) and all property defined by the term 'totam bona mobilitas et immobilitas' (34%). The calculation of additional *censum* in case of exceeding the loan repayment deadline or contractual penalty (*poena*) is recorded in 9% of cases. The remaining categories were used occasionally (less than 5%). In total, transactions insured with real estate goods accounted for as much as 78% of all additionally secured contracts. This shows not only the significant role of real estate in the loan trade registered in the books, but also, to a certain extent, the limitation of the market to the group of property owners. However, it is worth remembering that no additional form of insurance is applied to 40% of loans entered in the records, as well as nearly 20% of the percentage of agreements with other security than real estate. This allows us to state that in access to the credit market as debtors, the majority of debtors were owned, however, not owning real estate did not exclude a person interested in raising capital. Moreover, the declaration of assurance on all movable and immovable property was doubly advantageous for the debtor – apart from increasing his creditworthiness, in the event of potential enforcement, it allowed for flexible selection of objects to be auctioned and potential protection of key assets for the less basic ones. This is a direct reference to the 'de Soto problem', which, in the light of the results obtained, did not exist in Old Warsaw. This is indicated by the lack of transfer of legal ownership or physical possession of real estate during mortgage pledge (priority formula was used in the queue of creditors during the auction) and by the openness of the market to non-property owners.

## Social background

In the course of the analysed century, a total of 1,647 participants in credit turnover appeared in Old Warsaw, with an annual average frequency of 27 persons in the 15th century and 34 in the 16th century. The nature of the participation of most persons was characterized by one-time presence in all credit registers and one-sidedness when they acted only as a creditor or debtor. One-time participation concerned 81% of lenders and 73% of borrowers. On the other hand, unilateral actions were taken by as much as 90% of all registered persons. These figures and analyses of the personalities of the parties to the transaction prove the horizontality of the market which, in turn, is considered a testimony to its positive condition and the wide circulation of capital. In other words, apart from a large group of single debtors, there was an equally large group of single creditors who, having a certain cash surplus, undertook to invest in the market. What is very important in this context is the lack of dependence of many borrowers on a narrow group of those operating with serious capital, for example the wealthiest merchants (in such a case it would be a less favourable vertical structure). Only 9% of all people appeared on both sides of the market. The most active (more than tenfold presence) and proportionally smallest (less than 2% of all creditors and 1% of debtors) part of this group was formed by elites. However, their share was neither even nor equal. We see unevenness in the participation of only a part of the representatives of the wealthiest families, many wealthy merchants appeared in just a few contracts. On the other hand, inequality is expressed in different strategies adopted by the elites, some specialized in the role of creditors, another group mainly collected capital, while others operated on both sides of the market. In both cases, there is no uniform model of elite credit activity, characterized by clear differentiation.

The professional landscape of the medieval city was a real mosaic of various professions and specializations. Guild crafts were undoubtedly the most numerous but the leading position in terms of wealth was occupied by merchants; therefore, it is worth a closer look at the activity of both groups. The craftsmen of Old Warsaw comprised several main branches: construction, wood, metal, leather, food, services, and textiles, while the greatest wealth was achieved by goldsmiths and leather professions, which was also greatly influenced by the water-transported trade to Prussia. In the years 1427–1525 a total of 70 trades were recorded and the number of craftsmen increased five times (Koczorowska 1972). In the period covered by the analysis, 423 craftsmen taking part in the Old Town credit market (26% of the total number of people) were recorded. *Artifices* appeared in 596 cases with a total value exceeding 340,000 groszes. In total, their activity, against the background of general indicators describing the loan turnover, covered 41% of the number and 25% of the total value of all credit records. The median value of concluded agreements was 3 *sexagenae*, that is 1.5 *sexagenae* lower than the general market median. On the other hand, the annual frequency of occurrence was seven cases on average, which was twice as low as the average set for the whole market, with the highest activity occurring at the turn of the 15th and 16th centuries. Craftsmen most often used a loan authenticated in the books once (66% of people), mainly taking capital from the market twice as often as they invested. Investments were undertaken mainly by elites formed by goldsmiths, painters, some furriers, saddlers, and butchers. Nevertheless, the majority of master craftsmen treated the credit market as an incidentally used source of additional cash and not as an investment sphere. A completely different picture emerges from the analysis of merchants' activity. On the basis of the old town court records, a group of 155 merchants was separated, who constituted only 9% of the persons present on the market but, at the same time, were parties to almost half of all contracts (46%). The total value of transactions exceeded 842,000 groszes, that is over 60% of the total turnover recorded in the books. The wealth of this professional group is evidenced by the average (21 *sexagenae*) and median (6.5) exceeding by 2 *sexagenae* the median value of the obligation established in relation to the whole market. However, the frequency of occurrence of 6.6 cases per year was twice lower than the general city average. Merchants used the market for investment purposes as well as to obtain a loan, however, the tendency to invest capital was predominant. The custom of generating additional income from loan operations occupied a stable place in the investment strategy of Warsaw merchants for nearly eight decades which, at the same time, seems to be a positive sign of the stability and liquidity of the Old Town credit market.

The town of the Middle Ages and modern era did not make a closed environment limited only to the group of its inhabitants but concentrated economic activities of many social groups. Beside the burghers themselves, representatives of the nobility, clergy and peasants as well as the Jewish religious community participated in the life of almost every centre. The population growth of the city could not be achieved without migration and long-distance trade would not exist without a wide network of external relations to attract suppliers and business partners. After analysing the activity of particular groups, we will look at the territorial coverage of the Warsaw market.

According to the data presented in Table 10.1, the loan turnover was characterized by estate homogeneity expressed as a definite domination of burghers: 81% among lenders and as many as 96% among borrowers.

Table 10.1 Social structure of creditors and debtors in Old Warsaw in 1427–1527

| Social group | Creditors | | Debtors | |
|---|---|---|---|---|
| | Number of people | % | Number of people | % |
| Burghers | 476 | 80.7 | 633 | 95.6 |
| Nobility | 58 | 9.8 | 10 | 1.5 |
| Clergy | 33 | 5.6 | 4 | 0.6 |
| Peasants | 16 | 2.7 | 5 | 0.8 |
| Jews | 7 | 1.2 | 10 | 1.5 |
| Total | 590 | 100 | 662 | 100 |

Representatives of other estates acted mainly as creditors, although the scale of their activity was definitely marginal. Most often the burghers entered into credit relations with the nobility (10%) and clergy (6%), while peasants (2.7%) and Jews (1.2%) had a much smaller share. A characteristic feature of these unions was the one-time presence of the majority of creditors. The main source of cash and simultaneously the area of its investment was town market which sufficiently satisfied the capital needs of the inhabitants of Old Warsaw.

Considering not only the nobility, clergy, peasants, and Jews, but also townsmen from other centres, we can clearly see that the majority of external transactions covered villages and towns within a radius of about 30 km from Warsaw. There was also a close correlation between the increase in the transaction value and the distance from the city: if contractors came from the Kingdom of Poland, Lithuania, Prussia or Silesia, the median ranged from 22 to 50 *sexagenae* groszes and included the Warsaw elite, while the most numerous people in the immediate vicinity of the city concluded contracts for a median of 3 *sexagenae*, focusing on the middle and poorer strata. Moreover, we observe the phenomenon of one-time activity concerning as much as 90% of all persons coming from outside Warsaw and their role as creditors (75% of transactions). These facts seem to clearly indicate the lack of stability of credit ties, which were established sporadically, on the margins of conducted business and trade in goods. It also proves that there is a clear changeability in the composition of the retail network connecting Old Warsaw with other areas, which, especially in the context of the immediate vicinity of the city, indicates that the market is open to access by other people, while at the same time there is no long-term domination of one narrow group. Nevertheless, a more important conclusion is the statement that the intra-city credit market was characterized by estate and territorial homogeneity, expressed in the acquisition and investment of cash in the internal turnover created by private Christian burghers with a marginal, unstable network characterized by a short territorial range of the external relations.

## Conclusion

From the preserved urban sources of late medieval Old Warsaw emerges a picture of the credit market serving both the lower and middle classes, as well as the elites. Low-value agreements serving consumption purposes or small investments in small trade, workshops or house extensions dominated in terms of numbers. However, over 80% of total market turnover was made up of loans concluded by merchants with a value twelve times higher than the median of the consumer contract which directly illustrates the significant level of property differences between the middle classes and elites. The burghers were most often interested in an instrument with a short (of a few months) deadline but there was also a close correlation between a higher value of the contract and a longer loan duration. The demand for cash increased in the hungry gap period, spring and autumn, while the system of repayments was linked to the cycle of annual fairs which were the culminating points of the burghers' economic activity. Analyses of the additional security clauses of the agreement proved that there was no limitation of the market institutional framework resulting from the de Soto problem. Even as a result of repayment problems, the debtors were not threatened with a rapid loss of key assets and creditors had a flexible catalogue of recoveries at their disposal which encouraged both parties to participate in the market. Another optimistic signal is the fall in interest rates at the end of the 15th century.

The most important proof of the positive condition of the Warsaw economy is horizontality of the loan turnover. The credit instrument functioned in a broad social range, both among creditors and debtors. There was no dependence of broad groups of borrowers on a small group of wealthy elite members, investments were undertaken by numerous representatives of middle and poorer strata. There is also a visible pattern of credit relations based on a similar property group, that is the middle classes provided cash to their own group, just as the elites usually traded capital within their circle. This did not rule out a vertical flow of money. The homogeneity of capital turnover is also visible in the scale of the city's relations with other regions; external transactions did not constitute a significant percentage of the market (18% of the total number of entries) and, in their largest part, served primarily to contact the immediate surroundings of Warsaw, while, at the same time, the elites cooperated with merchants from hundreds of kilometres away. The most important were: Toruń, Gdańsk, Wrocław, Nuremberg, Wilno, Grodno, and Lwów. Thus, despite its average size for Central and Eastern Europe, Old Warsaw has become an important link in the trade chain connecting this part of Europe with the West. The boom (not the crisis) in the late Middle Ages created a convenient foundation for an even more dynamic development that came with the advent of premodern times.

## Note

1   In Old Warsaw, they calculated in the system of accounting groszes and *sexagena* of groszes, (*sexagena* = 60 groszes). The basic coin was a crown half-grosz of Władysław Jagiełło, 120 of which = *sexagena*.

## References

### Archival sources

Archiwum Główne Akt Dawnych w Warszawie /The Central Archives of Historical Records in Warsaw
AGAD, Stara Warszawa, 527, 528, 529, 530.

## Literature

Bartoszewicz, A. (2003). *Czas w małych miastach. Studium z dziejów kultury umysłowej późnośredniowiecznej Polski.* Warszawa: Aspra-JR.

Bogucka, M. & Samsonowicz, H. (1986). *Dzieje miast i mieszczaństwa w Polsce przedrozbiorowej.* Wrocław: Ossolineum.

Ehrenkreutz, S., ed. (1916). *Księgi ławnicze miasta Starej Warszawy z XV w.,* vol. 1: *Księga nr 525 z lat 1427–1453.* Warszawa: Warszawskie Archiwum Główne.

Guzowski, P. (2008). Kryzys gospodarczy późnego średniowiecza czy kryzys historiografii?. *Roczniki Dziejów Społecznych i Gospodarczych,* 68, pp. 173–93.

Kardasz, C. (2013). *Rynek kredytu pieniężnego w miastach południowego pobrzeża Bałtyku w późnym średniowieczu (Greifswald, Gdańsk, Elbląg, Toruń, Rewel).* Toruń: Towarzystwo Naukowe.

Koczorowska-Pielińska, E. (1972). Liczebność i specjalizacja rzemiosła w Starej i Nowej Warszawie w latach 1417–1526. *Rocznik Warszawski,* 11, pp. 5–22.

Kuklo, C. (2009). *Demografia Rzeczypospolitej przedrozbiorowej.* Warszawa: DiG.

Łozowski, P. (2020). *Kredyt i dom. Rynki obrotu pieniężnego i nieruchomościami w Warszawie okresu XV i początków XVI wieku.* Białystok: PTH.

Malinowski, M. (2016). Little Divergence revisited: Polish weighted real wages in a European perspective, 1500–1800. *European Review of Economic History,* 20(3), pp. 345–67.

Nightingale, P. (2007). Money and credit in economy of late medieval England. In Nightingale, P. *Trade, Money and Power in Medieval England.* Aldershot: Ashgate Publishing, pp. 51–71.

Pelc, J. (1935). *Ceny w Krakowie 1369–1600.* Lwów: IPPTN.

Samsonowicz, H. (1972). Warszawa w handlu średniowiecznym. In Gieysztor, A., ed. *Warszawa średniowieczna,* 2. Warszawa: PWN, pp. 9–31.

Schofield, P. (2002). Access to credit in the early fourteenth-century English countryside. In Schofield, P. R. & Mayhew, N. J., ed. *Credit and Debt in Medieval England c. 1180–1350.* Oxford: Oxbow, pp. 106–26.

de Soto, H. (2000). *The Mystery of Capital. Why Capitalism Triumphs in the West and Fails Everywhere Else.* London: Basic Books.

van Zanden, J., Zuijderduijn, J. & de Moor, T. (2012). Small is beautiful: the efficiency of credit markets in the late medieval Holland. *European Review of Economic History,* 16(1), pp. 3–22.

Wolff, A., ed. (1963). *Księga radziecka miasta Starej Warszawy (1447–1527).* Wrocław: Ossolineum.

Zuijderduij, J. (2009). *Medieval Capital Markets. Markets for Renten, State Formation and Private Investment in Holland (1300–1550).* Boston: Brill.

# Chapter 11

# Credit and finance
# in Rudolphine Prague

*Marie Buňatová*

## Introduction

Under the reign of the Emperor Rudolph II (Bohemian king from 1576 to 1611), Prague was an important Central European centre of power and culture and also a metropolis in which the capital of domestic and foreign companies and financiers was active. The population of the Prague agglomeration, which consisted of three royal towns – the Old Town, the New Town and Malá Strana, along with the town of Hradčany and the town of Vyšehrad, increased rapidly over several decades, rising from 25,000 at the beginning of the 16th century to 60,000–70,000 in the last third of the same century. Prague experienced an economic boom during this period, one which was boosted by the transferral of the imperial court to the city in 1583. This resulted not only in an overall increase in population, but also in the formation of a sufficiently strong group of consumers from among the courtiers, court officials, nobles, and wealthier burghers, who not only were interested in luxury goods from abroad, but also had the money to purchase them. Business opportunities attracted to the city more merchants, who chiefly came from neighbouring countries and from the north of the Apennine Peninsula, and subsequently from Holland or other parts of Western Europe at the turn of the 16th and 17th centuries. They all strove to supply the court, as well as the nobles and burghers, with desired goods of Italian, Western European, and overseas provenance (Ledvinka & Pešek 2000, pp. 336–9).

There had been Jews in the city since medieval times and their community had a population of around 8,000–9,000 during the Rudolphine period. Among them, there was also a large group of financiers, wholesalers, and smaller merchants, whose activities were not limited to just Jewish customers and the boundaries of the Jewish quarter, but co-created and influenced the entire nature and scope of trade in Prague. The economic elite consisted of families who we know resided in Prague from at least the end of the 15th century or first decades of the 16th century, such as members of the broader Horowitz-Munka, Sachs, Weisswasser, Weisel, and Impresor families. Marek

Mordechai Meisel, the Mayor of the Jewish community and the emperor's banker, held a very privileged position (Buňatová 2011; Vilímková 1993). Wealthy and smaller businessmen and financiers were also recruited from among Jewish immigrants who arrived here from the 1570s onwards from German lands, Poland and Italy. Moses Frankfurter, the Wechsler family, rabbi Jacob Kalman, the Italian Jews Abraham Sacerdoti, rabbi Ventura de Bacchi, and the brothers Samuel and Jacob Bassevi from Verona were particularly distinguished as businessmen and financiers with extensive foreign contacts (Buňatová 2019, pp. 257–63).

## The legal conditions for trade in early modern Prague

Separate commercial law did not exist in the early modern age and was included in private law at the time. In the Czech environment, the foundations of commercial law were embodied in estates law codified at the turn of the 15th and 16th centuries (Jireček & Jireček 1882; Kreuz & Martinovský 2007; Malý & Pánek 2001), and were also included in municipal law (Jireček 1876; Malý & Šouša 2013). Along with the Common Law of the Land and municipal law, the legislative terms for the business activities of Christians and Jews in Prague were also formed by the privileges granted by the rulers, instructions from the municipal governments of individual Prague towns, and the regulations of guild corporations (Buňatová 2013, pp. 52–100).

An important legal standard that influenced business life in Prague, with varying intensity, from the medieval ages to the 17th century was the so-called *guest law (Gastrecht)*. During the 13th and 14th centuries this developed in all economically advanced cities in Europe where it regulated the terms under which foreign merchants were able to trade there. In Prague, this law was codified in 1304 by the Bohemian King Wenceslaus II (1278/83–1305) and was subsequently amended several times during the 14th century (Buňatová 2013, pp. 54–9; Čelakovský 1886, pp. 19–21). Merchants from the Old Town had this law confirmed once again in 1498 by the Bohemian King Vladislaus II (1471–1516). The privileges were also confirmed by subsequent rulers and, for the last time, by Emperor Leopold I in 1671 (Urfus 1959, pp. 60–2).

Without going into a detailed analysis of Prague *guest law*, this was the most important restriction placed on foreign merchants (guests) in the 16th century because it prohibited retail sales. Guests, which included everyone who was not a Prague burgher, were only able to sell goods wholesale in Prague and were prohibited from selling goods 'in small quantities' directly to customers (apart from annual markets). Only burghers from Nuremburg, who were the main suppliers of foreign goods in Prague, were exempt from this prohibition on the basis of the Prague-Nuremburg Trade Agreement dating from 1488/89 (Buňatová 2016a, pp. 663–6; Janáček 1959, pp. 209–13).

Jews were also officially forbidden from conducting retail sales (outside the territory of the Prague Jewish Town) for many years. It was only Rudolph II who granted them the privilege of selling furs and leather in small quantities in 1585 but this more or less legalised the actual state of affairs because Prague Jews had been selling small quantities of various goods long before this despite the prohibitions (Buňatová 2013, pp. 87–8).

## Credit in light of the Land Constitution

Towards the end of the 15th century, European society's perception of money lending underwent a transformation, whereby Church authorities were forced to accept the constantly increasing money lending activities of Christians and gradually moderate the doctrine that prohibited Christians from performing this activity (Denzel 2010; North 1991). These changes also affected the Bohemian lands and the situation required new legislation at the turn of the 15th and 16th centuries (Urfus 1975, p. 65). Money lending and the related indebtedness at all levels of society, from nobles to subjects, was becoming a society-wide problem in Bohemia towards the end of the 15th century, one which Bohemian Diets and the Land Court repeatedly attempted to resolve. However, this task was not simple because, at that time, a number of burghers and nobles were openly lending money (Bůžek, 1989). In their resolutions, the Bohemian Diets attempted to regulate money lending by Christians and Jews by: (a) legalising maximum interest rates applied by Christian and Jewish creditors; (b) defining the legal and prohibited forms of money lending; and (c) defining the legal methods for securing loans and recovering debts (Buňatová 2011, pp. 105–36).

In 1484, the Bohemian Diet legalised money lending by Christians in Bohemia and permitted them to apply interest to loans at a rate of 10%. This principle was adopted in the Vladislaus Land Constitution in 1500 (Palacký 1862, pp. 190–1). The 10% interest rate on loans provided by Christians applied until 1543 when it was reduced to 6% (*Sněmy české I*, 1877, p. 565). This reduction is usually interpreted as an attempt to reduce the difference between the profits generated from lending money and the proceeds from farming on a noble estate (Ledvinka 1985, pp. 29–33) or as an attempt to approximate the terms of the financial market in Spain (with an interest rate of 5–7%), and in the Lutheran environment (with an interest rate of 6%) (Vorel 2005, p. 164). An interest rate of 5%, that is 1% lower than in Bohemia, was set in the territory of the Holy Roman Empire in 1577 by the Imperial Police Ordinance (*Reichspolizeiordnung*). From the time of codification of the Vladislaus Land Constitution, the Common Law of the Land gradually also defined the individual permissible and prohibited forms of money lending and determined the sanctions for failure to adhere to these terms. The term *usury* (*sedlání* or *lichva*) was used to identify the actions of a creditor who demanded a higher rate of interest from a debtor than that permitted for money lending, either publically or secretly, or demanded other services in addition to the interest (e.g. the gift of an item) (Jireček & Jireček 1882, pp. 345–6, 655).

The rapid increase in financial transactions during the last quarter of the 16th century resulted in an expansion of the register of various illegal forms of money lending which were intended to hide the actual interest rate imposed by the creditor. The Common Law of the Land underwent further amendments after this phenomenon became a society-wide problem. The punishments for *sedlání* were initially made stricter in 1575, and the guilty party would not only lose all his property but also own life (*Sněmy české IV*, 1886, pp. 288–90). This strict punishment was temporarily tempered in 1608 to just the forfeit of twice the loaned amount but, because the number of illegal cases of money lending did not fall, the Diet adopted new legislation in 1610. This described in detail the legal and particularly the illegal methods for arranging a loan (*partita*), and the punishments were again made stricter (Glücklich 1936, pp. 360–7). This regulation was adopted in the Renewed Land Constitution dating from 1627 (Jireček 1888, pp. 370–8).

The legislation concerning money lending by Jews underwent more complicated development during the 16th century when there were conflicts of interest between the monarch and the nobility. While the monarch was interested in making as much profit as possible from the Jews' business activities, the interests of the nobility were influenced by their concerns over not just the increasing indebtedness of their subjects, but also of the nobles themselves. The chief principles under which Jews were able to provide financial loans were stipulated by Vladislaus II in the Vladislaus Jewish Code dating from 1497 (Bondy & Dworsky 1906a, pp. 173–80). It permitted Jews to lend money against a lien on an item (e.g. jewels), and also allowed them to secure their loans by simple debt certificates (*schuldbrief*) or register their loans in official ledgers kept at town halls. Jewish creditors in Prague were also permitted to register their receivables in the Register of the Prague Burgravate whose court was competent to recover these debts. The permitted interest rate for Jewish creditors ranged between 20% and 24.76%, depending on the value of the loan.

Subsequent legislative developments in Bohemia were more regressive during the 16th century with constantly worsening terms under which Jews were able to lend money because the Bohemian Diets and the influential governments of the Prague towns regularly endeavoured to restrict the options of Jewish financiers as much as possible. As a result, the entire period until 1623 is characterised by worsening terms (with minor fluctuations) under which Jews were able to lend money and by the Jews' efforts to achieve the terms codified in 1497 as closely as possible.

The terms under which Jews were able to lend money worsened in the individual Bohemian royal towns, including Prague, during the first two decades of the 16th century. For instance, interest rates were reduced to 12.38% in the Old Town in 1515 and Jews were only permitted to lend money against a lien on items (Bondy & Dworsky 1906a, pp. 222–3). According to the legislation in the Land Constitution from 1530 (Jireček & Jireček 1882, p. 89), the text of which was incorporated in the amendments of the Land Constitutions from 1549 and 1564, Jews were prohibited from registering any loans in official (municipal) ledgers, or executing debt certificates with debtors, and were only permitted to lend money against a lien. It was only in the Rudolphine period that Jews were again permitted to conclude at least simple debt certificates with debtors.

The Diet resolution from 1596 brought about temporary legislative improvements for several years. According to this resolution, Jews were again able to recover their receivables before the court of the Prague Burgravate (Bondy & Dworsky 1906b, pp. 697–8); however, this was again forbidden in 1601, along with the possibility of securing loans by debt certificates. But, in practice, we know that financier Mordechai Meisel and other wealthy Prague Jews did recover their receivables before this court from at least the turn of the 1580s and 90s (Buňatová 2016b, p. 40). The Diet resolution from 1615, according to which Jews were able to conclude simple debt certificates for loans up to the value of 1,500–2,000 threescore of Meissen groschen and were again able to recover their receivables before the court of the Prague Burgravate, brought about another positive change (Bondy & Dworsky 1906b, p. 860). Other qualitative changes for Jews were the result of a privilege granted by Emperor Ferdinand II in 1623, in which he confirmed the interest rate of 24.76% (Čelakovský 1886, pp. 516–23). This rate was reduced to the level of Christian loans (6%) by a declaration in 1642 by Ferdinand III who conceived his order as an amendment to Article M XI of the Renewed Land Constitution from 1627 (Buňatová 2013, pp. 90–1).

## Credit practice by Christians and Jews in Prague

The general shortage of cash in the early modern society meant that loans were also an important pillar of the economy in Bohemia during the Rudolphine period. They were essential for wholesalers, who needed capital (cash) to purchase goods abroad, and also for medium-sized and small merchants who conducted business on the local market. The nobles were the ones most often interested in a loan in Prague (Bohemia) because their demanding lifestyle, court appearances, and construction of Renaissance residences as well as the every-day running of their households resulted in their constant need for money which they were often unable to fulfil using just the income from their estates. The monarch and his government apparatus were permanent clients requiring loans, the needs that increased after new military conflicts with the Turks flared up.

There were a number of moneylenders among the Christians and Jews in Prague whose services differed depending on their social standing and wealth. Some Prague burghers (both men and women) also lent money and mostly provided smaller loans to their neighbours – craftsmen or merchants – for their trade. These loans, up to a maximum of several tens of threescore of Meissen groschen, were usually registered by means of simple debt certificates (*cedule řezané*) or were possibly registered in the relevant municipal ledgers. However, there were also more ambitious individuals among these burghers, capable of providing very large loans to interested parties in the value of hundreds of threescore of Meissen groschen. Such loans were provided in the Old Town by, for example, Mikuláš Černohorský of Horoměřice († after 1588) or Magdalena Šípařová († 1579), the wife of the jurist Pavel Kristián of Koldín (1530–1589).

Other people who were interested in increasing the value of their money were the holders of various court and land offices. These included the imperial councillor and regional council president of the Old Town Jan Václav Popel of Lobkowicz (1561–1608), imperial councillor Jan Vchynský of Vchynice (†1590), and the Lord Chamberlain of the Bohemian Kingdom Bohuslav Felix Hasištejnský of Lobkowicz (1517–1583). Another group that had money were the imperial courtiers and general members of the monarch's court. Money lending provided them with the opportunity to increase their finances. This business was conducted by, for example, the court archivist and manager of the Rudolphine collections, Ottavio Strada Senior (1550–1606), his wife Barbora, and also by court architect Ulrico Aostalli de Sala (1525–1597), court gem cutter Ottavio Misseroni (1567–1624), and the most important artist of the Rudolphine court – Bartholomeus Spranger (1546–1611) (Buňatová 2011, pp. 164–6). Their clients were often also Prague Jewish merchants and financiers. Some of them certainly needed cash for trading on foreign markets. However, other cases indicate more speculative financial transactions in which these creditors from among court, land officials, and courtiers were involved together with the Jews.

From the end of the 15th century, the participation of Christians and Jews in financial transactions was the subject of legislative regulation that endeavoured to restrict them in their activities as effectively as possible by implementing prohibitions. In practice, this collaboration had various forms and degrees of participation by individual persons in the profits from money lending. This concerned various financial operations, the true content of which was often hidden in official (municipal) ledgers and masked by various fictional entries about debts or the purchase of goods. One model of a so-called prohibited collaboration was described in detail in the Diet resolution from 1601 (Bondy & Dworsky 1906b, pp. 749–50). This consisted of a Christian who had cash available and provided a Jew with funds at a 6% interest rate which the Jewish financier then lent to someone else at an interest rate of 24.76%. If we calculate in this model example that the Jew was able to legally apply an interest rate of up to 24.76% and equally divided the profits with his Christian associate, then the Christian's profits would be higher than if he had lent the money directly at the legal 6% interest rate.

This method, during which the Jewish financier conducted business using not only his own capital, but also the money he borrowed from nobles or wealthy burghers, was also practiced by Jews in Krakow in the 16th and 17th centuries (Bałaban 1912, pp. 168–70). This was an advantageous partnership for both parties. On the one hand, there was a group of Christians who had cash but sometimes lacked the necessary business experience or familiarity with the environment to appreciate their money suitably and safely. On the other hand, there were enterprising Jews on the Bohemian financial market with contacts; they were capable of quickly finding suitable parties interested in a loan but lacked the necessary cash to provide it. In these cases, both groups collaborated and participated in the profits from the loan (Buňatová 2011, pp. 167–8).

Money lending was also an important element in the business portfolio of Prague wholesalers who increased their income from the wholesale of foreign goods in this manner. This particularly concerned the wealthiest Prague merchants who were often first- or second-generation immigrants from Lutheran, German-language regions. For instance, Jan Nerhof senior of Holterperk († 1607), Valentin Kirchmajer of Reichvice († 1595), Tomáš Hebenštreit of Streitenfels († 1604), and his daughter Estera Teuflová († 1624) with her husband Jan Teufl of Zeilberk († 1607). They provided large loans to members of leading Bohemian noble families, to whom they also supplied foreign goods, but we can also find them among the creditors of Bohemian rulers. For example, in 1587 Emperor Rudolph II owed the merchant Tomáš Hebenštreit 9,142 threescore of Meissen groschen and owed Valetin Kirchmajer 2,000 threescore of Meissen groschen (*Sněmy české VII*, 1891, p. 149ff).

The financiers whose loans also helped cover the growing state expenditure of the Habsburg monarchy included a Prague wholesaler of small goods Lorenc Štark of Starkenfels († 1617) who managed his company for unbelievable 43 years. By 1617, he had lent the court treasury (*Hofzahlamt*) an amount of around 44,580 threescore of Meissen groschen which was secured by the Bohemian land tax and was also gradually paid off using the collected taxes. After his death, he left receivables owed by 140 debtors with a total value of over 123,219 threescore of Meissen groschen as well as other assets. Some of these debts were owed for supplied goods, some for loans provided mostly to noble clientele (Buňatová 2019, pp. 182–3).

The situation among Jews developed along similar lines. However, their legal options for providing loans were significantly constrained throughout the 16th century. They chiefly loaned money to the monarch who took advantage of the situation as Jews were considered servants of the royal chamber (*servi camerae*) from a legal aspect and were forced to pay the monarch for their protection. These enormous loans, which were free of interest in the best case and were of the nature of non-repayable loans in the worst case, were provided to monarchs by the Prague Jewish community as a whole.

Emperor Rudolph II also found a reliable loan provider in the banker Marek Mordechai Meisel (1528–1601). He provided financial services to members of the monarch's family as early as the 1580s. However, Meisel's loans to the emperor increased massively in 1597–1598 when he lent the court treasury *(Hofzahlamt)* a total of 126,000 Rhenish guilders, always at an interest rate of 24.76%. This money was intended for covering war expenses during conflicts with the Turks.

Banker Meisel was rewarded for his services with a number of privileges which His Imperial Majesty summarised in 1598 (Bondy & Dworsky 1906b, pp. 714–17). These rights concerned finance and the goods trade, the court jurisdiction applying to Meisel and his wife Frumet, and the privilege to execute a free will. The freedoms granted to Meisel were very close to those that the so-called court Jews *(Hofjuden)* enjoyed. To name a few of the privileges granted: when providing a loan, Meisel was permitted to execute a debt certificate with the debtor *(schuldbrief)*, to which the debtor was required to affix his seal (if he had one) and his personal signature. In other specific cases the debtor also had to have a guarantor. Meisel was also able to have his receivables registered in the ledgers of the Prague Burgravate and also potentially recover them before its court. However, the fickleness of the emperor's favour and of the privileges he granted is demonstrated by the fact that immediately after Meisel's death in 1601, all the privileges he had been granted were withdrawn and his property was mostly confiscated at the emperor's orders (Buňatová 2011, pp. 148–58).

While Meisel was chiefly involved in financial activities, there were a number of other Jews who combined money lending with trade. This was also the case of his father-in-law Isaac Rofe or, for instance, the branching Impresor, Altschul or Weisel families. They imported goods from abroad but were also active as buyers of agricultural crops from noble estates. They also lent money to the owners of these estates and provided them with other services. They sought out other customers interested in products from the estates (e.g. wool, grain, butter) with whom they negotiated the entire transaction and also arranged the relevant legal matters. The sale of these products was usually arranged under a business loan, which was interest-free for the first six months. Jewish brokers also prepared the text of debt certificates, negotiated the business terms with both parties, arranged the signatures of both parties, collected potential deposits, and subsequently also transported the crops to the customer at the arranged destination (Buňatová 2016b, pp. 44–8).

Jewish immigrants who moved to Prague at the end of the 16th century from Italy were also very enterprising. This was the case of Abraham Sacerdoti who conducted extensive transactions between Italy and Central

Europe and utilised his contacts at the courts in Innsbruck, Mantova, and his familiarity with the commercial environment in Verona, Bolzano, and Prague during his activities. The wholesalers rabbi Ventura de Bacchi and Israel Porta, who had settled in Prague, also had extensive business contacts with the Gonzago family in Mantova and at the Rudolphine court.

The notional successor to Mordechai Meisel in the role of banker to the Habsburg rulers was Verona native Jacob Bassevi (1570–1634) who was two generations younger and was the first Jew in the Habsburg monarchy to be granted noble status with the predicate *von Treuenburg*. He settled in Prague in 1611 but he had already been granted the position of court Jew *(Hofjude),* along with his brother Samuel, in 1590 by Rudolph II. He then provided financial services to Rudolph's successors, Matthias of Austria (1611–1617) and Ferdinand II (1617–1619, 1620–1637).

## Conclusion

Rudolphine Prague was a populous metropolis which attracted a number of foreign merchants in the last third of the 16th century, a time when significant entrepreneurs also emerged from the group of local merchants. The broad range of types of loan operations, which local merchants and financiers used and which the legislation was subsequently required to react to, also corresponded to the economic prosperity of the city. The repeated need to define illegal methods of money lending in the Common Law of the Land and municipal law indicates that money lending was a very common entrepreneurial activity and loans were an every-day matter of life in Prague society. The less advantageous legal conditions for money lending by Jews demonstrates the fact that Jews were strong competition which specific involved groups tried to eliminate in this manner. This meant that although Jews were able to apply an interest rate of up to 24.76% on their loans, they simultaneously had no way to sufficiently secure these loans which made them uncertain and difficult to recover. One explanation for the fact that Jews were able to lend money at such high rates, while Christians were only allowed to apply 6% interest to their loans after 1543, may be that the high interest rate permitted to Jews was supported by the monarch because Jewish taxes and loans were essential income for the state treasury. This interest was also shared by some nobles and burghers who were involved in the monetary transactions of Jews in the role of silent partners. On the other hand, there were the interests of owners of estates who were concerned about the constant indebtedness of their subjects and also the interests of Christian merchants and guilds for whom the Jews were strong and unwelcome competition. These two forces continued to oppose each other throughout the period when decisions were made about permitted and prohibited forms of money lending by Jews throughout the 16th century.

## Funding

The study was done within the research project Lumina quaeruntur LQ 300151901 *Migration and Mobility in Prague's Jewish Community at the Transition of the Middle Ages to the Early Modern Period.*

## References

Bałaban, M. (1912). *Dzieje Żydów w Krakowie i na Kazimierz, T. 1 (1304–1655).* Kraków: Izraelicka Rada Wyznaniowa w Krakowie.

Bondy, G. & Dworsky, F., eds. (1906a). *Zur Geschichte der Juden in Böhmen, Mähren und Schlesien von 906 bis 1620, 1 (906–1576).* Prag: Gottlieb Bondy.

Bondy, G. & Dworsky, F., eds. (1906b). *Zur Geschichte der Juden in Böhmen, Mähren und Schlesien von 906 bis 1620, 21 (1577–1620).* Praha: Gottlieb Bondy.

Buňatová, M. (2011). *Die Prager Juden in der Zeit vor der Schlacht am Weissen Berg. Handel und Wirtschaftsgebaren der Prager Juden im Spiegel des Liber albus Judeorum 1577–1601.* Kiel: Solivagus Verlag.

Buňatová, M. (2013). *Pražští kupci na cestách. Předbělohorská Praha a středoevropské trhy.* Praha: Mishkezy.

Buňatová, M. (2016a). Obchod mezi Prahou a Norimberkem v první polovině 16. století. *Český časopis historický,* 114 (3), pp. 652–76.

Buňatová, M. (2016b). Die wirtschaftlichen Beziehungen Prager Juden zum Adels in den böhmischen Ländern an der Wende vom 16. zum 17. Jahrhundert. In Hirbodian, S. & Torben, S., eds. *Juden und ländliche Gesellschaft in Europa zwischen Mittelalter und Früher Neuzeit (15.–17. Jahrhundert). Kontinuität und Krise, Inklusion und Exklusion in einer Zeit des Übergangs.* Wiesbaden: Harrassowitz, pp. 33–49.

Buňatová, M. (2019). *Hedvábí, sklo a koření. Obchod mezi Prahou a Itálií (1500–1620).* Praha: NLN.

Bůžek, V. (1989). *Úvěrové podnikání nižší šlechty v předbělohorských Čechách.* Praha: ČSAV.

Čelakovský, J., ed. (1886). *Codex iuris municipalis regni Bohemiae, Tomus I.* Praha: Grégr.

Denzel, M. A. (2010). *Handbook of World Exchange Rates 1590–1914.* London: Routledge.

Glücklich, J., ed. (1936). *Nová redakce zemského zřízení království českého z posledních let před českým povstání.* Brno: FF MU.

Janáček, J. (1959). *Dějiny obchodu v předbělohorské Praze.* Praha: ČSAV.

Jireček, H., ed. (1888). *Obnovené právo a Zřízení zemské dědičného království Českého. Verneuerte Landes-Ordnung des Erb-Königreichs Böhmen 1627.* Praha.

Jireček, J., ed. (1876). *M. Pavel Krystyan z Koldína. Práva městská Království českého a Markrabství moravského spolu s krátkou jich summou.* Praha: Všehrd.

Jireček, J. & Jireček, H., eds. (1882). *Zřízení zemská Království českého XVI. věku.* Praha: Všehrd.

Kreuz, P. & Martinovský, I., eds. (2007). *Vladislavské zřízení zemské a navazující prameny.* Praha: Scriptorium.

Ledvinka, V. (1985). *Úvěr a zadlužení feudálního velkostatku v předbělohorských Čechách (Finanční hospodaření pánů z Hradce 1560–1596.* Praha: ČSAV.

Ledvinka, V. & Pešek, J. (2000). *Praha.* Praha: NLN.

Malý, K. & Pánek, J., eds. (2001). *Wladislawské zřízení zemské a počátky ústavního zřízení v českých zemích (1500–1619).* Praha: HÚ AV ČR; Ústav právních dějin PF UK.

Malý, K. & Šouša, J., eds. (2013). *Městské právo ve střední Evropě. Sborník příspěvků z mezinárodní právnické konference "Práva městská Království českého" z 19.-21. září 2011.* Praha: Karolinum.

North, M. (1991). *Kredit im spätmittelalterlichen und frühneuzeitlichen Europa.* Köln – Wien – Wiemar: Böhlau.

North, M. (2000). *Kommunikation, Handel, Geld und Banken in der Frühen Neuzeit.* München: Oldenbourg.

Palacký, F., ed. (1862). *Archiv český čili Staré písemné památky české a morawské, V.* Praha: Výbor zemský v království Českém.

*Sněmy české od roku 1526 po naši dobu, díl I (1526–1547),* (1877). Praha: Královský český archiv zemský.

*Sněmy české od roku 1526 po naši dobu, díl IV (1574–1576)* (1886). Praha: Královský český archiv zemský.

*Sněmy české od léta 1526 až po naši dobu, díl VII (1586–1591),* (1891). Praha: Královský český archiv zemský.

Urfus, V. (1959). *Zdomácnění směnečného práva v českých zemích a počátky novodobého práva obchodního.* Praha: ČSAV.

Urfus, V. (1975). *Právo, úvěr a lichva v minulosti. Uvolnění úvěrových vztahů na přechodu od feudalismu ke kapitalismu a právní věda recipovaného římského práva.* Brno: Univerzita J. E. Purkyně.

Vilímková, M. (1993). *Židovské město pražské.* Praha: Avicenum.

Vorel, P. (2005). *Velké dějiny zemí koruny České, VII. (1526–1619).* Praha–Litomyšl: Paseka.

# Chapter 12

# The credit market of a small peripheral Polish town in the early modern period

*Monika Kozłowska-Szyc*

Credit was of great importance in the economic life of the early modern period. It played a special role in urban circumstances, hence trade economy developed there best. It was applied for consumption, as well as in investments and commodity exchange. The credit market functioning in small Podlasie towns, however, largely served private needs. The objective of this chapter is to show and discuss the phenomenon of credit in a small private town, which is the case of Białystok. Determining the size and the structure of turnovers, the duration of agreements as well as the way of their securing will allow us to outline the rhythm of the economic life of the urban centre under analysis and will help to determine the degree of its economic development. The analysis was based on the oldest preserved municipal registers. The material was complemented with promissory notes and documents kept in the Roskie Archives and the Branicki Archives. All the used archive records reside in the Central Archive of Historical Records in Warsaw (Księgi miejskie białostockie, 1744–1795; Archiwum Roskie, 1737–1794; Archiwum Branickich z Białegostoku, 1786).

Located at the borderline between the Crown of the Kingdom of Poland and the Grand Duchy of Lithuania, Białystok was one of larger urban centres in Podlasie (beside Tykocin and Bielsk Podlaski). In the 18th century, it had c. 2,500 residents, 41% of which were Christians, 35.5% Jews, and 23.5% soldiers (Łopatecki 2015, p. 351; Dobroński 2001, p. 38). It is important to emphasise that such small towns dominated in the landscape of the Polish-Lithuanian Commonwealth, hence they constituted over 90% of all urban centres of old Poland (Bogucka & Samsonowicz 1986, pp. 379–82). What is also worth noting is the fact that Białystok was the headquarters of the Podlasie latifundium of the Branicki family. The town emerged as a base of a magnate seat and formed along with the development of the landlord's manor. The development of such centres made up a characteristic quality of the modern era not only in the Polish-Lithuanian Commonwealth but also throughout Europe. However, residential towns in Poland differed from those in Western Europe by the fact that they were not a monarch's work but the magnates' (Stone 2001, p. 298; Bogucka 2001, p. 23; 2009, p. 18).

The Branicki family, as the owners of Białystok, had almost unlimited possibilities to intervene in all areas of life in the town. They were also of great importance on the Podlasie credit market. The most affluent residents of towns and estates belonging to the Branickis deposited their funds at Jan Klemens Branicki and Izabela Branicka, as well as people being at the top of the court hierarchy (Łopatecki & Kupczewska 2016, p. 490). Moreover, they had instruments controlling the local credit market. Through their officials they issued regulations limiting the opportunity of taking loans by the troops stationing in Białystok (Łopatecki 2015, p. 356), or permits allowing the local Jewish communities to run credit operations (Leszczyński 1980, p. 80). Moreover, the Branicki family created new town offices at their discretion: one of them was the position of governor, among whose tasks was, among other things, making sure that the properties of people who were not able to pay off debt claims were auctioned (Sztachelska-Kokoczka 2009, p. 21).

However, it was lack of bank institutions, where burghers, especially those more affluent, could take a loan or deposit their property, that affected the development of mutual loans at interest. A considerable role in the development of credit-monetary operations was primarily played by the Jewish population (Leszczyński 1980, pp. 188–202). It was the Jewish religious communities (kahal) that offered fringe banking services where not only burghers, but also neighbouring nobility and clergy lodged their money (Samsonowicz 1981, p. 128). The financial activity of Jewish communities had also its disadvantage: excessive liabilities of the kahal in the 18th century resulted in its insolvency and the necessity of the intervention from the dominion power (Dubnow 2001, p. 293). According to specification of liabilities presented in 1795, the Białystok kahal was in debt for almost 12,000 zlotys. It seems, however, that the liabilities could be much higher. The insolvency of the Białystok kahal was no exception; the community in nearby Tykocin struggled much more serious financial problems:[1] its debt of the mid-18th century is estimated for c. 90,000 zlotys; and also in Cracow (c. 508,000 zlotys), Lvov (438,000 zlotys) or Poznan (403,000 zlotys) (Leszczyński 1994, p. 141). It is estimated that the sum of Jewish communities' liabilities in the Polish-Lithuanian Commonwealth reached even 2.5 million zlotys (Stone 2001, pp. 306–7).

The first stage of the analysis of the Białystok credit market is examining the issue of the frequency of records. From the preserved documents records referring to loan agreements, we managed to extract reports for the appraisal of pledged properties or liabilities recorded in testaments. The most transactions were noted in the 1770s and 1780s but the most sources come from that period. It is also important to emphasise the fact that only part of credit turnover can be found in the preserved books. Not all transactions were recorded in the files. The evidence thereof is the part of the records which refer to the debts which were not paid off on time and include the reports for the appraisal of pledged movables. Moreover, recording a particular transaction in court registers was connected with

*Table 12.1* The structure of the value of credit market turnover in Białystok in the second half of the 18th century

| Value (in Polish zlotys) | Up to 50 | 51–100 | 101–500 | 501–1000 | Above 1000 | Unknown value | Total |
|---|---|---|---|---|---|---|---|
| Number of transactions | 108 | 29 | 64 | 23 | 25 | 15 | 264 |
| Value of transactions | 2,142 | 2,400 | 15,991 | 18,007 | 81,115 | – | 119,655 |
| % of the number | 41 | 11 | 24 | 9 | 9 | 6 | 100 |
| % of the value | 1.8 | 2 | 13.4 | 15 | 67.8 | – | 100 |

the necessity of notary fees. Thus, it could happen that the notary costs connected with recording the promissory notes in the files were equal or higher than the amount of liabilities; therefore, such transactions were not recorded in municipal books. It is also important to remember that part of Białystok merchants' liabilities could have been recorded in court books of other urban centres, for example, those where their business partners came from. Therefore, a full reconstruction of the credit market is impossible but the following analysis allows for general orientation in the scale and the nature of the phenomenon.

An important element in studies on economy is the analysis of the concentration of a particular phenomenon within particular wealth groups (as can be seen in Table 12.1). Unfortunately, for 6% of the transactions, we have no information of the amount of the credit agreement. The data presented in Table 12.1 demonstrate that even 67.8% of the value of all loan agreements was concentrated in the hands of a small group of people (9% of cases). In Białystok, credit turnover numerically dominated small transactions (up to 50 zlotys: 41%) but their value was a margin of the turnover (1.8%). Also, debts of 51–100 zlotys had little share in the market (2%). Also medium-value loans (101–500 zlotys) were popular: their value made 13.4% of the whole credit turnover. The highest interest was attracted, however, by transactions up to 100 zlotys: they made up jointly 52% of the number of all contracts, and their value did not exceed 4% of the total.

A certain facilitation in determining the weight of a particular debt is becoming familiar with the purchasing power of the money the local burghers traded in the 18th century. To illustrate this phenomenon, I will use, for example, prices of real estates in Białystok. For 100 zlotys, one could purchase the cheapest wooden house, a place of average value cost c. 300 zlotys, whereas the most expensive brick houses were worth even a few thousand zlotys (Kozłowska 2017b, p. 111). Simultaneously, wages of construction workers (builders, carpenters) available in the sources were 250 zlotys per year (Kozłowska 2017a, p. 210).

In Białystok, like in other Podlasie towns, petty consumption loans dominated, although there was also big credit. However, its share in the general market structure was quite small. Higher sums were mainly connected with big commerce and goods purchase and sale transactions. An example of such a loan is a series of credit transactions resulting from founding a trade company by Paliter Dawidowicz (a Białystok merchant and broker) as well as Jan Aleksander Lindsay (a major of an infantry regiment of the Grand Crown Buława). In the years 1761–1762, Dawidowicz, with a surety from Lindsay, borrowed altogether 5,425 zlotys, which allotted for a purchase of goods in Torun (Archiwum Roskie 1737–1794). It is important to bear in mind, however, that Podlasie towns were not considerable trade centres; like other towns of that rank, they were places of exchange of agricultural produce, craft products, as well as commodities brought by local merchants (Oleksicki 1985, p. 51; Sztachelska-Kokoczka 1992, pp. 101– 10). In the scale of the whole region, Jewish merchants from Tykocin had the largest shares in trade turnover (Wroczyńska 1995, p. 27).

The analysed credit agreements show that the loans were provided mainly by the people with Polish-sounding family names: they constituted c. 51.5% of the creditors. Many of them also incurred liabilities (they made up 51% of debtors). A quarter of all credit transactions took place within the population of Polish-sounding family names. They were largely petty loans, sometimes of just 4 zotys, even though we find also manifold higher liabilities, of over 300 zlotys.

Also Białystok Jews lent money: they made up 31% of all creditors in the contracts recorded in town books. However, we can suppose that their real share in the credit market was considerably higher, since certain Jewish transactions were recorded in kahal books, which have not survived. There must have gone primarily credit agreements between the Jews. Like in other Podlasie towns (Tykocin, Goniądz, Kleszczele or Orla), providing loans at interest was the fundamental source of income of many members of the Białystok Jewish community (Leszczyński 1980, p. 190). Source records also fail to indicate that Jewish bankers or merchants in Podlasie lent money to the clergy, which happened several times in other Polish towns (Morgensztern 1967, pp. 6–7; Hanejko 2011, p. 148). On the contrary, the Jews were debtors of numerous church institutions (Hundert 2006, p. 77). The Jews also often used money credit at the burghers. However, it is important to point out that the Jewish legislature attempted to reduce opportunities of borrowing money from Christians. From 1673 onwards, in Poland (from 1670 in Lithuania), the Jews had to abide by the so-called credit *chazoka*, which meant that if a Jew wanted to incur a debt from a Christian, he had to receive the kahal's permission. The *chazoka* was primarily expected to protect from reckless indebtedness; it was also a security for Jewish communities from executions which threatened them because of the collective responsibility of kahals for a bankruptcy of its every member (Leszczyński 1980, pp. 194–5; Pogonowski 1998, pp. 78–9). It seems, however, that those provisions were not always applied. In town books, we find many petty as well as more serious loans taken by the Jews. The debtors of the Christians were, for example, merchants and the kahal. For instance, Wolf Gołda, a rich merchant of long distance trade, owed to many Christian creditors a considerable amount of nearly 11,609 zlotys (Księgi miejskie białostockie, 1744–1795). Moreover, the Jews also incurred money liabilities from the town owner. In 1795, the Białystok kahal took a loan of 2,344 zlotys from Izabela Branicka, which allocated for paying off their outstanding debts (Archiwum Roskie, 1737–1794).

An inseparable component of loan turnover was a profit taken from the transactions by the creditors. Unfortunately, the interest was seldom mentioned in credit agreements. However, even on the basis of a few agreements including such data, we may calculate that debtors paid on average 8% of interest a year from the borrowed sum (the lowest interest rate was 5%, the highest rate: 12.5%). It is a relatively high interest rate, also in reference to the state legislature of those days. The Sejm Constitution (act of law) of 1775 introduced limitations on credit transactions which should not have a higher interest rate than 5% a year (Volumina legum, 1860, pp. 112–13). In other Podlasie towns (Tykocin, Orla, Bielsk), an annual interest rate ranged from 6% to even 10% (Leszczyński 1980, p. 198). A similar profit from providing loans was also noted in other Polish towns. For instance, in a small Małopolska private town of Tomaszów Lubelski, in most cases, the interest from the loan was 7–8% (Hanejko 2011, p. 148). On the other hand, in the royal town of Nowy Sącza at the turn of the 17th century, an annual interest rate reached 10% (in the case of the loans secured by the pledge of a real estate even 10–15%) (Dunin-Wąsowicz 1967, pp. 65, 72). A lower interest rate was noted, however, in the towns and regions connected with foreign and long-distance trade. For instance, in the 17th-century Toruń, 6% of interest was paid from the loan taken (the rate ranged between 4% to maximum 8%) (Mycio 1999, p. 65). On the other hand, in Żuławy Wiślane at the turn of the 18th century, burghers and peasants paid not more than 8.5% of interest, and in the 18th c. even 3% (Szafran 1985, p. 198). The aforementioned data show that the loan interest rate in the Commonwealth was higher than in the countries of Western Europe. For instance, in France, Portugal, and England, the interest rate reached maximum 5% annually (Dermineur 2018, pp. 209, 226; Costa, Rocha & Brito 2014, pp. 17–18). The reasons for this discrepancy were different; among them, we can count a weak development of credit instruments in Polish towns, lack of bank institutions, a higher risk of not receiving the money back, or different purposes of the loan.

Another important issue is the duration of loan agreements, which can be divided into short-term ones (lasting a year or shorter) and long-term ones (see Figure 12.1). Not in all cases, unfortunately, the source provides the duration of the loan agreement and we know the time for paying off the debt only in 23% of contracts. Burghers usually concluded agreements for

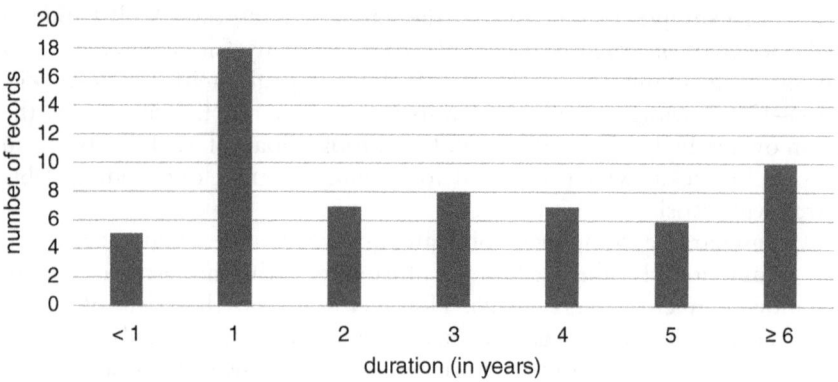

*Figure 12.1* Credit agreements by duration (in years) in Białystok, the second half of the 18th century.

a one-year period. It also observable that 62% of all credit contracts under scrutiny lasted more than a year. This is, however, a result of more frequent recording in town books – transactions not paid on time. In the case of such arrears, one of three possible solutions were applicable: the deadline was prolonged on the original conditions, or the time of contract was prolonged with sharpened contract conditions, or part of the debtor's property (commensurate with the scale of the debt) was taken over. Sometimes the debt was paid off in instalments. This phenomenon is, however, difficult to grasp, since the Białystok town books hardly ever noted payments of particular instalments. We usually learn about such operations only in reference to the return of the last part of the debt and the mutual acknowledging of the payment by both parties. With such a small number of cases, it is impossible to determine the dependencies between the number of instalments and the amount of the debt, as well as to answer the question, if spreading the payment over several parts affected the duration of the loan agreement, even though we can suppose that both tendencies known from other credit markets also occurred in Białystok. Moreover, we did not observe a mutual dependence between the amount and the duration of the credit transaction, which may result from too small a source basis.

It is also difficult to establish an exact date of incurring and paying off the liabilities, since a considerable part of the records concerns reporting for appraisal of pledged movables for debts not paid in due time. Moreover, certain records also include claims from previous periods. It seems, however, that loan agreements were mainly concluded in the period from April to June, which was connected with deficiencies of food and cash. The arranged day of payment often fell on the period of St John the Baptist fair. It was the greatest Białystok fair, organized on the name day (patron saint's day) of the town order (Sztachelska-Kokoczka 1992, p. 105; Grochulska 1973, p. 802).

All types of credit operations are connected with a risk of losing the lent money. Therefore, different methods of insuring loan agreements were developed. In the case of Białystok, 32% of transactions, beside a promissory note itself, a loan agreement, a bill of exchange, or a record in court books, was additionally secured by the pledge of movables and immovable property. The most often collaterals in Białystok were man's and woman's clothes (kontusz, żupan, skirts, vests, hats, pants, kerchiefs, belts, frock coats). Debt collaterals were also everyday objects (e.g. dishes, bowls as well as tin plates, spoons and knives, a brass iron, a silver jug, mugs). On the other hand, guarantees based on immovable properties as well as all possessions were mainly granted by the Jews, more rarely by the Christians. If the debtor was the kahal management, the whole community collectively guaranteed the loan. Moreover, such items as a violin, four pictures framed in glass, a military saddle, a clock, French pistols, or liturgical utensils were left to the debtors. The creditor could sell the items being a collateral of a loan agreement in the event of a default in due time. In this case the creditor should report the items for appraisal in the town office. They were assessed by an expert in a particular field (for example, clothes were priced by a tailor, a wooden house by a carpenter). After the appraisal the town authorities called the debtor for paying off the liability and buying out the pledge, usually within 30 days. In the event of the appraisal of the pledged items above the amount of the debt the creditor, having sold the items, should return the surplus to the office. If the collateral was assessed below the value of the debt, the creditor suffered a loss. It also happened that the town court, after the appraisal of the pledge, ordered the debtor to work off the missing part of the debt. Records in the preserved town books also show that certain Jews ran pawnshop activities in Białystok.

Knowing the ways of securing the loan, it is also important to investigate the amounts of loans reached in each of the distinguished groups of collaterals (see Table 12.2). It is clearly visible that the amount of collateral depended on the amount of the incurred debt. Petty debts were guaranteed by pledging clothes and other movables (up to 100 zlotys). Those slightly higher were secured on immovable property, usually land. High loans were insured by a record referring to the whole property. The situation was similar in other Podlasie towns. In Tykocin, considerable sums were secured on all types of immovable property (houses, plots of land, breweries). Smaller ones were guaranteed by different objects. Sometimes a collateral was even livestock: for example, in Goniądz, the loan collateral was a calf (Leszczyński 1980, pp. 192, 199).

The analysis of the oldest Białystok court books indicates that an important manifestation of economic activities of the burghers was credit operations. Loans were used not only in the turnover of commodities and investments but, primarily, for consumption purposes. The Białystok credit market was largely based on small value contracts (up to 100 zlotys), usually incurred for a one-year period, although most of transactions had no payment deadline.

*Table 12.2* Value of debts incurred in Białystok in the second half
of the 18th century by an additional way of their securing (arithmetical
average)

| Type of collateral | Number of records | Average value of the loan |
|---|---|---|
| Property | 12 | 577 |
| Land | 7 | 136 |
| Clothing | 37 | 29 |
| Everyday objects | 4 | 67 |
| Clothes and everyday items | 12 | 60 |
| Indefinite items | 7 | 93 |
| Others | 6 | 56 |

A considerable part of liabilities was also additionally secured by a collateral, the value of which depended on the amount of the debt. It is also important to note that the development of credit-monetary operations of the town under scrutiny was considerably affected by the Jews, who, according to data in the preserved sources, constituted at least 31% of all creditors, even though their real share in the market, perhaps much more considerable, is difficult to determine because of the lack of preserved kahal books. Despite the growth of the number of recorded transactions from the 1770s onwards, on the Białystok credit market there is no sign of modernization processes, so visible in, for example, Warsaw (Łozowski 2018, pp. 177–78), and the vast majority of transactions belong to the sphere of traditional private credit, the recognition of which should be one of the priorities of Polish economic historiography. Small towns like Białystok constituted the vast majority of urban entities in the Commonwealth but the evaluation of their economic life standard requires specific studies, which are still missing.

## Note

1 Tykocin, like Białystok, was a private town belonging to the Branicki family. In the 18th century, it had c. 3,000 inhabitants, 51.7% of whom were Christians and 48.3% Jewish (Kusiński 1966, p. 272, Choińska 2009–2010, p. 38). The Jewish community in Tykocin was the fifth largest community in old Poland and supervised c. 50 neighbouring settlements in Podlasie. In 1771, as a result of the intervention of dominion power, it transferred the supervision of those villages and towns to the younger Białystok kahal (Kaźmierczyk 2002, p. 148; Rogalewska 1995, p. 17).

## References

Archiwum Branickich z Białegostoku. (1786). Warsaw: The Central Archives of Historical Records. 48.

Archiwum Roskie: akta osobisto-rodzinne i majątkowo-prawne (1737–1794). Warsaw: The Central Archives of Historical Records. 628, 633, 634, 636.

Bogucka, M. (2001). *Miasta a władza centralna w Polsce i w Europie wczesnonowożytnej (XVI–XVIII w.)*. Warszawa: Wydział I Nauk Społecznych PAN.

Bogucka, M. (2009). Miasto i mieszczanin w społeczeństwie Polski nowożytnej (XVI–XVIII wiek). *Czasy Nowożytne*, 22, pp. 9–49.

Bogucka, M. & Samsonowicz, H. (1986). *Dzieje miast i mieszczaństwa w Polsce przedrozbiorowej*. Wrocław: Zakład Narodowy im. Ossolińskich.

Choińska, M. (2009–2010). Powinności mieszczan w mieście królewskim a w mieście prywatnym: przykład Tykocina w XVI–XVIII wieku. *Studia Podlaskie*, 18, pp. 7–110.

Costa, L. F., Rocha, M. M. & Brito, P. (2014). *Money Supply and the Credit Market in Early Modern Economies: The Case of Eighteenth-Century Lisbon*. Lisboa: Gabinete de História Económica e Social.

Dermineur, E. M. (2018). Rural Credit Markets in Eighteenth-Century France: Contracts, Guarantees and Land. In Briggs, Ch. & Zuijderduijn, J., eds. *Land and Credit: Mortgages in the Medieval and Early Modern European Countryside*. Basingstoke: Palgrave Macmillan, pp. 205–31.

Dobroński, A. (2001). *Białystok – historia miasta*. Białystok: Zarząd Miasta.

Dubnow, S. M. (2001). *History of the Jews in Russia and Poland 1: From the Beginning until the Death Of Alexander I (1825)*. Skokie: Varda Books.

Dunin-Wąsowicz, A. (1967). *Kapitał mieszczański Nowego Sącza na przełomie XVI/ XVII wieku. Wpływ na ekonomikę miasta i zaplecza*. Warszawa: Państwowe Wydawnictwo Naukowe.

Grochulska, B. (1973). Jarmarki w handlu polskim w drugiej połowie XVIII wieku. *Przegląd Historyczny*, 64(4), pp. 793–821.

Hanejko, E. (2011). Miasto w okresie od wielkiego sporu o Ordynację do I rozbioru Polski. In Szczygieł, R., ed. *Tomaszów Lubelski. Monografia miasta*. Lublin–Tomaszów Lubelski: Tomaszowskie Towarzystwo Regionalne, pp. 127–215.

Hundert, G. D. (2006). *Jews in Poland-Lithuania in the Eighteenth Century: a Genealogy of Modernity*. Berkeley: University of California Press.

Kaźmierczyk, A. (2002). *Żydzi w dobrach prywatnych w świetle sądowniczej i administracyjnej praktyki dóbr magnackich w wiekach XVI–XVIII*. Kraków: Księgarnia Akademicka.

Kozłowska, M. (2017b). Rynek obrotu nieruchomościami w Białymstoku w XVIII wieku. *Studia Podlaskie*, 25, pp. 103–27.

Kozłowska, M. (2017a). Rynek kredytowy w XVIII-wiecznym Białymstoku w świetle analizy ksiąg miejskich. *Roczniki Dziejów Społecznych i Gospodarczych*, 68, pp. 199–222.

Księgi miejskie białostockie. (1744–1795). Warsaw: The Central Archives of Historical Records. 1, 2, 3.

Kusiński, W. (1966). Przemiany funkcji Białegostoku w przeszłości. *Rocznik Białostocki*, 6, pp. 267–96.

Leszczyński, A. (1980). *Żydzi Ziemi Bielskiej od połowy XVII w. do 1795 r. (studium osadnicze, prawne I ekonomiczne)*. Wrocław: Zakład Narodowy im. Ossolińskich.

Leszczyński, A. (1994). *Sejm Żydów Korony 1623–1764*. Warszawa: Żydowski Instytut Historyczny w Polsce.

Łopatecki, K. (2015). Ustrój XVIII-wiecznego miasta Białystok. *Miscellanea Historico-Iuridica*, 14(1), pp. 349–79.

Łopatecki, K. & Kupczewska, M. (2016). Dyspozycje majątkowe Izabeli z Poniatowskich Branickiej na wypadek śmierci. *Kwartalnik Historii Kultury Materialnej*, 64(4), pp. 485–93.

Łozowski, P. (2018). The Social Structure of the Real Estate Market in Old Warsaw in the Years 1427–1527. *Economic History of Developing Regions*, 33(2), pp. 147–82.

Morgensztern, J. (1967). Operacje kredytowe Żydów w Zamościu w XVII w. (wierzytelności I zadłużenia). *Biuletyn Żydowskiego Instytutu Historycznego*, 64, pp. 3–32.

Mycio, A. (1999). Formy kredytu mieszczańskiego na początku XVII wieku w świetle ksiąg ławniczych Starego Miasta Torunia. *Rocznik Toruński*, 26, pp. 55–70.

Oleksicki, A. (1985). Socjotopografia Białegostoku w XVIII w. w świetle inwentarza miasta z 1771/72 I planu Beckera z 1799 r. In Majecki, H., ed. *Studia i materiały do dziejów miasta Białegostoku, 4*. Białystok: Białostockie Towarzystwo Naukowe, pp. 41–56.

Pogonowski, I. (1998). *Jews in Poland: A Documentary History*. New York: Hippocrene Books.

Rogalewska, E. (1995). Rozwój giny żydowskiej w Tykocinie. In Rogalewska, E., ed. *Żydzi tykocińscy 1522–1941*. Tykocin: Towarzystwo Przyjaciół Ziemi Tykocińskiej.

Samsonowicz, H. (1981). Początki banków prywatnych w Polsce. *Sobótka*, 36(1), pp. 127–38.

Stone, D. Z. (2001). *The Polish-Lithuanian State, 1386–1795*. Seattle: University of Washington Press.

Szafran, P. (1985). Kredyt na Żuławach Gdańskich w XVII-XVIII wieku. *Rocznik Gdański*, 45 (1), pp. 139–48.

Sztachelska-Kokoczka, A. (1992). Handel w miastach dóbr podlaskich Jana Klemensa Branickiego. In Dubas-Urwanowicz, E. & Urwanowicz, J., ed. *Miasto, region, społeczeństwo. Studia ofiarowane profesorowi Andrzejowi Wyrobiszowi w sześćdziesiątą rocznicę Jego urodzin*. Białystok: Dział Wydawnictw Filii UW, pp. 101–10.

Sztachelska-Kokoczka, A. (2009). *Białystok za pałacową bramą*. Białystok: Urząd Miejski.

*Volumina legum*: vol. 8 (1890). Petersburg: Jozefat Ochryzko.

Wroczyńska, E. (1995). Rozwój żydowskiego osiedla w Tykocinie do końca XVIII w. In Rogalewska, E., ed. *Żydzi tykocińscy 1522–1941*. Tykocin: Towarzystwo Przyjaciół Ziemi Tykocińskiej.

# Chapter 13

# Jewish credit business in the urban context of late medieval Austria

*Birgit Wiedl*

## Introduction

Medieval Jewish settlement in today's Austria[1] took place rather late compared to other parts of the German-speaking area. In the south, the first Jewish settlement can be traced in Friesach, an enclave of the archbishop of Salzburg in the Duchy of Carinthia, in the 12th century (Wenninger 2015, pp. 341–3); in Austrian and Styrian cities, full-fledged Jewish communities developed from the early 13th century onwards, particularly in Vienna, Krems, Wiener Neustadt, and Maribor (today's Slovenia). Although it was the urban centres that attracted the majority of Jewish settlers, the number of Jews dwelling in the countryside should not be underestimated.

The legal position of the Austrian Jews living was for the most part defined and assigned by the ruler. Therefore, legal provisions dealing with Jews and the (urban) Jewish credit market can mainly be found in documents issued by territorial princes: general privileges for the Jews were issued by the ruler and applied to all Jews living under their governance, and also town charters were for the most part issued not by the municipality, but by the lord of the town. A single exception for Austria is Emperor Frederick II's privilege for the Jews of Vienna, that repeats his imperial privilege from 1236 and emphasises his claim to the *Judenregal* during his power struggle with the Austrian duke (Brugger & Wiedl 2005, pp. 31–2, no. 20). Yet apart from remaining immediate subjects to the ruler throughout the Middle Ages, Jews in Austrian towns were subjected to a variety of legal systems – the town laws and legal systems of manorial lords (and ladies) as well as the common law, be it codified or oral.

The legal basis for Jewish life was the ducal privilege of 1244 that put the Jews of Austria under the sovereign rule of the duke (see the contribution of Eveline Brugger) and was extended to their other territories by the Habsburg dukes, and also adapted in most of the neighbouring countries (Magin 1999, pp. 354–60). The privilege emphasised the duke's interest in Jewish monetary business and laid claim to his judiciary prerogative, which was stressed by an explicit exclusion of the municipal court (Brugger &

Wiedl 2005, pp. 35–7, no. 25). Economic control was in part given to the office of the *Judenrichter* (*iudex iudeorum*, Justice for the Jews), usually a member of the respective town's upper-class citizenry, who had limited rights of supervision over the selling of unredeemed pledges. Despite the strong ties to the ruler many of the *Judenrichter* enjoyed, the towns were generally interested in expanding the office's competences, gradually transforming the office into an at least partly municipal one.

Due to the duke's financial interest, the regulations of the privilege focussed mainly on moneylending and pawnbroking and thus laid the basis for both the Jewish credit business and the cities' continuing attempts to modify them to their benefit. While many of these articles were a genuine creation of the ducal chancellery, the central part, the right of the Jews to clear themselves of the suspicion of having accepted stolen goods as pledges by taking an oath (= Statute of the Market, Toch 2013a, p. 211), stood in the tradition of the imperial regulations from the late 11th century (Toch 2013b, pp. 46–7). Most territorial rulers within the Holy Roman Empire had granted this right to their Jewish inhabitants; over time, it became a major point of contention between the territorial princes and their cities, with the latter seeking to abolish or at least curtail the Statute (Magin 1999, pp. 352–400).

## Urban policy regarding Jewish moneylending

The policies of the Austrian cities were aimed at mitigating the regulations of the 1244 privilege or, at least, at benefiting in some ways from the Jewish community. Already late-13th-century town charters therefore addressed two concerns that became the main conflict issues between ruler and towns: the questions of jurisdiction and of control over the Jews' economic activities. Due to the cities' limited power base, their 13th-century attempts at modifying the regulations to their benefit remained restricted to altering single articles. Towns strove to weaken the Jews' legal position by changing the place of jurisdiction (the synagogue), by at least partially involving the municipal judge, and by replacing the required Jewish witness with one or more Christians, a development that was by no means unique to Austrian towns (Gilomen 2009, pp. 24–6). Other issues raised in the 1244 privilege such as penalties for hurting and killing Jews, for devastating cemeteries and synagogues, and for rape, were hardly ever touched upon by municipal legislation (Wiedl 2013, pp. 209–11). In economic regards, the main issues that remained predominant throughout the town charters of first half of the 14th century were, apart from excluding Jews from specific professions, directly connected with moneylending: the limitation of interest rates, and the regulation of pawnbroking.

### Early attempts

In 1308, the citizenry of the Carinthian town of St. Veit, seat of the ducal court, took advantage of the ongoing struggle between the Carinthian

Duke Henry VI and the Austrian Duke Frederick the Fair for the Bohemian crown. The latter, having managed to take hold of the Carinthian towns, was willing to acquiesce to the citizens' demands. The articles introduced by the St. Veit citizenry therefore represent a prime example for a town's wishes regarding the regulation of Jewish credit business: in a quasi-negation of the Statute of the Market, Jews were forbidden to accept any potentially stolen goods in pawn at all, and were furthermore forbidden to take anything in pawn from a person unknown to them, a regulation that must have proven extremely harmful to the everyday business of Jewish pawnbrokers who at least partially relied on walk-in customers. Most town charters of the 14th century did (or could) not go that far and thus strove at expanding the list of items the 1244 regulation forbade the Jews to accept in pawn: to the bloodstained or soaked (i.e. illegally appropriated) objects, towns added specific items that were mostly of ecclesiastical (chalices, tunicles) and economic or agricultural provenance (unprocessed yarn and cloth, unground corn; Wiedl 2013, pp. 211–12). Comparison with other cities shows that defining and limiting the range of pawnable objects was a core interest of towns throughout the Holy Roman Empire, and that the objects chosen were rather similar (Maimon 2003, p. 2184; Müller 2012).

Apart from pawnbroking, the reduction of the Jewish interest rate was the central bone of contention between the towns and their respective rulers. The maximum rate of eight pennies per pound per week that had been set by the 1244 privilege was already being undermined by late-13th-century efforts: the forged town charter of Wiener Neustadt from the late 1270s cut down the interest rate to three or four pennies and combined this with additional improvements for the debtor such as denying the creditor's right to compound interest during the first month after default of payment. Other towns went along the same lines and tried to at least sneak in small benefits, such as the Carinthian town of Villach: while the privilege issued by the town lord, the bishop of Bamberg, followed the 1244 privilege to a large extent, the loss of compound interest in the first month was added, as was the addition of chalices and tunicles to the forbidden pawn objects (Brugger & Wiedl 2005, pp. 255–7, no. 302).

## Municipal policies after 1338

Throughout the Holy Roman Empire, the complete dependence on the ruler's protection left the Jews in a precarious situation (Müller 2004, pp. 254–6). In Austria, this first came to pass in the wake of the persecutions that followed an accusation of host desecration in the Lower Austrian town of Pulkau in 1338. The persecutions went far beyond the local scope and affected many Jewish settlements in Austria, Moravia, Bohemia, and Carinthia, whereas the largest Jewish community in Vienna remained safe, albeit at a(n) (economic) price. Recognising danger the Jews were in, the Viennese citizenry seized the chance to make use of the persecution to their own advantage: in

June 1338, with the persecutions only just abating, the Jewish community had to agree to a severe reduction of the interest rate for loans given to Viennese citizens in return for protection. In their charter, the Jewish community of Vienna spoke of the 'clemency' the citizens were showing them in times of their distress, and to show their 'gratitude', they had promised to lend the pound only against a maximum interest of three pennies per week, a serious decrease from the 1244 interest rate of eight pennies. The Jewish community's consent alone was however not considered sufficient – as sovereigns over all Austrian Jews, the dukes would consider the city's action an interference into their rights as well as a threat to diminish the income of the ducal treasury due to its negative affect on the Jews' fiscal power. Therefore, the city of Vienna sought ducal approval, which the Austrian Dukes Albrecht II and Otto had to grant due to the precarious situation of their Jews (Brugger & Wiedl 2005, pp. 336–8, nos 439 and 440). Business documents from the mid-14th century indicate that the interest rates had indeed decreased notably, yet this is true for transactions in both urban and rural areas, correlating with a general weakening of the ducal protection.

Vienna was not the only town that seized the opportunity to exploit the Jews' precarious situation: in September 1338, the bishop of Passau granted a new municipal law to his Lower Austrian town of St. Pölten that included two articles aimed at limiting Jewish credit and pawnbroking business: no Jew was allowed to accept houses, tunicles, unground corn, and bloodied clothing as collateral from citizens or other episcopal subjects living within the city, unless they could produce a concession by the municipal judge. Furthermore, every Jewish moneylender had to present their debenture bonds and moveable pledges thrice annually to the municipal judge, who would in return confirm the submission in writing. Should a Christian debtor die within a year and the Jew not be able to present the judge's corroboration, the debtor's heirs were no longer liable to pay the debt (Brugger & Wiedl 2005, pp. 341–2, no. 444). These articles show for the first time in Austria a more encompassing municipal control exerted by the town judge; it is all the more interesting since no Jewish presence can be traced in St. Pölten after 1338 when the city's Jewish population had most likely been murdered (Wiedl 2013, p. 217).

## Attempts at a more encompassing control

From mid-14th century onwards, Austrian towns strove to achieve a more encompassing control over the Jews. The increasing decline of the ducal protection offered considerable leeway for the towns to shift competences to their favour, allowing them to tighten their grip on the Jews perceptibly. In addition to limiting the pawnable objects, particular attention was paid to the extent to which their citizens indebted themselves, especially with regard to the mortgaging of houses and real estate. In this regard, municipalities used the office of the *Judenrichter*: according to the 1244 privilege, Jewish debtors could submit a request to the *Judenrichter* for permission to sell the collateral after one year of the pawning, provided that the capital and interest of the original loan had not exceeded the pledge's value; after a year and a day, the Jewish creditor had the general right of disposal over the collateral (Wiedl 2009, pp. 290–2), a time frame generally common in the pawnbroking business (Shatzmiller 2013, pp. 10–11). While the *Judenrichter* played an important role in the municipal supervisory measures of the late 14th century, he often had to share responsibility of the control over Jewish credit and pawn business with the municipal judge. In the Salzburg-ruled town of Ptuj (Lower Styria, today's Slovenia), the task was divided between the municipal judge, to whom the Jews had to submit their promissory notes annually, and the *Judenrichter*, who supervised their moveable pledges on a weekly basis; according to St. Pölten's town law of 1338, it was the exclusive right of the municipal judge to request the town's Jews to submit their debenture bonds and pledges thrice annually for approval. In 1396, several towns in Styria received a privilege by Duke Wilhelm that, among other articles, gave equal control to the municipal judge and the *Judenrichter* by ordering that debenture bonds from citizens of the respective municipality to Jews had to be corroborated by seal by both of them. It is however still unclear to what degree this regulation was put into practice on an everyday level; this double-sealing has only been evident in some cases in the materials analysed to date (and had not been unheard of before the privilege). For example, a document issued by the Jew Gutel from Graz in 1398 was sealed by both the municipal judge and the *Judenrichter* but concerned her sale of a forfeited pledges to a third party and not a debenture bond as such (Brugger & Wiedl 2018, p. 203, no. 2170). Furthermore, in only four of the nine privileged cities a Jewish presence can be traced for the time period; it is however not uncommon for ducal privileges and municipal laws to include articles concerning Jews irrespective of an actual Jewish presence (e.g. Brugger & Wiedl 2015, pp. 11–12, no. 1145: municipal law of Kitzbühel that included articles on the selling of meat by Jews, without any trace of Jewish settlement).

### Jews as subjects of municipal administration

In the late 14th century, the towns' aim of monitoring Jewish business was extended beyond the producing and certifying of documents; municipal administration most notably strove to include the many transactions of small(er)-scale lending and pawnbroking, most of which had not been documented in writing at all until then. Of particular interest to the municipal administration was control over the mortgaging of houses and their potential subsequent forfeiture, whereas registers of moveable pledges, particularly jewellery, as can be found in many cities (Shatzmiller 2013, pp. 45–50), are not transmitted for Austria. To ensure the control over the mortgages, many towns set up a *Judenbuch* (*liber iudeorum*, Peter 2007) as well as registers of Jewish house-ownership. The *Judenbuch*, usually administered by the *Judenrichter*, was the place where all the business transactions conducted by and with Jews had to be registered in but it also provided some protection for the Jews: the entries rendered it impossible for debtors to claim that bonds presented by Jews were forgeries, and Jews could produce the *Judenbuch* as proof before court. It is important to note that these tightening municipal control measures were not exclusive to the Jewish inhabitants: some of the *Judenbücher* were included in the general *Satzbuch* (mortgage register), as is the case for the *Judenbuch* of the Scheffstrasse (Goldmann 1908). The Scheffstrasse, a small community outside the Vienna city walls and subjected to the duchess of Austria, had its own register, kept by both ducal officers and representatives of the city of Vienna. While the manuscript's first part was a cadastral register, the second and third parts are dedicated to loans among Christians and Jews respectively. The entries of the *Judenbuch* registered loans granted by Jews, Viennese as well as Lower Austrian and Bohemian Jews, to inhabitants of the Scheffstrasse, who were mostly small-scale craftsmen, for the years from 1387 to 1421 (Wiedl 2014, pp. 140–2).

The setting up of *Judenbücher* was not exclusive to the cities: rulers and monasteries, as well as the Estates of Styria and Carinthia in the 15th century tried to keep track of their debts by means of *Judenbücher* (Brugger et al. 2013, pp. 161–2). The setting up of a *Judenbuch* also seemed to be subjected to ducal approval (e.g. Duke Albrecht III's permission to Bruck/Leitha, Brugger & Wiedl 2018, p. 26, no. 1886), signifying the duke's sovereignty over the Austrian Jews.

Apart from the *Judenbücher*, most of which were lost during the persecutions of 1420/1421 that ended Jewish settlement in the duchy of Austria, the Jewish credit market within towns can also be traced in the general municipal cadastres and title registers that document the pawning of houses and real estate by Christian debtors to their (not only) Jewish creditors. It is however crucial for an extensive survey of an urban credit market to include the administrative records of manorial lords, particularly monasteries, within a city; for example for Vienna, there are over 30 manuscripts to add to the (already extensive) municipal records, stemming from provenances such as the Scottish Monastery, the Teutonic Order, and the Citizens' Hospital (Geyer & Sailer 1931).

## Jewish moneylenders and their clientele

The earliest (traceable) business connection of citizens of an Austrian town with a Jewish creditor dates back to the year 1264 when two citizens of Krems that housed the second-largest Jewish community (after Vienna) took out a loan with the Jew Ismael of the same city (Brugger & Wiedl 2005, pp. 56–7, no. 42); the transaction also marks the first actual appearance of a *Judenrichter* in Austria who corroborated the business deal. Up until the mid-14th century, only the urban upper classes appear in the business documents due to a general lack of written source material for the lower strata of the social scale. Usually, the urban debtors take out the credit together with their wives, while widows are commonly accompanied by other relatives but do appear on their own as well (e.g., Geyer & Sailer 1931, pp. 434–5, no. 1449). Jewish women played an important role as moneylenders particularly in the smaller-scale pawnbroking business, as the high number of entries concerning female moneylenders into the *Judenbuch* of the Scheffstrasse indicates, whereas Jewesses from prestigious families counted high-ranking citizens and nobility among their clientele and could grant high credit sums (Keil 1999). The amounts taken out in loan varied greatly and could be as small as a few pound pennies (mostly Viennese pennies, although also Hungarian and Bohemian florins and the Aquileian mark appear), depended not only on the debtor's needs, but also their credit-worthiness which could result in more, or more valuable pledges, and the Jewish moneylender's financial capacities. Sums exceeding 100 pounds were rare among the urban clientele.

The majority of the records do not inform us about the debtor's reason to take out the loan. Credit periods were usually sought to be kept short and varied between a few days and several months; if a loan was intended to run over a longer time period, the business partners normally agreed upon partial repayments. Otherwise, on the due date that was fixed in the obligation (and usually also noted down in the cadastre and mortgage registers), a pre-agreed-upon amount of money had to be paid back that included not only the capital but also the interest accrued over the initial credit period, meaning that with a few exceptions, the actual interest rate for the original capital cannot be deduced. Only in the event of default, the interest rate mentioned in the document would become effective as of the due date; in addition to this default interest, compound interest could apply in a long-standing loan. To evade these higher interest rates, many debtors sought new agreements shortly before the due date, usually by either a partial payment or, even more commonly, by pawning additional collaterals. In the late 14th century, interest rates seem to have been rather fixed at three, sometimes only two pennies per pound, meaning that the interest rate of eight pennies allowed to Austrian Jews in the 1244 privilege had long vanished from everyday business reality. The interest rates of what is referred to as 'daily interest', a (mostly) short-term loan where the debtor was subjected to interest with immediate effect, could go up to five pennies per week; this type of loan was the most unfavourable for the debtor and usually only taken out in dire need.

Municipalities themselves as debtors appear sparingly in the Austrian source material. A few small-scale loans from Sopron (Brugger & Wiedl 2015, pp. 204–5, no. 1477 and p. 220, no. 1506) with Jews from the neighbouring Wiener Neustadt can be traced, the only city that appears (rather) frequently as a debtor to Austrian Jews is Bratislava who had business contacts with Jews from the small Lower Austrian towns of Marchegg, Hainburg, and Weiden that were close by, or with Jews from Vienna who had migrated there from Bratislava (Brugger & Wiedl 2018, index lemma *Pressburg*). When in need of a higher loan however (of over 400 Hungarian florins), the city approached Jews from Vienna (Brugger & Wiedl 2018, pp. 228–9, no. 2215), as did the city of Brno, who, when taking out the considerable loan of 1000 pound pennies, turn to the Steuss family in Vienna, the wealthiest Jewish moneylenders of the duchy (Brugger & Wiedl 2018, p. 82, no. 1973). Brno also appears in a long list of debtors that includes the Moravian Margrave Jobst and the Bohemian marshal who had taken out a loan of over 2000 pounds from an equally long list of Jewish creditors from Vienna, Salzburg, Krems, Wiener Neustadt, and Herzogenburg (Brugger & Wiedl 2015, pp. 410–11, no. 1840).

## Jews before court

Disputes over loans and forfeited pledges make up a large part of trials before municipal and manorial courts, where Jews appear both as plaintiffs and as defendants and can be seen exhausting the same legal remedies that were accessible to their Christian counterparts (Wiedl 2016). Jews and Christians sued each other over all sorts of economic issues, from overdue outstanding debts and unredeemed pledges to disputes over duties and levies as well as every-day neighbourhood conflicts. These trials not only show the inclusion of Jews into the municipal system of duties and rents but give evidence of their knowledge of the various judicial systems they were subjected to. Apart from municipal and manorial courts, Jews could appear before what is referred to as the *Judengericht* ('court for the Jews'), a court established to adjudicate in conflicts between Jews and Christians that consisted of an equal number of Jewish and Christian assessors and was headed by the *Judenrichter* (not to be confused with the Bet Din, the internal rabbinical court). Traces of this court are almost non-existent before 1400 and scarce still in the 15th century, which indicates that the *Judengericht* might not necessarily have been a comprehensive entity. In the few existing documents, all from the duchy of Styria and concerning the *Judengericht* of the towns of Graz (1404) and Judenburg (1451, 1465, and 1474), the respective *Judenrichter* settled economic disputes over outstanding debts (Rosenberg 1914, pp. 167–8, no. 20, pp. 170–2, nos 24 and 25), assigning the respective Jews their right to the thus forfeited pledges.

## Economy in polemics

The Jewish usurer is a central figure in anti-Jewish polemics. Apart from general fantasies about the rapacious Jewish nature, many polemics also centred on the Statute of the Market. Stigmatised as the 'very old but truly diabolic law' that allowed Jews to 'be fattened and revel in luxury' by Peter the Venerable, it does not surprise that municipal anti-Jewish expressions, that were often economy-focussed, targeted the Statute. 'Since the accursed Jews have much better rights towards the Christians than the Christians towards the Jews', a paragraph in a privately commissioned compendium of legal regulations of Vienna from before 1360, scathingly sums up the right of the Viennese Jews to clear themselves from the suspicion of fencing by oath, and further identifies the Christian pawnbroker as 'the poor man [who would] lose his pennies he had borrowed on the pledge' if said pledge turned out stolen beforehand. In contrast, pledges 'caught up in the Jew's power' remained in the Jew's possession regardless of (as the compendium suggests) the questionable legitimacy of their acquisition. Half a century later, the chronicle of the monastery of Klosterneuburg draws upon a similar image in its comment on the fire that had ravaged the Jewish quarter of Vienna in 1406: it had impoverished more Christians than Jews, since the Christians had lost their pledges that had been kept in the burnt-down houses of the Jews, while, implicitly, the Jews still could, or would, demand their loans back and benefit from Christian misery (Wiedl 2018, pp. 67–8).

## Conclusion

Jewish life in the Duchy of Austria came to a violent end during the Viennese Gesera of 1420/21 instigated by Duke Albrecht V. The citizenries profited from the murder and expulsion of the Austrian Jews by an at least partial annulment of their debts and by donations of the former Jewish houses the duke had confiscated. In the late 15th century, it was the Estates of the Duchies of Styria and Carinthia as well as the Archbishopric of Salzburg who were the driving forces behind the expulsion of the Jews from these territories in 1496 and 1498, respectively; the city of Graz requested that the Jewish houses were given to their citizens of Graz even before the expulsion decree had been issued (Brugger et al. 2013, p. 203, pp. 221–7). Similar developments had taken place all over the Holy Roman Empire where territorial princes and municipal authorities had expelled their Jews, with economic reasons being but one of the arguments.

The Austrian cities had never played that much of a defining role in Jewish medieval life. Their citizens, however, had not only been the Jews' business partners, debtors, and occasionally also creditors, but also their next-door neighbours with whom the Jews had lived for centuries. With the rise of the citizenry in the financial sector, Jewish moneylenders were not needed any more (Wenninger 1981) and it was their neighbours who, without hesitation, exploited their loss of ducal protection that had, at that time, been reduced to a mere financial exploitation.

## Funding

Research for this chapter was funded by the Austrian Science Fund (FWF): P32396 and preceding projects P28610, P24405, P21237, P18453, P15638.

## Note

1   The geographical realm of this chapter focusses mainly on the cities within the medieval duchies of Austria, Styria, and Carinthia as well as the archbishopric of Salzburg.

## References

Brugger, E., Keil, M., Lichtblau, A., Lind, C. & Staudinger, B. (2013). *Geschichte der Juden in Österreich*. Vienna: Ueberreuter.

Brugger, E. & Wiedl, B. (2005). *Regesten zur Geschichte der Juden in Österreich im Mittelalter 1*. Innsbruck: Studien Verlag.

Brugger, E. & Wiedl, B. (2010). *Regesten zur Geschichte der Juden in Österreich im Mittelalter 2*. Innsbruck: Studien Verlag.

Brugger, E. & Wiedl, B. (2015). *Regesten zur Geschichte der Juden in Österreich im Mittelalter 3*. Innsbruck: Studien Verlag

Brugger, E. & Wiedl, B. (2018). *Regesten zur Geschichte der Juden in Österreich im Mittelalter 4*. Innsbruck: Studien Verlag.

Geyer, R. & Sailer, L. (1931). *Urkunden aus Wiener Grundbüchern zur Geschichte der Wiener Juden im Mittelalter*. Wien: Deutscher Verl. f. Jugend u. Volk.

Gilomen, H. (2009). *Juden in den spätmittelalterlichen Städten des Reichs: Normen – Fakten – Hypothesen*. Trier: Eigenverlag des Instituts.

Goldmann, A. (1908). *Das Judenbuch der Scheffstraße zu Wien (1389–1420). Mit einer Schriftprobe*. Wien: Wilhelm Braumüller.

Keil, M. (1999). "Maistrin" und Geschäftsfrau. Jüdische Oberschichtfrauen im spätmittelalterlichen Österreich. In Hödl, S. & Keil, M., eds. *Die jüdische Familie in Geschichte und Gegenwart*. Berlin: Philo, pp. 27–50.

Magin, C. (1999). *"Wie es umb der iuden recht stet". Der Status der Juden in spätmittelalterlichen deutschen Rechtsbüchern*. Göttingen: Wallstein-Verl.

Maimon, A. (2003). *Germania Judaica*. Tübingen: Mohr.

Müller, J. (2004). »Erez gezerah« – »Land of Persecution«: Pogroms against the Jews in the 'regnum Teutonicum' from c. 1280 to 1350. In Cluse, C., ed. *The Jews of Europe in the Middle Ages (Tenth to Fifteenth Centuries)*. Turnhout: Brepols, pp. 245–60.

Müller, J. (2012). 'Gestolen und ainem juden versetzt'. Jüdische Pfandleiher zwischen legaler Geschäftspraxis und Hehlereivorwurf. *Aschkenas*, 20(2), pp. 439–78.

Peter, T. (2007). Judenbücher als Quellengattung und die Znaimer Judenbücher. Typologie und Forschungsstand. In Kießling, R., Rauscher, P., Rohrbacher, S. & Staudinger, B, ed. *Räume und Wege: Jüdische Geschichte im Alten Reich 1300–1800*. Berlin: Akademie, pp. 307–34.

Rosenberg, A. (1914). *Beiträge zur Geschichte der Juden in Steiermark*. Wien: Wilhelm Braumüller.

Shatzmiller, J. (2013). *Cultural Exchange. Jews, Christians, and Art in the Medieval Marketplace*. Princeton: Princeton University Press.

Toch, M. (2013a). *The Economic History of European Jews. Late Antiquity and Early Middle Ages*. Leiden: Brill.

Toch, M. (2013b). *Die Juden im mittelalterlichen Reich*. Munich: Oldenbourg.

Wenninger, M. (2015). Zu Friesach im Jahr 1124: *Vi[ll]a Iudeorum* oder *Via Iudeorum*? Die Neuinterpretation einer Urkunde und ihre Folgen für die frühe Geschichte der Juden im Ostalpenraum und die Geschichte der Stadt Friesach. In Grabmayer, J., ed. *800 Jahre Stadt Friesach*. Klagenfurt: University of Klagenfurt, pp. 341–68.

Wenninger, M. (1981). *Man bedarf keiner Juden mehr. Ursachen und Hintergründe ihrer Vertreibung aus den deutschen Reichsstädten im 15. Jahrhundert*. Vienna: Böhlau.

Wiedl, B. (2009). Jews and the City: Parameters of Jewish urban life in late medieval Austria. In Classen, A., ed. *Urban Space in the Middle Ages and the Early Modern Age*. Berlin: De Gruyter, pp. 273–308.

Wiedl, B. (2013). Codifying Jews: Jews in Austrian town charters of the thirteenth and fourteenth centuries. In Price, M. & Utterback, K. (2013). *Jews in Medieval Christendom – »Slay Them Not«*. Leiden: Brill, pp. 201–22.

Wiedl, B. (2014). Juden in österreichischen seriellen Quellen in der ersten Hälfte des 14. Jahrhunderts. In Haverkamp, A. & Müller, J, eds. *Verschriftlichung und Quellenüberlieferung. Beiträge zur Geschichte der Juden und der jüdisch-christlichen Beziehungen im spätmittelalterlichen Reich (13./14. Jahrhundert)*. Peine: Hahnsche Buchhandlung, pp. 123–46.

Wiedl, B. (2016). "…und kam der jud vor mich ze offens gericht." Juden und (städtische) Gerichtsobrigkeiten im Spätmittelalter. *Mediaevistik. Internationale Zeitschrift für Interdisziplinäre Mittelalterforschung*, 28, pp. 243–68.

Wiedl, B. (2018). Anti-Jewish polemics in business documents from late medieval Austria. *Medieval Worlds*, 7, pp. 61–79.

# Economic, political, legal and other consequences of debts and loans

# Chapter 14

# Economical and political consequences of the limiting of the statutory maximum interest rate in Central Europe from 10% to 6% since 1543

*Petr Vorel*

## Introduction

For the late medieval and early modern society, the issue of debt loans and maximum interest rates was of great importance for both religious and economic reasons (Kindleberger 1985, pp. 41–2). Since ancient times, the society discussed the question of the maximum interest rate especially in relation to usury. Nonetheless, the interest rate level was generally a regulated element of the economic system and interest-bearing loans were either completely banned or allowed within certain boundaries.

Central Europe also reflected the contradiction between the Christian doctrine which, until the Middle Ages, refused any interest on borrowed money as undesirable usury, and the economic reality that could not do without interest-bearing loans. In this regard, the development of the British Isles significantly differed from continental Europe. Even as late as 1521, in England, there was confirmed a strict ban on lending money at interest (Bacon 2002, pp. 89–91; Blanchard 1996, pp. 57–73). This would not have been possible on the continent at the time, as credit from large banking houses was commonly used to finance policies of imperial and papal power already in the 15th century.

Major part of Europe of the Late Middle Ages already generally accepted the concept of interest (North 1991) but each state used its political instruments to regulate the maximum interest rate. Demanding an interest rate above the legal limit was severely punished as the forbidden usury but only as long as both parties to the transaction were Christians. In fact, an important part of the credit system of that time was represented by Jewish merchants and bankers whose business activities were not restricted by the standard statutory interest rate but followed different rules.

## Specifics of the economic system of medieval Bohemia

In the second half of the 14th century, the Kingdom of Bohemia was one of the most advanced financial centres in Europe of that time. During the reign of Emperor Charles IV of Luxembourg (1356–1378), the first permanent imperial court in the history of the Holy Roman Empire was established in Prague and Bohemia was a major European exporter of silver. Thanks to these circumstances, Bohemia developed an advanced credit system.

The extraordinary economic and cultural development of this region was disrupted by the deep internal crisis of the Holy Roman Empire at the beginning of the 15th century that resulted in religious wars in Bohemia. These also fundamentally disrupted the development of the domestic economy and severed its connection to international market networks. However, accepting interest at the statutory maximum interest rate remained part of the economic system even in times of crisis. Nonetheless, the most prominent recent publications dealing with the historical evolution of interest rates do not pay attention to this part of Europe (Homer & Sylla 2005, pp. 96–108; Geisst 2013, pp. 58–75). As the situation in Bohemia in the corresponding period represents a certain anomaly in terms of wider European development, I have taken the liberty of summarizing the basic information in this study which may serve well as comparative material.

At the end of the 15th century, during the restoration of the country's economic system in the time of the post-war boom, a prominent Czech lawyer, Professor Viktorin Kornel of Všehrdy (Dean of the Faculty of Arts at Charles University and later an official of the Land Court) created a factual overview of legal regulations. The elaboration was based on the situation of several generations earlier which he reconstructed by studying archival sources. At the same time, he explained how to apply the former legal procedures in view of the recent political instability when the judicial system was not functioning and proper property records were not kept (Jireček 1874, p. 8).

It is clear from this source that in Bohemia at the end of the 15th century, interest was perceived as a normal, long-term accepted and stable part of the country's economic practice with clearly defined rules. For example, for duration of the obligation, if the creditor did not request the payment of interest for a continuous period of 'jural years' (3 years and 18 weeks), the debt was annulled. However, this did not apply during the time when the judicial institutions that could be used to demand the payment of interest did not work. If the creditor applied for a court-mandated freezing and subsequent seizure of part of the debtor's land property, he could claim not only the 'principal amount' (property at the book value of 'one third higher', i.e. 1.5 times the owed amount), but also the unpaid interest. Already at the end of the 15th century, there was a separate register of the so-called 'interest books' at the Land Boards office. These books recorded significant receivables and regular interest payments, and the official entry in the 'interest books' had the same legal power as the land property records in the Land Books (Jireček 1874, pp. 28, 206, 361–2).

The standard interest rate in Bohemia at that time was 10% (Jireček 1874, p. 324). The country's economy adapted to this relatively high interest rate. However, it mainly relied on the development of the internal market and the rapid formation of a dense network of towns and townships controlled by nobility. Until the end of the 15th century, the still-continuing religiously motivated economic blockade of the 'heretical' Bohemia prevented any significant involvement in international trade. On the political level, this situation was exacerbated by the non-confrontational but unambiguous constitutional exclusion of the Bohemian lands from the newly consolidated Roman-German Empire. At the time of the establishment of the Imperial Diet structured by estates' principles (1495), the Bohemian lands were no longer part of this Empire (Vorel 2017a, pp. 184–6).

These circumstances also contributed to deepening the economic isolation of the Kingdom of Bohemia. However, this isolation was paradoxically accompanied by significant economic prosperity. The explanation for this phenomenon is rather complex. It is related to the development of large nobility-administrated manors, weak ruling power, the political system of the so-called Estates Monarchy, and the specific role of Bohemia as the Europe's main silver producing region, up to the advent of mass import of this precious metal into Europe from America in the 1540s (Vorel 2013, pp. 41–62; Vorel 2019a, pp. 52–7).

Another characteristic of the Czech lands was the different structure of land tenure. Except for minor remnants, there was practically no system of feudal hierarchy in relation to the sovereign or among the nobility themselves. Most of the territory consisted of allodial ('free') properties registered in the Land Books, or 'enrolment' properties (mostly medieval royal or ecclesiastical estates). Property rights to the land held by the nobility were thus not restricted by the ruler or the ecclesiastical hierarchy as was the case with hereditary fiefdoms and other forms of legal subordination in Western Europe.

During several decades at the turn of the 15th and 16th centuries, major magnates systematically purchased smaller nobility estates for which they paid not in cash but in issued interest-bearing bonds. For some time, this was beneficial for both parties: a large territorial domain made it possible to introduce new forms of enterprise by the central administration and to increase profit. The former owner of the small estate regularly received high interest payments from his properties and did not have to worry about its management.

Most of the large dominions created in this way were based on an interest-bearing loan. Under the standard conditions, the first half of the annual interest was paid in spring on the name day of St George (5%) and the second half in autumn on the name day of St Gall (5%). This also corresponded to the usual six-month notice period. This system appeared stable as the bonds were collateralised by credible guarantors but, generally, also by the value of the debtor's land properties. Each nobleman could put up a guarantee for his debts only up to the value of his land properties. Any violation of this rule was considered a serious crime. For this reason, the financial chambers of great magnates served as regional financial houses where a large part of the rural nobility deposited their interest-bearing assets.

## Debt of the Royal Chamber

The model described above worked even at a high interest rate, as the country had not been at war for a long time and there was effectively no strong ruling court that would unproductively tap funds from the economy in the form of taxes or forced loans. This significantly changed after 1526 when the Austrian Archduke Ferdinand of Habsburg was elected the King of Bohemia. Czech estates rejected Ferdinand's claims for recognition of the hereditary ruling rights through his wife (sister of the previous King Louis). They insisted on an election because it included the acceptance of an election waiver by the candidate for the throne. This undertaking also included the acceptance of all financial liabilities of the previous rulers in relation to the domestic estates which were secured by pledges of former medieval royal property, property of secularized ecclesiastical institutions, and by the continuous income sources of the ruler including mint revenues and other assets. Although the Lands of the Bohemian Crown were the economically strongest region in the newly established Bohemian-Austro-Hungarian personal union and they were also in a politically safe zone (the Hungarian and Austrian lands were under an imminent threat of invasion by the Ottoman Empire), they yielded only irregular income from ad-hoc tax levies which were, however, subject to the approval of the Land Diet.

From the very beginning of his reign in Bohemia, King Ferdinand tried to change this situation which was disadvantageous for him. Yet the King managed to find one effective tool to force the domestic nobility to pay his expenses. Most of the medieval royal and ecclesiastical properties were held by great magnates but legally, they represented long-term pledges that the king could theoretically redeem. In view of the long-term inflationary development, the difference between the nominal amount of the pledges (determined in the 15th century) and the real value of the dominions at the beginning of the second third of the 16th century was considerable. Therefore, the king enforced money loans in high amounts, especially from great magnates that did not bear interests and were never expected to be repaid by the King. He only continuously 'credited' the loan amount to the original pledge amount up to the real market price of the relevant dominion. Naturally, the King also took into account the real political situation, and he therefore used such economic instruments individually with regard to the position of the specific noblemen within the aristocratic opposition or in the newly emerging power structures at the court.

However, these gradual steps were not sufficient for King Ferdinand to solve the long-term internal indebtedness of the Royal Chamber that he partially 'inherited' from his predecessors on the Bohemian royal throne and partly exacerbated himself. Loans to the Royal Chamber also carried the standard 10% interest meaning that even servicing of the sovereign debt represented considerable costs, although the debt itself was not being repaid.

The prospects of any significant change were fundamentally limited by the financial costs of the war in the Balkans. The defence costs of the rest of the Lands of the Hungarian Crown and the hereditary Austrian lands in the Danube region also absorbed the vast majority of tax revenues from the Bohemian lands. Thus, using a tax instrument to reduce the internal debt was also not an option. At the beginning of the 1540s, the interest rate of 10% was already too high for Czech economy both in terms of the cost of servicing the sovereign debt (which amounted to approximately half a million threescore of Czech groschen) and also for the financial chambers of great magnates.

## Interest rate in Central Europe in the early 1540s

The process of decreasing the maximum tolerated interest rate in Bohemia basically reflected the more general trend observed in Central European economy of the period. Especially in the context of the rapid process of reformation, most German states in the early 1540s were considering the introduction of a lower interest rate in the range of 5–7% (Brady 1996; Geisst 2013, pp. 74–5). By contrast, large South German banking houses maintained an interest rate of 10%, even in terms of financing the Habsburgs (Homer & Sylla 2005, pp. 115–16), as did the Florentine bankers who, at that time, also maintained their usual (10–12%) interest rate (Bruscoli 2009, p. 90). However, in the absence of knowledge of the exact terms of the loans and their collateral, a mere overview of the documented levels of interest rate in 16th-century Europe may seem quite chaotic (Homer & Sylla 2005, pp. 119–20). Nonetheless, the statutory maximum interest rate was legally binding. If someone was willing to lend money at a lower interest rate or interest-free, they were free to do so.

For King Ferdinand, the idea of forced reduction of the maximum interest rate in Bohemia from a 'normal' 10% to a lower level was certainly attractive as he was the country's largest debtor. However, the first step he took in the early 1540s was aimed against Jewish financiers. They were expelled from the Kingdom of Bohemia by the royal decree of November 9, 1541 and this decree was (with a few exceptions) actually enforced. The formal pretext for the expulsion of the entire Jewish population from Bohemia was their alleged participation in starting the fire of Prague Castle in the same year. However, this did not make much sense because the anti-Jewish decree concerned the whole kingdom, not just Prague (Vorel 2005, pp. 147–8).

The Jewish population was granted only a very short period of time to organize their departure from Bohemia, during which they were also supposed to settle their property matters. For the monarch, such an intervention could only have a short-term economic benefit, as long as the expulsion of the Jewish financiers and their families was also accompanied by the amortization of their claims against the Royal Chamber. However, we do not have any specific data on the 'unchristian' interest rate at which it was possible to obtain a loan from the Jewish bankers in Prague at that time.

A certain comparison is provided by the situation in contemporary Rome where Pope Paul III indulged the Jewish business community during the same period but under very harsh economic conditions. The Jewish financiers paid much higher fees than Christian bankers to the papal treasury for legal protection and for the privilege of granting higher-interest loans. In 1543, the twenty 'old' Jewish banking houses that had been active in the city for a long time had their maximum interest rate reduced from 60% to 48%. For the next twenty 'new' Jewish families that extended the financial sector of the papal Rome, the maximum interest rate was set to a significantly lower level of only 30% (Simonsohn 1991, pp. 413–14; Vorel 2017b, pp. 39–44). The temporal link between the exodus of an influential and large group of Jewish financiers from Prague and other Bohemian towns and the growth of their numbers in Rome only a little later (but under less favourable conditions than those of the 'old residents') cannot be supported by material sources for the present but it is a logical assumption.

However, by expelling the Jewish financiers, King Ferdinand deprived himself of the possibility of obtaining flexible loans at a time when he needed them most. Such a situation occurred at the turn of 1541 and 1542 when King Ferdinand, in agreement with his brother Emperor Charles V, tried to organize a campaign of a large Christian army against the Ottoman Empire in the Balkans. The immediate impulse for this action was not only the destruction of the imperial and Spanish fleets off the coast of Algiers, but also the occupation of the capital of the Kingdom of Hungary (nowadays Budapest in Hungary) by the Ottoman army (1541).

From the end of 1541, King Ferdinand sought to convince the Christian rulers of Europe of the necessity of a joint campaign against the Ottoman Empire. The aim was not only to reconquer the capital of Hungary, but all the lands all the way to the south of the Balkan Peninsula. This resonated positively mainly at the Imperial Diet where significant support for the Hungarian campaign was offered to the Habsburgs by the Lutheran princes, associated in the so-called Schmalkaldic League. It was a clear political agreement: Protestant princes and cities in the Roman-German Empire will pay the soldiers to regain Hungary in exchange for a greater leniency of the Habsburgs in religious matters. At that time, an agreement between the Catholic Church and the Lutheran Reformation seemed to be a viable solution to the confessional schism. Therefore, Pope Paul III supported the Hungarian campaign with his own troops. He also announced the long-promised General Council of the Church. This was supposed to start in

Trentino, South Tyrol, already in the autumn of 1542 when everybody would have returned from the supposed victorious campaign against the common confessional adversary.

The Imperial Assembly held at the end of 1541 even approved the financing of the common imperial army but it stipulated the following condition: King Ferdinand was supposed to provide, from his own resources, for another army of nearly the same size. However, King Ferdinand did not have the money to fulfil such task nor did have many options to borrow. To secure the basic needs and pay for the soldiers, he needed at least 100,000 Rhenish guilders in cash. He asked the Bohemian Land Diet for one half; he wanted to get the other half in Austrian countries.

Regarding the economic potential of the Kingdom of Bohemia, the amount of 50,000 guilders was not a major problem. However, the tax system was very cumbersome and it took a long time for the tax to be gradually collected in small amounts from individual taxpayers. Yet, for the purpose of the military campaign, it was necessary to collect the money in a short time and in cash which was not possible without fast lending operations. These could have been arranged by the Jewish financiers who had been expelled from the country by King Ferdinand a few months earlier.

## Technical implementation of interest rate reduction in Bohemia

The entire campaign of the Christian troops to Buda ended in October 1542 in a great disaster and disgrace. The limited scope of this study does not allow me to examine the broader political significance of this unsuccessful military enterprise which has not yet been fully appreciated by European historiography and which I have attempted to interpret elsewhere (Vorel 2019b). However, the negotiations on securing financing for the military campaign in Hungary in 1542 in cash were the main impulse for the subsequent change in the maximum interest rate in Bohemia.

Technically, the change was made as follows:

In the undated royal proposition from the beginning of 1543, the monarch complained, among other things, about the high expenses he incurred with the campaign in 1542. He had to borrow money at a high interest rate that he was due to start repaying soon. Therefore, at the Land Diet that convened on April 30, 1543, he asked for further financial contributions. The Assembly refused to pay the King any money in cash but approved a new tax for the year 1543 in the amount of 1% of all property value. On this occasion on April 30, 1543, the Land Diet decided to reduce the maximum interest rate from 10% to 6%. The record indicates two reasons for this: by this reduction, the Assembly intended to prevent the usual practice whereby a nobleman preferred to sell his estate and to live unproductively on the income from interest yielded by the principal sum. This was assessed by the Assembly as an undesirable social phenomenon that caused other problems. As a second reason, the Assembly stated that the current interest rate in neighbouring countries was already considerably lower. Under the new standards, all loans taken were to be remunerated at only 6% starting from the earliest name day of St Gall (October 16, 1543). In his reply, the King very much welcomed the decree to reduce the maximum interest rate to 6% and stressed the importance of putting this resolution into practice (*Sněmy české*, 1877, pp. 557, 561, 565, 569).

For the majority of the politically active Czech nobility, which at that time consisted mainly of holders of larger estates, the reduction of the maximum interest rate seemed to be very advantageous because most of them were debtors rather than creditors. Like the monarch, they assumed that the economic cycle would continue reducing the costs of servicing their debts and making cheap credit more affordable. However, the consequences of this political decision were much more complex.

## Immediate consequences of the interest rate reduction in 1543

The resolution of the Land Diet of April 30, 1543 to reduce the interest rate from 10% to 6% was implemented immediately. However, on the nearest date when this change was to take effect (October 16, 1543), the existing credit system completely collapsed. Nobody wanted to lend money at the lower interest rate. The creditors terminated the credit agreements *en masse* and demanded the repayment of their assets in cash, as the future development with regard to credit market regulation was uncertain. The ad-hoc general disruption of the cycle of revolving credit contracts constituted an economic catastrophe, especially for great magnates. In most cases, they did not have the liquid funds necessary to repay their old loan contracts, and the failure to meet their financial obligations threatened to result in an official freezing and subsequent seizure of properties of a greater value than the amount of debt to be recovered. In the mid-1540s, several large territorial units thus disintegrated. The most affected person was John of Pernštejn, resident at the Pardubice Castle, the owner of the largest complex of land holdings in Bohemia at that time who, already in 1543, began to gradually sell off his estates to satisfy the creditors.

The collapse of the Bohemian credit market completely changed the sovereign's opinion on the role of the Jewish financiers in the country's economy. The anti-Jewish measures mentioned earlier were abolished in 1545.

The deep credit crisis came unexpectedly fast but did not last long. Its immediate consequences were overshadowed by the problems caused by the drawing of the Bohemian lands into the war between the Habsburgs and the imperial opposition in Germany in 1546–1547. King Ferdinand took advantage of a temporary victory in the Roman-German empire for his goals in Bohemia. Under the pretext of an alleged participation in the Estates Resistance, he carried out a politically and religiously discriminative punishment of the Czech estates that disproportionately impacted royal towns and members of the Unity of the Brethren (Vorel 2015, pp. 193–201). Thus, the year 1547 brought a one-time debt relief for the Royal Chamber: most of the sovereign debts were simply cancelled as a punishment to the creditors for real or alleged participation in the Estates Resistance. By confiscating the land property of the royal towns and that of a part of the aristocratic opposition, the king gained sufficient land for the restoration of his own estates subject to the Royal Chamber.

## Long-term consequences of the interest rate reduction in 1543

The interest rate reduction in 1543 brought one long-term effect: significant growth in market prices of aristocratic land property. The official price of an aristocratic dominion was calculated based on two main items:

The first item was the so-called current income. This was determined as the expected revenue from business activities of the estate administration (fish farming, farmyard business, sheep, production, and sale of beer, etc.). The estimated value of the dominion included ten times the current income, which corresponds exactly to the 'old' interest rate of 10%.

The second part consisted of the so-called fixed income. This was the total value of the obligations of serfs to the nobility based on the possession of properties used by the serfs (rustic tenure). The holders of rustic properties were obliged to semi-annual payments of a specified relatively low amount either in cash or possibly in goods or by physical performance (statute labour). These rights held as assets by the nobility could easily be converted into the corresponding amount in money. The estimated value of the estate then included the annual income calculated in this way at a higher value (twenty times the annual income).

However, the reduction of the interest rate from 10% to 6% brought considerable chaos to this system which had been applied for long decades. After 1543, the model estate apprised the 'old way' yielded much more than its holder would have earned on interest if he had sold the estate and lent the money to someone. Therefore, the market price of the allodial aristocratic dominions rose sharply within a short time. Although neither the amount of the current income nor the fixed income changed, the income of the estate started to be included as a multiple of 15 (current income) and 30 (fixed income).

## Conclusion

In Bohemia at the end of the Middle Ages, the interest rate was one of the items strictly regulated by the state. Due to the specific development in terms of land tenure, whose expansion at the turn of the 15th and 16th centuries was accompanied by frequent capitalization maintaining the constant interest rate of 10%, constituted a long-term stabilizing element that was made possible also by sufficient amount of quality currency on the internal market. A change occurred after 1526 when the demands of the ruling court on the tax and credit system increased significantly. The immediate impetus for the reduction of interest rates was given by the financial problems in need of flexibly securing a large amount of cash to raise an army to fight in Hungary in 1542. The interest rate in Bohemia was reduced to 6% by an unexpected ad-hoc decision of the Land Diet on April 30, 1543. The consequences of this decision became apparent as early as October 1543 when the credit system in Bohemia collapsed. This led to rapid disintegration of many large aristocratic estates whose holders, given the new conditions, were not able to meet all the obligations burdening their land tenures. In the long term, the consequences of this interest rate reduction were reflected in a rapid increase in the formal accounting value of land tenures. This process was not yet related to the consequences of the so-called 'price revolution' that started affecting Central Europe much later.

## References

Bacon, F. (2002). Of usury (1601). In Boyle, D., ed. *The Money Changers (Currency Reform from Aristotle to E-Cash)*. London: Routledge, pp. 89–91.

Blanchard, I. (1996). English Royal Borrowing at Antwerp 1544–1574. In Boone, M. & Prevenier, W. eds., *Public and Private Finances in the Middle Ages (Proceeding of the Colloquium Ghent, May 5th and 6th 1995)*. Studies in Urban, Social, Economic and Political History of the Medieval and Modern low Countries, 4, Leuven, pp. 57–73.

Brady, T. (1996). *Zwischen Gott und Mammon (Protestantische Politik und deutsche Reformation)*. Berlin: Siedler.

Bruscoli, F. G. (2009). *Papal Banking in Renaissance Rome (Benvenuto Olivieri and Paul III, 1534–1549)*. Ashgate: Routledge.

Geisst, Ch. R. (2013). *Beggar Thy Neighbor (A History of Usury and Debt)*. Philadelphia: University of Pennsylvania Press.

Homer, S. & Sylla, R. (2005). *A History of Interest Rates*. Hoboken: Rutgers University Press.

Jireček, H., ed. (1874). *M. Viktorina ze Všehrd O právích Země české knihy devatery*. Praha: Spolek českých právníků "Všehrd".

Kindleberger, Ch. P. (1985). *A Financial History of Western Europe*. London: George Allen et Unwin.

North, M. (1991). Kredit im spätmittelalterlichen und frühneuzeitlichen Europa. *Quellen und Darstellungen zur Hansischen Geschichte*, Bd. 37.

Simonsohn, S. (1991). *The Apostolic See and the Jews VII (History)*. Toronto.

*Sněmy české od léta 1526 až po naši dobu* (1877). Vol. I. (1526–1545). Praha: Královský český zemský výbor.

Vorel, P. (2005). *Velké dějiny zemí Koruny české VII (1526–1618)*. Praha: Paseka.

Vorel, P. (2013). *From the Silver Czech Tolar to a Worldwide Dollar (The Birth of the Dollar and its Journey of Monetary Circulation in Europe and the World from the 16th to the 20th Century).* New York: Columbia University Press.

Vorel, P. (2015). *The War of the Princes: The Bohemian Lands and the Holy Roman Empire 1546–1555.* Santa Helena – California: Helena History Press LLC.

Vorel, P. (2017a). Conditions for the Integration of Central Europe at the End of the Middle Ages (1356–1495). *Comenius – Journal of Euro-American Civilization*, 4, New York: Comenius Academic Club, pp. 173–96.

Vorel, P. (2017b). Funding of the Papal Army's Campaign to Germany during the Schmalkaldic War (Edition of the original accounting documentation 'Conto de la Guerra de Allemagna' kept by the Pope's accountant Peter John Aleotti from June 22, 1546 to September 2, 1547). *Theatrum Historiae*, 21, pp. 9–96.

Vorel, P. (2019a). European merchant trading firms and the export of the precious metals from the Kingdom of Bohemia during the sixteenth century. In McWatters, Ch. S., ed. *Mercantilism, Account Keeping and the Periphery-Core Relationship.* London–New York: Routledge, pp. 49–60.

Vorel, P. (2019b). Habsbursko-osmanské soupeření v Uhrách v kontextu říšských a papežských dějin (Tažení křesťanského vojska k Budínu roku 1542). *Český časopis historický*, 117, pp. 935–91.

# Chapter 15

# Legal regulation of the credit market in Bohemia and Moravia

*Pavla Slavíčková*

## Introduction

As Urfus (1975, p. 45) has already pointed out, the need to regulate the credit markets in the countries of Central Europe most likely became necessary during the 14th century in the context of economic development and outgoing political and social transformation. While the ideas of medieval scholastics regarding the credit market were often far removed from economic reality, increasing business and monetary relations generated the demand for a legal framework. At that time, the law in the countries of Central Europe operated under the principle of legal particularism where different laws applied to different social groups of feudal society, such as nobility, burghers, peasants, clerics, etc., and even to different territorial units (Gábriš 2018, p. 54).

Besides the canon law of the Catholic Church, the *law of the land* consisted of the laws of nobility, the peasant laws that defined the particular rights and obligations of landlords and peasants, the constitutional laws that contained the relationship between the nobles, the monarchs, and the leadership of the state, and the municipal laws that governed the inhabitants of the so-called royal and dowry towns. With this system legal unity did not exist, even within a particular section of law. The body of valid law was formed partly by legal books, by the legislation, and by court judgments in various jurisdictions (Slavíčková 2012). Although there had been several attempts to unify these laws within the countries of Central Europe since medieval times, the process was completed no earlier than the very end of the early modern period. Regulating the credit market was only one part of a long process of codification.

Based on this background, this chapter discusses how the legislature treated the credit market, what the attitude of the law was regarding interest on loans, and how legal opinion evolved during the medieval and early modern periods. Moreover, this chapter describes the differences between particular rights in the Czech lands, it compares the findings with the opinions of the most influential personalities of economic thought of the time and, finally, it considers the influence of foreign law on Czech rights and, vice versa, the influence of Czech law on the legal regulation of the credit market in other countries in Central Europe.

## Early opinions on the credit market

The body of law used in the countries of Central Europe during the Middle Ages was chiefly unwritten. It was based on the legal customs that had been settled upon within a community and were universally recognized, sanctioned, and respected (Gábriš 2018, pp. 53–61). References to the regulation of interest rates on loans can be found in even the oldest of texts such as legends and chronicles. Almost without exception, these ancient sources condemned lending money for interest and considered it a form of usury (Slavíčková 2015, p. 896). In contrast, the later theoretical treatises of the 14th century from the Czech lands made it possible to lend money for profit. This was most likely through the influential thoughts of Thomas Aquinas (1223–1274), as can be seen in the works of Štěpán of Roudnice (around 1300–1365). In the treatise known as *Quaestiunculae* he declared an understanding of trade and associated loans. According to Svoboda (2008, pp. 379–84), these opinions formed the basis for a liberal approach to the credit market that was typical of the High Middle Ages.

The *Maiestas Carolina*, the legal code proposed by the Roman Emperor and Czech King Charles IV in 1350, also allowed cash loans, but only in connection with playing dice, and prohibited all other types of loan, especially those connected with a pledge of personal property (Maiestas Carolina, art. XXXI, p. 190). This code was based both on previous legal customs as well as the *Liber Augustalis* of 1231, the legal code for the Kingdom of Sicily promulgated by Emperor Frederick II. However, due to strong resistance from the nobility, King Charles IV had to withdraw the code and it never came into effect.

Several mixed views of the credit market were included in many early legal texts. The oldest preserved text from the Czech lands is the so-called *Book of Rosenberg* (Brandl 1872). It was written by an unknown author and is a body of noble law that most likely comes from the 13th century. As a reflection of traditional Czech law, it also included the earliest regulation of the credit market; although only in the form of a few brief references. The book mainly describes procedural law as used in the *Territorial Court* (Zemský soud), similar to the *Ordo iudicii terrae* (Palacký 1842), a legal book from the second half of the 14th century. Articles 159 and 210 of the *Book of Rosenberg*, and article 61 of *Ordo iudicii terrae* contained instructions on how to judge the repayment of loans (Brandl 1872, pp. 78–9, 156; Palacký 1842, pp. 108–9). The peak in the evolution of law in the pre-Hussite era featured the *Czech Territorial Law* (Čáda 1930) written by Ondřej of Dubé (around 1320–1412/13). As Marečková points out, his perfect knowledge of Czech procedural law was supplemented by extensive practical experience (Marečková 2006, p. 27). In several articles, Ondřej of Dubé declared that the creditor had the right to recover not only the loan, but also interest from the debtor, and defined the procedures for doing this in court (Čáda 1930, art. 5, 9, 39, 69, 72, 74, and 144, pp. 118–19, 120–2, 138, 148, 149, 150, and 177–8). The articles also included the situation where a debtor could not pay a debt even after the term had been extended three times. In this case, the court could order the seizure of property (Čáda 1930, art. 73, pp. 149–50).

Later, Jan Hus (1369–1415), Czech theologian, philosopher, church reformer, and key predecessor to Czech Protestantism, turned to a more conservative concept of the credit market that was viewed though strong moralism. He relied on the argument that time belongs to God and therefore does not deserve to be sold (Erben 1865, p. 214). He identified many types of trade as usury, not only placing interest on loans, but also pledges of property, adding penalties for delay, and even the resale of goods at increased prices and the sale of unnecessary goods. The only 'proper' business was when a farmer or craftsman sold the goods he produced without profit. According to Jan Hus, this was good business that could be described as pleasing to God (Erben 1865, pp. 127–8).

Thomas Štítný (1333–1401/9) was already urging buyers to run their business with respect to both the common good and the benefit of the people. Those who traded for profit were committing the 'sin of covetousness'. Based on this presumption, he considered money to be sterile; interest should not be taken on a loan (Slavíčková 2015, p. 899). Other adherents of the Hussite movement were of the same opinion, such as Mikuláš of Dresden (d. 1417) and Jakoubek of Stříbro (1371/3–1429). Their treatises known as *De usura* argued for the rule of *sola spes facit usuram*, which is contrary to the later attitudes of other church reformers such as Luther, Calvin, or Zwingli (Urfus 1975, pp. 49–51).

### Regulation of the credit market in the first codifications

The process of legal codification achieved success throughout Central Europe in the 15th and 16th centuries (Slavíčková 2012, pp. 31–3). This happened in the Czech lands after the Hussite Revolution, under the strong influence of the Estate, various especially powerful social groups with different kinds of political rights (Marečková 2006, p. 38). After a long period of resistance, the nobility used the codification of territorial law as a tool to consolidate power under the rule of Vladislav II (1471–1516). The *Territorial Constitution* (Kreuz & Martinovský 2007), approved by the Estates in 1500 and signed by the king two years later, collected constitutional, procedural, administrative, criminal property, and family law provisions. However, it had a non-exclusive character and an inconsistent structure. Even in this legal codification, the regulation of the credit market was not comprehensive. In article 431, the codification explicitly prohibited usury which was defined as an amount in excess of ten out of one hundred borrowed. The usurer was to be punished and the money to go to the state (Kreuz & Martinovský 2007, p. 222). More often, loans and interest were treated in the context of procedural law (art. 117, 118, 167, 315). While the creditor could have asked the court for support in cases when the debtor had not paid the debt properly and in time, the usurer was not entitled to judicial protection (Kreuz & Martinovský 2007, art. 402, p. 213). This article referred to the *Czech Territorial Law* by Ondřej of Dubé, which may be considered a continuation of the content of the private legal books.

The quality and importance of the private legal books can be seen in the books of Viktorín Kornel of Všehrdy (1460–1520). The author was a famous lawyer and humanist, and his book known as the *Nine Books on the Laws of the Czech Lands* (Jireček 1874) represents the most comprehensive publication on Czech territorial law at the end of the 15th and the beginning of the 16th century. Kornel's legal book is a critical discourse of Czech territorial law, supported by exact citations of not only the Czech common and territorial laws, but also the Bible and various works of ancient and medieval philosophers (Marečková 2006, pp. 29–31). It defined the basic requirements for business contracts, ordered the registration of real estate sold as debt, and determined rules for repayment and possible recovery of debt (Jireček 1874, art. 16, 17, pp. 60–7). The increase of debt by interest was considered a matter of course (Jireček 1874, art. 24, pp. 87–91).

The territorial law of the Moravian nobility was included in the legal book written by Ctibor Tovačovský of Cimburk (around 1438–1494) and its amendment by Ctibor Drnovský of Drnovice (d. 1543). The works known as the *Tovačovský Book* (Brandl 1868a) and the *Drnovský Book* (Brandl 1868b) were used in practise at the Moravian territorial court during the 16th century despite the official release of the codification of Moravian territorial law in 1535 and 1562 (Slavíčková 2012, p. 32). Compared to Czech territorial law, the Moravian legal books also contained the full wording of a loan agreement, which, if observed, had the certainty of legal enforceability at the Moravian territorial court (Brandl 1868b, pp. 96–8; Brandl 1868a, pp. 84–5). Significant parts of these books were incorporated in the official codification of Moravian territorial law from 1535 and 1562 (Čáda 1937), together with the older resolution of the territorial parliament and judgments of the territorial court. According to Čáda (1937, p. XXXIII), the resolution of the territorial parliament from 1500 mainly concerned Jews and usury. Based on previous arrangements, the Moravian territorial law accepted loans provided by Jews with a maximum interest of '*two coins out of ten coins*' per year (Čáda 1937, art. 111, p. 123). All such loans had to be made under the supervision and knowledge of the municipal authorities.

Credit business performed by Jews outside of towns was forbidden (Čáda 1937, art. 111, p. 126).

The highlight of the evolution of law in the Czech lands in the early modern period was the *Renewed Territorial Constitution* of 1627 for Bohemia, and 1628 for Moravia (Obnovené zřízení zemské, 1890). This constitution was issued by the Habsburg king Ferdinand II after his victory over the Protestant opposition and brought many fundamental changes to build a bureaucratic and centralized state (Marečková 2006, pp. 66–71). Compared to previous codes and legal books, the *Renewed Territorial Constitution* treated the legal relations of the credit market in a very detailed and systematic way. It ordered forms of procedure for lending money and all its consequences, including protections for the creditor as well as the debtor (Obnovení zřízení zemské, part LXX, and LXXI, pp. 265–73, 273–7). All disputes over debt were to be settled in court. According to article 317, those who did not pay the loan were to be imprisoned; on the other hand, those who falsely accused someone were to be sentenced to death. In the case of several borrowers, they all guaranteed the loan equally. Debts were to be paid in a quality coin and, last but not least, if the creditor lost the contract, he had to witness the existence of the debt (Jireček 1890, pp. 265–73). According to article 349, usury, whether conscious or subconscious, was forbidden. The constitution set 6% as the maximum interest rate. However, usury was defined more broadly. Examples were when someone entered into a contract for a different amount than what was lent, selling goods with undue profit, or lending goods for sale instead of cash (Jireček 1890, pp. 279–89).

The *Renewed Territorial Constitution* reflected the interests of the Catholic monarch and remained valid until 1848. All members of Protestant churches were forced to emigrate and their property was confiscated by the state. This included, among others, John Amos Comenius (1592–1670), who was a philosopher and pedagogue, led several schools, and advised governments across Protestant Europe (Polišenský 1996). His views on the credit market reflected the attitudes of Protestant society and suitably complemented the legislative dimension of the issue. One example is the work called *Letters to Heaven* (Listové do nebe, 1970) from 1619 which was published before Comenius was forced to depart and was intended for the Czech audience. It is a dialogue of Christ with poor people on one side and rich people on the other. The poor complained, inter alia, about a lack of money, high interest rates, and injustice in borrowing money from the rich. According to Comenius, this social inequality should never occur because it is not desirable and the poor should be satisfied with their situation. Moreover, he criticized them for their complaints; they should work hard instead. He encouraged the rich to care for and be kind to the poor (Imrýšek 1970). In his later book *General Consultation on an Improvement of All Things Human* (De rerum humanarum emendatione consultatio catholica) published abroad in

Latin in 1666 (Sedláček 2008), Comenius openly condemned borrowing money, especially from Jews. He claimed that this is not the solution; one was supposed to save rather than lend and to take care of the family rather than property. However, if necessary, lending money had to follow rules and fairness as guaranteed by the state (Sedláček 2008, chapter V). This is an obvious reference to the existing legislative background and a significant advancement compared to the works of medieval authors.

## Obligation and business law in municipal codes

The municipal law in Central Europe was based on the customary law of local communities, mixed with the law of German colonists, and adapted in later developments through statutes enacted by the towns proper (Gábriš 2018, p. 60). The connection between towns based on the system of appellation (the mother town served as appellate instances for filial towns) created a more or less coherent region that followed the law of the leading municipal authority. Three different types (areas) of municipal law could be found in the Czech lands before unification (Hoffmann 1975).

The municipal law of Brno, the capital city of the South Moravian Region, is usually considered the most important for future developments. In its very early history, it was influenced by the privileges of Vienna (Weizsäcker 1953), later it adopted some of the principles of Roman law and also created its own statutes containing both public law norms and private law regulations (Gábriš 2018, p. 84). As Flodr points out, it was especially the law of obligations and business law which underwent the greatest transformation from its origins due to the incorporation of judgments from the municipal courts (Flodr 2001, p. 248). This shows the frequent occurrence of these cases in municipal courts.

The municipal law of Brno divided loans according their origin: *debita ex delicto*, which means unlawful debts awarded to the creditor by the court, and *debita ex contractu*, those based on a contract between creditor and debtor. Further criteria were the amount of the loan (small, medium, large), whether the debtor was a single person or a group, and if the observance was joint or separate (Flodr 1990, art. 128, and 131, pp. 192–4). All these factors were considered by the court when deciding on the procedure to recover the debt. Especially in the case of small debts, the court's decisions were complicated by formal shortcomings in contracts and therefore pressure grew to record loans by official means (Flodr 2001, p. 249).

The law defined a loan as handing over a thing for temporary use. The legal and factual ownership of the thing continued to belong to the creditor. The loan could be money, but also things including real estate or even animals (Flodr 1990, art. 132, p. 194). The loan contract also included a pledge of property called *pignus* or *ipoteca vel pignus*. (Flodr 1990, art. 546, p. 336) It was formed from part of the debtor's assets, both current and future; however, some things were excluded by law such as bed linen, the clothes of the debtor, as well as religious artefacts or stolen items. (Flodr 1990, art. 397, 548, pp. 219, 336) The municipal law of Brno was the first to define an exchange in the market as either the exchange of thing for thing or thing for money, known as *permutatio*. (Flodr 2001, pp. 260–1) A contract could be in verbal or written form and concluded before witnesses. The influence of Roman law on these provisions is obvious, which could be described as a typical feature of municipal law. It adopted not only the main ideas, but also the specific Roman law terminology that eventually became used in daily practice (Boháček 1924).

The main principles of the municipal law of Brno were generalized and compiled in the compendium known as *Manipulus vel directorium iuris civilis*, whose influence exceeded the borders of Moravia and fundamentally influenced the law in Prague. (Slavíčková 2012, p. 21) It was also used in 1534 as the basis for the first failed attempt to codify municipal law in the Czech lands, as well as in 1579 for the more successful draft written by Pavel Kristián of Koldín known as the *Town Privileges of the Kingdom of Bohemia* (Malý 2013). This codification was of very high quality and contained provisions for town administration, duties of the council, property rights, procedural law, obligation law, inheritance law, family law, and a few rights from criminal law. The issues of the credit market and of usury were treated in several chapters. The first, known as *De Venditionibus*, dealt with sales and the different types of markets (Malý 2013, art. G.XXXV–H.XXII, pp. 207–22). A section on loans and pledges of debt followed (Malý 2013, art. H.XXIII–XXXVIII, pp. 222–7). The content of the chapter was mostly based on rules defined by the municipal law of Brno with an even greater inclusion of Roman law together with generalization of its key principles (Skřejpková 2013, p. 712). In this form, *Town Privileges* received subsidiary validity in relation to the *Territorial Law* in the second half of the 17th century and remained in force until the issuance of the *General Civil Code of the Austrian Monarchy* in 1811.

*Town Privileges* was approved by the King and was used as a tool to unify municipal law in all countries belonging to the Kingdom of Bohemia. Towns that followed the *Magdeburg Rights* resisted this unification for long time (Slavíčková 2013). This alternative legal system was found in many parts of Central Europe including North Bohemia with Litoměřice in its centre, and in North Moravia with Olomouc in its centre (Spáčil & Spáčilová 2018). Throughout the existence of these legal islands, close relations with mother cities outside of the Czech lands were maintained, which had Litoměřice aligned with German Magdeburg and Olomouc with Polish Wroclaw (Biedrzycka & Kutylak-Hapanowicz 2007). Yet the provisions of the *Magdeburg Rights* were not incorporated in the *Town Privileges* at all, despite official requests by the councils of these towns (Slavíčková 2013, pp. 48–51). Their proposals in 1571, known as the *Extract of the Main*

*Articles* (Jireček 1883), included rules for lending money. However, most of these articles focused on procedural matters relating to the recovery of outstanding loans before the courts (Jireček 1883, art. 17, 19, 38, 39, pp. 16, 17, 27) and brought nothing new to the issue. The towns in North Bohemia eventually agreed to use the *Town Privileges* and abandoned the *Magdeburg Rights* in 1610. The towns in North Moravia followed them by the end of the 17th century (Slavíčková 2013, pp. 51–3).

## Conclusion

In the early period of customary law, the basic rules of the credit market were already in place. We can see this in the earliest theoretical treatises by authors from the pre-Hussite period, whose views match the content of the oldest legal books. While the law during the Middle Ages focused on procedural rules for the recovery of outstanding loans, the concept of the credit market was defined by the regulatory texts written by theologians such as Jan Hus and his followers. Change came with the first codifications that treated the credit market as an integral part of business law and the laws of obligation. The inclusion of Roman law played an important role and formed the basis of the early modern business law as well as the laws of obligation. The resulting municipal laws found themselves incorporated into foreign legal provisions. The process of development was led by the municipal law of Brno, which had a significant influence on Prague. Despite the long history and development, the regulation of the credit market as contained in the *Magdeburg Rights*, was not taken into account in the unification of municipal law.

The contents of the *Territorial Law* reflected the political and religious changes to the Czech lands in the early modern period. While the *Renewed Territorial Constitution* was open to lending money with interest, Comenius, a member of the Protestant opposition, refused it and recommended more diligence instead. Although he was forced to leave the Czech lands, it seems most likely that neither his opinions nor any other legal regulations of the credit market used in the Czech lands influenced other countries in Central Europe. Although the development of nobility, peasant, and municipal law within the countries of Central Europe was quite similar, as was already shown by Gábriš (Gábriš 2018), the ruling power usually preferred domestic customs. It was the *Magdeburg Rights*, the most widespread legal system used in Central Europe, that was first able to adapt itself to local conditions, but was eventually pushed out. Last but not least, we should mention the territorial law in Upper Silesia, such as the territorial law of the Duchy of Opole and Racibórz, that first adopted the content of Moravian territorial law during the 15th and 16th century (Kapras 1922). However, this was due to the annexation of this territory to the Czech lands after the Hussite wars and it had no effect on future development.

## Funding

The research was funded by the Czech Science Foundation, Grant No 19-07805S.

## References

Biedrzycka, A. & Kutylak-Hapanowicz, A., eds. (2007). *Europejskie maista prawa magdeburskiego. Tradycja, dziedzictwo, identyfikacja*. Kraków: Muzeum Historyczne Miasta Krakowa.

Boháček, M. (1924). *Římské právní prvky v právní knize brněnského písaře Jana*. Prague: Jan Kapras.

Brandl, V., ed. (1868). *Kniha Drnovská*. Brno: Josef Šnaidr.

Brandl, V., ed. (1868). *Kniha Tovačovská, aneb pana Ctibora z Cimburka a z Tovačova Pamět obyčejů, rádů, zvyklostí starodávných a řízení práva zemského v Markrabství Moravském*. Brno: Josef Šnaidr.

Brandl, V., ed. (1872). *Kniha Rožmberská, kritické vydání opatřené poznámkami a glosářem*. Prague: Jednota právníků.

Čáda, F., ed. (1930). *Nejvyššího sudího Království českého Ondřeje z Dubé Práva zemská česká*. Prague: Česká akademie věd a umění.

Čáda, F., ed. (1937). *Zemské zřízení moravské z roku 1535 spolu s tiskem z roku 1562 nově vydaným*. Prague: Česká akademie věd a umění.

Erben, K. J., ed. (1865). *Mistra Jana Husi sebrané spisy české I*. Prague: Bedřich Tempský.

Flodr, M., ed. (1990). *Právní kniha města Brna z poloviny 14. století I. Úvod a edice*. Brno: Archiv města.

Flodr, M. (2001). *Brněnské městské právo*. Brno: Matice moravská.

Gábriš, T. (2018). *Prolegomena to Legal History of East-Central Europe*. Prague: Wolters Kluwer.

Hoffmann, F. (1975). K oblastem českých práv městských. *Studie o rukopisech*, 14, pp. 27–64.

Imrýšek, I., ed. (1970). *Listové do nebe. Jan Amos Komenský*. Nový Jičín: Vlastivědný ústav.

Jireček, H., ed. (1874). *O právích země české knihy devatery M. Viktorina ze Všehrd*. Prague: Všehrd.

Jireček, H., ed. (1883). Extrakt hlavnějších a přednějších artikuluov z práv Sasských anebo Magdburských. In *Spisy právnické o právu českém v XVI-tém století*. Vienna: H. Jireček, pp. 98–147.

Kapras, J. (1922). Zemská zřízení opolsko-ratibořské a těšínské. *Sborník věd právních a státních*, 22, pp. 395–412.

Kreuz, P. & Martinovský, I., eds. (2007). *Vladislavské zřízení zemské a navazující prameny*. Prague: Scriptorium.

Maiestas Carolina (2003). In Bláhová, M. & Mašek, R., eds. *Karel IV. Státnické dílo*. Prague: Karolinum, pp. 153–249.

Malý, K. et al., eds. (2013). *Práva městská Království českého. Edice s komentářem*. Prague: Karolinum.

Marečková, M. (2006). *Czech Legal & Constitutional History*. Prague: Linde.

Palacký, F., ed. (1842). *Řád práva zemského. Latině i česky.* In *Archiv český čili stare písemné památky české I morawské II.* Prague: Stawy Králowstwj Českého, pp. 76–135.

Polišenský, J. (1996). *Komenský, muž labyrintů a naděje.* Prague: Academia.

Sedláček, M., ed. (2008). *Jana Amosa Komenského Všenáprava: Panorthosie.* Brno: Soliton.

Slavíčková, P. (2012). Vývoj městského a zemského práva v českých zemích v předmoderní době. In Slavíčková, P., ed. *Právní ochrana dětí v období prvních kodifikací.* Praha: NLN, pp. 18–35.

Slavíčková, P. (2013). Der Prozess des Untergangs des Sächsisch-Magdeburgischen Rechts im Leitmeritzer und Olmützer Rechtskreis in Böhmen und Mähren. *Zeitschrift für Neuere Rechtsgeschichte,* 35(1/2), pp. 41–54.

Slavíčková, P. (2015). Počátky českého ekonomického myšlení. In Slavíčková, P. & Tomčík, J., eds. *Znalosti pro tržní praxi 2015. Sborník z mezinárodní vědecké konference.* Olomouc: Societas Scientiarum Olomucensis II, pp. 895–902.

Skřejpková, P. (2013). Majetková práva. In Malý, K. et al., eds. *Práv městská Království českého. Edice s komentářem.* Prague: Karolinum, pp. 695–715.

Spáčil, V. & Spáčilová, L. (2018). *České překlady Míšeňské právní knihy.* Olomouc: Memoria.

Svoboda, J. (2008). Štěpán z Roudnice a jeho Quaestiunculae. In Kraft, P., ed. *Sacri canones servandi sunt.* Prague: Historický ústav AV ČR, pp. 379–84.

Urfus, V. (1975). *Právo, úvěr a lichva v minulosti.* Brno: Univerzita J. E. Purkyně.

Weizsäcker, W. (1953). Wien und Brünn in der Stadtrechtsgeschichte. *Zeitschrift der Savigny-Stiftung für Rechtsgeschichte,* 70, pp. 125–58.

# Chapter 16

# The trade in farm money in rural areas in the 16th and 17th centuries (using the example of small towns on the Pardubice estate)

*Tereza Siglová*

## Introduction

The trade in farm money (*gruntovní peníze*) was connected to the exchange of farm holdings and mainly with a specific system of repayments. It was a sale of claims on farm holdings secured in land transfer registers, which were called farm money. When a farm holding was sold, only a part of the market price was paid in cash, the so-called deposit (závdavek), with the remaining amount being paid off using repayments. The farm holder gradually settled the claims of previous owners or their heirs. As a result, as many as five groups of people could have claims on a single farm holding. The practice was the same with inheritances – one of the heirs bought out the shares of the other heirs. The unpaid balances of market prices were often bought and sold. Subjects frequently sold their claims only after a long period of time for a cash sum which amounted to merely a fragment of the original amount (Chocholáč 2007, p. 300; Mainušová 1965, p. 1).

The essence of the sale of farm money meant that a seller sold the farm money to which they had a claim for a specific farm holding. The buyer purchased it for a lower price and expected that, in the future, the whole claimed sum would be repaid. When farm holders bought out the farm money themselves, they could deduct it from the repaid sum as if they had repaid them themselves. In these cases, purchasing farm money could be considered a means to reduce the indebtedness of a farm holding and to pay off the farm more efficiently, that is more quickly and for a lower amount. When the money was bought by a third party, it was primarily a way to invest free financial resources or to save capital with profit. The buyer could expect a gradual return of the invested amount in the future and repayment of the whole sum. There were also rare cases of buyers changing their minds and selling off the purchased money, which could have been profitable.

Farm money was usually purchased for a sum of money and was therefore a type of financial credit with the possibility of solid appreciation of the invested money. The farm money was occasionally paid in kind, for example in livestock, grain, beer or wood. In these cases, it was a form of business credit (Chocholáč 2001, pp. 71nn, 80). On the Pardubice estate, no case of purchasing farm money for labour was found, as is documented on Moravian estates (Chocholáč 2001, p. 81).

I have chosen three small towns for this analysis (Bohdaneč, Dašice and Týnec nad Labem), which were part of the large Pardubice estate in East Bohemia. This estate was situated along the Elbe River and included two large towns, five small towns and approximately 120 villages. From 1560, it belonged to the monarch. The selected towns varied in population size and were evenly distributed across the estate. According to the tax register (*berní rula*), which recorded payers of the tax from tenant farms, after 1650, there were 89 such farm holdings in Bohdaneč, 80 in Dašice, and 46 in Týnec. In Bohdaneč, there were said to be 463 persons excluding small children, with 344 in Dašice, and 175 in Týnec (Siglová 2011, p. 75).

The sale of unpaid farm money was recorded either in orphan books or in land transfer registers (Siglová 2017, p. 230). These sources contain information about the name or the surname of the seller and buyer, about the amount of the bought out sum, and the sum which the seller usually received immediately. The date of the sale is also given.

## The attitude of landlords to the trade in farm money

Judged by a different number of sales of farm money on various estates, not all landlords had the same attitude to this type of transaction. The trade in farm money appeared quite often in records in the orphan books on the Pardubice estate, with approximately one-quarter of farms sold after the death of the tenant holder. On one household, there could even have been several (as many as five) such transactions. Sales of farm money were at least formally approved by the local landlord or estate manager (Vs Pce, bk. no. 302, fol. 318r, 1655; bk. no. 282, fol. 363v, 1579). On the Mělník estate, sales of farm money were not a very common transaction and appeared more often before the Thirty Years' War (Koumar 2010, p. 261). On the Frýdlant estate, the practice of purchasing farm money was not at all common (Štefanová 2009).

The negative attitude of landlords to the selling of farm money resulted from their efforts to protect their own claims to escheat and to prevent the impoverishment of their subjects. The landlords did so from the position of the supreme owners of the land. On the Strážnice estate, the landlord did not intervene in subjects' right of disposal when the sales were within the borders of the estate. Some sales, for example to Jews and guilds, were tied to the consent of the landlord (Mainušová 1965, p. 2). It is clear from the landlord's decrees, orphan books, and land transfer registers that the landlords on the Pardubice estate wanted to have these transactions under control. They primarily aimed to restrict the involvement of their own administrators in this type of trade (Kalousek 1905, pp. 378n). Even though an administrator did occasionally purchase the repayments, this was rare (Vs Pce, bk. no. 327, fol. 80v). The landlords were apparently concerned that the administrators could have misused the disadvantageous position and poverty of the subjects and used buy-out of the money for their own enrichment.

The landlords oversaw the transactions mainly for the protection of orphans' rights and also occasionally cancelled a whole transaction. One of the possible reasons was when the seller sold farm money belonging to somebody else (for example, to stepchildren or siblings) (Vs Pce, bk. no. 336, fol. 27r). Another scenario was when the sum of sold farm money was higher than the rightful claim of the seller which meant that the sold sum was higher than the share of the inheritance to which the seller was entitled. Both these cases caused confusion in the settlement of inheritance claims and due to invalid sales some groups of heirs could have received less than they were entitled to (Vs Pce, bk. no. 336, fol. 460r, 1704). There were also exceptional cases of orphans who abandoned a part of their financial claims for 'social' reasons.

In contrast, the landlord's decrees positively encouraged people to purchase money from people who wanted to sell it because of their poverty or some other reason. The estate manager was also tasked to support purchasing farm money of orphans, whose shares of the inheritance or their parts lay unused in orphan chests (funds) or church endowments (Kalousek 1905, pp. 378n; Černý 1930, p. 90).

## The motivation of buyers and sellers

The most common reasons for sales which are mentioned in orphan books and land transfer registers are only general, such as *'from necessary, important or great need'* or *'out of necessity'*. These references to need were made particularly in the second half of the 17th and at the beginning of the 18th centuries when the buyers were mostly institutions (Vs Pce, bk. no. 336, fol. 155r, 1685; bk. no. 321, fol. 671r, 1657; bk. no. 338, fol. 196r, after 1702).

More specific reasons for selling farm money are found only rarely. Some sellers were motivated by the necessity to obtain cash quickly to cover various expenses and by their own worsening social, health or economic situation. Some sellers needed to get cash quickly to purchase their own farm holding and to pay for related expenses, such as furnishings (Vs Pce, bk. no. 336, fol. 396r, 1692, fol. 213v, 1686; bk. no. 327, fol. 524r, 1657). The owner may have needed the money to repair the buildings on a farm holding (Vs Pce, bk. no. 325, fol. 953v, 1659). Selling farm money may have been connected to providing financial help to a family member, for example a husband (Vs Pce, bk. no. 336, fol. 486v, 1707, fol. 46v, 1688).

Some sellers were motivated by health problems that made them pay for medical care for their relatives or themselves (Vs Pce, bk. no. 336, fol. 474r, 1692; bk. no. 327, fol. 614r, 1704). Their deteriorating health and efforts to provide for themselves in old age were reasons for some people to prefer an immediate cash payment to a long-term repayment (Vs Pce, bk. no. 336, fol. 59r, 1664; bk. no. 327, fol. 430v, 1688). Another circumstance which could have prompted the seller to sell was old age (Vs Pce, bk. no. 327, fol. 568v, 1697).

Social reasons would include cases where a widow decided to sell the farm money in order to provide financial resources for expenses connected to the upbringing and sustenance of orphans (Vs Pce, bk. no. 336, fol. 335r, 1716). Widows were sometimes forced to pay off their late husbands' debts and they evidently needed the consent of the orphans in these situations (Vs Pce, bk. no. 336, fol. 46v, 1692; bk. no. 320, fol. 717r, 1596; bk. no. 285, fol. 70r). The obligation to pay funeral expenses could also have accelerated the sale of farm money (Vs Pce, bk. no. 336, fol. 206v, 1716).

Some sellers sold their money in order to acquire resources for satisfying creditors and repaying debts (Vs Pce, bk. no. 327, fol. 174v, 1659; bk. no. 320, fol. 717r, 1596; bk. no. 336, f. 396r, 1698). Others needed to pay fees and the financial demands of the state (Vs Pce, bk. no. 336, fol 179r, 1719; bk. no. 338, fol. 196r, 1704).

A farm holder occasionally sold farm money on his already repaid farm. He would definitely have been motivated by the need to obtain cash which he could not acquire elsewhere. In this way, the tenant farmer obtained a loan similar to a mortgage (Mainušová 1965, p. 8). The sale could have been a symptom of his economic problems. But even this kind of sale was permitted by the landlord. Some sellers probably decided to sell a part or a whole share because the period for repayment of farm holdings was extended and they had to wait longer to receive their own share of the inheritance. There was also a chance that they would never receive it.

On average, after 1625, the period for repaying orphans or whole groups of heirs increased in the towns being studied. Before that, repaying a group of orphans took almost 22 years but during the Thirty Years' War, it was almost 39 years. This period was not shortened until the beginning of the 18th century when it was more than 42 years. An heir who, as a rule, anticipated that they would be paid their share of an inheritance after many years and who would know the current economic situation of the holder and other circumstances, such as his abilities, preferred to give up their share of an inheritance. For many orphans, it was more acceptable to sell their farm money at a loss and to obtain at least some cash. It was common that a seller gradually sold their share of the inheritance, money inherited from parents or siblings or purchased money depending on how much cash they needed or inherited. The moment the farm money was sold apparently depended on a number of various factors and a seller's individual motives played an important part in the process.

Understanding the motivation of buyers is even more difficult than understanding the sellers, since the records in orphan books do not contain sufficient information. For example, in Podůlšany, these financial activities were related to building a new church instead of the existing chapel and securing financial income for the church endowment.

Some buyers managed to transfer the repayments which they had to pay from their own farm holding, to the farm where they had purchased money. This was a rare situation and it is not clear to what extent these buyers could rely on exchanging the claims of their creditors for their own claims on other farm holdings.

## The extent of the trade in farm money and its buyers

In the 16th and 17th centuries, a total of 737 sales of farm money were recorded in the three small towns of the Pardubice estate. Most of them were made in Bohdaneč (57.5%); in Dašice, it was 30.5% and 11.9% in Týnec. The size and number of farm holdings in each town played an important part in this. The high percentage of sales in Bohdaneč might have been caused by financial possibilities connected to the large output of local beer which was supplied to the part of the estate north of the Elbe River until the beginning of the Thirty Years' War.

In the first half of the 16th century, there were surprisingly few documented sales which was caused by the gradual introduction of the administrative books by the estate and by the fact that in the oldest period many records were made only retrospectively and mutual claims were not registered in detail. Almost a half of the sales was recorded after 1650. It is mainly orphan books which reveal the increasing number of these transactions. The amounts of purchased repayments reached their maximum in the second half of the 17th century when the buyers were mostly holders of the farms whose farm money was purchased. In (myslím, že tam není velké I) land transfer registers, most sales were recorded in the second half of the 16th century. The number of sales decreased afterwards, which was due to the few preserved registers of patrimonial duties. The higher number of recorded sales is also reflected in large amounts of purchased repayments in these periods. The amount of purchased money ranged from one *kopa* (a bag of threescore groschen) to 454 kopas. The highest sums were paid in the last quarter of the 16th century and in the first half of the 17th century.

Three groups of buyers participated in the money trade to varying extents. The first group was holders of the tenant farms whose farm money was purchased. The second one was buyers who did not hold this tenant farm or it was not recorded about them, which means a third party. The last group was institutions. The farm holders predominated after 1650 – from that date, they bought more than half of the farm money sold. The amount of purchased money ranged from 1.33 to 370 kopas and the paid amounts varied from 0.67 to 165 kopas. Buying up farm money became a more common way for tenant farmers to pay off their own farm holdings more quickly and cheaply and it also reduced the indebtedness of tenant farms. It is clear from the records that farm holders had a right of first refusal to buy out farm money, which they did more and more frequently. An institution or a third party buyer purchased the money only after the farm holder refused to do so, either because he did not want to, or because he did not have sufficient cash (Vs Pce, bk. no. 336, fol. 206v, 1710, fol. 337v, 1731, fol. 616r, 1713; bk. no. 327, fol. 167v, 1646, fol. 348r, 1662; bk. no. 282, fol. 574r, 1582).

Institutions participated in about one third of sales, mostly in the last quarter of the 16th century. In general, they bought out larger amounts and on average they had a higher proportion of the purchased sums than of the number of sales. The most common institutions which bought farm money were local towns and villages (in almost half of the cases). Church endowments constituted one third of buyers, but unlike towns and villages, these for the most part were not local. The proportion of towns and villages was larger until 1675, afterwards church endowments started to participate in this trade much more. The growing activity of church endowments was connected to the gradual consolidation of their property in the second half of the 17th century (Pumpr 2010, p. 294nn). It was also supported by landlords who secured the right of first refusal after farm holders. The next institutional creditors were guilds from Bohdaneč, chiefly butchers (9) and tailors (7). The final frequent buyers were found only in Bohdaneč – a literary brotherhood (church choir) (6) and a hospital which surprisingly appeared only once (Vs Pce, bk. no. 319, fol. 79r 1594, fol. 194v, 1591; bk. no. 336, fol. 506v, 1706, fol. 703v, 1692; bk. no. 283, fol. 110r, 1588; bk. no. 279, fol. 207r, 1561).

The share of third-party buyers on the whole decreased, although not evenly. They were represented more strongly between 1551 and 1575 and then between 1601 and 1625. Third parties were later replaced by other groups of buyers who had the right of first refusal, that is by farm holders and probably institutional buyers, mainly church endowments and apparently also towns and villages.

The group of third-party buyers also included orphans for whom the farm money was purchased as a form of appreciation of the cash which had remained on the farm holding after their father's death or of invested orphan money. This practice was supported by landlords who stated in their decree that farm money 'was better purchased for our poor orphans, whose money would have lain in chests otherwise' (Kalousek 1905, p. 378n). Out of 13 cases of purchasing farm money for orphans, only four occurred in the 17th century. The trade in farm money on behalf for orphans in general was certainly bigger. Farm money in surrounding villages was bought for orphans from towns and at the same time farm money in towns was purchased for orphans from villages.

In the group of third-party buyers, there are also individuals for whom purchasing farm money was a strategy for investing or saving surplus cash. In the 16th century, some buyers appeared repeatedly, particularly in the town of Bohdaneč. Some of them were presumably involved in the lucrative brewing of beer which they supplied to inns across a designated area. The profit and cash they made in this way could have been invested afterwards, for example in buying out farm money. However, landlords gradually restricted brewing by the inhabitants of Bohdaneč until it ended completely at the beginning of the Thirty Years' War. Involvement in the trade with demesne fish, which reached far beyond the borders of the estate to approximately 100 km-distant Prague, represented a rather more short-term investment (Vs Pce, bk. no. 315, fol. 64r, 1562).

The profitability of purchasing farm money is reflected in the percentage of purchased money to money paid out in cash. Procházka states that this figure ranged from 15% to 70% of the purchased amount (Procházka 1963, p. 352). On the Strážnice estate at the turn of the 16th century, it was between 8% and 40% (Mainušová 1965, p. 4). On the Pardubice estate, this range was even wider than Procházka suggested – from 11% to 92.7%. Chocholáč indicated that the paid amount was around one third of the purchased sum in several Moravian localities before the Thirty Years' War. Based on an analysis of one locality, this ratio decreased even more after the war, due to the shortage of cash and uncertainty over repaying shares on farm holdings (Chocholáč 1999, p. 128). If the first half of the 16th century is not taken into account, the average percentage of purchased money to money paid out in cash gradually decreased. After 1650, it was common that farm money was purchased for one third of its real value on average. The sample did not prove that this percentage was influenced by the type of buyer or the purchased amount. Judging from the average values, it seems that it was more profitable to sell the farm money to a third party or to relatives who were represented mainly in the group of farm holders. The seller could usually expect a higher share of the sold amount from them than from the other two groups of buyers. Nevertheless, the differences are not significant.

## Conclusion

The trade in farm money was connected to the exchange of farm holdings and mainly to the specific system of repayments. It was a sale of claims on tenant farms guaranteed in the land transfer registers. The seller sold their farm money which they were entitled to on a farm holding. The sellers needed to obtain cash quickly in order to cover various expenses related to worsened social, health, and economic conditions. During the 17th century, they were probably more motivated by prolonging the repayment of farms and by the necessity to wait sometimes even decades to be paid their own share of the inheritance. The sellers therefore preferred to obtain at least a part of their share immediately. Buyers usually purchased farm money for a third of their value. If the buyer was the holder of the farm where the money was purchased, they could deduct the whole amount from the repaid amount as if they had paid it themselves. In other cases, the buyer expected repayment of the whole purchased sum and considered it an investment. The security of claims was tied to regular payment of repayments which was heavily influenced by the economic situation of tenant farms. It can be assumed that during the Thirty Years' War and in the second half of the 17th century the farm holdings had very low reserves and were unstable. Any fluctuations caused by crop failure, death of livestock or other disasters disrupted the economic balance of the farm and made it impossible for tenant farmers to meet their liabilities. This instability was probably a reason why third-party buyers participated less in this trade. It was the third-party buyers and institutions who risked the irretrievability of the investment. In contrast, the number of buyers–farm holders who reduced the indebted-ness of their homestead in this way increased. From this point of view, it seems logical that landlords aimed to oversee these transactions. Landlords supported the practice of farm holders' and institutions' purchasing farm money by invoking their right of first refusal and they also tried to prevent third-party buyers from undertaking risky financial operations.

## References

Černý, V. (1930). *Hospodářské instrukce. Přehled zemědělských dějin v době patrimonijního velkostatku v 15.–19. století.* Praha: Československá Akademie Zemědělská.

Choholáč, B. (2007). Poddaní na venkově. In Chocholáč, B., Borovský, T. & Pumpr, P., eds. *Peníze nervem společnosti. K finančním poměrům na Moravě od poloviny 14. století do počátku 17. století.* Brno: Matice Moravská, pp. 292–336.

Chocholáč, B. (2001). Poddanský úvěr na Moravě v 16. a 17. století. *Český časopis historický*, 99, pp. 59–84.

Chocholáč, B. (1999). *Selské peníze. Sonda do finančního hospodaření poddaných na západní Moravě koncem 16. a v 17. století.* Brno: Matice Moravská.

Kalousek, J., ed. (1905). Instrukce hejtmanská na panstvích komorních, č. 157. In *Řády selské a instrukce hospodářské 1350–1626. Archiv český čili staré písemné památky české i moravské 22.* Praha.

Koumar, J. (2010). *"Má doplaceno a žádnému nic nedluží". Aspekty transakce s poddanskou nemovitostí na mělnickém panství v 17. století.* Dizertační práce, FF UK. Praha.

Mainušová, H. (1965). Obchod gruntovními penězi na strážnickém panství na konci 16. a počátku 17. století. *Ceny, mzdy a měna*, 10, pp. 1–10.

Odehnal, P. (2011). *"Paměť se činí, že se peníze gruntovní pasírují." K hospodaření poddaných na východní Moravě v 17. a na počátku 18. století.* *Východní Morava*, 1, pp. 42–64.

Odehnal, P. (2000). Měšťané a předměšťané klobúčtí (Příspěvek k poznání hospodářských poměrů poddaných na broumovském panství ve druhé polovině 16. století na základě rozboru pozemkových knih. *Časopis Matice moravské,* 119, pp. 45–64.

Procházka, V. (1963). *Česká poddanská nemovitost v pozemkových knihách 16. a 17. století.* Praha: Československá akademie věd.

Pumpr, P. (2010). *Beneficia, záduší a patronát v barokních Čechách (Na příkladu třeboňského panství na přelomu 17. a 18. století).* Brno: Matice Moravská.

Siglová, T. (2011). *Soudové zisku nenesou. Spory obyvatel městeček pardubického panství v 16. a 17. století.* Brno: Matice Moravská.

Siglová, T. (2017). *Úvěr a zadlužení obyvatel městeček pardubického panství v 16. a 17. století.* Pardubice: Univerzita Pardubice.

Štefanová, D. (2009). *Erbschaftspraxis, Besitztransfer und Handlungsspielräume von untertanen in der Gutsherrschaft. Die Herrschaft Frýdlant in Nordböhmen, 1558–1750.* Wien–München: Oldenbourg Wissenschaftsverlag.

Vs Pce. State Regional Archives in Zámrsk, the Pardubice estate (Velkostatek Pardubice).

# Chapter 17

# Investments of a south Bohemian 'banker' in the first half of the 16th century

## The credit operations of Knight Petr Doudlebský of Doudleby

*Tomáš Sterneck*

## Introduction

The boom of the lending business in the early modern Bohemian lands is inseparably connected with the activities of the lower nobility. Knights as lending investors represent an important phenomenon of the economic and political history of Bohemia and Moravia in a period between the middle of the 16th century and the outbreak of the Thirty Years' War, as their activity considerably contributed to the transformation of the social elites of that time.

There are many documented cases when the aristocracy's requirements for self-representation within the spontaneous reception of the new, Renaissance lifestyle led to far-reaching indebtedness and, in more than one case, even to the disintegration of large aristocratic dominions (Ledvinka 1985; Vorel 1998). Skilful knightly entrepreneurs were capable of using client relationships to their nobler patrons to develop lucrative financial deals. Some grew tremendously rich in this manner and used the means to build their own large land complexes, often through the purchase of immovable property from indebted aristocrats. As an illustrative example, we can name members of the knightly family of Malovec of Malovice, who acquired the extensive Hluboká domain in southern Bohemia from the lords of Hradec in the late 16th and early 17th centuries (Bůžek 1989; Bůžek 1996; Maťa 2004).

Another remarkable personage connected with the southern Bohemian milieu is Knight Petr Doudlebský of Doudleby, who developed his own systematic lending business as early as the first half of the 16th century. Doudlebský's activities heralded the behaviour of many later knightly financial entrepreneurs; at the same time, however, his lifestyle was specific or even atypical in many respects. Rather than as an isolated phenomenon, Petr's lending investments need to be studied with regard to his origin, family ties, and personal life, as they conditioned his business to a considerable extent (Sterneck 2004).

## Origin, inheritance, and first business activities

The father of Petr Doudlebský of Doudleby, Diviš (d. 1516), belonged to the large circle of South Bohemian lower nobility that found employment in the services of the leading South Bohemian magnate family, the lords of Rosenberg. He himself worked in the administrative apparatus of the Rosenberg dominion but his precise official function is unknown. Other members of Diviš's generation of the knights of Doudleby were also engaged as officials of the lords of Rosenberg – especially his brother Vilém, who is documented as the burgrave of Český Krumlov in 1479–1483 (SOA Třeboň, rkp. A 22, I. historický kvatern, pp. 169, 180).

Along with Vilém and his other brothers, Petr and Jan (i.e. uncles of our Petr Doudlebský of Doudleby), Diviš granted loans to his aristocratic employers in the 1460s and 1470s. A notary in Rosenberg services unflatteringly describes the brothers as *maledicti usurarii*. When ticking off debt entries in Rosenberg *Libri obligationum*, however, the zealous clerk makes similar caustic glosses also about many other creditors whose behaviour cannot yet be regarded as a targeted lending strategy of later entrepreneurs (Pelikán 1953, pp. 153–4, no. 422).

Diviš left four sons; after Petr, the eldest, came (in the order of birth) Jiřík, Bohuslav, and František Doudlebský of Doudleby. They preliminarily agreed on a property settlement on June 30, 1516; its definitive form was approved by parchment deeds of March 19, 1518. Petr, Bohuslav, and František split among themselves the father's estates east of Soběslav and north of Jindřichův Hradec (the Budislav farmstead with a fortified house and nearby properties), while second-born Jiřík kept the remnants of the family property near České Budějovice including a part of the village of Doudleby, which gave name to the Doudlebský family, and the village of Nedabyle (SOA Třeboň, CR – listiny, z Doudleb 2, 2b, 2c, 3, kart. 6, no. 351–3, 356–8).

A considerable shift in the property situation of Diviš's sons was in the offing, however. Jiřík Doudlebský of Doudleby suddenly died late in 1521 or early in 1522. Even though his younger siblings Bohuslav and František also had inheritance rights to a part of the deceased's property, they waived their claims in favour of their eldest brother. Petr Doudlebský's land possessions were thus suddenly increased by the addition of estates near České Budějovice (SOA Třeboň, CR – listiny, z Doudleb 5, kart. 6, no. 371).

The 1520s were a time of a revived interest in silver-bearing areas near České Budějovice (Kořan & Koutek 1947, p. 15). Petr Doudlebský made use of the fact that land plots inherited from his brother stretched into these areas. Together with Knight Václav Metelský of Feldorf, he asked King Louis Jagellon for a license for precious metal mining near Nedabyle. The sovereign confirmed his consent with the commencement of mining in a privilege of November 4, 1522. For a period of 15 years, the knights did not have to pay fees connected with mining activity to the royal chamber; moreover, they were granted the right of free sale of the yield (SOkA Č. Budějovice, AM ČB – chronologická řada, no. 1522/9). Counting on the approval of their request, the two knights had started to mine silver in the new mine of St Anne before July 22, 1522 (Kalousek 1893, pp. 58–9, no. 1403 and 1405).

Still in the first half of the 1520s, before mining near Nedabyle got fully under way (regrettably, we have no information about its profitability), Petr Doudlebský sold all his property from his brother Jiřík to his partner in the mining business for 900 threescore of Meissen groschen. As he did not want the sale of the silver-bearing land to exclude him from participating in the possible proceeds of the mining, however, he conditioned the sale by retaining a claim to one-half of the prospective profits (SOkA Č. Budějovice, AM ČB – knihy, Kniha konceptů 1538–1550, f. 147r).

## In the services of the lords of Rosenberg

By selling the inheritance from Jiřík, Petr Doudlebský of Doudleby lost the newly acquired estates but gained a considerable amount of ready money while, for a certain period, remaining a partner in Nedabyle mining (he later lost the claim to half of the proceeds from the mining under unclear circumstances). The motivation for his steps in the first half of the 1520s needs to be sought in an effort to create a financial reserve in connection with entering the services of the lords of Rosenberg where Petr is documented from October 16, 1523. His employment in the dominion of the South Bohemian magnates was undoubtedly connected with self-representation costs. It is possible, however, that the knight already linked the perspective of such work with considerations of utilizing new contacts for launching a lending business.

In his first years among the servants of the lords of Rosenberg, Petr was among the group of 'senior courtiers'. He left it on January 1, 1528 to become the burgrave of Český Krumlov, an office in which he is documented until 1531. In 1532–1540, he held the same post at another Rosenberg residence, Třeboň. The knight's career culminated on October 16, 1540, when he became the governor of the Český Krumlov domain – that is, the leading official of the whole Rosenberg dominion at that time. He held this position until his death on March 18, 1550 (SOA Třeboň, CR – registratura, z Rožmberka 10, fasc. I, 1441–1553, ff. 97r, 110r, 118r, 126r and pp. 172–4; SOA Třeboň, rkp. A 22, I. historický kvatern, pp. 170, 171, 183, 219, 223).

An important milestone in the knight's professional life was the death of Peter V of Rosenberg on November 6, 1545. The subsequent guardianship period lasting until May 1551 placed considerable demands on the governor of Český Krumlov. He became a leading member of the official council that took over some powers of the Rosenberg guardians in their absence (Pánek 1989, pp. 42–3). At that time, Doudlebský participated in an effort to economically strengthen the dominion by seeking new financial resources and restricting the expenditures of the Rosenberg chamber as much as possible (Pánek 1985, pp. 18, 20, 32, 34, 36–8, 40, 46–7, 53, 236).

The entering of the services to the lords of Rosenberg introduced Petr Doudlebský to a prominent social milieu, providing the knight with numerous opportunities to establish contacts with a wide circle of noblemen, many of whom needed ready money for various reasons. He made use of the simplified access to potential debtors to commence credit investments.

## Credit investments and their resources

The earliest document of lending activity of Petr Doudlebský of Doudleby is a debenture dated December 6, 1526 with which Linhart Ekhart of Urtvinovice confirms receipt of a loan of 500 threescore of Meissen groschen (SOkA Č. Budějovice, AM ČB – chronologická řada, no. 1526/4). Petr's further credit investments involved members of various knightly families as well as the chambers of the lords Krajíř of Krajk, of Sternberg, of Hradec, of Pernstein, Zajíc of Házmburk, Ungnad of Sunek, of Gutnštejn, Kavka of Říčany – and of Rosenberg. The knight's financial business even outgrew the boundaries of the Bohemian lands, as he found debtors also among members of the Austrian families of the barons of Hohenfeld and the counts of Starhemberg. (SOA Třeboň, CR – registratura, Doudlebští z Doudleb; SOA Třeboň, CR – listiny, z Doudleb 7, 9, kart. 7, no. 409, 423; SOA Třeboň, pobočka Č. Krumlov, VS Č. Krumlov, sign. I 5AE 7a, I 7B gamma 3e).

As initial capital for launching his lending business, Doudlebský could use part of the cash he gained from the sale of the estates from his brother Jiřík. Petr's later investments were undoubtedly also based on further extraordinary income to a considerable extent. His property grew thanks to his siblings also at the beginning of the fifth decennium of the 16th century through inheritance from his youngest brother, František. Having sold his inherited part of the Budislav farmstead, František lived in Soběslav and died childless there in 1540. Among other things, František's estate included a debenture on 600 threescore of Meissen groschen lent to Lady Anna Hradecká of Rožmitál. She repaid this debt to Petr on the holiday of St George in 1544 along with 1,700 threescore she had borrowed directly from him. Later, towards the end of 1547, she borrowed money – this time 400 threescore – from him again (SOA Třeboň, CR – registratura, Doudlebští z Doudleb, no. 7, 10; SOA Třeboň, pobočka Č. Krumlov, VS Č. Krumlov, sign. I 5AE 7a).

Petr's property was considerably augmented by a one-off appreciation of his professional qualities by Peter V of Rosenberg. In his will dated July 8, 1544 in Český Krumlov, he remembered his loyal official with a large bequest of 2,000 threescore of Meissen groschen (SOA Třeboň, CR – listiny, z Rožmberka 27/15a, 27/16, kart. 75, no. 410, 413; NA Praha, Desky zemské, DZV 7, f. H 27).

Petr's mining activities, which did not remain limited to the opening of the mine near Nedabyle, probably also added to his financial potential. While in the service to the south Bohemian magnates, Doudlebský participated in Rosenberg precious metal mining (Pánek 1985, pp. 36–7). He bought the first mining shares as early as the 1520s, at the time of the greatest boom of mining activity near Český Krumlov. He further extended his activities in this field later, having invested in many mines in the wider neighbourhood of Český Krumlov and near Kamenný Újezd in the 1540s. Since the mid-40s, he financed above all the mine he had founded himself. Although period sources do not allow us to assess the return on these investments in a complex manner, they probably also played a part in the knight's property rise (SOA Třeboň, pobočka Č. Krumlov, VS Č. Krumlov, sign. I 7B gamma 3e).

## Regular income structure

Regular incomes of Petr Doudlebský of Doudleby can be divided into three basic categories: land rents from Land-Table estates, the salary paid to him from the Rosenberg chamber and, finally, interest profits. It was especially the numerous entries in the last category that prompted the knight to keep running records of his incomes. Registers in his own hand of the incomes expected on the individual accounting dates (St George and St Gall of each year) with additional marks denoting paid off receivables are preserved for 1546–1549. In other, occasionally made, records, Doudlebský registered the principals of the loans along with the names of debtors and other information about his property (SOA Třeboň, pobočka Č. Krumlov, VS Č. Krumlov, sign. I 5AE 7a, I 7B gamma 3e).

These sources make it possible to study the structure of Petr Doudlebský's incomes and the development of the value of his debentures in the last years of his life. On the other hand, we are lacking a more complex overview of the knight's expenditures, apart from those that were a direct part of his business activities. A certain part of Petr's incomes must have necessarily been paid in various taxes. Naturally, his expenses included payment for ordinary life necessities as well as the costs of his household and self-representation.

The table shows that Petr's regular income from land rents dropped by almost a third between 1547 and 1548. The amount of the salary paid out to the Český Krumlov governor from the Rosenberg chamber was stable in 1546–1549. On the contrary, a steep increase in regular incomes from the lending business is visible during the very brief period preceding his death: on St George's in 1546, he was to receive 255 threescore and 54 Meissen groschen from his debtors; as of St Gall 1546 and on both dates in 1547, it was already 297 threescore and 54 groschen and in 1548, 315 threescore and 54 groschen on St George's and 333 threescore and 54 groschen on St Gall's.

Table 17.1 Basic categories of the regular income of Petr Doudlebský of Doudleby in 1546–1549 – amounts and relations

| Year | Date | Incomes (in Meissen groschen; thr. = threescore, gr. = groschen) | | | |
|------|------|-----------|--------|-------------------|-------|
| | | Land rents | Salary | Interests claimed | Total |
| 1546 | George | ? | 20 thr. | 255 thr. 54 gr. | ? |
| | | ?% | ?% | ?% | |
| | Gall | 32 thr. 6 gr. | 20 thr. | 297 thr. 54 gr. | 350 thr. |
| | | 9.171% | 5.714% | 85.114% | |
| 1547 | George | 32 thr. 6 gr. | 20 thr. | 297 thr. 54 gr. | 350 thr. |
| | | 9.171% | 5.714% | 85.114% | |
| | Gall | 32 thr. | 20 thr. | 297 thr. 54 gr. | 349 thr. 54 gr. |
| | | 9.145% | 5.716% | 85.139% | |
| 1548 | George | 23 thr. 47 gr.[1] | 20 thr. | 315 thr. 54 gr. | 359 thr. 41 gr. |
| | | 6.612% | 5.560% | 87.827% | |
| | Gall | 87 thr. (*) | 20 thr. | 333 thr. 54 gr. | 440 thr. 54 gr. (*) |
| | | 19.732% | 4.536% | 75.731% | |
| 1549 | George | 89 thr. (*) | 20 thr. | 327 thr. 54 gr. | 436 thr. 54 gr. (*) |
| | | 20.371% | 4.578% | 75.051% | |
| | Gall | 22 thr. 39 gr.[2] | 20 thr. | 442 thr. 54 gr. | 485 thr. 33 gr. |
| | | 4.665% | 4.119% | 91.216% | |

Notes:

1) For this date, we also have separately quantified the amount of tax money Doudlebský was to take over from his peasants: 11 threescore and 54½ groschen.

2) The claim of 24 threescore and 11 groschen was reduced by 1 threescore and 32 groschen from peasants whose homesteads had been damaged by fire.

The sums denoted (*) include other entries added to land rents and not falling into the knight's regular incomes. Apart from land rents, the amounts in question include also tax money Doudlebský collected from his peasants and delivered to tax collectors under his name.

After Anna Rožmberská of Rogendorf repaid 200 threescore of Meissen groschen, the knight's interest profit slightly deceased to 327 threescore and 54 groschen as of St George 1549. However, subsequent investments in loans totalling 2,300 threescore of Meissen groschen to Austrian noblemen considerably increased the source of Petr's income under study. On the last accounting date of his life, St Gall in 1549, Doudlebský was to receive 442 threescore and 54 groschen in interests.

We need to point out, however, that while the amounts from land rents and the salary usually arrived on time, the interest profits of Petr Doudlebský of Doudleby suffered from frequent delays of the individual instalments sometimes even stretching over several accounting dates. Petr was therefore forced to send the debtors reminders of interests; some arrears for the last accounting dates even had to be collected by his heirs (SOA Třeboň, CR – listiny, z Doudleb 9, kart. 7, no. 423; SOA Třeboň, CR – registratura, Doudlebští z Doudleb, no. 6, 7, 20).

Profit from the lending business was by far the knight's most important regular income in 1546–1549. Even with the delays of some of the instalments, the total of the interests received well exceeded Petr's land rents and service salary combined. Until St Gall of 1547 inclusive, the salary reached less than two-thirds of the value of the income from his peasants. Then (based on dates for which we know the incomes not distorted by the inclusion of other entries) the income from land rents dropped almost to the level of the salary, which nevertheless remained the knight's lowest income. Regular incomes from the Rosenberg chamber, thus did not play a more considerable part in the extension of Petr's fortune. We know, however, that it was the service to the South Bohemian magnates that brought Doudlebský to the prominent social milieu, which provided ideal opportunities for the development of his business activities.

## Value of debentures

A precondition for the steep increase in Petr Doudlebský of Doudleby's interest revenue was a fundamental rise in the amount invested in the loans. Petr's capital in debentures rose from 6,810 threescore of Meissen groschen as of St George in 1546 to 11,710 threescore of Meissen groschen as of St Gall in 1549; the increase amounted to 4,900 threescore, or 71.95% of the initial amount. The knight's lending business thus reached an astonishing volume, with debentures becoming clearly the most important part of his property. The repayment of the principal by some of the debtors did not reduce the value of the debentures for long, as Petr strove to quickly re-invest the money. If he momentarily lacked ready money when concluding new credit deals, Petr did not hesitate to borrow the needed sum himself for a short time (SOA Třeboň, pobočka Č. Krumlov, VS Č. Krumlov, sign. I 5AE 7a; SOA Třeboň, CR – registratura, Doudlebští z Doudleb, no. 13, 16).

Petr's strategy concerning the profitability of the particular receivables deserves attention. The regulations concerning credit operations in the lands of the Bohemian Crown underwent an important change in 1543, as the legal annual interest rate was reduced from 10% to 6% (Gindely & Dvorský 1877, pp. 565–6, 569, no. 309, 310; Ledvinka 1985, pp. 28–35). While receivables based on his earlier credit investments continued bearing Doudlebský the contractually fixed 'higher interest', with new loans in the Bohemian lands, he was already bound by the lower, 6% interest. Towards the end of his life, however, Petr found a way of circumventing the interest rate reduction in the form of new high loans to Austrian noblemen. On the holiday of St George in 1549, he lent 1,300 threescore of Meissen groschen to Jerome and Paul James of Starhemberg and doubled an earlier loan of 1,000 threescore to Christopher of Hohenfeld – all with 10% interest (SOA Třeboň, pobočka Č. Krumlov, VS Č. Krumlov, sign. I 5AE 7a; SOA Třeboň, CR – registratura, Doudlebští z Doudleb, no. 18, 20).

*Table 17.2* Value of interest-bearing receivables of Petr Doudlebský of Doudleby in 1546–1550

| Year | 1546 | | 1547 | | 1548 | | 1549 | | Inheritance to divide 30/6/1550 |
|---|---|---|---|---|---|---|---|---|---|
| Date | St George | St Gall | St George | St Gall | St George | St Gall | St George | St Gall | |
| Amount lent out (in threescore of Meissen groschen) | 6,810 | 8,410 | 8,410 | 8,410 | 9,010 | 9,610 | 9,410 | 11,710 | 11,330 |
| Change against previous date | – | +1,600 | 0 | 0 | +600 | +600 | –200 | +2,300 | –380 |

The comparison of the value of Petr Doudlebský's credit investments in 1546–1549 with his income at that time shows that the newly lent amount could not by far have been covered by his regular incomes, especially as he financed his mining business as well. The same is undoubtedly true also of his earlier credit operations before 1546. We have said already that Petr relied on other, extraordinary sources of money. Without them, his lending business would have not grown into its gigantic dimensions, even with repeated reinvestment of the interest profits. Apart from means gained from inheritance and the money received in connection with his employment in Rosenberg services (besides the regular remuneration), the knight's extraordinary incomes probably included also yields from precious metal mining. One more source needs to be added to those mentioned above, however: a continuous rearrangement of Petr's property from immovable to movable.

## Immovable property

The core of Petr Doudlebský of Doudleby's land possessions was his portion of the inheritance of his father's estates. To this Land-Table property, Petr added – we do not know when – a part of a nearby village. The knight's subsequent activity concerning land property, however, already had the form of a reduction in favour of the accumulation of financial means. Apart from the aforementioned sale of family possessions near České Budějovice acquired after the death of brother Jiřík, Petr gradually divested himself also of properties east of Soběslav and north of Jindřichův Hradec. We have written documents of that until 1539 (SOA Třeboň, CS – listiny, Budislav

II-70–1, kart. 17, no. 114; SOA Třeboň, CS – registratura, II-30A-1, kart. 101, no. 24; NA Praha, Desky zemské, DZV 8, f. A 3; Sedláček 1885, p. 92).

Further reduction of Petr's land possessions can only be followed indirectly, through sources testifying to the decline in its valuation and to the reduction of land rents he received from his estates (Sterneck 2004, pp. 278–82). Even so, it is evident that rather than building his own domain, Doudlebský preferred capital investments, not hesitating to partially cover them by the sale of real property.

Petr Doudlebský made valuations or lists of his assets for his own needs. In some of these records, he quantified the market value of some of his Land-Table estates using the method common at that time, that is the multiplication of their annual revenue by a corresponding capitalization coefficient (Kostlán 1986). Based on these sources, we can state that the market value of the knight's Land-Table property in 1543–1546 amounted at least to 2,679 threescore and 30 Meissen groschen. Between 1546 and 1547, it dropped to approximately 2,285 threescore and 35 groschen and on the accounting date of St Gall in 1547, it only amounted to 2,000 threescore.

In a private property valuation from the last months of his life, Doudlebský divided his assets into two categories and quantified the value of each of them separately. He counted ready money and invested capital worth 11,515 threescore of Meissen groschen, while his Land-Table property and the equipment of his household were worth 3,350 threescore according to his valuation (SOA Třeboň, pobočka Č. Krumlov, VS Č. Krumlov, sign. I 5AE 7a). Preserved inventories of Petr's inheritance show that it included various articles of daily use as well as of luxury character – clothing, bed linen, cook- and tableware, tools, weapons, hunting, bird trapping and fishing equipment, furs as well as jewellery (Sterneck 2004, pp. 296–308, 316–23, 329–32). The value of the knight's real property evidently did not increase since the end of 1547. The total estimate of 14,865 threescore of Meissen groschen can be regarded as a reliable quantification of the value of Petr Doudlebský of Doudleby's fortune near the end of his life.

## Rich old bachelor and his bequest

On the absolute level, 16th-century property estimates made for the purposes of taxation need to be taken with reserve. With a certain level of caution, however, they can be used as indicators of property proportionality of tax payers (Míka 1967; Sterneck 2006, pp. 10, 187, 221–3). According to a preserved list for the Bechyně Region in 1523, the tax estimate of Petr Doudlebský of Doudleby's own property was 2,000 threescore of Meissen groschen (the knight did not show any land rent property at that time). He probably had 900 threescore from the sale of the estates from his brother Jiřík at his disposal already but it did not reflect in the valuation because it had not been invested in loans as yet. Even so, a comparison with the assessments of other payers from among the lower nobility indicates that, at that time, Doudlebský was one of the less affluent knights in the region (Bůžek 1985, p. 79). In 1543, however, Petr's *dominicalis* property was valued at 5,940 threescore of Meissen groschen for tax purposes, and his peasants' property at 630 threescore. By that time, the invested capital certainly already comprised a considerable part of the knight's own property (Sterneck 2004, pp. 287–8).

Regrettably, we do not know the property proportionality of the lower nobility in the Bechyně Region at the very end of the first half of the 16th century. As regards Petr Doudlebský, the (solitarily recorded) tax valuation of his property as of 1543 is not followed by any other we would have at our disposal. Let us call to mind, however, the reliable estimate of his property Petr made for his own needs in the last months of his life. An absolute majority of the total of 14,865 threescore of Meissen groschen was covered by the value of debentures and land possessions (c. 13,650 threescore), that is of regularly taxed parts of property. In view of the temporally closest preserved earlier and later tax sources depicting payers in the Bechyně Region (from 1523 and 1557), we can say that towards the end of his life, Doudlebský was among the property elite of the knighthood (not only) in this region (Placht 1950, pp. 24–32, 81–4).

Petr Doudlebský did not start his own family; he never married and probably had no illegitimate children, either. He therefore faced the question of to whom he would bequeath his considerable fortune. King Ferdinand I of Habsburg complied with the knight's application for the right to freely make his last will on June 7, 1536. In a testament drawn up in Český Krumlov on January 28, 1547, Petr established two groups of heirs between which his estate was to be divided after his death. He bequeathed half of his property to William and Peter Vok of Rosenberg, minor sons of Jobst III of Rosenberg (d. 1539), and the other half to his own relatives, Diviš and Fridrich Doudlebský of Doudleby. Before the division of the inheritance, however, William and Peter Vok of Rosenberg as well as their three unmarried sisters were to receive a hundred threescore each for gold chains in memory of the Český Krumlov governor (SOA Třeboň, CR – listiny, z Doudleb 6, 8, kart. 7, no. 394, 414; NA Praha, Salbuchy, Majestalia 283, f. 110v; SOA Třeboň, CR – listiny, z Rožmberka 27/17, kart. 75, no. 415).

Petr died on March 18, 1550 at Český Krumlov Castle. His last will was registered in the Land Tables on April 23, and the division of his estate took place in several stages by the summer of that year. Lady Anna Rožmberská of Rogendorf gained numerous garments, textile, furs, and other items within the framework of the settlement, and some of Petr's weapons were ceded to the Rosenberg armoury (NA Praha, Desky zemské, DZV 9, ff. E 16–17; SOA Třeboň, CR – listiny, z Doudleb 9, kart. 7, no. 423; SOA Třeboň, pobočka Č. Krumlov, VS Č. Krumlov, sign. I 5AE 7a).

The heirs did not retain Petr Doudlebský's Land-Table estates. On May 12, 1551, William of Rosenberg, acting also on behalf of his younger brother Peter Vok, together with Diviš and Fridrich Doudlebský of Doudleby, sold them for 1,940 threescore of Meissen groschen (SOA Třeboň, CS – listiny, Katov II-195-1, II-195-2, kart. 48, no. 342, 343; NA Praha, Desky zemské, DZV 16, f. C 12; DZV 49, f. D 27; DZSt 45, f. E 21). As for the deceased's debentures, documents are preserved of inheritance claims made to the relevant receivables (SOA Třeboň, CR – registratura, Doudlebští z Doudleb, no. 20). The heirs used the respectable fortune of the deceased knight above all to strengthen their financial potential.

## Conclusion

Petr Doudlebský of Doudleby could base his property rise on capital inherited from his forebears and on economically favourable circumstances under which he started his career in the service of the Rosenbergs. Later, he also repeatedly enriched himself thanks to good fortune rather than his own merit. However, he was always capable of making perfect use of his luck for business activities in which he found a resource for another, systematic augmentation of his property. His motivation demonstrably did not lie in an outlook of building his own extensive knightly domain or in an effort to secure his offspring. Next to Petr's generous investments, however, we can see manifestations of his excessive parsimoniousness in relation to minor amounts. Several preserved documents prove his unwillingness in the fulfilment of his financial obligations towards persons standing on lower levels of the social ladder (SOA Třeboň, pobočka Č. Krumlov, VS Č. Krumlov, sign. I 5AE 7a).

The unmarried and childless knight found a home in the proximity of his aristocratic employers, the lords of Rosenberg, whom he served in a loyal and model manner. The main content of his bachelor life, however, was diligent 'multiplication' of money, not only through efficient large-scale lending investments but also on the level of petty skimping (bordering on ludicrousness in the context of his large financial transactions). It was from this contradictory and somewhat curious background that one of the pioneers of systematic lending business of the Bohemian lower nobility grew in the early modern period.

## References

### Archival sources

NA – Národní archiv Praha.
SOA – Státní oblastní archiv Třeboň.
SOkA – Státní okresní archiv Č. Budějovice.

## Literature

Bůžek, V. (1985). Majetkové rozvrstvení stavů Bechyňského kraje v letech 1523–1557 (Edice berního rejstříku Bechyňska z roku 1523). *Hospodářské dějiny*, 13, pp. 65–87.

Bůžek, V. (1989). *Úvěrové podnikání nižší šlechty v předbělohorských Čechách*. Praha: Ústav československých a světových dějin ČSAV.

Bůžek, V. (1996). *Nižší šlechta v politickém systému a kultuře předbělohorských Čech*. Praha: Historický ústav AV ČR.

Gindely, A. & Dvorský, F., eds. (1877). *Sněmy české od léta 1526 až po naši dobu I. 1526–1545*. Praha: Královský český zemský výbor.

Kalousek, J., ed. (1893), *Archiv český čili Staré písemné památky české i moravské, sebrané z archivů domácích i cizích XII*. Praha: Bursík & Kohout.

Kořan, J. & Koutek, J. (1947). *Rudní ložiska v oblasti rudolfovské a jejich dějiny*. Praha: Státní geologický ústav ČSR.

Kostlán, A. (1986). K rozsahu poddanských povinností od 15. do první poloviny 17. století ve světle odhadů a cen feudální držby. *Folia Historica Bohemica*, 10, pp. 205–48.

Ledvinka, V. (1985). *Úvěr a zadlužení feudálního velkostatku v předbělohorských Čechách. Finanční hospodaření pánů z Hradce 1560–1596*. Praha: Ústav československých a světových dějin ČSAV.

Maťa, P. (2004). *Svět české aristokracie (1500–1700)*. Praha: Nakladatelství Lidové noviny.

Míka, A. (1967). Majetkové rozvrstvení české šlechty v předbělohorském období. *Sborník historický*, 15, pp. 45–75.

Pánek, J. (1989). *Poslední Rožmberkové. Velmoži české renesance*. Praha: Panorama.

Pánek, J., ed. (1985). *Václav Březan: Životy posledních Rožmberků I*. Praha: Svoboda.

Pelikán, J., ed. (1953). *Rožmberské dluhopisy z let 1457–1481*. Praha: Nakladatelství ČSAV.

Placht, O., ed. (1950). *Odhad majetku stavů království českého z r. 1557*. Praha: Královská česká společnosti nauk.

Sedláček, A. (1885). *Hrady, zámky a tvrze království Českého IV. Vysočina Táborská*. Praha: Knihtiskárna Františka Šimáčka.

Sterneck, T. (2004). K majetkovému zázemí a domácnosti rytíře Petra Doudlebského z Doudleb. *Husitský Tábor*, 14, pp. 259–362.

Sterneck, T. (2006). *Město, válka a daně. Brno v moravském berním systému za dlouhé války s Vysokou Portou (1593–1606)*. Praha: Historický ústav AV ČR.

Vorel, P. (1998). Úvěr, peníze a finanční transakce české a moravské aristokracie při cestách do zahraničí v polovině 16. století. *Český časopis historický*, 96(4), pp. 754–78.

# Chapter 18

# The Lithuanian Evangelical Reformed Church as a credit institution in the 17th century

*Marzena Liedke and Piotr Guzowski*

## Introduction

As for present-day discussions on economic development, religion constitutes an important institution (Acemoglu & Robinson 2012; Rubin 2017). Protestantism, in this context, is of particular importance (Becker, Pfaff & Rubin 2016) as a significant element explaining differences between regions in Europe (van Zanden et al. 2012). Max Weber pointed it out in his well-known work *The Protestant Ethic and the Spirit of Capitalism* (2005) that Protestant theologians (in comparison with the Catholic Church) developed different attitudes towards the role of usury, work, and profit.

The aforementioned theses became arguments in the discussion aiming at answering the general question, if the changes in Christianity affected forming capitalism as a dominating economic system, or the economic transformations at the end of the Middle Ages and the beginning of the modern era affected the new religious currents.

In this discussion, so far, there has quite seldom been taken up an attempt to study activities of economic institutions of religious nature, functioning in religiously differentiated communities. Researchers try to compare countries dominated by reformed denominations with Catholic regions and if someone takes up studies including religiously complicated political structures, they do it with econometric methods using models which considerably simplify the historical past and consider phenomena in the macro scale (Nunziata & Rocco 2018). However, it is worth considering what signs of Weber's protestant ethic can be traced in societies of diverse denominational composition in their day-to-day functioning. To what extent can we observe the ethic described by Weber in the countries where the Protestants made up a minority and had to adapt themselves to the socio-economic circumstances where other Christian denominations dominated? An example of such a country is the Polish-Lithuanian Commonwealth (hereinafter: PLC) where basically existed freedom of religion, although not all religions or denominations enjoyed the same social status. In political sense, as well as regarding the number of followers, the Catholic Church dominated but, in various regions of the country, denominations prevailing in the population were Lutherans (Pomerania), the Orthodox or the Uniates (Ukrainian lands, most of the territory of the Grand Duchy of Lithuania). An important element of the religious landscape was a very numerous Jewish minority settling all over the country.

Among Protestant denominations of the PLC, representatives of the Evangelical Reformed Church were of particular importance. They were not numerous but followers of this branch of Protestantism were representatives of the noble elite or, as in the case of the Grand Duchy of Lithuania (hereinafter: GDL), also the wealthiest magnates: mainly the members of the extremely politically and economically powerful Radziwiłł family (whose members used the title of dukes) who protected and financially supported the Evangelicals.

The Evangelical Reformed Church in GDL (called Jednota) was organized within a synodal-presbyterian system, with the provincial synod as the principal authority, consisting of clergy and lay members of the community. For most of the 17th century, the provincial synod of the Lithuanian Calvinists gathered every year in Vilna and was attended by representatives of ca 110 parishes. The highest position in the clergy hierarchy occupied the so-called superintendents who supervised particular districts grouping a few parishes. The Jednota was organized in six districts: Vilnian, Zawilejski, Samogitian, Novogrodek, Ruthenian, and Podlasie. The *actor*, that is a lay officially responsible for legal, administrative, and financial management of the whole Calvinist community was of almost equally high importance.

## The aim and sources

The objective of this chapter is an attempt to present the results of a search for Weber's capitalist protestant ethic in the credit activities of the Calvinist Church in the GDL.

Financial settlements presented to the Synod annually by *actor*, bills and acts of provincial synods themselves constitute a source basis for this chapter (Akta synodów, 1915; Akta synodów, 2011; LLAS, f. 40, man. 1136). The latter show that economic problems concerned the Evangelical elite no less than theological or disciplinary questions. Nearly a half of canons referred to financial and economic questions and, in 1642, it was explicitly said 'That bills are *anima* of all affairs discussed at the Synod' (LLAS, f. 40, man. 1136, p. 48). Two financial documents were also analysed in more detail: to the canons of 1668 of the Vilna provincial synod, the register called 'District sums of the churches of the GDL' was added, containing data from four districts: Samogitian, Novogrodek, Zawilejski, and Ruthenian (LLAS, f. 40, man. 1136, pp. 303–6); therefore, another document called 'Sums of the Vilna district' of 1674 is an important supplement to our knowledge (LLAS, f. 40, man. 168, k. 59). Although we do not have data for the sixth district in the framework of the Jednota – Podlasie, we may outline a general financial situation of the Calvinist Church in the GDL.

## The Calvinists' approach to usury

Although Weber himself in his book did not start a large discussion on usury and credit (Kaelber 2007, pp. 59–86), he mentioned, as a side note, Calvin's little more liberal attitude towards the problem (Weber 2005, p. 149, note 29). The followers of his studies often underscored the significance of the turn in this matter which had taken place in the Geneva community. The progressing commercialization of economy required evolution in the moral assessment of banking. The Catholic Church throughout the Middle Ages was not able to cope with the problem of usury and despite the theoretically clearly negative attitude towards it, from the days of Thomas Aquinas onwards, there always remained a certain margin for free interpretation which enabled banking activities (Wood 2004). Lithuanian Evangelicals also dealt with a similar problem.

Protestants gathered in 1621 at the synod of Vilna expressed their opinion in the canon 'On Usurers': 'It is certain that any usury is prohibited in the Word of God, and it does not become a Christian man to deal therewith; on the contrary, he should help his neighbor in need with his property and goods…' (Akta synodów, 1915, p. 62). This statement shows an attempt to maintain the tradition, characteristic of all Christianity, of condemning usury activities, and simultaneously a will to leave a way out enabling running necessary lending activity which was visible in the views of Calvin (Schultze 2000, pp. 198–211; Kerridge 2002). Calvin's seemingly precise guidelines left, however, much room for interpretation and the criteria of just profit did not have to be readable for an average follower of Reformation views in other countries. Members of the Polish-Lithuanian protestant community realized that economic life without credit would not have been possible, hence the synod did not reject the credit activity completely but only imposed certain restrictions. A potential moral dilemma of the Evangelicals was to be solved by a clergyman.

## The financial situation of the Jednota in the 17th century

Over the 17th century, the situation of the Evangelical Reformed Church in the PLC worsened along with the political and demographic situation. The counter-Reformation action resulted in taking over Calvinist temples, especially those which used to be Catholic churches. The Catholics also took churches built from scratch which were located in the estates of their patrons who decided to convert into Catholicism. Those processes naturally resulted in the deterioration of the financial situation of the Lithuanian

Calvinist religious community. Therefore, affairs connected with the material functioning of the Jednota had to take quite a great deal of time during the debates of provincial synods.

The material and financial basis of the Jednota in the GDL were private foundations of churches, as well as material and financial legacies. Among the latter, there occurred land estates and urban immovable properties, and also smaller donations in the form of money or silver and gold items. A certain variety of such donations was fundraising (*kolekta*) among the faithful, initiated in synods and organized in particular intentions or for particular people. An additional position in the Jednota's revenues was profits from managing immovable property: from leasing manor farms or renting town houses. Income, at least theoretically, also came from capital turnovers and providing loans.

The material situation of the Lithuanian Evangelical Reformed community in the 17th century is also reflected in two financial documents from 1668 and 1674. The resources registered in both are the sums to which the Jednota was legally entitled: foundation bequest, confirmation of the legacy (donation), a bond guaranteeing the return of the loan with the interest, or a mortgage loan collateral (Figure 18.2). A part of them are legacies (12.9% of the value) which were donated to particular churches and meant an obligation to pay a certain amount of money in the future in total or in instalments. In practice, donators could manage them as amounts of the capital from which the endowed churches were paid a yearly rent. The tentative analysis of the legacies for the Jednota in the files of provincial synods in 1611–1655 demonstrates that merely 32% of the declared donations were paid out immediately at the moment of the bequest (Liedke & Guzowski 2017, p. 124). Widowed spouses or children were often not very willing to give away the legacies of the dead spouses or parents. Realization of most of them required many years, efforts and legal operations.

The vast majority of the bequeathed sums (65.3%) were the loans secured in two ways (Figure 18.1): either on immobile property (27.4%) or a bond (37.9%). The former form of guarantee was derived from the concept of purchasing a rent which, in our case, meant a transaction, the result of which was that the immovable property owner sold the Jednota a particular regular income from the property for a certain amount of money. The other form meant an ordinary money loan secured by bond. Also, foundation bequests were secured by immovable property income (16% of the value of the bequeathed sums). Because of the laconic form of the source, it was impossible to reconstruct the nature of a group of bequests (5.8% of value).

The analysis of the two documents under scrutiny shows that bequests connected with the Vilna district were of the highest value, over 123,000 zlotys, which should not come across as surprising because of its exceptional, capital character, the importance of the Jednota, as well as a pursuit, so visible over the 17th century, of creating a central archive of the Evangelical

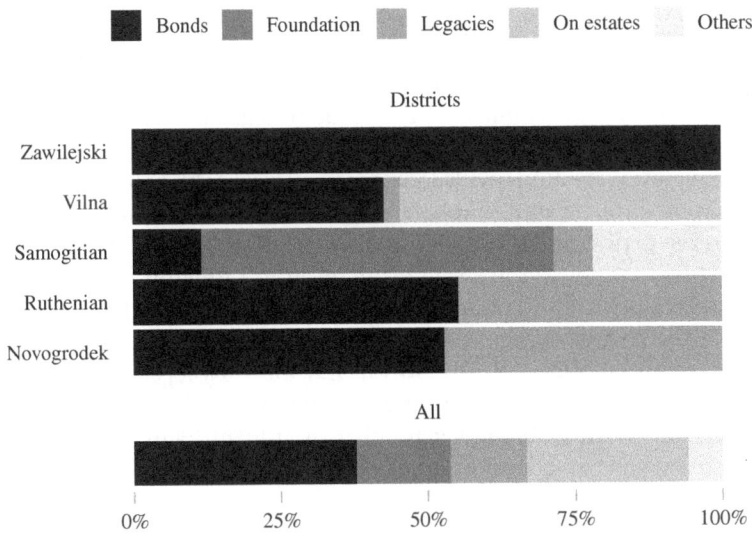

*Figure 18.1* The nature of the sums to which particular districts were entitled.
*Source:* LLAS, fond 40, man. 1136, pp. 303–306; fond 40, man. 168, p. 59r.

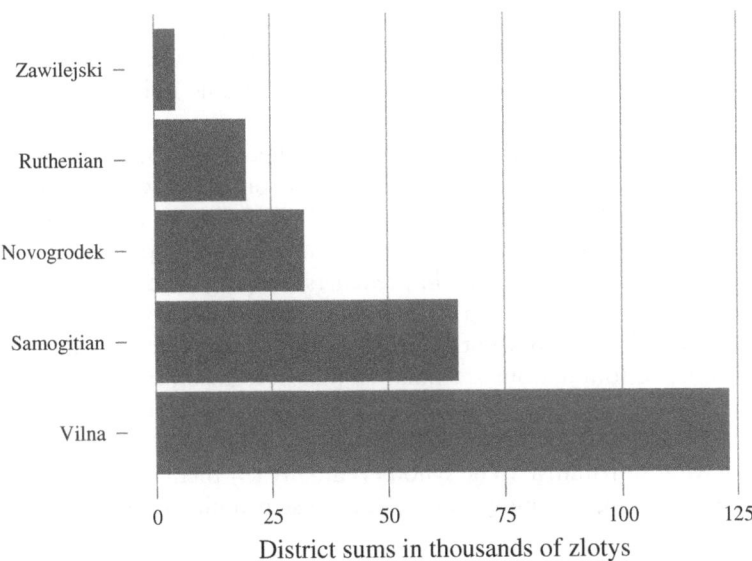

*Figure 18.2* Value of the sums to which particular districts were entitled.
*Source:* LLAS, fond 40, man. 1136, pp. 303–306; fond 40, man. 168, p. 59r.

Reformed Church in Vilna (Figure 18.2). Monetary legacies for the Vilna church came from not only people who had their estates in that district. Many inhabitants of lands belonging to the other districts, beside donations for churches in their maternal district, made bequests for the community in Vilna. Nearly half as much of the value of legacies (65,100 zlotys) was noted in the case of the Samogitian District, to which belonged the churches of the magnates: the Radziwiłłs (Kiejdany) or rich noblemen (Dziewałtów). After all, the affluent and middle Samogitian nobility remained religiously active in the period under examination, whereas, among the magnates, only the Radziwiłł family still protected Calvinism in Lithuania. Furthermore, a half of the value of Samogitian bequests were registered at the Novogrodek District (32,125 zlotys), and of considerably smaller value are the sums of the Ruthenian District (19,600 zlotys) and the Zawilejski District (4,512 zlotys). The particularly poor resources of the vast Ruthenian District could result from a considerably lower number of affluent Evangelical noblemen settled in the most easternmost areas of the GDL.

## Rent purchase

Although legacies, in respect of value, make up the smallest of the categories of sums recorded in the source that we distinguished, undoubtedly resulted from the donors' piety. Among the issuers of charity obligations in favour of the Jednota, mentioned in the two documents we analysed, dominates middle nobility. However, there also occur representatives of poorer noblemen, burghers, and even foreigners. In the group of the most generous donors, eight people, usually members of the middle nobility, bequeathed 1,000 zlotys and more.

Similar to legacies, which probably resulted from primarily spiritual needs, are high bequeathed foundation sums connected with the church in Kiejdany (25,000 zlotys) and Dziewałtów (14,000 zlotys). The former is part of the foundation of Krzysztof Radziwiłł and his wife Anna who granted resources to build a new church, preachers' lodgings and school buildings in 1631 (LLAS, f. 40 nr 1, pp. 1–7). The latter, in turn, was connected with the donation (before 1630) of 10,000 by Brasław marshal Jerzy Podbereski. The history of foundations is similar to that of legacies, the enforcement of which was not easy, as in the case of the sums, mentioned in the list of 1668, donated both by the mother and the sister of Nowogródek ensign Stefan Frąckiewicz Radzimiński. The synod eventually left them in his hands, probably not wanting to annoy one of the most prominent co-religionists of that time.

We can guess that the sums of legacies and foundations recorded in the sources, or basically rents derived from them every year, served current needs of particular churches. The foundation document of a new Kiejdany church shows that from 25,000 zlotys donated by the Radziwiłł family, 'a ready rent of 2,500 Polish zlotys' (VUL, f. 4, man. 16408, p. 4) were paid for the needs of the church, the school, and the hospital. The acquired funds could be and probably often were a source of capital saved by particular communities and secondarily allocated for the credit market.

## Loans

Even though the aforementioned canon of the Synod in Vilna in 1621 pointed at somewhat negative attitude towards usury, it does not mean aversion to capital turnover. Among the tasks of the church actor defined by the Synod of 1644, were, as it was written:

> So that, over the *expensa* and expenditures, for the working at different churches, for buildings and rights some of the aforementioned benefits were left, the actor is expected to preserve *fideliter in integro,* and if someone well-settled and reliable occurred, he is supposed to provide profits.
>
> (LLAS, f. 40, man. 1136, p. 69)

It was no novelty. Even earlier the synods formulated instructions for the supervisors of the church material property, as in 1629, recommending the actor and his assistants 'not to lend money sums, especially those larger, on bonds but on a secure bequest of a secure and legally reliable property' (Akta synodów, 2011, p. 53).

The two collations of district sums we analyse confirm the little effectiveness of the synod's recommendations as regards the loans, since only four (absolute minority) were secured on estates (in comparison with 45 secured by bond). However, their amounts were high. Among them, there were loans granted to Jerzy Wolan (7,000 zlotys), Elżbieta Abramowicz (7,000 zlotys), and the amount of 5,000 zlotys to be paid off by Marcjan Ogiński (the only borrower who was not Calvinist). A particular role in the Jednota's financial fate was also played by a loan provided for Krzysztof Radziwiłł (48,000 zlotys).

The synod had such serious problems with reclaiming the first two sums, as well as the interest therefrom, that in 1654, a special canon was adopted ordering the church actor: 'if the aforementioned debtors refused to return the sums sponte and in a friendly manner, His Grace the actor legally bring the satisfaction and immediately, if God allows for that, presented the future Synod with the sum' (LLAS, f. 40, man. 1136, p. 191). Within a year, however, they did not manage to reclaim both sums and again the actor was ordered to 'proceed legally after still friendly and second requisition' (LLAS, f. 40, man. 1136, p. 205). The following war turmoil was not conducive to paying off the liabilities. Still, the Synod of 1665 recommended the actor to reclaim the sum from Lady Abramowicz (LLAS, f. 40, man. 1136, p. 257) and, in the following year, they proposed she has to pay five zlotys from a hundred, or in various grain being in trade or in ready money (LLAS, f. 40, man. 1136, p. 271).

The largest liability recorded in both sources was a loan of 48,000 zlotys granted in 1636 to Vilna voivode, Krzysztof II Radziwiłł. As the borrower confirmed himself in the Vilna Tribunal books: 'being in need for a sum of money, I took the sum of ready money of forty and eight thousand Polish zlotys from the churche's own treasury' (NLL, fond 93, man. 1, p. 135 v.). With the borrowed sum, Radziwiłł was expected to pay an annual rent of 3,360 zlotys in two instalments and the loan was secured on his estates. After Krzysztof II Radziwiłł's death in 1640, his liabilities were inherited by his son Janusz but he did not meet them according to the agreement. In 1643, the Synod asked him for regular payments or, at least, giving them another estate as a collateral guaranteeing the inflow of cash to the Jednota's treasury (LLAS, f. 40, man. 1136, p. 59). In subsequent years, Janusz's financial obligations to the Evangelicals increased. Their scale is recorded in the files of provincial synod of 1650. According to them, it was necessary to add to the old loan of 48,000 zlotys another sum of 13,250 from which the combined annual rent should bring the Church 4,277.5 zlotys (7% per year) and was to be returned to the Vilna church.

Moreover, Janusz Radziwiłł brought in bonds for 13,600 zlotys for the unpaid rent of the previous years which was to be paid off after three years (without interest). The remaining liabilities, which Radziwiłł had promised to pay back 'without fail', were 4,992 zlotys (LLAS, f. 40, man. 1136, p. 150).

To a certain degree, Janusz settled the arrears in 1651 when he paid to the Vilna Evangelicals 5,000 zlotys and 3,570 zlotys in the next year (LLAS, f 40, man. 711, p. 1). The capital, however, was paid off neither by Janusz Radziwiłł nor his son-in-law and nephew Bogusław Radziwiłł. There were also more and more problems with reclaiming the interest from the loan. In 1663 the Synod asked to return 'both repurchase and bond sums being in His Grace the Duke's hands [...] to the Vilna church' (LLAS, f 40, man. 1136, p. 223). A year later, the synod ordered the Samogitian super-intendent 'to write to His Grace the Duke with a fervent request so that he ordered to return the sum of 2,000 to the seniors of the Kiejdany church' (LLAS, f. 40, man. 1136, p. 230). In response to the demand from the synod, Bogusław wrote a letter informing that from the capital sum secured on Kiejdany 'I assign 3,000 Polish zlotys for each year [...] They are supposed to be returned to the hands of the seniors of the Vilna church' (LLAS, f. 40, man. 711, p. 2). Unfortunately, this liability also had probably no chance for being paid off since the synod of 1666 received another declaration of Radziwiłł that the duke equerry wants, in return for 'the interest from the sums, to give an estate in possession to the God's Church' (LLAS, f. 40, man. 1136, p. 265). This did not come to force and Bogusław Radziwiłł's death at the end of 1669 undermined the stability of financial relations between the

Radziwiłłs and the Evangelicals even more. In 1672, stewards of Ludwika Karolina (Bogusław's daughter) 'declared [to the Synod] to return the bond sums (...) next year' (LLAS, f. 40, man. 1136, p. 342) but, in 1675, the synod ordered the church actor to legally assert the sums remaining with the duchess (LLAS, f. 40, man. 1136, p. 382). The register of the sums belonging to the Vilna church of 1674 shows that the Radziwiłłs, altogether, beside 48,000 secured on the estates, owed additionally 39,150 zlotys guaranteed by bonds. Part of the bond sums was paid off in the subsequent years but, in 1687, their debt (resulting from the loans) to the Vilna church was still 61,000 zlotys, the interest from which was 4,400 zlotys a year (NLL, f. 93 man. 8, pp. 1–2). The capital sums were practically not returned, whereas, at least theoretically, they guaranteed a stable income. The interest registered in 1687 was slightly above 7.2% a year and did not differ considerably from that determined at the moment of signing the agreements between the Evangelicals and Krzysztof II and Janusz Radziwiłł (7%) in the first half of the 17th century. A simple economic calculation shows that, for instance, 48,000 zlotys lent in 1636 should be returned to the Evangelicals as soon as in nearly 15 years, which is before the war with Moscow and Sweden (1654/55), but the problems with the enforcement of the interest, signalled by the Synod, show that this certainly did not happen. The warfare, political turmoil connected with the Radziwiłłs, and the crisis in managing their property in the second half of the 17th century resulted in no growth in effectiveness of reclaiming the income from the lent resources. Meanwhile, there also occurred a considerable fall in the money value. At the moment of taking the resources by Krzysztof II Radziwiłł, the ducat rate was maximum 180 zlotys and when Karolina Ludwika issued her document, over a half century later, nearly 400 zlotys were paid for one ducat. From a purely financial point of view, the loans granted by the Evangelicals to Krzysztof and Janusz Radziwiłł and never paid back were an unsuccessful venture. However, maybe the aim of the Lithuanian Evangelicals was not a financial profit but a guarantee of political protection from the mighty family and survival of the whole religious community.

In the case of other borrowers, those who secured their debts with bonds only, the Jednota's debt collection was no much more successful, even though the group was dominated by wealthy and moderate well-off nobility. In the period of the deep economic crisis mostly resulting from warfare (1654–1667), the authorities of the Jednota came to the conclusion that it is more beneficial to gather resources than their turnover. In 1665, the Synod decided that: 'The church sums, when reclaimed are not to be lent to anyone against the bond, or a collateral, but will remain *in loco certo*, because *temporum experiencia* demonstrated how *difficultates* their parties were and still are' (LLAS, f. 40, man. 1136, p. 241).

A certain chance of improving the debt collectability was seen in manipulating the interest rate. A normal rate with loans was 7% but, in 1666, they decided to lower it for the people in arrears down to 5%, especially in the lands conquered by the enemy (LLAS, f. 40, man. 1136, p. 272). A year later, the Synod came to the conclusion that after the cessation of hostilities in the GDL, the economic situation would improve and decided: 'Now, at the peace decision, Their Graces Lords debtors should pay the interest *ab hinc octo pro centum* from the church sums' (LLAS, f. 40, man. 1136, p. 279). Thus, it was an ordinary rate, not different from the market rate. More or less at the time when Krzysztof II Radziwiłł borrowed 48,000 zlotys from Jednota (1636), he also signed a contract with the Stołpec Dominicans (1639) by virtue of which he took 10,000 zlotys. He secured the loan against the estate Ostaszyn and promised to pay an annual rent worth 8% of the loan value (CAHRW, AR, dz. VIII, man. 557, p. 1). In the 1660s, Bogusław Radziwiłł borrowed money at the same rate several times from the Minsk Dominicans (CAHRW, AR, dz. VIII, man. 248, pp. 2–14). In both cases: 'Catolic' loans, likewise 'Evangelical' loans, the capital sums were not paid off by the debtors and the rent from them was still paid by Ludwika Karolina (CAHRW, AR, dz. VIII, man. 248, p. 60; man. 557, pp. 5, 7). We can also note that the contracting parties ignored the Parliament Act of 1635, which pointed out that 'We guarantee for the future repurchase rents to churches, orders, hospitals, colleges and other clergy persons [...] seven zlotys from a hundred' (Volumina Constitutionum, vol. 3, part 2, 2013, p. 259).

## Conclusion

It is difficult to find Weber's spirit of capitalism in the sources produced by the authorities of the Evangelical Reformed Church in the GDL. Indeed, concern of the material security of the temples and the faithful occurs in the synod files quite frequently but it does not differ from the Roman Catholic Church documentation. Evangelical clergymen and lay patrons of churches were not more open to the phenomenon of usury than Catholic or Orthodox clergymen and they ran credit business because it did not require from the community members the involvement that would be necessary in, for example, managing estates. Moreover, it is difficult to talk about full opening to market mechanisms and not all loans were granted by the Calvinist Church voluntarily. It is obvious that it was impossible to refuse the needs of the most prominent patrons from the Radziwiłł family but also in the case of other sums registered in both documents the circumstances of the liabilities considerably exceeded the principles of a market contract. Almost all debtors (except one) were Reformed Evangelicals but the analysis of provincial synod files, beside many examples of successful financial operations, also delivers information about several problems.

The involvement of church institutions in credit market is the evidence of its poor development mainly based on private credit without strong public banking institutions. The backwardness in this matter probably resulted from not only economic, but also doctrinal reasons common to all Christian denominations. As in the case of the activities of Catholic monasteries, in the sources under discussion, we deal with the repurchase rent. However, it is interesting that, against Calvin's suggestions and in certain situations, the Lithuanian Evangelicals demanded higher interest rates than the state regulations allowed for. In the case of pious legacies and foundations, the benefactors were usually to deduct 10% of their value a year to the churches of the Jednota and the interest rate of the loans secured by bonds was between 5% and 8% per year. Despite the problems the Jednota actors had with reclaiming the sums 'kept' by Church members, the trust in the co-religionists was so high that the prohibitions of bond loans repeated by the Synod were ignored.

The observations of other aspects of the economic activity of the Evangelical Reformed Church in Lithuania (Liedke & Guzowski 2017) demonstrate that the financial activity yielded higher revenues than potential investments in purchasing property. Besides, the Calvinist Church was not always good at managing estates; therefore, they rather tried to find effective tenants, according to the rule that 'the estate was leased to a *viro integro* of our religion'. A serious obstacle in achieving profits from agricultural and breeding economy at the beginning of the second half of the 17th century was the occupation of the country by foreign troops. Thus, the circumstances forced the Evangelical community to undertake the credit activity, even though it was connected with visible risks. This, however, was not far from the practice of other religious institutions, especially Catholic ones, in that period.

## Funding

The research for this chapter was financed from the grant received from the Ministry of Science and Higher Education of the Republic of Poland, through the National Programme for the Development of the Humanities for the years 2016–21 (nr 11H16019684).

## References

Acemoglu, D. & Robinson, J. A. (2012). *Why Nations Fail: The Origins of Power, Prosperity, and Poverty*. New York: Crown.

Becker, S. O., Pfaff, S. & Rubin, J. (2016). Causes and Consequences of the Protestant Reformation. *Explorations in Economic History*, 62, pp. 1–25.

CAHRW (The Central Archives of Historical Records in Warsaw), AR (Archiwum Radziwiłłów), dz. VIII, manuscripts 248, 557.

Grodziski, P., Kwiecień, M. & Karowicz, A., eds. (2013). *Volumina Constitutionum*, vol. 3 (1611–1640), part 2. (2013). Warszawa: Wydawnictwo Sejmowe.

Grużewski, B. et al., eds. (1915). *Akta synodów prowincjalnych Jednoty Litewskiej 1611–1625*. Wilno: E. Wende i SP.

Kaelber, L. (2007). Max Weber and usury: implications for historical research. In Armstrong, L., Elbl, J. & Elbl, M., eds. *Money, Markets and Trade in Late Medieval Europe*. Leiden-Boston: MA, pp. 59–86.

Kerridge, E. (2002). *Usury, Interest and the Reformation*. Aldershot: Ashgate.

Liedke, M. & Guzowski, P., eds. (2011). *Akta synodów prowincjonalnych Jednoty Litewskiej 1626–1637*. Warszawa: Semper.

Liedke, M. & Guzowski, P. (2017). Problemy finansowe ewangelickiej Jednoty Litewskiej w pierwszej połowie XVII w. w świetle akt synodów prowincjonalnych. *Roczniki Dziejów Społecznych i Gospodarczych*, 78, pp. 95–130.

LLAS (The Wróblewski Library of the Lithuanian Academy of Sciences), fond 40, manuscripts: 1, 168, 711, 1136.

Nunziata, L. & Rocco, K. (2018). The Protestant ethic and entrepreneurship: Evidence from religious minorities in the former Holy Roman Empire. *European Journal of Political Economy*, 51, pp. 27–43.

NLL (Martynas Mažvydas National Library of Lithuania), fond 93, manuscripts 1, 8.

Rubin, J. (2017). *Rulers, Religion, and Riches. Why the West Got Rich and the Middle East Did Not*. Cambridge: CUP.

Schultze, L. (2000). Calvin's view on Interest and Usury. *Studia Historiae Ecclesiasticae*, 26, pp. 198–211.

van Zanden, J. L., Buringh, E. & Bosker, M. (2012). The rise and decline of European Parliaments, 1188–1789. *Economic History Review*, 65, pp. 835–61.

VUL (Vilnius University Library), fond 4, manuscript 16408.

Weber, M. (2005). *The Protestant Ethic and the Spirit of Capitalism*. London: Routledge.

Wood, D. (2004). *Medieval Economic Thought*. Cambridge: Cambridge University Press.

# Chapter 19

# Debts and claims as a part of administration and everyday life of Bohemian chamber estates in the early modern period

*Zuzana Vlasáková*

## Introduction

The following text deals with various manifestations of debts and claims captured in archival sources reflecting everyday life of chamber estates Pardubice, Kolín, and Poděbrady in the early modern period. Bohemian Chamber dominium belonged to the ruler of the Kingdom of Bohemia and it was meant to provide resources for the needs of the monarch (from 1526 member of Habsburg Dynasty), his family, and the court. As we will see later, the ruler established a sophisticated system of control and administration of chamber-goods with the Court Chamber (*Hofkammer, Dvorská komora),* central financial authority of the monarchy on the top, and Bohemian (Royal) Chamber (*Böhmische Kammer, Česká komora*) as a subordinate agency (Hochedlinger, Maťa & Winkelbauer 2019, Tb 1, pp. 382–5, Tb 2, pp. 825–55, 896–902). Among other things, the Bohemian Chamber coordinated the administration of chamber estates belonging to the Czech lands and represented the main authority for patrimonial apparatus and local authorities such as town councils, headmen, and village officers. Branched systems of administration gave birth to various types of archival records including instructions, orders, relations of visitation commissioners, accounting books, biannual accounts, land registers, report from land books as well as 'regular' correspondence between central authorities, estates and its communities. Those that have been preserved show us that aspects such as debt, claims or remarkable 'phenomenon' of large arrears steadily visible in biannual accounts (in very blunt terms called embezzlement) represented important parts of patrimonial as much as town and rural economy. The chapter is largely based on the analysis of these sources, placed mostly in National Archives in Prague (Národní archiv, NA) and State Regional Archives in Zámrsk (Státní oblastní archiv Zámrsk, SOA Zámrsk) but deals also with published edition of archival sources (Černý 1930), (Kalousek 1905) and literature related to the topic (Maur 1966, 1975, 1976 et al.), (Beránek 2004, 2005), (Pešák 1929, 1930, 1933).

## Bohemian chamber estates and its administration

### Definition and structure of the dominium

Before we come to the theme of the chapter itself, I consider it important to introduce the dominium of Bohemian chamber estates, its genesis, and the system of administration. Only with this brief excursion could we fully understand the complex (and sometimes even complicated) relations within particular estates, the circulation of money and therefore also the dynamics of debts and claims. In the strictest sense of the term, Bohemian chamber estates after 1526 meant the property purchased (or confiscated) by Ferdinand I or his descendants and was considered as private property of the sovereign. He could thus manipulate them without supervision of the Bohemian noblemen (and traditional land institutions in which they usually had a key word). The revenues generated from the estates (*camerale*) were intended to finance the court and the administration of the estates (Hledíková, Janák & Dobeš 2005, p. 107).

In the course of the 16th century, thanks to original and newly associated territories, two chamber complexes were established. The smaller part consisted of estates Zbiroh, Točník, Králův Dvůr, Křivoklát with Krušovice, and Přísečnice and it was well known for forestry and iron deposits. However, the core of the dominion laid along the river banks of the Elbe, expanding from Brandýs in the west through Přerov, Lysá (Beránek 2004), (Beránek 2005), Poděbrady, and Kolín to Pardubice in the east. Even after some territorial losses, which the dominium suffered at the end of the 16th century and the first half of the 17th century, with its length of 116 km and the size of 2580 km², it occupied a considerable part of the Czech lands (Maur 1966, pp. 151–2). The largest estate was Pardubice (745 km²) which, in the middle of the 17th century, consisted of an eponymous administrative centre Pardubice, town Přelouč, five other small towns, and approximately 130 villages or its parts (Šebek 1990, pp. 184, 202). Just for a point of comparison, the size of Poděbrady estate (at the same period consisted of two towns and 47 villages) was 315 km² and estate Kolín 118 km² (Maur 1976, pp. 15–17).

### Administrative hierarchy

As already stated, the owner of chamber–goods was the ruler of Kingdom of Bohemia, i. e. in the early modern period representative of the Austrian branch of the Habsburg family. Ferdinand I, brother of the Holy Roman Emperor Charles V, ruler of the Habsburgs' Austrian hereditary lands and (from 1526) king of Bohemia and Hungary, established new bureaucratic apparatus to centralise and rationalise the administration of these territories and its finances. Also, as previously mentioned, regarding Bohemian chamber-goods, on the top of the hierarchical pyramid stood Court Chamber

(*Hofkammer, Dvorská komora*) supreme financial authority of the monarchy (Volf 1980, pp. 62–109) and then Bohemian (Royal) Chamber (*Böhmische Kammer, Česká komora),* the superior authority and administrator of the estate (Pešák 1929, pp. 58–68), (Pešák 1930), (Pešák 1933, pp. 66–178, 195–216, 279–96). Last but not least, both chambers had departments that took care of accounting books (*Buchhalterie, hlavní účtárna*) and those which collected money from particular estates – *Rentamt,* in Bohemia called *úřad mistra komory,* later *rentmistrovský úřad* (Kubátová 1975). Both offices also regularly sent visitation commissions (*vizitační komise*). The designated commissioners were given instruction (or instructions) indicating not only which estates they should visit but also which fields and topics they should investigate. Instruction and relations of visitation commissioners from the second half of the 16th century, 17th and 18th century can be found in (NA, SM, karton 1707) or (NA, SM, karton 2260–2265).

Beside these central authorities, each chamber estate also had its officers who should administrate and take care of the area. That meant constantly try to improve economic conditions of the estate, propose ideas that could help to increase income, record all income and expenses, and also guaranteed judicial and executive acts (edited instructions for officers Kalousek 1905, pp. 366–481; original texts for Pardubice in SOA Pardubice, Vs Pardubice, kniha 169–173 or NA, ČDKM IV–17/4–18/1, 18/1–2, 1–3, karton 37 and 39, for Kolín, Poděbrady NA, ČDKM IV–K, ČDKM IV–P, karton 107 and 180). Members of apparatus were also entrusted to collect taxes as well as help with recruitment and other claims of state, etc. *Hejtman* stood at the head of the majority of all estates and represented the main authority on the estate. Sometimes he had 'a deputy' (*místohejtman*) who helped him with some tasks, especially those that required travelling and therefore longer absence from residence of the estate. This person took on some responsibilities relating to financial agenda as well. It applies partly in regard to burgrave (*purkrabí*), a person who was entrusted to care about the main residence of the estate as well as manor farms belonging to the ruler. Estates in question also had their tradition in forestry and therefore each of them had its forest management for which the representative was called *forstmistr (lesmistr).* Likewise, fish pond farming was a very important part of the estate´s economy so it was provided with its own administrative 'unit' with an appointed fishmistr (*fišmistr*) at the head ('personal' information and lists of officers for Kolín NA, NM, karton 367, for Pardubice NA, NM, karton 592–603, 624 and for Poděbrady NA, NM, karton 646–649).

Very important and also quite numerous parts of the administrative machinery were represented by local offices of scribes. They were responsible for bookkeeping as well as for dealing with correspondence of the office (or – if they were asked and usually against payment – of inhabitants of the estates), for recording all income and expenses in the 'section' they were entrusted to supervise. They also had to regularly (instruction demanded once a week) make total sums of income and expenses, submit it for control, and defend the treasuries against trespassers during the entire period of time. The main accountant and bookkeeper of the estate (*důchodní písař*) had to send biannual accounts to Bohemian Chamber and handed revenues from the estate (references about different instructions for scribes in NA, SM, karton 1647, b.f). It means he was also responsible for controlling other scribes, their accounts and cash in their treasuries. Second 'persona' responsible for very important 'resort' was the scribe that took care of the property of the estates' orphans (*sirotčí písař*). There were also scribes who took care of the finances and accounts of landlord breweries (*útratní písař*), those who recorded cereal crops (*obročníobilní písař*), transfers and sales of real estates or composed wedding contracts, testaments, and inventories of the property that belonged to the lately departed inhabitants (*písař pojezdný*), etc. (Růžková 2013, pp. 86–113) In the context of this chapter, it is important to emphasize that most of them (and especially the 'main' scribes and those who dealt with orphaned properties) were instantly in contact with money (or other resources of 'wealth' from the estate), thus they were also first 'suspects' if some discrepancies in the accounts were found.

## Monarch, nobles, burghers, and sefs as debtors and creditors

All revenues from the overhead economy and hereditary taxes coming from inhabitants of the estate were meant to flow to the hands of the ruler. Originally, treasuries of the estates were supposed to finance the court of the monarch and his family as well as administration of estates and his lands. In fact, a large majority of resources was used to redeem his debt to other people and subjects – to representatives of aristocracy as well as 'lower' nobility royal and patrimonial towns and its burghers, serfs or Jewish communities (Volf 1947/1948, pp. 110–71). The amount of the debts (as well as amounts of unpaid interests) was still increasing during the early modern period, and even members of Habsburg family sometimes used the phrase 'forests of debts' for describing the situation (Kohler 2003, pp. 72an). House of Habsburg was even sometimes forced to pawn some estate (or rather its profits) to their creditors, mostly to merchant houses like Fugger, Welser, Henckel, and others (Volf 1947/1948, pp. 119–27). Monarchs therefore constantly demanded from both chambers, visitation commissioners as well as hetmans and other officers to find ways how to increase revenues of the dominion. They also – again and again (and with the same, virtually zero result) – forbade loans from both patrimonial treasury and orphan's treasury. It was very common praxis (especially with regard to orphan's money) that different subject were granted loans from treasuries and rulers repetitious prohibitions issued in the course of 16th, 17th and 18th centuries had not change that. After all, even the ruler himself did not keep his own commands and he was often the one who owed large (or even the largest) sums of money to orphan's treasuries – both dominical as municipal (Chocholáč 2003, pp. 43–8).

Orphan's treasuries were a great temptation for representatives of different groups within the estates, not only as orphan's book, but also as other records (testaments, patrimonial accounts, records of municipal courts, etc.) prove. Manorial officers or town council (existed only in towns entitled to have their own treasury and evidence of town orphans and their property) provided a great amount of loans with interests, (based on cash deposited in treasuries) and remarkably wide clientele took advantage of it. Not only the Habsburg sovereign and some of his patrimonial officers themselves, but also local noblemen, usually representatives of 'lower' nobility, burghers (or burghers with coat of arms), and serfs were among them. Orphans were promised to gain some extra sum to the amount of their funds and those who obtained a loan could use it to his (or even her) profit. In case the debtor would not be able to repay the debt (during his life or by his family members after his death), there should be some person (or persons, *rukojmí*) who were able to guarantee (usually with their property) that they could possibly repay it themselves. Unfortunately, despite all of these arrangements, large amount of loans remained unpaid for a very long time, some of them even for eternity. That was a big problem which sometimes escalated to complaints, pauperism, and even escape of newly adult orphans (NA, SM, karton 1646, b. f.).

Not only orphan books, but also other documents of central, patrimonial as well as 'local' (town and village) authorities, presented us with different types of credit operations. Trade with homestead money and different other aspects visible within the rural space and small towns are described in detail in other chapters of this monography. Yet, it would be useful to point out some general information about debts and claims and its manifestations within the estates in question. Firstly, it is obvious that loans served specifically to cover the basic needs of debtors – in the case of serfs for buying food or other basic needs, investment into equipment or staff needed for agriculture or craft, for paying different taxes, in the case of burghers and noblemen, furthermore also for representation, extending their property, and (especially in the families of patrimonial and town officers) for paying for the education of their children. Thanks to a variety of records, we could assume it was more common to take/provide loans among people who had history – they usually knew each other and trusted each other (Siglová 2016, pp. 42, 47). Therefore, it is quite likely that our knowledge about debts in the area is not complete because some of them were never recorded. We know exactly only about those that are specified in sources like the aforementioned orphans book, testaments or court protocols (in case a creditor or debtor ask the authorities to judge their dispute regarding some aspect of the debt). The next point worth mentioning is that debt and claims were one of those aspects that crossed the borders – both physical and social. It meant that we could see a burgher as a creditor and a noble person as a debtor and vice versa. They both had the same duties which should lead to one conclusion – to pay their debt. It should happen (just as with orphan's money) personally (in money or by other ways), by members of family or by his guarantors. Last but not least, in case of a deceased debtor, all instructions and ordinance required payment firstly of all arrears to patrimonial (and then town) treasuries, then came debts to other creditors. The remainder of property was preserved for heirs (as transcripts of testaments as well as orders of hetmans prove, e.g. NA, SM, karton 1646, b.f., et al.).

## Arrears ('rest') of the patrimonial officers as neuralgic part of the administration

References to different type of arrears *('rests')* are often found in the archival sources recording (not only) administration of chamber estates. *Rest* essentially meant the difference between the expected profit, specified by comparing all incomes and expenses recorded in the accounting books, and the real amount of money deposited in patrimonial treasuries at the time of comparison (Stejskal 1995, pp. 6–8). The largest arrears were usually detected during biannual controls of accounts and revenues or thanks to inspections and visitations conducted by the Bohemian chamber. Sometimes, one of the officials pointed to the unfair practices of other members and that launched an investigation. It can be tempting to assume that all of these amounts of money (attributed to individual officials and in particular to the 'main' scribe, *důchodní písař*) can be clearly identified as embezzlement. However, references in accounting books, correspondence or visitation reports prove that it is not that simple because different items were included among *'rests'* (at least at the beginning of the control). Firstly, all sums that (according to the proclamations of the scribe or other officer in question) were given to the Chamber officer, commissioners, envoies of ruler, merchant houses or Habsburg creditors but cannot be proven with quittance *(kvitance)* were counted in. The fact that the Bohemian Chamber did not withdraw money only twice a year, but sometimes also during visitation or control of other persons authorized by Bohemian as well as Court Chamber, did not help to clarify the situation. All expenses that exceeded the limits of financial and natural resources earmarked for manorial office *(deputát)* and were not approved by the Bohemian chamber beforehand were also classified as arrears (discussions about *deputát* NA, SM, karton 2261, pp. 1 or karton 1707, pp. 37an). Last but not least, Chamber officers counted in also the debts of merchants and other persons who did not pay for the goods purchased from chamber estates – for example, Pardubice and Poděbrady provided great amounts of fish for Prague burghers (Maur 1975, pp. 53–114).

Only when the Chamber's 'accounting department' deducted these sums, the remaining arrears was considered as a personal debt of the officer and he was obliged to foot the amount in arrears. Czech historian Václav Černý once wrote that after revelation of any machinations of the manorial officer, 'the person in question was punished and replaced by a new officer who usually received a new instruction' (Černý 1930, p. 14). However, the reality, as archive sources show, was different. It is clear that disproportions between accounts and cash (or quittances) did not have to lead to immediate punishment. Firstly, the official had been given a certain period of time during which he had to justify the deficiencies. And even if he did not manage to prove that he was not the one who should have been blamed, the penalties were in most cases limited to (sometimes only temporary) deposing the person from his position and pay the arrears. The officer was not forbidden to continue with his 'career' in the future and his honor was not questioned. Nevertheless, the ruler and both his Chambers did not turn a blind eye to this problem and tried repeatedly to prevent such behavior by fixing salaries and fulfilling material needs of manorial staff, by emphasising permanent vertical and horizontal control, by ordering hetmen and other officers to lead parallel accounts (beside those who were recorded by scribes) and checking them periodically, etc. Yet, large amounts of arrears appeared continuously throughout the period as well as complaints of officers that their services were not sufficiently appreciated (more about this topic Vlasáková 2019, pp. 37–59).

It can be assumed that all of the circumstances mentioned above together with the disorderliness of officers, often criticised in correspondence and other sources, contributed to the confusion in both accounts and treasuries. But they could also create some space for the conscious machinations of officials and for what we can actually define as embezzlement (even with our contemporary terminology).

## Conclusion

The purpose of this chapter was to present the chamber estates as the place where debts and claims were an indisputable part of day-to-day life of almost every inhabitant of the dominion including serfs, burghers, local nobility, manorial officers and, last but not least, Habsburg's ruler himself. Firstly, genesis of Bohemian chamber dominium and structure and hierarchy of the administration were presented because, without this step, it would be difficult to understand the financial flows, credit operations, and relationship within the estates and its inhabitants. Then, it is focused on different manifestation of debts and claims, how representatives of various social groups dealt with credit operations, and whether it is possible to track some patterns in their behavior, in the mechanism of giving loans, treating money lent at interest or repaying debts. The last part deals with the topic of officers' arrears and warns against marking them automatically as embezzlement, without closer examination and analysis of wider archival sources, as such an approach proved itself incorrect in the past research.

## Funding

This chapter has been prepared thanks to the support of a specific project of University Pardubice called SGS_2019_008 Support of scientific and presentation activities of students of the doctoral program History and the master program of Cultural History (*Podpora vědeckých a prezentačních aktivit studentů doktorského programu Historie a magisterského programu kulturní dějiny'*).

## References

### Archival sources

Národní archiv (NA), České oddělení dvorské komory (ČDKM), IV– Čechy – 17/ 4–18/1, karton 37.
Národní archiv (NA), České oddělení dvorské komory (ČDKM), IV– Čechy – 18/ 1–2, 1–3, karton 39.
Národní archiv (NA), České oddělení dvorské komory (ČDKM), IV– Čechy –K, karton 107.
Národní archiv (NA), České oddělení dvorské komory (ČDKM), IV– Čechy –P, karton 180.
Národní archiv (NA), Nová manipulace (NM), sg. K35/4, karton 367.
Národní archiv (NA), Nová manipulace (NM), sg. P 9/1, karton 592–6.
Národní archiv (NA), Nová manipulace (NM), sg. P9/2. karton 597–603.
Národní archiv (NA), Nová manipulace (NM), sg P9/11, karton 624.
Národní archiv (NA), Nová manipulace (NM), sg. P26/1, karton 646–9.
Národní archiv (NA), Stará manipulace (SM), sg. P 70/5–13, karton 1646.
Národní archiv (NA), Stará manipulace (SM), sg. P 70/30, karton 1647.
Národní archiv (NA), Stará manipulace (SM), sg. P 100/5I, karton 1707.
Národní archiv (NA), Stará manipulace (SM), sg. S 195/3–11, karton 2260–5.
Státní oblastní archiv Zámrsk (SOA Zámrsk), Velkostatek Pardubice (Vs Pardubice), inv. č. 165–169, kniha 169–73.

### Literature

Beránek, V. (2004). Osedlé obyvatelstvo na komorních panstvích Brandýs nad Labem, Přerov nad Labem a Lysá nad Labem v předbělohorském období. In Svoboda, M., ed. *Pax bello potior. Sborník věnovaný doc. PhDr. Rudolfu Andělovi, CSc.* Liberec: Technická univerzita v Liberci, pp. 115–25.
Beránek, V. (2005). Proměny dvorového hospodářství na komorních panstvích do prvních let třicetileté války (panství Brandýs nad Labem, Přerov nad Labem a Lysá nad Labem). *Časopis Národního muzea. Řada historická,* 174(1–2), pp. 23–55.

Černý, V. (1930). *Hospodářské instrukce. Přehled zemědělských dějin v době patrimonijního velkostatku v XV.–XIX. století*. Praha: Nákladem Československé Akademie Zemědělské.

Hledíková, Z., Janák, J. & Dobeš, J. (2005). *Dějiny správy v českých zemích od počátků státu po současnost*. Praha: NLN.

Hochedlinger, M., Maťa, P. & Winkelbauer, T., eds. (2019). *Verwaltungsgeschichte der Habsburgermonarchie. Hof und Dynastie, Kaiser und Reich, Zentralverwaltungen, Kriegswesen und landesfürstliches Finanzwesen*. Band 1, Teilband 1.-2. Wien: Böhlau Verlag.

Chocholáč, B. (2003). Sirotčí truhlice. In Dvořák, T., Vlček, R. & Vykoupil, L., eds. *Milý Bore: profesoru Ctiboru Nečasovi k jeho sedmdesátým narozeninám věnují přátelé, kolegové a žáci*. Brno: Historický ústav AV ČR: Historický ústav FF MU: Matice moravská, pp. 43–8.

Kalousek, J. (1905). *Řády selské a instrukce hospodářské, Archiv český XXII*. Praha: Domestikální fond království Českého.

Kohler, A. (2003). *Ferdinand I. 1503–1564. Fürst, König und Kaiser*. München: Verlag C. H. Beck.

Kubátová, L. (1975). K otázkám ústřední a české zemské finanční správy v 16. až 19. století. *Sborník archivních prací*, 25(1–2). Praha: Archivní správa Ministerstva vnitra ČSR, pp. 95–142.

Maur, E. (1966). K utužení feudálních vztahů na komorních statcích v době pobělohorské. In Fiala, Z., ed. *Z českých dějin. Sborník prací in memoriam prof. dr. Husy*. Praha: Univerzita Karlova, pp. 151–69.

Maur, E. (1975). Český komorní velkostatek a trh v druhé polovině 17. století. *Sborník historický*, 24, pp. 53–114.

Maur, E. (1976). Český komorní velkostatek v 17. století. Příspěvek k otázce 'druhého nevolnictví' v českých zemích. *Acta Universitatis Carolinae. Philosophica et historica. Monographia 59*. Praha: Univerzita Karlova.

Pešák, V. (1929). Hospodářství a správa komorních panství v Čechách za Maxmilliána II. *Časopis pro dějiny venkova*, 16, pp. 58–68.

Pešák, V. (1930). Dějiny královské české komory od roku 1527. Část 1. Začátky organisace české komory za Ferdinanda I. *Sborník archivu ministerstva vnitra republiky Československé*, 3. Praha: Archiv ministerstva vnitra republiky Československé.

Pešák, V. (1933). *Studie k dějinám královské české komory, Sborník archivu ministerstva vnitra republiky Československé, 6*. Praha: Archiv ministerstva vnitra republiky Československé, pp. 66–178, 116–34, 195–216, 279–96.

Růžková (Vlasáková), Z. (2013). *Mezi kladivem a kovadlinou. Vrchnostenský aparát pardubického panství v letech 1560–1630*. Master's thesis. Univerzita Karlova v Praze.

Šebek, F., ed. (1990). *Dějiny Pardubic I*. Pardubice: Městský národní výbor.

Siglová, T. (2016). Dluhy a zadlužení poddanského obyvatelstva na příkladu městeček pardubického panství v 16. a 17. století. *Východočeské listy historické*, 35, pp. 35–49.

Stejskal, A. (1995). Nedoplatek a zpětná dotace – sociálněekonomické kategorie rožmberských velkostatků (1550–1611). *Časopis Národního muzea v Praze. Řada historická*, 164(1–4), pp. 6–39.

Vlasáková, Z. (2020). Defraudace jako neuralgický bod raně novověké vrchnostenské politiky (nejenom) na příkladu polabských komorních panství v 16. a první polovině 17. století. In Jílková, M., Macková, M. & Valová, E., eds. *Jak se u nás podvádělo: za monarchie i za republiky*. Pardubice: Univerzita Pardubice, 2019, pp. 37–59.

Volf, M. (1947/1948). Královský důchod a úvěr v 16. století. (Příspěvek k historii českých státních financí). *Český časopis historický*, 48–9 (1947–1948), pp. 110–71.

Volf, M. (1980). Dvorská komora a české finance před Bílou horou a po ní (1610–1640). *Sborník archivních prací*, 30(1), pp. 62–109.

# Chapter 20

# Financial aspects of the property transactions of rural subjects in Moravia in the 16th and 17th centuries

*Bronislav Chocholáč*

## Introduction

Since the end of the 20th century, as mentioned in the preface of this book, there has been a significant expansion of research into the financial management of the subject population in Moravia. The research focused mainly on a comprehensive analysis of records of various forms of property transactions with tenant farms, while the most frequently used source for this study was land registers (Procházka 1963). However, there has not been a deeper comparison of the achieved results from several manorial estates in Moravia or the Czech lands which would affect the existence and scope of the instalment system, farm holding prices, size of earnest payments, farm money, and credit business of individual subjects and institutions operating in the rural milieu (or the milieu of small towns) in a long time frame without the comparison being limited to a short period of the Thirty Years' War (Chocholáč 2017). The aim of the chapter is to generalize the achieved knowledge with this broadly conceived comparison.

Nevertheless, it is also necessary to draw attention to the limitations and parameters of the comparison conducted in the Introduction. Research on individual estates was carried out in the form of a probe at different number of localities (one to five), one of which was usually a small town. Namely, they were the estate Pernštejn and villages Černovice, Chlébské, Olešnička, Sejřek, and the township Štěpánov (Chocholáč 1989, 1990), the estate Telč and villages Doupě, Nevcehle, Strachoňovice (Valůšek, 1998), Hostěnice, Růžená and the township Mrákotín and the estate Žďár (nad Sázavou) and the villages Počítky, Radešín, and the township Dolní Bobrová (Chocholáč 1999); the estate Bojkovice with the homonymous small town (Janík 2002); the estate Brumov and the villages Lipina, Mirošov, Smolina, Tichov, and the town Valašské Klobouky (Odehnal 2007, 2011) and the estate Nový Světlov and the villages Sehradice (partially), the estate Boskovice and villages Krhov, Skalice, Sudice, and Žďárná (Vaněk 1997) and the estate Dřevohostice with the homonymous small town (Vohnický 2014). With regard to the preservation of the sources (especially land registers) there was no research on the individual estates in precisely limited periods despite the fact that three basic time intervals could be defined for comparison which showed the highest frequency of research conducted: the Pre-White Mountain Period (from the 1580s to 1618), the Thirty Years' War and the second half of the 17th century. Possible overlaps into the earlier or later periods were independently taken into account for the individual examined issues.

## Prices of farm holdings and the instalment system

Before proceeding to the actual comparison, it is necessary to emphasize the property rights of the examined properties. In all cases without exception, these were purchased farmsteads (Procházka 1963, pp. 95–105). At these farm holdings in the 16th century, there was an instalment system of their prices. Its beginnings likely reach back to the late Middle Ages (Chocholáč 2007, p. 300). The expansion of this system was aided by the frequent alternation of the farmers at the farmsteads (especially at the smaller farm holdings), the lack of cash on the part of the purchaser, with which he could pay for the purchase of the homestead immediately or in the short term, and the overall price increase due to the price revolution. Its accompanying phenomenon was an increase in the prices of agricultural crops and wage labour of subjects and, in terms of financial penetration, of highly inflationary tendencies into the money circulation which were caused by the use of large amounts of small coins with low silver content (Vorel 2000, p. 145). Practically, this meant that the buyer did not have sufficient funds to pay the homestead immediately and therefore the agreed price was distributed (for the prices of farm holdings, their creation, and difficulties in interpretation, see Chocholáč 2005, pp. 98–103; Štefanová 2009, pp. 86–94). The first part was the earnest money, that is usually the largest instalment paid immediately after the property transaction or shortly after it took place; the remainder was divided into several annual instalments (Procházka 1963, pp. 308–9, 314–21). These instalments of the prices of farmsteads, from which interest was never paid, were usually labelled as vejrunky (annual payments), annual or farm money (for other labels in Czech and German, see Procházka 1963, p. 318). They were mainly paid to the creditors by the farmer working on the farm holding, less often the widow or the village headman as the so-called money deposited *on the right*. The recipients of the farm money were most often individuals, less often institutions, such as the orphans' cash boxes and church endowments, sporadically guilds, municipalities, etc. Part of the means were also acquired by the manorial lords, for instance, as money of fugitive subjects, etc.

Thanks to several land registers, which were kept regularly already from the 1540s, research in these localities on the Pernštejn estate have proved a permanent growth of the prices of farmsteads in all size categories for the second half of the 16th century; on the contrary, their slight decrease by about a tenth of the previous value was observed at the beginning of the 17th century (Chocholáč 1989, pp. 67–73, 81). A different price development was recorded at the end of the 16th and at the beginning of the 17th century at the Boskovice and Telč estate because the prices of farm holdings stagnated here or even rose slightly (Vaněk 1997, pp. 34–46; Chocholáč 1999, pp. 79–80). From this, it is clear that there was no continuous rise in farmstead prices everywhere at the turn of the 17th century as the older literature postulated for Bohemia (Petráň 1964, p. 25). Whether and to what extent the differentiation in the development of farmstead prices in individual estates was related to the current level and state of the serf economy, however, cannot be determined at present and is a question for further study.

The comparison of price data from the pre-White Mountain period with the war period, which could be realized for the Boskovice, Dřevohostice, Telč, and Žďár regions, provided interesting information. There was a significant drop in the price of the farmstead if the farm holding was directly hit by the looting of soldiers, a fire and subsequently its desolation. In such cases, however, of which a small number was recorded (Chocholáč 1999, pp. 77, 89–90), the price set in the next property transaction was only a fraction of the original value.

If the farm holdings were not directly affected by the above-mentioned interventions, the decrease of their prices on the mentioned estates were zero or only minimal, at most a tenth of the original pre-White Mountain value (Vohnický 2014, p. 55; Vaněk 1997, p. 35 f.). It is even still possible, in the first war years (the beginning of the 1620s), to observe a slight increase of the price with some farm holdings (Valůšek 1998, pp. 63–7). It was similar also at the Mělnik estate in Bohemia (Koumar 2011, p. 88). Unfortunately, it was not possible to determine whether the inflationary moves of the coins were projected in the rise of the prices (Kostlán 1985, p. 285 f.). The absence of a distinct reduction of the prices of the majority of the farmsteads indicated that the actual fact of an ongoing military conflict did not influence the value level of the villagers.

In the framework of the property transactions in all of the examined localities, further data with an influence on the instalment system of the farmsteads besides the prices – the earnest money and annual (vejrunkové) instalments – were also negotiated. The solvency of those interested in the farmstead can be seen in the size of the proportion of the really paid earnest money (without the values of the hereditary shares of the new farmer on the farm holding or his wife, gifts of relatives, permanent burdens, etc.) as compared to the price of the farmstead (Chocholáč 1999, pp. 98–9; Janík 2002, p. 65). In the pre-war period, the share was around (Bojkovice, Kuřim region, Pernštejn region, Telč region, Žďár region) 10 to 16% of the price on average (Chocholáč 1999, pp. 100–2; Janík 2002, p. 66). The share of earnest money in the price of a farmstead was similar (18%) in localities on the Brumov estate, even though the methods for processing the data were different – all found amounts of the earnest money were included (Odehnal 2007, pp. 98–9, 213). In contrast, a high share of earnest money in the price was proved in the research of small towns on the Pardubice estate where it reached 40% in the period between 1601 and 1621. Despite a small decrease in the following years, the share remained high (between about a quarter and third of the price) until the end of the 17th century which probably reflects less serious damage of the localities during the Thirty Years' War (Siglová 2017, pp. 202–4). Considering practically stable prices of homesteads in small towns throughout the whole 17th century, buyers must have had quite large amounts of cash in order to acquire them.

Other than the municipalities from the Kuřim region, Hostěradice on the Telč and Počítky on the Žďár estates, with which the statistical processing of the comparison could not be carried out because of the absence of sources or the limited number of data, there was a decline in the share of the earnest money in the price in all the examined localities on the Bojkovice, Telč, and Žďár manorial estates in the course of the war (Chocholáč 1999, p. 100). With the small town of Mrákotín in the Telč region, the reduction was minimal; similar values were found also on the Mělník estate (Koumar 2011, p. 90), whereas with Bobrová in the Žďár region, the drop was the greatest where the paid earnest money only reached a fifth of the pre-White Mountain values (Chocholáč 1999, p. 100). A larger amount of financial means from the earnest money in the pre-war period gave the seller (if he received it) a greater change of a new purchase on another farmstead. In this way, it was possible to support the exchange of farm holdings in the surveyed localities and a certain trade approach of the subjects to the farm holding is observable on the estates of West Moravia in the pre-White Mountain period, especially among holders of smaller-property farms. The farm was held to the extent that it was beneficial to the landlord and the size matched to the abilities and energies of his own family. If the owner of the homestead felt he could handle 'more', it was not usually possible to buy more fields so he sold the old farmstead and bought a larger one for it (it was similar in the opposite case) (Chocholáč 1999, pp. 155–6). Nevertheless, the decline of the actually paid earnest money in the course of the war while maintaining farmstead prices almost unchanged significantly reduced these options.

In the post-war period, if the instalment system did not disappear on the estate (as, for instance, in the Pernštejn region) and payment of the earnest money was maintained, the pre-White Mountain values of its share in the price were not mainly (with the exception of Mrákotín) renewed. Their amount was low and almost the same as the data from the period of the Thirty Years' War. Completely different amounts of earnest money were found for the town of Valašské Klobouky. In spite of different methods for processing the records (all found amounts of earnest money were included) in comparison with previous studies, the share of earnest money in the price increased throughout the whole 17th century with the exception of the period 1660–1679. It was due to a growing tendency to buy homesteads in the town for cash, in such a case, the earnest money equalled the price of the homestead (Odehnal 2007, pp. 211–12). This practice, if compared with findings from other estates in Moravia, where the price of farmstead paid in cash was lower than the price of the same farm holding paid in instalments, apparently decreased the prices of farm holdings, disrupted the instalment system in the town, increased the number of paid homesteads and secured the payment of financial means to the seller (creditor) but required the buyer to have quite a large amount of cash. When these financial means did not suffice as a result of the worsening economic situation in the town, which was caused by frequent invasions from Hungary to East Moravia during the 17th century, the number of gratuitous transfers increased and accounted for as much as one quarter of all exchanges (Odehnal 2007, p. 221). In order to ensure that the farm had a holder, all claims of creditors were lost.

In the course of the entire period in question (for the Pernštejn region already from the middle of the 16th century) on the estates where data comparisons were possible (Dřevohostice, the Pernštejn region, the Telč region, the Žďár region), there was a reduction of the annual (vejrunkový) instalments set within the conditions of the property transaction. If this fact was accompanied by a more significant decrease in really paid farm money, this led to an extension of the ideal and mostly real maturity of the farm holdings. As a result, the number of long-term or permanently indebted farms with instalments increased in those localities.

The researches carried out so far have generally confirmed the very good payment discipline of farmers for the pre-White Mountain period which was reflected both in the amount of the instalments and in their regularity of their use. Despite that, the extent of indebtedness with farm instalments was different at the individual estates. In the Pernštejn region in the period from 1550 to 1580, only not quite 45% of the farm holdings were in debt (Chocholáč 1989, data from graphs Nrs. I, III, V, VII, and IX), on the Nové Hrady estate, it was even only 39% of the farmsteads in the middle of the 16th century (Holakovský 1993, pp. 77–8). The Telč region at the end of the 16th and beginning of the 17th centuries (1580–1619) showed roughly half of the farm holdings to be in debt (Valůšek 1998, pp. 83–5), the Pernštejn region, at the same time, was already two-thirds of the farmsteads (Chocholáč 1989, data from graphs Nrs. I–X). It was similar at the Mělník estate (1584–1620), where 67% of farms and 61% of cottages were indebted with instalments (Koumar 2011a, p. 38). So far, the greatest indebtedness of farmsteads with instalments before White Mountain at a level of 71% was found at the Český Krumlov estate in the first quarter of the 17th century (Holakovský 1993, pp. 77–8). When interpreting the growth of the indebtedness of the farm holding with instalments, it is not possible to settle for the primary reference to the worsening economic conditions of the subjects, it is necessary to put this phenomenon in the broader context of ongoing property transactions. The indebtedness was influenced not only by the ideal maturity, which reflected the negotiated terms of the transaction between the buyer and the seller or the acquirer of the farm holding and heirs concerning the amount of the price, the earnest money and annual payments, but also the actual maturity of the farm holdings. It reflected both the payment discipline of the farmer which depended on the actual yield of the farmstead and the number of people it had to existentially and socially secure as well as the frequency of the exchanges of the farm holdings. The frequent alternation of the farmers (especially at the smaller farm holdings) in the pre-White Mountain period, on the one hand, maintained or increased the indebtedness of settlements with instalments, on the other, reflected the trade access to these properties on the part of their holders.

During the war, there was a deepening of the indebtedness – it was almost 70% in the Telč region, nearly 80% in the Pernštejn region and more than 85% of the farm holdings in the Žďár region (Chocholáč 1989, graphs II, IV, VI, VIII, and X; 1999, pp. 113–5). This trend (if the entire instalment system did not collapse) then continued even in the post-war period and reached 90% indebtedness of the farm holdings. The research on the Mělník estate in Bohemia also came to the same results (Koumar 2011a, pp. 38–39). At the end of the 17th century, the existence of paid-off farmsteads was already an exception (Chocholáč 1999, graphs pp. 113–5). The long ideal maturity, little or no earnest money and almost non-payment of the annual instalments practically precluded the payment of the farmstead and, at the same time, created conditions for the actual collapse of the instalment system (on the reasons of the collapse of the system, see Chocholáč 2005, p. 117), as happened, for instance, in the Boskovice, Pernštejn or Strážnice regions. In the case of a long-term absence of the instalment system in the locality (at the estate), the awareness that the farmsteads had been purchased may decline.

The indebtedness of the farm holdings with instalments at the Světlov estate (specifically in the village Sehradice) in the east of Moravia at the end of the 17th and beginning of the 18th centuries was resolved in other ways: gratuitous acquisition of the farm holdings, or payment of a farmstead with cash (neither case required the existence of an instalment system), or setting low prices of farm holdings (only to 50 Moravian gulden) in maintaining a certain level of the instalment system of the farm holdings (Odehnal 2011, p. 47).

On the contrary, a completely different state of the payment system of tenant farms in comparison with research in Moravia or with the research in the Mělník region was presented by Dana Štefanová for several villages of the Frýdlant estate in North Bohemia because the farmers there in the second half of the 17th century paid their annual instalments very regularly and systematically. They acquired enough financial means not only from their agricultural products, but also through participation in protoindustrial domestic production (Štefanová 2009, pp. 122–4).

## Sale/purchase of farm money

The existence of a repayment system was linked to a credit transaction in which unpaid financial stakes in farmsteads were traded. The sellers were individual subjects – holders of the shares (creditors). The range of entities on the buyer side was more diverse. Most often, farm money was bought up by the farmers on their farmsteads but, besides them, not only other subjects, including village headmen, could be involved in the transaction, but also municipalities themselves, guilds, orphans' cash boxes and church endowments, the manorial lords' administrators, or even owners of the estate (Valůšek 1998, pp. 89–90; Chocholáč 1999, p. 136). If the farmer bought the farm money on his farmstead, he thus lowered his indebtedness, or sometimes could even achieve its complete payment. In the case of the other entities, it was the placement of excess financial means into one of the forms of loan transactions that could provide large profits above even the period legitimate interest rate (6%). In all of the examined Moravian localities, including the smallest of them, the sale of farm money was recorded. That was also the case on the Mělník estate. The appearance of this transaction in the records of the land registers, which must be taken to be minimal (see below), was possible to determine for localities in the Telč region. At each farmstead there in 1580 through 1700, there were, on average, almost three sales (Chocholáč 1999, determined from the values on pp. 118, 119, 126). The same value was found for small towns on the Pardubice estate in the period 1576–1700 (Siglová 2017, pp. 230–1). On the contrary, this transaction is entirely absent on the North Bohemian Frýdlant estate. The cause could be the legal situation on the domain, because, at some farms, these transactions were forbidden in the effort mainly to protect the financial shares of the orphans.

Before actually comparing, it is also necessary to realize what the data is. Mainly credit transactions, which led to the debt settlement of the homestead, that is mainly the purchase of money by a farmer on his own farm holding, were recorded in the land registers. In the case of purchases of money for the benefit of other entities, the amount of the indebtedness of the farmstead did not change, therefore the records of these transactions were only important in knowing to whom the respective instalments are to be paid which was less important information than the amount of the indebtedness. This is one of the main reasons (besides the effort itself of the farmstead holder to relieve it of debt) that the owners of farm money were dominated by other farmers on their farm holdings over other entities on the examined estates farms.

The research conducted so far also showed that a large part of the records of the sale of farm money did not contain all of the required values – the amount of the purchased amount was missing or the amount of means paid out (or instead of money, the purchased amount was paid by domestic animals, cereals, beer, temporary lease of fields, work tasks, etc.) or both were absent. More often, money was bought up for farm animals and grains in the middle of the Thirty Years' War in the Boskovice region which could have been caused by the decline of local markets and the rise in prices of agricultural products (Vaněk 1997, p. 115). Of the total number of the sales of farm money, all the data was contained on them in Bojkovice only with 17% of the transactions (Janík 2002, p. 81), it was approximately 35% in the Boskovice region (Vaněk 1997, p. 99), perhaps 40% in the Telč and Žďár regions (Chocholáč 1999, pp. 126–7).

Only these complete records made it possible to ascertain the percentage of the funds purchased in real terms. In the pre-White Mountain period, this value could be statistically ascertained for the villages in the Boskovice region and for the small towns of Deblín, Dolní Bobrová, and Mrákotín. In the West Moravian towns, the amount paid reached, on average, the amount of one-third of the bought-up means (Chocholáč 1999, p. 128) – the share of about two-fifths was in small towns on the Pardubice estate (Siglová 2017, p. 231) – but in the villages, it did not reach even one-fourth of the bought-up share (Vaněk 1997, data from the tables on pp. 101–4). The difference between the small towns and the villages could be caused by the fact that there was a larger number of solvent candidates in the first-mentioned settlement area. Increased competition between buyers may have enabled sellers to negotiate better terms of the transaction but this hypothesis needs further investigation. If it was possible to monitor the proportion of funds paid to the amount of bought-up money by farmers on their farmsteads and other entities, its amount was several percent higher for other entities. As in the case above, the seller of farm money, unless the farmer was not interested in the transaction, negotiated slightly more favourable terms of the transaction. Unfortunately, comparisons for the next period can no longer be made due to the lack of statistically relevant data.

## Orphans' cash boxes and church endowments

As already mentioned above in the buying up of farm money, not only the subjects, but also institutions that inter alia dealt with credit in the village and small town milieu were also present within the instalment system. These included orphans' cash boxes and church endowments. Funds were given to the orphanages from the farmstead holders who paid the annual instalments for the inheritance shares to juveniles. These funds were usually kept here until they reached adulthood (earlier pay-outs could have occurred when the money was used, for example, to pay for the education of the child).

Only the amount of the financial means, which were transferred to the orphans' cash box as covered annual instalments, can be investigated from the land registers. It is therefore not possible to discover the total amount of the means in them. In all of the examined localities in West Moravia during the pre-White Mountain period (with the exception of Radešín and Počítky on the Žďár estate where it was impossible to determine these values before 1618), several tens of Moravian gulden came to the orphans' cash boxes in this way in the villages and several hundred in the small towns (Chocholáč 1999, pp. 133–4). Thus, the existence of funds in the orphans' cash box gave farmers some hope of obtaining a loan (credit) in the event of an economic crisis on farmsteads caused, for example, by a natural disaster. It was thus possible to obtain money to repair the house, to buy grain, etc. During the war, the shift of these monies to the orphans' cash boxes significantly declined and in the second half of the 17th century it was practically none with the exception of Bobrová. The provision of loans from these monies was thus impossible.

The financial means generated by the instalment system were also paid into church endowments. They were the annual payments, which ageing farmers or their wives willed, payments that children paid as requiems for the masses celebrated for their deceased parents or fulfilment of previous buying up of farm monies which were conducted in the name of the church endowment by the sextons who were to take care of their functioning.

In West Moravia in the pre-White Mountain period, less money came into the church endowments than the orphans' cash boxes – in the Kuřim and Telč regions, it was approximately only a fifth of the amount, not quite a third in Dolní Bobrová. In the post-war period, unlike the orphans' cash boxes into which, with the exception of Dolní Bobrová, in fact no money from instalments came, the church endowments from all of the localities in the Telč and Žďár regions acquired more means that had been the case in the pre-White Mountain period. The growing share of church endowments in the purchasing of farm money in the second half of the 17th century was also visible in small towns of the Pardubice estate (Siglová 2017, p. 235). This situation was probably influenced by two factors. The first was increased activity of sextons, especially in small towns that bought up a lot of farm monies and thus expanded the property of the requiems. The second factor could have been the growing Baroque piety which could have led to a closer attachment to the Catholic Church and, consequently, to an increase in its support of wills on the part of the subjects.

## Conclusion

The presented comparison of research results devoted to the basic financial aspects of property transactions with subject farmsteads enabled a greater generalization of the achieved findings. If it was possible to compare prices of settlements in the surveyed localities at the end of the 16th and early 17th centuries with the previous period (the Pernštejn region), their amount at that time stagnated or declined which did not confirm the conclusions of the earlier literature on their permanent growth. Apart from the prices that dropped significantly as a result of the destruction of the farmsteads by fire, looting by the soldiers, which led to their desolation, the prices of other farm holdings persisted and, in some places, they even slightly increased at the beginning of the 1620s. The value standard of the subjects was thus preserved even at the time of the conflict. On the contrary, it is possible to generalize in the research conducted (with the exception of Valašské Klobouky) that, during the war, there was a decrease in the payment of the earnest money in comparison with the pre-White Mountain Period. This payment, if it did not disappear with the collapse of the instalment system, remained low in the post-war period. Permanent decline was seen also in the amount of the annual instalments which was, moreover, accompanied from the war period by the declining ability of the holders of the farmsteads to realistically pay these instalments. The accessibility of these funds that allowed them to buy a farmstead or eased their life situations was thus extended and complicated for the recipients of the instalments, that is the creditors, especially if they were widows, orphans, subtenants (*inquilinus*) or retired farmers. On the contrary, the decline or even the end of the claims of their holding of the farmstead helped the debtors, that is the farmers working the farm holdings from whom the money was to be paid.

The decline in the purchase contracts of the set and subsequently actually paid earnest money and annual instalments increased the indebtedness of the farmsteads with these receivables, which was manifested on the estates to different degrees. Despite this, roughly a quarter of all the farm holdings managed to get rid of these debts at least for a short time at the end of the pre-White Mountain period. In the course of the 17th century, the indebtedness deepened and at its end it was possible to find a paid-off farmstead only in sporadic cases. If the worsening economic situation of the subject population was the likely reason for the increasing debt in the war and post-war period, in the pre-White Mountain period an increased exchange rate of farms was found on several estates, especially for less wealthy classes in which a certain trade approach to the farm holding could have been reflected on the part of their holders.

The sale of farm monies was also connected with the existence of the instalment system of the farmsteads. The trade with instalments was proved in all of the examined localities which indicates the common appearance of loan transaction in the milieu of the rural area in Moravia in the 16th century. The majority of the receivables were bought up by the farmers on their farmsteads who reduced the debt of the farm holding in this way, or sped up its repayment. For buyers from other entities, it was usually advantageous appreciation of the invested funds. The lack of full-fledged data for statistical processing on the individual estates makes it difficult to analyze this phenomenon more thoroughly. Despite that, it was possible to determine the share of the bought-up money for cash for several localities in the pre-White Mountain period. It was higher in small towns than in villages and the fact that the other entities paid on average slightly more for the same amount of bought-up money than the farmers on their farmsteads did.

Part of the receivables that arose under the instalment system were also transferred to orphans' cash boxes and church endowments. Thanks to that, in West Moravia in the pre-White Mountain period, there was a reserve of funds in the orphans' cash boxes from which it was possible to provide loans to farmers who found themselves in a difficult economic situation. During the war, the shift of receivables to orphans' cash boxes declined until it ceased almost completely in the post-war period, thus the possibility for farmers to obtain credit from these monies also ended. With the church endowments, the development was the opposite. The relatively smaller amount of means in the endowments in the pre-White Mountain period increased in the post-war period, whether through the influence of the agile credit activities of the sextons or the activity of the growing Baroque piety of the populace in all of the surveyed localities.

## Funding

The research was supported by the Faculty of Arts, Masaryk University.

## References

Chocholáč, B. (1989). *Zadluženost a poddanské dávky. Příspěvek ke studiu sociálně-ekonomických problémů poddaných v 2. polovině 16. a v 1. polovině 17. století na základě rozboru pernštejnských pozemkových knih.* Nepublikovaná diplomová práce. Brno: Historický ústav Filozofické fakulty Masarykovy univerzity.

Chocholáč, B. (1990). K hospodaření poddaných na pernštejnském panství v druhé polovině 16. a v první polovině 17. století. *Časopis Matice moravské*, 109, pp. 83–111.

Chocholáč, B. (1999). *Selské peníze. Sonda do finančního hospodaření poddaných na západní Moravě koncem 16. a v 17. století.* Brno: Matice moravská.

Chocholáč, B. (2001*). Poddanský úvěr na Moravě v 16. a 17. století. Český časopis historický*, 99, pp. 59–84.

Chocholáč, B. (2005). *Güterpreise, Verschuldung und Ratensystem. Eine Fallstudie zu den finanziellen Transaktionen der Untertanen bei Besitzübertragungen in Westmähren im späten 16. und im 17. Jahrhundert*, in Cerman, M. & Luft, R., eds. *Untertanen, Herrschaft und Staat in Böhmen und im "Alten Reich". Sozialgeschichtliche Studien zur Frühen Neuzeit*, München, Oldenburg Verlag, pp. 89–125 (Veröffentlichungen des Collegium Carolinum, Band 99).

Chocholáč, B. (2007). *Poddaní na venkově*, in Borovský, T. & Chocholáč, B. & Pumpr, P., eds. *Peníze nervem společnosti. K finančním poměrům na Moravě od poloviny 14. do počátku 17. století.* Brno: Matice moravská, pp. 292–336.

Chocholáč, B. (2017), Gruntovní peníze a válka. *K majetkovým a finančním poměrům poddaných na Moravě během třicetileté války*, in Balcarová, J. & Kubů, E. & Šouša, J., eds., *Venkov, rolník a válka v českých zemích a na Slovensku v moderní době*. Praha, Národní zemědělské muzeum, s. p. o., pp. 127–33.

Holakovský, M. (1993). Finanční hospodaření na selských gruntech v předbělohorských jižních Čechách. *Jihočeský sborník historický*, 62, pp. 70–92.

Janík, P. (2002). *Poznámky k hospodářskému postavení obyvatel Bojkovic v 17. století*. Nepublikovaná diplomová práce. Brno: Historický ústav Filozofické fakulty Masarykovy univerzity.

Koumar, J. (2011). "… k velikému ztenčení skrze vojáky a jinou vojenskou zběř týž statek přišel…" Odraz třicetileté války v transferu poddanských nemovitostí na mělnickém panství. *Historie – Otázky – Problémy*, 3(1), pp. 77–91.

Koumar, J. (2011a). "Má zaplaceno, žádnému nic nedluží…" Finanční aspekty majetkového transferu poddanské nemovitosti na mělnickém panství v 17. století. *Ústecký historický sborník*, 1, pp. 7–43.

Kostlán, A. (1985). Finanční zhroucení ve střední Evropě na počátku třicetileté války. *Folia Historica Bohemica*, 8, pp. 265–316.

Odehnal, P. (2007). *Po spálení města Klobouk*. Hospodaření poddaných na jihovýchodní Moravě ve stínu válečných událostí 17. a počátku 18. století. Nepublikovaná disertační práce. Olomouc: Katedra historie Filozofické fakulty Univerzity Palackého.

Odehnal, P. (2011). "Paměť se činí, že se peníze gruntovní pasírují". K hospodaření poddaných na východní Moravě v 17. a počátkem 18. století. *Východní Morava*, 1, pp. 43–64.

Odehnal, P. (2013). Nad zlomkem gruntovní knihy vsi Šanov z druhé poloviny 17. století. *Východní Morava*, 3, pp. 19–35.

Petráň, J. (1964). *Poddaný lid v Čechách na prahu třicetileté války*. Praha: Československá akademie věd.

Procházka, V. (1963). *Česká poddanská nemovitost v pozemkových knihách 16. a 17. století*. Praha: Nakladatelství Československé akademie věd.

Siglová, T. (2017). *Úvěr a zadlužení obyvatel městeček pardubického panství v 16. a 17. století*. Pardubice: Univerzita Pardubice.

Štefanová, D. (2009). *Erbschaftspraxis, Besitztransfer und Handlungsspielräume von Untertanen in der Gutsherrschaft. Die Herrschaft Frýdlant in Nordböhmen, 1558–1750*. Wien–München: Verlag für Geschichte und Politik & Oldenburg Verlag. (Sozial- und wirtschaftshistorische Studien, Band 34).

Valůšek, D. (1998). *Zákupní držba na Telčsku od konce 16. století do roku 1800 (na základě rozboru pozemkových knih vesnic Nevcehle, Strachoňovice a Doupě)*. Nepublikovaná diplomová práce. Brno: Historický ústav Filozofické fakulty Masarykovy univerzity.

Vaněk, P. (1997). *Postavení poddaných na boskovickém panství na konci 16. a v 1. polovině 17. století ve světle pozemkových knih*. Nepublikovaná diplomová práce. Brno: Historický ústav Filozofické fakulty Masarykovy univerzity.

Vohnický, A. (2014). "Léta Páně koupil jest dům za sumu področní…" Proměny ekonomických a sociálních poměrů obyvatel městečka Dřevohostice od konce 16. do začátku 18. století. In *Sborník Státního okresního archivu Přerov*. Přerov, pp. 49–61.

Vorel, P. (2000). *Od pražského groše ke koruně české 1300–2000. Průvodce dějinami peněz v českých zemích*. Praha: Rybka Publishers.

# Chapter 21

# Debt in the life of a Gdansk merchant

*Anna Paulina Orłowska*

## Introduction

While analysing the town books of Gdansk, Cezary Kardasz presumed that the merchants of Gdansk had either no financial surpluses or were not interested in investing into short and middle-term credit as those credits were only rarely mentioned in the town books (Kardasz 2013, p. 115). In this chapter, I would like to demonstrate that, on the contrary, a merchant of Gdansk used a multitude of credit forms due to the development of pragmatic literacy. Those private credits were, therefore, not registered in the town books and their variety is often not recognized enough in the historiography.

This chapter is a case study based on a merchant account book. This microhistorical approach offers us insights in the diversity of credit forms and allows to examine the functioning of credit in its full extension hence, in the merchant account books, we can also find information on credit on small sums, as well as given in the informal way and under the circumstances of high level of trust.

## The merchant and his book

The merchant in question was active for 35 years, from 1421 till 1455, the year in which he probably died. He spent all this time in Gdansk where he lived in houses of city's aldermen. Although his origin is unknown, what we know about him is that he neither got married nor had children and in 1421 he immigrated to Gdansk. Due to his language, we can assume that his birthplace in the south-eastern part of the Baltic Sea basin is very likely. The man was rather a middle-range merchant with a maximum of the annual turnover of 6,500 Mark Pr (Stark 1985). His main economic activities involved trading along the East–West axis typical for Hanseatic trade, connecting his partners from Riga and Prussia with counterparts in Flanders and Lubeck. He also traded intensively with English merchants and maintained various contacts with Lithuanians from Vilnius. The range of his merchandise was very wide, covering fishes, grains, oils, fats, leathers, beverages, clothes, spices, metals, and wood but the four most important groups were wax, furs, cloths, and salt (Slaski 1905; Schmidt-Rimpler 1915; Stark 1985; Orłowska 2020/1).

The primary source for the analysis of his activities is his account book preserved in the Gdansk archive (Archiwum Państwowe w Gdańsku). It is a paper notebook bounded in plain leather, containing 113 sheets and three additional pieces of paper, two of them were issued by the merchant's partners. Nearly all entries of the book were written by one hand and in Middle Low German, in a version typical for the south-eastern part of the Baltic Sea basin.

For years, this account book had been the only source of information about its author and his business activities. He never wrote down his name but, in a promissory note preserved in the book, he was named as the creditor. On this basis, he was identified as Johan Pisz. After having analysed all town books of Gdansk from the given period of his activity, I was able to correctly determine his name as Johan Pyre (also written as Pyr or Pire). This name is repeated a few times in the primary sources in Gdansk, however, it was not found in any documents outside of this town. The information from further primary sources offers us additional clues and allowed to refute some of the hypotheses regarding the merchant but his account book remains the main source to examine the business activities of Pyre.

The question is what was the practice of using a credit in everyday life of a merchant? To better understand the limitations of examining the credit notes in the merchant book, a short description of the accounting techniques shall be provided.

### The bookkeeping

Pyre structured his notes in the typical North German fashion which means that he largely worked with slips of paper on which he made notes ('*Zettelwirtschaft*') (Arlinghaus 2002). They were kept inside a book by a fold-over flap. Only the most relevant or long-term transactions were registered in his merchant book. Unfortunately, with two exceptions, those slips of paper were lost so that we only have his book at hand. This way of taking and keeping notes was very common for merchants of the Hanseatic region who, unlike their Italian counterparts, noted also only a minority of their transactions in cash and this rule applies also for Pyre's bookkeeping (Arlinghaus 2000).

Furthermore, he employed a typical North German notation style but in an extreme shorthand of his own creation as he did not mention his name nor even a praenomen and he also omitted some verbs and did not properly register the dates of transactions (Tophinke 1999). Pyre also tended to omit the word '*schuldich*' ('due') as he wrote, for example: '*Item soe ys my Hans*

*Monyk ½ mk'* ('therefore Hans Monyk is [due] to me ½ mk') (Orłowska 2020/2, 95v 6).

Pyre started writing his merchant book in a quite traditional way, trying to use some techniques regarding the double-entry accounting. Therefore, during the first years, he annotated personal accounts and multiplied entries about diverse transactions in which a growing number of partners were involved. However, already in the fourth year of his economic activity, 1424, he introduced a major change and arranged the notes according to the transactions and not to his business partners. In this new system, all the data regarding one transaction was written down in direct vicinity. The final due was clearly put at the end of a note, also in typical North German fashion (Tophinke 1999). The final due was usually calculated in the local currency poor Mark Pr.

The merchant split the transactions into two main categories – the simple purchase and sale transactions as well as more complicated transactions. The latter, he used to place in one segment of the book and described usually in a traditional way, one transaction after the other, using merchant signs of his partners in the headline of notes for a quick recognition of the notes. He developed a different system for purchase and sales. This system, called *Methode der Gegenseiten* ('method of opposite sides'), was unique and very innovative (Schmidt-Rimpler 1915). The merchant registered all the details of a given transaction on the left page of the book and the information including the name of the trade partner, the description of the merchandise, the amount, the price per unit, the sum to be paid, the payment date and, in some cases, also the date of the transaction, and further details. He did not have to leave any empty space underneath the note, contrary to other merchants of the same period. He instead described the next transaction directly under the previous one. The details of the payments were noted on the right page, parallel to the description of a transaction. As the details of a payment were usually shorter than the description of the transaction, he had enough space to elaborate on even most complicated payment processes. This is how he avoided the problem of lacking space for the description (a problem which led other merchants to write down this information in randomly chosen empty spaces in their books). This approach allowed him to maintain a clear structure and to diminish disarrangements. Additionally, such a structure better fulfilled the function of memory aid and allowed to omit details of the notes such as dates.

Since Pyre was able to collect all details of a given transaction in the same place, so that they followed each other chronologically, he could retrace them at a glance. This made noting down dates largely redundant which is why Pyre's merchant book contains few time stamps – usually at the beginning of each page and, on average, one more in the middle of the page. The book in its final state therefore contains mostly crossed-out notes without any temporal data on when a transaction was initiated and when it was paid. Thus, determining those dates is challenging and often downright impossible.

The main influence on whether a note contained both a date of the transaction and a due date was its position in the book and on the page. As the entries at the top of a page were usually dated, they contain both dates with a higher likelihood. In addition, Pyre dated his notes in the middle of the page (usually about the tenth note on a page) more often when a larger amount of time had passed since the date at the top so that his memory needed another prompt. Furthermore, Pyre dated almost half of the entries in the last ten years of his activities with both dates, the majority of which in the last five years. Since Pyre also reduced his activities in this time frame by reason of the loss of faculties due to aging, this trend can be attributed to dealing with his decreasing memory. The net effect is that the portion of dated transactions was many times higher in those last years of Pyre's life.

## Credit

As the Hanseatic merchants have rarely noted the cash transactions, most of the entries in Pyre's account book describe credit transactions. He used a variety of credit forms such as cash credits, trade credits, annuities, and so-called *wedderlegynge*. The loan was described either with some form of verb *'lenden'* ('lend') or with the adjective *'schuldich'* ('due'). However, it occurred very often that the credit transaction was not explicitly described but can be interpreted from the merchant's remarks.

### Cash credit

Pyre mentioned cash credit he granted or received in more than 130 instances. The sums varied a lot, from just half a Mark to up to nine hundred Mark Pr.[1] Usually, no collaterals were involved, neither in the form of deposits nor with warrantors. The omission of securities might be due to the fact that all those credits were granted within existing business relationship. Nevertheless, promissory notes could have been used in addition (which will be explained below). A significant fraction of Pyre's credit transactions was processed in foreign currencies. We can assume that some monetary loans could have been granted to permanent business partners when they suddenly needed a specific currency. The paybacks were either in the same currency or in Mark Pr. Therefore, in some transactions, the credit in foreign currency evolved into currency exchange.

Unfortunately, it is not possible to deduce the interest rate in spite of the notable number of mentions in his book because Pyre did not use to add information regarding the loaned and the paid back sum, and the complete dates when the credit was granted and cleared.

## Credit in commodities

In Pyre's merchant book, we can observe that he used to lend and borrow not only coins but also commodities. The description of such transaction is very similar to the description of cash credits. In 1423 he noted '*Item noch Hans gelent 500 clesemes, ed stont 30 ½ mk. Item noch gelent 1 gulden sware krone [ed stont] 6 ferd*' ('Furthermore, I lent Hans 500 [furs], it was 30,5 mk. Furthermore, I lent [him] 1 gold heavy crown, [it was] 6 ferd) (Orłowska 2020/2, 3r 10). Such transactions could occur similarly to the transactions regarding foreign currencies, when particular merchandise was needed, that the merchant did not own. Consequently, in 1445, Pyre should provide wax to Bernd Pynyg but he was not able to purchase enough wax before the delivery so he borrowed one piece of wax from Hynryk Vosse '*Item soe lende my Hynryk Vosse 1 stucke wasses, dat Bernd Pynyg untffenk* [...]' (Orłowska 2020/2, 82v 5). As it happened with currencies, the return could be done with the same merchandise or later paid up, converting a loan into a simple sale.

## Trade credit

An even significantly larger portion is the trade credits. While Pyre only explicitly noted that a payment was done on borrow ('*tho borge*') in five transactions (Orłowska 2020/2, fol. 68r 1, 71r 7, 91r 13, 106r 9, 107v 6), analysis of the source, however, demonstrates that most of the sales and purchases were done by borrowing. Thus, the number of implicit trade credits constituted the majority of entries in Pyre's merchant book.

There are only roughly 25 records per year in which any date is mentioned, however, it is usually the day of payment. Only in 71 transactions (ca. two per year) both the date of the transaction and of the payment were recorded.

The spread of the payment periods is huge and varied between 14 to 289 days. The median was 99 days, the average 115. If the payment should be done in two rates, the first payment was, on average, due already on the 71st day, the second on 138th day. However, there were only six fully described cases of payment with two rates so that the analysis of this type of payment has to be done very prudently. Even if we examine all the cases with two requitals, including those where the day of the payment was not noted, there is no pattern regarding merchandise or the size of a transaction. The only pattern that can be observed is that the business partners were usually living in Gdansk which probably made the split payment easier as no additional effort or cost of money transfer arose.

Within these 71 transactions, for which both the date of transaction and payment were noted, 11 partners are named twice, seven of them traded additionally with the same merchandise so that ceteris paribus a comparison can be made. The hypothesis was that the development of the transaction should have influenced further transactions: the more punctual the repayment was the better conditions should be offered in the second transaction. This assumption turned out to be false. Neither the price of the merchandise nor the length of the payment period changed in favour of the punctual partner or got worse for partners that were very late with their first payment. The only exception is the monger Herman van Eymken, who bought oil twice. As for the first transaction made in 1448, the amount was small and the payment period very short as it spanned only over 21 days. One year later, he bought threefold and the payment period was extended to 283 days. Furthermore, in the second transaction, his surname was also noted while, in the first one, he was described only by his given name and occupation (Orłowska 2020/2, fol. 77r 7, 75r 9). However, it has to be admitted that all partners with the exception of monger van Eymken were Pyre's long term partners and thus trust could have been established and, therefore, the delayed repayment had no influence on the relation.

The current date of a payment was documented in approximately every tenth note (Orłowska 2020/2 fol. 68r 7, 69r 5, 74r 5, 75r 1, 76r 1,2, 106r 6). The analysis of these seven cases has not revealed any patterns other than that the requital was never on time. The payment periods varied from 57 to 218 days, the requital was late by at least eight days with a maximum of 333 days (14–222%). Even very late remunerations were not higher than the sum named in the loan transaction therefore the delay in repayment was not punished with an additional fee.

The payment scheme of these seven transactions reflects the majority of the cases, however, in some cases, the debts were paid before the due date. The date of debt clearing was much more determined by the presence of the debtor, or one of his partners, in Gdansk than by any calculations. Therefore, dates were seen rather as indices than as strict terms. Sometimes, this ambiguity is obvious by the definition of the date. In a number of transactions, Pyre noted that the payment (or delivery) should be done in spring with the 'first open water', when the water is free from ice ('*toe betalen op ed vorjar met den eyrsten oppen water*', Orłowska 2020/2, 83r 12). The further case, in which this term was used, shows quite clearly the understanding of payment dates as Pyre noted 'to be paid on Easter, with the first open water' ('*op Ostern betalen med dem eyrsten open water*', Orłowska 2020/2, 84r2). This is one of the reasons why Easter was the second most popular payment date and was chosen 75 times. Nearly as popular as Easter was Pentecost which was mentioned 72 times, followed by the date of the only annual fair of Gdansk – St Dominic (August, 4), that was chosen 70 times. St Michael's Day (September, 29) was the most popular date in Pyre's business, chosen 84 times, and the second popular date of clearing, St Martin's Day (November, 11) selected 64 times.

Often, credit was also repaid in different rates than initially agreed upon, usually divided into more but smaller rates. In addition to the local currency, Mark. Pr., payments were often made in foreign currency or in different currencies at the same time. Pyre's descriptions of such payments clearly demonstrate that the use of coins was purely conceived in the amount of precious metals. As we could prove, he was able to quantify the gold content of the coins as he correctly appraised the price of gold coins of rapidly changing quality. He often just noted the type of metal and their converted value in Mark Pr. Rates were often cleared with debts of other merchants thus a debtor paid his dues by having one of his own debtors pay them. The debt clearing could include multiple stages. Despite this convolution, the portion of debts paid was very high so that very few credits in the merchant book remained unpaid. This demonstrates the enormous importance of reputation and credibility to a Hanseatic merchant.

### Warrantors, promissory notes, entries in town books

Due to such high reliabilities, warrantors for credits rarely play a role in Pyre's merchant book. There were only two situations in which Pyre used a warrantor. A promissory note, on the other hand, was much more common.

Johan Pyre's merchant book constitutes a valuable example of the prevalence of promissory notes in the Hanseatic sphere. A detailed analysis of his documentation offered only scarce evidence of using a promissory note or a demand for payment. Pyre called those papers 'letters' ('*breyve, breyffe*'). The most interesting case, where a promissory note was used, occurred in 1437: Pyre paid 100 Mark Pr. to Tomas Schenkendorp for a promissory note issued by Nychawes Otten, which had initially been issued to Hynryk van den Berge. This transfer of the promissory note is the first known example of such a procedure.

However, transferred duties are relatively often present in Pyre's merchant book. Due to its convenience, this pattern emerged especially often with business partners who did not travel to Gdansk and therefore could use promissory notes to move capital from afar.

The use of promissory notes must have drastically exceeded the cases in which Pyre registered them. How they were employed can be seen with the promissory note which remained in Pyre's book and helped to identify his name (Orłowska, 2020/2, 66v). Said note is not mentioned anywhere in the book. The transaction connected to the note can be identified (Orłowska 2020/2, 67r 1) but Pyre did not consider the use of a promissory document noteworthy. Thus, the use of promissory notes and transferred promissory notes was such an ordinary occurrence that it often did not even make it into our sources. This could cause an illusion of their rarity and create an image of a credit-unfriendly Hanseatic League.

The other method to guarantee the payment was to register a debt in the town books. In the case of Pyre, who was commercially active for 35 years and involved in the multiple credits and loans, there is only one mention in the town books as, in 1442, Vincentius Schulte confessed in front of judges that he owed Pyre 64 Mk. Pr. (*Liber scabinorum*, 1435, ff. 359v). The conditions of payment were very generous, as the first rate of 24 Mk. Pr. was expected to be paid after more than a year, at Easter of next year, the second and third should also be paid at following Easter, respectively. Vincentius Schulte was not mentioned in the merchant book of Johan Pyre nor was he very well known in Danzig as he is mentioned only twice in the town books. These two factors – the limited relation and the very unusual scheme of repayment spread over three rates and three years – could be the argument for the choice of credit guarantee.

Regarding the land register, Pyre mentioned having three entries in this register. However, the entries from the 15th century were erased in the book of land register which is the reason why we cannot confront his notes and entries from the land register (Grulkowski 2009).

### Life annuities

Pyre acquired an annuity for life three times. All transactions were made in summer and autumn of 1453, two years before his death, probably when he struggled with health problems. In all those cases mentioned, the life annuities were paid out in money. On the other hand, the purchase price was not covered in coins but in goods. Therefore, those annuities can be considered as a delayed payment for goods sold by Pyre.

The first transaction entailed two purchases of one bale of cloth each which Peter Bemen bought on June 24 and July 12 (Orłowska 2020/2, 68r 5, 6, 67v, 5–6). The total value of both bales was 865 Mk. Pr. Peter Bemen promised to pay 100 Mk. Pr. per year, each on St Martin, November 11. The interest rate was set at 12.12%. Pyre noted that the annuity was secured by an entry in the town ground book so that Peter Bemen's real estate functioned as collateral. This runs in parallel with the currency flow in Prussia because the sum noted in official town sources had to be expressed in good Mk. Pr. (as opposed to the lower quality variety of the poor Mk. Pr.) which Pyre mentioned in his notes. For his convenience, he also wrote down the amount in poor Mk. Pr. which was more commonly used in mercantile practice.

The second transaction is worth analysing because the annuity was not fixed during the initial purchase but rather agreed upon as the payment was due (Orłowska 2020/2, 68r 8, 67v, 8). On August 2, 1453, Jacop Vligen bought 12 pieces of Russian wax from Pyre which cost 476 ½ poor Mk. Pr. minus 4 ½ Schilling Pr. After the first rate of 150 poor Mk. Pr. had been paid, Vligen and Pyre agreed on a life annuity. 229½ poor Mk. Pr. should be converted into an annuity sum with an interest rate of 11.33%. The annuity was to be paid to Pyre in rates of 26 Mk. Pr. The due dates were not specified. Similar to the case above, the house of the debtor served as collateral, recorded in the town book as a guarantee. The remaining 97 Mk. Pr. minus 4 ½ Schilling Pr. were paid by regular means.

The last transaction was initiated on September 8, 1453: Leyffart Blomendael bought one bale of *Merdesches* worth poor 215 Mk. Pr. (Orłowska 2020/2, 67r 3, 65v, 3). In this case, the payment in the form of an annuity was also agreed upon later. Pyre wrote down neither collateral nor the height of the rates or their due dates. Yet, he noted that he was paid 15 Rhein Gulden (ergo 17.5 Mk. Pr.) on St Michael in 1455. Below that, he remarked that 27 Mk. Pr. were still due. If this was the annuity rate or a different debt, it cannot be determined due to the brief note. Thus, we cannot determine the interest rate.

Furthermore, in this entry, Pyre clearly defined what a life annuity is: 'when I am dead, it shall be dead, too' (*'wan yk dot sye, soe sal ed ok dot syen'*). He states the central concept of an annuity for life: it ends with the death of the recipient. The interest rate of two of those life annuities was 12.12% and 11.33%. Thus, they were set significantly above the interest rate common in Gdansk in that period, which was approximately 8.3% (Grulkowski 2009). On the other hand, this fits the pattern which C. Kardasz identified for annuities for life – i. e. a higher age resulted in higher interest rates (Kardasz 2013). In addition, Pyre had a strong stance in the negotiations since all those annuities were agreed upon as payments for already existing debt and he could just as well have demanded immediate payment from a debtor in line with the original contract.

As a result, we can observe that Pyre never paid for the purchase of life annuities in hard currency, instead, they were used as a form of payment that Pyre used as an indirect exchange for his merchandise. As most of the time this kind of payment had not been written into Pyre's original note but came up over the course of a business venture, the reasons for this change should be better investigated. They might simply reflect a temporal lack of liquidity of the relevant business partner.

### Wedderlegynge

The *wedderlegynge* constituted the typical form of passive income in the Hanseatic League and was also a form of loan given to a young merchant in order to allow him to run his own business, in most of the aspects similar to *comenda* (Cordes, 1998). This traditional form of business was implemented by two partners, one of which purely offered capital (*socius dormiens*) while the other took the holdings of the *wedderlegynge* with him to travel and trade. The partners usually contributed in equal parts to the capital of the venture. Since the *socius dormiens* did not take part in the activities, merchants mainly employed this type of capital investment in their later years. They were even employed by people who were no merchants at all. This was largely due to the low risk of such an investment.

Four instances of *wedderlegynge* can be identified in Pyre's merchant book. Atypically, they were formed in the first phase of his activities, rather than as a capital investment at a higher age. The founding capital of those *wedderlegynge* differed a lot: 29.5 Mark Pr., 82 Mark Pr. and 150 Mark Pr. In one case, the founding capital cannot be reconstructed. In three cases, neither the duration nor the profits can be determined. The *wedderlegynge* with Steven van Ummen constitutes the exception from this rule: his business with Pyre was already documented in 1421. It lasted until 1425, *id est* five years. Over the course of those five years, van Ummen and Pyre made 213% of the profit.

## Conclusion

According to what Agnieszka Bartoszewicz stated about the use of account books and promissory notes, they were a standard solution of merchants in the big towns of Vistula basin in late Middle Ages (Bartoszewicz 2017). The economic implications of this development should not be underestimated: the ability to secure a loan without engaging the town officials or even warrantors gave the late medieval merchants new financial tools. The credit market boomed without leaving traces outside of merchant books.

During the 35 years of his business activity in Gdansk, which are documented in his account book, Johan Pyre used the official town books only four times in order to secure his loans – he used the ground books three times in order to secure his life annuities but he secured his merchant credit by using an entry in the town bench book only once. In the same period, he granted more than 130 cash credits for sums up to over 900 Mark Pr. and a multitude of trade credits. He used no collaterals and nearly no warrantors. His primarily guarantee was the relationship of trust with his partners and the entry in his book. However, we can also presume that the promissory notes were often used but not mentioned, as in the case of the promissory note that survived in the book. In addition, Pyre's merchant book provides evidence on transfer of the promissory note as early as in 1437.

## Note

1  The highest loan in town books of Gdansk achieves 1,800 Mark Pr. (Liber scabinorum, 1435, ff. 73r).

## References

Arlinghaus, F. J. (2002). Die Bedeutung des Mediums "Schrift" für die unterschiedliche Entwicklung deutscher und italienischer Rechnungsbücher. In Pohl, W. & Paul, H., eds. *Vom Nutzen des Schreibens. Soziales Gedächtnis, Herrschaft und Besitz im Mittelalter*. Wien: Verlag der österreichischen Akademie der Wissenschaften, pp. 237–68.

Arlinghaus, F. J. (2000). *Zwischen Notiz und Bilanz. Zur Eigendynamik des Schriftgebrauchs in der kaufmännischen Buchführung am Beispiel der Datini / di Berto-Handelsgesellschaft in Avignon (1367–1373)*. Frankfurt a.M.: Lang.

Bartoszewicz, A. (2017). *Urban Literacy in Late Medieval Poland*. Turnhout: Brepols Publishers.

Cordes, A. (1998). 'Widerlegung'. In *Lexikon des Mittelaters*. München: LexMA-Verlag, v. 9, p. 64.

Grulkowski, M. (2009). Rynek renty w Głównym Mieście Gdańsku w świetle najstarszych ksiąg gruntowych w XIV–XV wieku. In Kizik E., ed. *Studia i materiały do dziejów domu gdańskiego*. Gdańsk: Wydawnictwo Uniwersytetu Gdańskiego, pp. 21–98.

Kardasz, C. (2013). *Rynek kredytu pieniężnego w miastach południowego pobrzeża Bałtyku w późnym średniowieczu (Greifswald, Gdańsk, Elbląg, Toruń, Rewel)*. Toruń: Towarzystwo Naukowe w Toruniu.

Orłowska, A. P. (2020/1). *Ein Kaufmann und sein Handelsbuch im spätmittelalterlichen Danzig, Darstellung*. Köln: Böhlau Verlag.

Orłowska, A. P., ed. (2020/2). *Ein Kaufmann und sein Handelsbuch im spätmittelalterlichen Danzig, Edition*. Köln: Böhlau Verlag.

Schmidt-Rimpler, W. (1915). *Geschichte des Kommissionsgeschäfts in Deutschland, v. 1.*, Halle a.S: Verlag der Buchhandlung des Waisenhauses.

Slaski, W. von (1905). *Danziger Handel im XV. Jahrhundert auf Grund eines im Danziger Stadtarchiv befindlichen Handlungsbuches geschildert*. Heidelberg: Druck von C.F. Beisel Nachf.

Stark, W. (1985). *Untersuchungen zum Profit beim hansischen Handelskapital in der ersten Hälfte des 15. Jahrhunderts*. Weimar: Hermann Böhlaus Nachfolger.

Tophinke, D. (1999). *Handelstexte: Zur Textualität und Typik kaufmännischer Rechnungsbücher im Hanseraum des 14. und 15. Jahrhunderts*. Tübingen: Gunter Narr Verlag.

# Index

*Note*: Page numbers in *italics* indicate figures and in **bold** indicate tables on the corresponding pages.